THE

PARISH OF

A SERIES OF BIOGRAPHICAL, ECCLESIASTICAL, HISTORICAL,
GENEALOGICAL, AND INDUSTRIAL

SKETCHES AND INCIDENTS.

BY

JOHN CAMERON, J.P.,

KIRKINTILLOCH.

𝔚𝔦𝔱𝔥 " 𝔠𝔞𝔩𝔦𝔠𝔬 𝔓𝔯𝔦𝔫𝔱𝔦𝔫𝔤 𝔦𝔫 𝔠𝔞𝔪𝔭𝔰𝔦𝔢" 𝔞𝔭𝔭𝔢𝔫𝔡𝔢𝔡.

KIRKINTILLOCH:
D. MACLEOD, 47 COWGATE STREET.
1892.

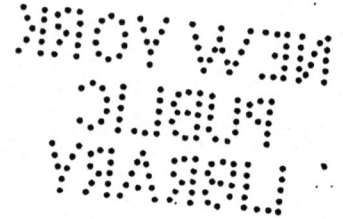

ISBN 978-0-282-21011-3
PIBN 10844525

1 MONTH OF
FREE
READING

at
www.ForgottenBooks.com

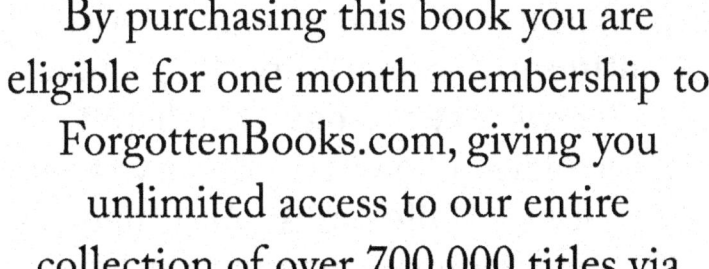

By purchasing this book you are eligible for one month membership to ForgottenBooks.com, giving you unlimited access to our entire collection of over 700,000 titles via our web site and mobile apps.

To claim your free month visit:
www.forgottenbooks.com/free844525

PREFACE.

THE following papers originated in a very simple way, and without any previous intention or plan on my part. I had presided at the Campsie Re-union in Glasgow, in 1876; and when again requested by the committee to take the chair, in February, 1885, I accepted with reluctance, owing to the difficulty of getting anything new to say about the parish which had not been dilated on year after year at the then annual soirees. To impart some freshness to my speech as Chairman, I referred to some matters connected with the early history of the parish. My remarks created the desire to hear something further, and this led to my receiving an invitation from the committee of the Campsie Mechanics' Institution to deliver one or two lectures in the Town Hall, Lennoxtown, in connection with their following winter course.

I accepted this invitation, and gave two lectures—one on "The Ecclesiastical History of the Parish," and another on "The Parish of Campsie: its Physical Features and Geology, its Landed Families, and the Rise of its Manufactures," &c. Both lectures were very fully reported in the *Lennox Herald* and *Stirling Observer* newspapers, and their publication led to correspondence with some interested in one or other of the topics referred to, and opened to me sources of additional information from original charters, old minute books, pamphlets, and correspondence on Campsie affairs, the existence of which I knew nothing of previously, and to which very few had means of access. It was also the means of putting me in communication with several individuals who had long resided in the parish, whose reminiscences of old times were freely imparted to me, and by whose assistance I have been enabled to collect some of the old parish traditions which are now passing rapidly away, and owing to the great changes that have occurred in the population, both agricultural and industrial, much interesting parochial history has now been entirely lost.

It thus came about that it became one of the relaxations of a busy life to revisit my native parish, in which I ceased to reside as long ago as 1864, in order to collect the materials which have been partially utilised in the following papers. When in quest of information I have always been received with the greatest kindness and courtesy, information was freely imparted, and much trouble was sometimes taken to obtain it for me, or to sift out the truth from conflicting accounts or narratives.

The subject matter naturally divided itself into either particular subjects or localities, and as details accumulated these grouped naturally into their various sub-divisions, referred to in my second lecture under the rise of its manufactures. I had been asked to publish the two lectures delivered in Lennoxtown, but had decided to delay this and re-write and extend them when I was asked by the Young Men's Association to give the opening lecture of their literary course in 1889. I chose local subjects in that and the two subsequent years, in order to encourage the study of parochial subjects by the members of the Y.M.A. In this way, a brief reference to the pastorate of the Rev. James Lapslie in the lecture on the Ecclesiastical History of the Parish expanded into " The Rev. James Lapslie : a Sketch of his Life and Times," as now printed. The reading of this lecture was followed by the usual discussion. I was favoured with the presence of some old friends who took part in this, from whom additional information was obtained, and also some anecdotes which were quite new to me, and these have been incorporated with the text of the lecture. In the following year (1890), having again received an invitation from the Y.M.A. to open their winter's course with a lecture, I took up the subject of "Calico Printing in Campsie," as nearly all the members were more or less connected with Lennoxmill. The introduction of calico printing had been briefly referred to in my second lecture under the rise of manufactures. It was treated in much greater detail in the lecture to the Y.M.A. This lecture was very fully reproduced in the columns of the *Kirkintilloch Herald*, and awakened considerable local interest, and again publication led to my being put in possession of additional facts and anecdotes, which were duly incorporated. To suit the convenience of Campsonians no longer resident in the parish it was published in pamphlet form, and the first edition has been completely exhausted.

On the suggestion of those interested in the subject a second edition of "Calico Printing in Campsie" is issued with the present series of papers.

When again asked to open the Y.M.A. course, in 1891, I took as my subject the ministry of the Rev. Dr. Norman Macleod and Dr. Robert Lee in Campsie, and at the close of the lecture the meeting unanimously expressed a request that I should publish that lecture as well as the other one that was to follow in the same course on "The Clachan and District," and I consented.

It occurred to me afterwards that it would be a pity to print "The Clachan and District" and take no notice of Lennoxtown and district, with which I was more particularly identified, so I wrote out in the form of a lecture the paper on "Lennoxtown and District" which appears in this volume. In doing this I had occasion frequently to refer to the Lennox family, and I wrote the paper on the "Lennoxes of Lennox Castle" in the form of a lecture. Lennox Castle led to Woodhead, which led to the earliest seat of the family at Balcorrach, and this naturally suggested the next paper on the genealogies of the old landed families and their original towers or mansions.

I had obtained information about the original feuars of Torrance and their ploughgates, which I considered deserved a place in any parish history. Birdston had a history of its own, which has more than a merely local interest, and which could not well be omitted in a series of papers dealing with the parish as a whole, as it completes all the districts which the parish naturally divides into.

This volume has attained a size never anticipated by me when, at the request of the Y.M.A., I consented to publish the two lectures of last winter's course. I have, therefore, withheld papers on the etymology of place names, the physical features and geological history of the district, the Auld Wives' Lifts, and the sun worship which prevailed there in pre-Christian times, &c., &c. Perhaps at some future time I may be able to publish these papers and also complete the ecclesiastical history down to the appointment of the late Rev. Dr. Monro, of which the papers on Lapslie, Macleod, Lee, and Govane, and sessional affairs are sub-divisions, as the time has hardly arrived when "Sunday Racing in Campsie" and "Ecclesiastical Electioneering" can be dealt with in the strictly impartial spirit in which all history should be written.

I cannot conclude without thanking all who have so kindly assisted me in the preparation of these papers. In this connection I cannot refrain from mentioning the following gentlemen, nearly all of whom are natives of the parish, to whom I am under great obligations :—Mr. John Young, F.G.S., Hunterian Museum, Glasgow University; Mr. James Millar, 17 Monteith Row, Glasgow; Mr. John Cowan, Wycliffe House, Anlaby Road, Hull; Mr. Rowland Hill Eadie, 108 Woodlands Road, Glasgow; Mr. Malcolm Baird, registrar, Lennoxtown; Mr. Robert Blair, session clerk, Campsie Glen; Mr. John Russell, Milton; Dr. A. T. Wilson, Kirn; and others who may not wish that their names should appear here.

J. C.

SOUTH BANK HOUSE,
KIRKINTILLOCH, *May, 1892.*

CONTENTS.

REV. JAMES LAPSLIE.

NORMAN MACLEOD, D.D.

ROBERT LEE, D.D.

THE CLACHAN OF CAMPSIE.

LENNOXTOWN AND DISTRICT.

THE LENNOXES OF LENNOX CASTLE.

GENEALOGIES AND PARISH TOWERS.

THE ELEVEN PLOUGHS OF BALGROCHAN.

BURSTON, BURDSTON, NOW BIRDSTON.

REV. JOHN GOVANE AND "SESSIONAL AFFAIRES."

APPENDIX.

CALICO PRINTING IN CAMPSIE.

REV. JAMES LAPSLIE,

MINISTER OF CAMPSIE.

A SKETCH OF HIS LIFE AND TIMES.

Inhoduate (handwritten)

REV. JAMES LAPSLIE,

MINISTER OF CAMPSIE.

A SKETCH OF HIS LIFE AND TIMES.

Rev James Lapslie (handwritten)

~~f all the ministers~~ of the parish since the ~~Reformation—perhaps~~ ~~one is no one whose incumbency stands out in such bold relief~~ ~~the~~ Rev. James Lapslie, ~~who~~ held office for a period of pwards of forty years, namely, from 1783 till 1824. His ~~a~~storate forms quite an epoch in the parochial annals. ~~few persons still~~ survive who have heard him preach, ~~or recollect~~ ~~is pastoral visitations,~~ but we are all familiar with his name, nd have heard something about his eccentricities. I venture to ~~ope that a sketch of his life, with~~ some of the incidents of the ~~irring times in which he lived, will prove to the members of the~~ 'oung Men's Association ~~an~~ interesting chapter in our Campsie nnals.

Mr. Lapslie belonged to an old parish family. In 1660 the ame of a John Lapslie appears as " tenant of Baghrochan," the same year another John Lapslie is a " cotar in Boghous." Ir. Lapslie was probably descended from one of those. The urying-place of his father and mother is marked by a tombstone the Clachan churchyard, which may be familiar to many of ou. This stone has a shield, with armorial bearings on the top, nd this motto below—" *Corona mea Christus*," and the following scription :—

> JOHN LAPSLIE,
> LATE OF GREENFOOT AND
> TACKSMAN OF BANCLOICH
> MILLN. DIED 21 SEPTR.,
> 1774, AGED 73.
> MARGARET LOCKHART,
> HIS SPOUSE. DIED DEC. 19,
> 1754, AGED 24.

Greenfoot, the farm of which John Lapslie was tacksman, was small one at the clachan, from which a piece of land was taken 1660 to enlarge the graveyard. It was ultimately merged into

B

Balcorrach farm. At the time of his birth Mr. Lapslie's father was tenant of Bencloich Mill. Young Lapslie displayed aptitude as a scholar. He had an excellent memory, ~~keen observation, and some~~ little rustic wit. His boyish cleverness encouraged his friends to aid him in the struggle to obtain a university education, with the view of his entering the ministry. If the parish tradition is correct Lapslie had the entire sympathy of his father in prosecuting his studies, ~~but his stepmother had small~~ the boy's talents as ~~likely to ensure~~ success in the pulpit, and she is reported to have expressed her opinion that " the craws would never ~~drite on our~~ kirk," a saying which became a proverbial expression in Campsie.

Lapslie studied in Glasgow ~~College~~ University, a seat of learning of which John Mayne wrote—

> " If ye've a knacky son or twa,
>   To Glasgow College send them a';
>   Wi' whilk, for gospel, or for law,
>   Or classic lair,
>   Ye'll find few places here awa',
>   That can compare !

> There ane may be for sma propyne
> Physician, lawyer, or divine ;
> The gem, lang bury'd in the mine,
>   Is polished here,
> Till a' its hidden beauties shine
>   And ~~sparkle clear !"~~

He was licensed by the Glasgow Presbytery on 29th March, 1780. He then became tutor and travelling companion to Sir James Suttie, of Prestongrange, with whom he made a tour on the Continent. Lapslie, ~~who had a~~ aug splendid physique, now cultivated an aristocratic manner, and became an extreme Tory.

~~LIVING OF CAMPSIE BECOMES VACANT.~~

While abroad with his pupil the living of Campsie became vacant by the death, on the 7th May, 1783, of the incumbent, Mr. William Bell, who had been minister since 1747. During the whole thirty-six years of Mr Bell's ministry there was unbroken peace and concord throughout the parish. The people had long been privileged ~~with a succession of earnest, godly ministers,~~ and they appear to have fully appreciated their advantages in this respect. The patronage of the parish vested in the crown. ~~There appears to have been no representation made by any local influential heritors to the Government indicating the wishes of the parish in regard to the filling up of the vacancy. Had this been done there might then have been a chance of the parishioners obtaining their wishes, as they did in the case of Mr Lapslie's successors, Mr Macleod, Mr Lee, and Mr Monro, when the Crown presented the man who was the selection of the heritors and people.~~

Mr. Lapslie aware of the *above*, and
asked the influence of the Suttie family with the Government, on
his behalf. and within
seven weeks of the late minister's death the Crown issued a presentation in favour of James Lapslie,
The people were angry at the
unnecessary haste, and were also dissatisfied with the presentee,
who was not spiritually minded enough for the more devout
parishioners, while his new airs and opinions were not relished by
his old acquaintances. It then transpired that there was a very
general feeling in favour of the appointment of Mr. Crawford,
who had been Mr. Bell's assistant. Mr. Crawford had discharged
the duties with much acceptance, and had thoroughly earned the
goodwill and kindly interest of the people of all classes.

In the temper of the Church Courts of that day any open
resistance would have had no chance of success, and although
much feeling and strong opposition had been aroused and continued to gather in volume and intensity, Mr. Lapslie was
ordained and inducted in November following.

Mr. Lapslie is the only native of the parish as far as I am
aware who has ever been a minister within its bounds.

The result was the secession of all who were opposed to him,
who thereupon resolved to erect a Chapel of Ease, as near the
centre of the parish as possible, where, in respect of their voluntary contributions, it was understood that the communicants
would have the election and appointment of the minister. A site
for this chapel was selected on the estate of Mr. Lennox of
Woodhead, who gave a feu for one hundred years at a
nominal He also laid the foundation
stone and contributed to the funds. Farmers and others assisted
by contributions in money, materials, cartages, or labour. The
contractor for the mason work was Mr. Stevenson, a grandfather
of the late Mr. Stevenson of Alton. The edifice was completed
for an expenditure of about £600 in money. The building was
substantial, *The seats were all of clay*
earth, and wooden forms without backs served for seats.

When the Chapel was a deputation,
consisting of the leading members of the Kirk-Session,
appointed to wait on the Glasgow Presbytery, and make
them acquainted with the state of matters regarding the erection
of the Chapel, and also acquaint them with the unanimous wish
of the promoters that Mr. Crawford should be appointed its first
minister. Dr. Porteous,
afterwards first minister of St. George's,

~~one of the clerical leaders of the day, "a sound divine and a dexterous politician,"~~ informed them that it was in vain for them to think of having Mr. James Crawford, lately assistant, as their minister, as the Presbytery were determined he should not be settled in Campsie. This was duly reported by the deputation, and the people, ~~after consideration,~~ resolved that they would not be dictated to by the Presbytery, ~~and be it happened in Campsie,~~ as in many other parishes, ~~that the si......~~ ~~.....~~ of the members of ~~the Presbytery of the bounds.~~

~~RELI....... ....TION IS ORIGINATED.~~

Fortunately the promoters had still in their own hands the titles of the property, and they could, and did, retain their new church. They were quite unanimous in the course they decided to follow—to forsake the Church of Scotland and apply to the Relief Presbytery to take them under their charge and grant them sermon.

On the 6th October, 1784, eleven months after Mr. Lapslie's induction, "the Relief Presbytery formally agreed to take them under their inspection and give them what supply of sermon they can afford."

KIRK SESSION APPOINTED.

When Mr. Lapslie entered on his duties he found no Kirk-Session in existence, all the elders having withdrawn before his ordination, and the appointment of deacons, which had been revived by Mr. G...... 1701, had ...... fallen into disuse. He had, therefore, to apply to the Presbytery for advice and assistance. After consideration, they empowered the ministers of Kirkintilloch, Cumbernauld, and Kilsyth to act along with him in managing Session affairs and in electing a new Session. A Kirk-Session was in due course appointed. Each elder had assigned to him a district. The members and some of their districts were:— James Muir, Aulton, who had Woodhead, Clachan, and the Eleven Ploughs; John Gray, Birdston, who had Birdston, Kincaid, and the new Printworks; James Calder, Highdykes, who had Auchinreoch, Antermony, Craigbarnet, and Kirkton. J. Hunter, Hayston; John Calder, Baldorran; James Calder, Spithead, were the other members, who also had their districts. There were also admitted afterwards to the eldership, during Mr. Lapslie's ministry, Sir John Stirling of Glorat; John Gardiner, Lennox Mill; William M'Leroy, and John M'Farlan, of Kirkton.

It has been reported of Mr. Lapslie that, at the beginning of his ministry at the Clachan, he occasionally left the pulpit while the first psalm was being sung, walked into some of the cottages and entreated or ordered the members to leave and go into church.

Quite a customary thing

This was ~~zeal exceeding discretion, and was soon discontinued.~~
That he was considered an unwelcome intruder was forced upon
his notice in many ways which would seriously have discouraged
most men. But he, no doubt, had the consolation that a brother
minister had who when his beadle deplored, " What a lot o' folk
are leaving the Kirk the day and gaun to the meeting house,"
jocosely said, " Very true, John, but we dinna see ony o' the
stipend gaun after them."

LUNARDI'S VISIT.

The year following his induction Lunardi ascended in a balloon
from Glasgow and alighted in Campsie, and was hospitably
received by Mr. Lapslie, who returned with him to Glasgow in the
afternoon, and appeared along with him in the boxes of the
theatre the same evening. ~~Having regard to the religious feelings
of the period such an action was calculated to shock~~ the religious
~~sentiments or prejudices of his people, but Mr. Lapslie disregarded
public opinion for the temporary notoriety~~ the incident gave him.

HIS ACCOUNT OF THE PARISH.

It fell to him to write the history of the parish for the *Statistical
Account of Scotland*, edited by Sir John Sinclair, and he performed
his task with great ability and success. ~~No one can read that
production without observing that the~~ writer was a naturalist, a
sportsman, and an agriculturist; in particular, his love of nature
and his keen observation of its varying moods are exhibited. He
describes with the minuteness of a specialist the wild animals and
birds then found within the parish, but no longer to be seen in
it—the different kinds of badgers and foxes, the weasels, otters,
polecats, hedgehogs, wild cats* and the different species of hawks.
" So common (Mr. Lapslie notices) was the glade or kite that its
various modes of flight were considered as an almanac for the
weather, and its note a symbol of moral conduct. Every boy will
tell you that it is not for nought that the glade whistles, alluding
to the note of the bird when it glides through the air, watching
its prey. The golden eagle used formerly to build in our rocks.
Till within these two years (that is up to 1790), we had a regular
bred huntsman, who hunted the district. His salary was paid by
the tenants at so much per plough."
Mr. Lapslie also describes the mineral workings of that period
the parish roads and their maintenance, and the methods of the
Kirk-Session in administering relief to the poor.

*The late Mr. George Miller ~~of the Valley~~ ~~Mr. Lapslie's statements~~ ~~and also~~ about the golden
eagle, ~~though~~ ~~surely~~ have been an erne.

FUNERALS.

His description of the customs that then obtained at funerals is most interesting. Practically the whole parish was invited to attend the funeral of a laird or farmer. Those bidden were invited by special messenger to come to such an one's burial to-morrow against ten hours. Although the invitation was for ten o'clock in the forenoon, the corpse was never interred till the evening. At what Mr. Lapslie calls the old funeral entertainment in Campsie, the routine was as follows:—A prayer was pronounced before and after the "service." The service consisted of, first, a drink of ale, then a dram, then a piece of shortbread, then another dram of some other species of liquor, then a piece of currant bread, and a third dram either of wine or spirits. This was followed by loaves and cheese, pipes and tobacco. This was sometimes repeated, in which case it was a double service. It was sure of being repeated at the "dredgy."* However distant any part of the parish from the place of interment, it was customary for those attending the funeral to carry the corpse on handspokes in easy stages, and with frequent changes of bearers. Before the funeral it was customary to have at least two lyke-wakes, where the young neighbours watched the corpse, being merry or sorrowful according to the situation or rank of the deceased. A funeral cost at least a hundred pounds Scots to any who followed the old course.

Not less interesting is his account of the state of the parish at the three different periods which he brings before us for comparison. In 1714, he tells us that very little butcher meat could have been used, for, the gentry excepted, only three cows are said to have been killed for winter beef in the whole parish. No wheaten bread was used in the parish. The men wore bonnets and plaids, plaiding waistcoats, and plaiding hose. No English cloth whatever was worn by the inhabitants, the gentry excepted. There were no enclosures except about gentlemen's gardens or woods. There was neither cart nor chaise; and the gentry rode to church on horseback. The rental of the whole parish was only £800. Thirty years later, in 1744, there was still no wheaten bread, nor were potatoes, carrots, or turnips used by the inhabitants. Only a few kail were planted in the yards for the pot. There was still no chaise in the parish, but some few carts were used to carry out manure in spring. The wheels were not shod with iron, and the moment the manure was carried out they were taken down till next spring. The bulk of the farmers ploughed their land with what was styled the broad plough, four horses being yoked

---

* The "dredgy," according to Dr. Jamieson, means (1) the funeral service, (2) the compotation of the funeral company on their return to the house of the deceased after the interment had taken place. Some derive it from *Dirigi nos Domine*, one of the psalms sung in the office for the dead.

abreast. In 1748 the rental of parish was £1500, but in 1763 it had risen to £3000. The population in 1783, the year in which Mr. Lapslie was inducted, was 1627, and consisted of 317 householders or " Reeks," giving an average of over five for each family or reek. In 1793 the rental was £7000, and the population had risen to 2517, owing to new Printfields.* In 1794 there were nearly 200 carts in the parish. Mr. David Dunn, grazier and famed cattle breeder, while paying a rental of £1400 per annum for grass lands, did not so much as grow a cabbage plant. Potatoes were now used by all classes for six months of the year. Wheaten bread was common, and there were actually two bakers in the parish. Three hundred fat cows were killed annually, about Martinmas, for winter provision. Every lad was now dressed in English cloths and fancy vests, with thread or cotton stockings; and every girl in cotton stuff, black silk cloaks, and fancy bonnets. Inclosures were now gradually being made. Up to 1763 farms were possessed in run-rig, and as soon as the crop was cut the cattle of the neighbouring tenants grazed in common till next spring. Mr. Lapslie says there had been a sudden transition from strict to loose manners, caused by a number of wandering people settling at the different printfields, but that was now improved. His strong political bias comes out when he refers to the operative part of this community, whom he writes of as conceiving themselves to be groaning under the most abject slavery. Their associations for Parliamentary Reform he terms Jacobin Societies. He rails at the Relief meeting, which had drawn off a considerable number from the Establishment, and made them in some measure hostile to the powers that be. Then he goes on to " be doubtful but the spirit of innovation was encouraged by their public teachers with a view to increase the adherents to their own tabernacle."

Mr. Lapslie also gives a brief sketch of the ecclesiastical history of the parish, and details his ministerial duties in 1794, which consisted of visiting and regularly examining the congregation once in the year, preaching three discourses every Sunday from 10th April to 10th October, and in winter two discourses, one of them always a lecture. The sacrament was given once a year; three discourses on the Fast-day, two on Sunday, the action sermon in the church and the evening sermon, besides preaching in the tent; and two on Monday. He states that " the ecclesiastical discipline of this parish is still kept up. As for discipline against fornicators, two days doing public penance in the church are required, besides a fine of a crown for each guilty person to the poor. Public baptism is regularly adhered to, parents requiring private baptism for their children pay half-a-crown to the poor."

*In 1891 the population of the parish was 5338, being a decrease of 535 since 1881, and the valuation for 1891-2 was £25,926 1s 2d.

Great changes took place during Lapslie's ministry. His own boyhood was spent in the parish, and he has recorded that at the time of writing his Account (about 1793), he had not heard of a salmon being seen in the Glazert for eighteen years. Yet, in former times, salmon were plentiful in that stream and it was a great deposit for salmon spawn, which greatly recruited the fisheries in the Clyde. It was customary, though unlawful, to burn the water for them in spawning time. This method of killing salmon by torches made of the dressings of lint, and long spears with which to strike the fish, was then a common sport, both on the Glazert and on the Blane. Notwithstanding the statement that he had not heard of a salmon in the Glazert, salmon came up that stream till 1798, when a weir was placed on the Kelvin at Killermont, which effectually barred their passage. The older weir at the Partick Mills, while an obstacle, did not entirely prevent the fish getting over, as it was low. From the erection of the Killermont weir salmon have been unknown in the Campsie waters, but printworks, alum works, bleach works, distilleries were soon in evidence on these streams as injurious to the fish lower down, and their pollutions might have caused the fish to disappear had the burns above them not been well stocked and able to replenish them.

CASE OF THOMAS MUIR.

Mr. Lapslie came into the most enviable notoriety in connection with the political prosecution of Mr. Thomas Muir of Huntershill. He was on terms of intimacy with Muir's family, from whom he had always received the greatest kindness and hospitality. He had been their guest for weeks at a time. But when the Government decided to institute a prosecution against Muir, he exerted himself most strenuously in fishing out evidence to be used against him. He attended the preliminary precognition of the witnesses for the Crown, some of whom he sought to influence, and in order to influence a witness to do so, he, in the presence of the Sheriff, hinted "that it was in the power of the Sheriff of Lanarkshire to procure him a berth." He was not himself cited as a witness by the Crown, but he went to Edinburgh and voluntarily tendered himself as a witness. To his being accepted Muir objected, stating his reasons for doing so, and intimating that it was his intention as soon as he was at liberty to do so, to institute proceedings against him. After discussion, the court sustained Muir's objection, and Lapslie was ordered to stand down. The cruel sentence of fourteen years' transportation, the harsh treatment after sentence, the rescue under such peculiar circumstances, the adventures, and the tragic death of Muir made a deep impression throughout this country and America. Lapslie's conduct alienated many of his friends, and it drove his opponents in the parish to exasperation. It was remarked that he never prospered afterwards, a blight seemed to fall on his whole life, his usefulness and influence for good were impaired, and he was harassed by personal worries and family troubles. The national interest taken in the political trial of Muir gave him a wide notoriety. The Government, in 1793, appointed him chaplain to the Blue Gown Beggars, for which he received £50 a year. The duties of the office consisted in preaching a sermon annually in Stirling. This appointment to an ecclesiastical post was at once understood to be a recognition of his officious political zeal. That this was so indeed was seen from the fact that it was continued to his family after his death. Such a reward gave rise to heated controversy; it inspired the satirist, and gave the rhymster a popular theme. The minister of Campsie was honoured with a cartoon in Kay's Portraits. Under the name of Pension Hunter, he is represented dressed in black, with top boots and white stockings, reading a book on the "Management of Bees," of which he was said to be the author. He is standing on an open Bible, inscribed with Rev. xiii.—"And the world wondered after the beast." In the letterpress to the portrait it was remarked of him that "in settling accounts he was the dreichest of the dreich, and nothing in the shape of a gift came amiss to him." The sting of this was its truthfulness. He was everywhere held up to contempt for his ingratitude to the Muir family, and for extreme political servility. Even in the streets of Glasgow and Campsie ballads were sung in doggerel like this—

> "My name is Jamie Lapslie,
> I preach, and I pray,
> And as an informer
> Expect a good pay."

Long afterwards the same hostile feeling was reproduced in the poems and songs of Alexander Rodger, who in his day gave a great deal of attention to the Campsie folks, some of whom he introduced into his verses and sarcasm. He refers to Lapslie in "Black coats and cravats sae white" :—

> "There's pensioner Jamie, corruption's chief tool,
> Whose tears flow as freely as whisky at Yule;
>   Wie his black coat and cravat sae white.
> So keenly he feels for the suffering poor
> That he'd willingly do what he did for Tom Muir—
> To get them sent off to a far better state,
> By hanging or starving them out at the gate;
>   Wie his black coat and cravat sae white."

HIS FIGHT WITH FORREST, THE MILLER.

It was during the period of great local excitement which followed Muir's trial that the incident occurred in which Lapslie's name as Minister of Campsie got published far and near, as having fought with one of his parishioners. It is, I believe, an undoubted fact that a regular pitched battle took place between the minister and a miller named Forrest. Forrest was an admirer of Thomas Muir of Huntershill, and in common with a great many in Campsie was very wroth at the part taken by Mr. Lapslie in connection with Mr. Muir's prosecution. Meeting Lapslie one day he gave the minister a bit of his mind, adding "that were it not for his black coat, he would have thrashed him then and there." Lapslie, who was a tall powerfully built man, accepted the challenge at once. He threw off his black coat, and casting it on the ground, said, "Lie there divinity. Now here am I, Jamie Lapslie!" A regular fight then took place, in which the minister proved the better man. The fight with the miller occurred about 1793. The alacrity with which the minister doffed his black coat, and the success with which he emerged from the contest, gave the incident a world-wide currency. The late Rev. Dr. Monro encountered the story in South America, in 1860. He had been commissioned by the General Assembly to proceed to British Guiana, on a mission to the churches there. It was advertised that on a certain day, in a church named, a sermon would be preached by the Rev. Thomas Monro, M.A., Minister of the parish of Campsie. A Scotchman of rather an enquiring turn of mind, came to the vestry after the service and asked if he was the minister who had thrashed the miller. Dr. Monro was greatly amused at being thought capable of taking rank with those military clerics who could thrash a miller in a stand up fight or "pitch on" a farmer.

ENFORCEMENT OF NEW MILITIA ACT.

In 1797 an Act of Parliament was passed anent the militia in Scotland. Under it all persons not labouring under bodily infirmity and not specially exempted as a class, such as peers, half-pay officers, clergy, teachers, and persons over 45 years of age, were liable to be chosen by ballot to serve in the militia, unless they found a substitute. The introduction of this Act was unpopular, and its enforcement caused many riots throughout Scotland. That it was a Government measure ensured Mr. Lapslie's support. He threw himself with characteristic energy into giving effect to the Act within his own parish. This was strongly resisted by those liable to be called on to serve—the block printers, block cutters, and weavers being specially prominent. The hostility became so strong that it found vent in action, and on the 22nd August, 1797, when Mr. and Mrs. Lapslie were absent, the outbuildings at the manse were deliberately set on fire and burned to the ground, and but for the prompt assistance rendered by the people in the Clachan, the manse itself would have shared the same fate. The parties to this wilful fire-raising were said to be well known, but no proceedings were ever instituted to bring them to justice. When the minister realized the volume and intensity of the hostility against him, he took the more prudent course of allowing it to die down. To have instituted a prosecution would only have intensified it.

THE ORGAN QUESTION IN GLASGOW.

In the year 1806, Dr. Ritchie, of St. Andrew's Church, Glasgow, supported by his whole congregation, wished to obtain the use of an organ as an accompaniment to the church psalmody. This, according to Dr. Strang, "at once roused the intolerant spirit of Glasgow Presbytery, who at once saw in this reform the most insidious and fatal of all engines to destroy the venerable Kirk of Scotland. The tender conscience of the redoubtable Mr. Lapslie of Campsie was at once stung, the unimaginative brain of Dr. Rennie was at once set on fire," &c.

In course of time, without leave either from Town Council or Presbytery, an organ was placed in the Church. This roused the Presbytery to madness, and the Town Council were also displeased; but Dr. Ritchie, in January, 1808, obtained an appointment to the High Church in Edinburgh, and he left the battle to be fought out by others. The Presbytery, before he could be loosed from his charge, tried his conduct before the Court. After several of the most violent and wordy of the objectors had poured out their wrath on their brother, they succeeded in getting the majority of the Presbytery to agree to the following resolution :—"The Presbytery did and do hereby declare that the use of organs in the public worship of God is contrary to *the law of the land* and to *the law and constitution of the Established Church*, and, therefore, the Presbytery did and hereby do prohibit the use of organs in all churches and chapels within their bounds." The question excited great interest at the time, and gave rise to much discussion and bickering.

Mr. Lapslie was in the hottest of the fight. He published " A Statement of the Proceedings of the Presbytery of Glasgow, relative to the use of an Organ in St. Andrew's Church in the public worship of God." This was written in a spirit intensely hostile to the proposal. On the other side, a satirical political squib, entitled " Dulness," was published in 1807, in which amongst other opponents, Mr. Lapslie came under the lash. This is what is said of him—

> " The great Profundus rose,
> Broad was his forehead, pointed was his nose ;
> His swelling cheek and wildly rolling eye
> Betokened pride that aimed at something high.
> Fat had he grown beneath the Royal hand—
> A famed protector of a sinking land ;
> (For much he talked in troublous times now past,
> And got a pension for his talk at last.)
> Man of great words but man of little sense,
> Now, rise, and use thy boisterous eloquence ;
> Be thou the mighty bulwark to defend
> The Church from all the dangers that impend ;

Rise and display thy law, thy classic lore,
Each innovation of the times deplore;
Condemn whate'er thy fathers did not know,
And all thy pedantry and dulness show.
And much he spoke, the goddess foe to sense
Listened with joy to his frothy eloquence.
She iuly hailed her kingdom now begun,
And hailed Profundus an adopted son."

PRESERVES COLLINS' GRAVE.

The first act which put him really in sympathy with his parishioners was his resolute conduct in preserving the grave of the
Rev. John Collins, the murdered minister, from being appropri-
ated as a burying-place by one of the parishioners. The memory
of Collins had always been cherished. Notwithstanding the great
scarcity of ground, his grave had always remained undisturbed.
About 1806, John Brown, of the Newton of Campsie, made some
claim to obtain this ground for himself and family. Mr. Lapslie
prevented him from opening Collins' grave, and, in consequence,
had an action raised against him in the Sheriff Court of Stirling.
Unsuccessful there Mr. John Brown appealed to the Court of
Session, who confirmed the decision of the lower court. Mr.
Lapslie this time had the hearty support of his Kirk-Session, who
entered the following minute in their Record :—

" CLACHAN OF CAMPSIE,
"5th Feb., 1807.

" Considering it is of the utmost importance for the interest and peace of
the parish that the graves and burial-places of our dead should not be encroached upon and disturbed by violent possession, therefore, we, the Kirk-
Session of Campsie, most heartily approve of and sanction, as we did formerly in a verbal manner, the Rev. Mr. Lapslie's conduct in defending the
grave of the Rev. Mr Collins, formerly minister of this parish, from the
encroachment and violent possession of John Brown, cottar and labourer,
in Newton of Campsie. That, in order that there be no dubiety concerning
our hearty approbation and sanction of Mr. Lapslie's conduct in carrying
out the law plea against the said John Brown, now before the Sheriff of
Stirling, we order a mandate to be made out for this purpose, to be subscribed by us respectively and individually, as elders and members of the
Kirk-Session of Campsie.

(Signed) " JAMES LAPSLIE, Moderator.
" JOHN M'FARLAN Session Clerk."

For the time being Mr. Lapslie became the champion of popular
feeling. This did much to allay the old irritation against him
and to engender a better disposition towards him in many who
had hitherto been always in antagonism.

PROPOSED NEW CHURCH.

The question of a new church was one of the deepest interest to
Mr. Lapslie. Even as early as 1794 Mr. Lapslie wrote in the
Statistical Account of Scotland :—" If the population of this
district continues to increase there will be absolute necessity for
building a more commodious church in a more centrical site for

the better accommodation of the inhabitants." The large secession to the Relief which his induction caused had relieved the pressure in the parish church for a time, but as population was continuing to increase the want of accommodation was becoming year after year more clamant. With the cry for more seats came also that for a church on a more suitable site, and nearer to where the bulk of the population resided. The great increase of population had taken place at the Newtown and the Milltown, and the unsuitableness of the Clachan site to the existing requirements of the parish was generally acknowledged. It was found to be an excuse for only attending church for a Sunday or two before and after the communion, and when the defaulters were remonstrated with, the long distances from Torrance, Birdston, Milton, and Lennoxtown, were urged in excuse, in addition to which there was the want of room if they did attend. The interest was getting deeper and deeper, two parties forming, holding opposite views—the one wishing to retain the church in the Clachan, the other desirous to have a new church in the centre of the parish. Miss Lennox of Woodhead was strongly in favour of retaining the Clachan site. At a meeting of the heritors on 15th September, 1821, it was unanimously agreed that a new church should be built as early as possible in the year 1823, and that it was impossible that it could be built within the churchyard. A new site was therefore agreed on, to the east of the Clachan Green, where there is still a large elm tree. almost directly in front of Mr. Jamieson Provan's cottage. Mr. Stirling of Craigbarnet and Mr. M'Farlan of Kirkton were appointed to wait on Miss Lennox, to ascertain whether she approved of this site, or if she would suggest any others. Miss Lennox approved of the site, on certain conditions, provided the heritors adopted the plan of new church submitted by Mr. David Hamilton, architect, Glasgow, and provided also that the ground required would be paid for at a fair valuation. The plan which Miss Lennox was determined to have shewed a Gothic building to seat 1200. On certain objections being made to the size as being larger than what was necessary, and the expense in consequence greater than the occasion called for, it was agreed to reduce the width shewn on the plan and give accommodation for only 1000, in order to meet the objections of these grumblers. On 2nd April, 1822, a committee was authorised to invite offers to execute the work in conformity with Mr. Hamilton's plan and specification, and the meeting separated under the impression that the whole affair had been happily settled. On the 6th August of that year a meeting of the heritors was called to decide as to the offers sent in, when, instead of proceeding to discuss the offers and accept the most favourable, Mr. Buchanan of Carbeth submitted the following motion:—" That the building of the new church should be put off till 1826, in consequence of the pressure of the times, and that the church is not ruinous, but in a condition to afford public worship, notwithstanding of the minute of the heritors of date 15th September, 1821. Sir Samuel Stirling seconded this motion. Mr. Kincaid moved as a counter-motion:—" That this meeting follow out the former resolution of the heritors and proceed to examine the estimates." This having been seconded the meeting proceeded to vote. *Delay* (Mr. Buchanan's motion)—Buchanan, Sir S. Stirling, Thomson, Maitland, Downie, Buckie, Angus, M'Nichol, Fergus, Ewing, Peat, Wilson, and Turner—13, being a majority in number. *Proceed* (Mr. Kincaid's counter-motion)—Stirling of Craigbarnet, Kincaid, Kincaid, jun., Davidson (factor), Gordon, Gray, Reid, Dick, J. Buchanan, M'Farlane, and Samson—11, a minority in number but a majority in value. This surprise vote upset the whole scheme on the very day when it was expected the matter would have been settled by the acceptance of tenders. No one could have been more deeply disappointed than Mr. Lapslie. The tactics pursued by the majority were severely criticised, and controversy followed, which was about to end in litigation, when Mr. Lapslie died suddenly at the end of the year following, and his death caused a truce.

HOME AND FAMILY.

On 10th Sept., 1792, Mr. Lapslie was married to Elizabeth Ann, third daughter of Sir John Stirling, the fifth baronet of Glorat, then in her eighteenth year. Tradition has it that the lady did not look with favour on the advances of her reverend suitor, who was considerably her senior in age, but Sir John had a very large family of sons and daughters and a limited income, and he took a very prosaic and unsentimental view of the situation, declaring there was no use for old maids if honest men could be got to marry them. The young lady took the hint and yielded to parental suggestion, and the marriage followed in due course. It could not be called a happy one, different tastes and incompatibility of temper manifested themselves, and the Clachan gossips had it that sometimes for weeks together the husband and wife did not speak to each other. Where it was necessary to communicate this was done in writing. Those gossips further alleged extravagance at home, and it was known that the minister was in debt wherever he could obtain credit. There was also said truly feckless management, as it frequently happened that the manse domestic had to be sent out late on the Saturday night to borrow tea, sugar, bread, &c., of which it had just been discovered that the stock was insufficient for family use till Monday. The children grew up proud and self-willed, and did not seem to receive careful home training. Even their manners were not attended to, and the boys were wild and under no restraint. In 1806, when Mrs. Gartshore Stirling was making her first call at the manse after her marriage, while seated in the drawing-room with Mrs. Lapslie, a boy rudely rushed into the room, roaring out, "Father! father! leather Sandy for biting Mary (the house-maid) and kicking "——. Here he discovered that his father was not in the room, but that his mother and a lady were, where-upon he bolted out as unceremoniously as he had rushed in.

Being without any restraint at home, where their mischief was allowed to pass unpunished, the boys proved very troublesome pupils in the parish school, where they sorely tried the temper and patience of Mr. M'Farlane, the teacher. One day, during the morning prayer, three boys—a Lapslie, a Stewart of Blairturnach, and a Muir of the Clachan, an older brother of the late R. C. Muir—set the teacher's coat tails on fire while his eyes were shut. The teacher ascertained who were the parties to the trick, but re-mained ominously silent. He carefully examined his tawse, and was evidently not satisfied, but he said nothing. At the play hour, however, he took a walk up the Glen, where he selected a switch, which he carefully dressed, and with this he administered such a thrashing to the three delinquents as had probably never been seen in that schoolroom before. On another occasion one of the Lapslie boys, on being reproved or punished by Mr. M'Farlane, struck him. The teacher promptly expelled both him and his brother. Mr. M'Farlane had already endured much provocation, he was receiving no fees for his labours, and his patience was completely exhausted. But the father took the boy back in the afternoon, and the scholars saw the minister standing weeping at the door of the school, entreating the schoolmaster to take his son back. The old teacher's heart relented at the pitiful sight, and the boy was allowed to resume his place in the school. There is another story of a "lark" of one of the boys. On one occasion a minister was officiating in the absence of Mr. Lapslie. He had returned to the manse and was waiting for his dinner. The ser-vant entered and placed a gigot of mutton on the table, but almost immediately thereafter one of the sons came into the room, seized the mutton, and ran off. Having heard something of the wildness of the family, he realized that if he were to get anything to eat he should not lose the mutton. He therefore pursued the runaway almost to the end of the road at Haughhead Bridge, and forcibly took possession of the mutton, which he carried back in triumph, and then had his dinner. There is another story in which one of the boys was the principal. A dinner party was being given which Mrs. Lapslie was particularly anxious should pass off with as much style as possible. To contribute to this, one of her own boys was dressed up as a page in buttons, and had to assist to wait table. He was carefully drilled in his duties by his mother, who promised the largest plum on the table as a reward. Everything passed off well till the fruit was being handed round. In order to secure the plum, Mrs. Lapslie thought of lifting it and putting it on her own plate, to give the boy after-wards. She was taking it up when the page, looking frightened, exclaimed in the hearing of all the guests, " Oh! mother, mother, that's my plum!" ~~The tableau can be easily imagined.~~

Lapslie had a family of four sons (John, James, Alexander, and Andrew) and two daughters (Margaret and Gloriana). With him Gloriana, the youngest, was a great favourite.

LAPSLIE AS A PREACHER.

Lapslie's preaching was said to be very irregular. He had a few crack sermons, but was often very unprepared for his pulpit duties ; but he had the frankness to confess this himself, apologising from the pulpit " that there was nothing new to-day, but if they would all come back next Sabbath he would have something better." He had a strongly emotional nature, on which he placed no restraint ; a certain fervid eloquence, which was accompanied by an extraordinary amount of physical exertion. One who heard him preaching at Milton described him as beginning to fumble with a vest button, then button by button the vest was unbuttoned, until at the end he appeared to be undressing, all the while he was laying off his sermon, with the perspiration streaming off him. But the most peculiar feature about his speaking was that he was frequently moved to tears by his own utterances, and when this was the case his tears were both freely and copiously shed. The sight of a man moved to tears by his own speeches, and especially in public, in the pulpit or on the platform, is so unusual that his " greeting " added a zest to all his public appearances, which were considered flat when there was no good display. The facility with which he could " turn on" the "greet" was wonderful. His brother-in-law, the late Mr. Joseph Stirling, who died unmarried, at Hillhead, Kirkintilloch, in 1878, remarked of him—" Mr. Lapslie is an awful man for greeting. Man, he would greet reading an almanac!" Lapslie had seen the Rev. George Whitfield and had heard him preach. Whitfield's preaching made a deep impression on him, and afterwards he seems to have taken Whitfield as his model. Whitfield's preaching has been thus described:—" He gesticulated, stamped, and wept with a tempestuous abandonment to which the most successful efforts of counterfeit passion on the stage seemed poor."

After a severe snowstorm Lapslie was accompanying his sons a part of the way to Glasgow, where they were going to resume attendance on the classes at the College, and John Edwards joined the party going through Lennoxtown. The conversation turned on Whitfield, whom Lapslie said he had heard, and whom he declared to be the greatest preacher since the days of the Apostle Paul. Lapslie suddenly stopped, and raising his arms to heaven, in imitation of Whitfield, declared he could never forget the impression made upon himself of awed solemnity when Whitfield lifted up his arms in appealing to heaven. This incident perhaps, gives the clue to Lapslie's manner of speaking in the pulpit. While there was often an apparent straining after dramatic effect, with but indifferent success, his addresses were sometimes strikingly eloquent. He took advantage of local incidents with which the congregation were all familiar to point a moral and reach their hearts. There was one occasion on which he did this effectively.

RAB'S PRAYER.

A "natural" in the Clachan, named Rab, one day accidentally set himself on fire. In his distress he threw himself down on his straw bed, and in this way ignited it also. He was terribly burned, and after lingering in great agony for a short time died. To his great physical sufferings were added mental distress. In prospect of death he was alarmed about his soul. A neighbour, distinguished as Red Rab, called on him to inquire for him. He revealed his state of mind, and piteously entreated his neighbour—" Oh, pray for me, Rab; pray for me." " Oh, man," replied Red Rab, " I canna pray." Then said the poor natural—" Oh, the Lord help us baith, then ! " Those who heard Mr Lapslie tell this story and point its moral were never likely to forget it.

There is a very vivid description of his appearance when addressing the General Assembly. The case itself was a charge of immorality against a minister, who was accused of having been too familiar with his housekeeper. ~~For the people to seek to get rid even of an immoral minister awakened all his hatred to~~ the accused. The writer is Lockhart, in " Peter's Letters to his Kinsfolk," and Lapslie is thus described :—" Mr. Lapslie is undoubtedly the most enthusiastic speaker I ever heard. He is a fine, tall, bony man, with a face full of fire and a bush of white locks, which he shakes about him like the *thyrsus* of a Bacchanal. He tears his waistcoat open, he bellows, he sobs, he weeps, and sits down at the end of the harangue trembling to the finger ends, like an exhausted pythoness."

MISSIONS—REV. EDWARD IRVING'S SPEECH.

In politics Lapslie was an ultra Tory. ~~Democracy was to him~~ He saw it ⅄ missions to the heathen, in Sabbath schools, and he was rather hostile to these movements in consequence; but he consented to take the chair at a public meeting of the inhabitants, held on 30th January, 1819, in the Lennoxtown Public School-house, when the Campsie Bible, Missionary, and School Society was constituted. At its third annual meeting, on 14th August, 1821, in the Relief Meeting-house, after sermon the Rev. James Brown, Relief Church, the Rev. James Lapslie called to the chair. Although presiding, Mr. Lapslie, in his opening address as chairman, showed little or no sympathy with the cause of Christian missions. It appeared to him that the conversion of the heathen was far too vast and difficult a matter to be attempted by human organization. In his opinion it could only be affected by the direct visitation of the Lord God Almighty. The adoption of the report was then moved by the Rev. Edward Irving, assistant to Dr. Chalmers, Glasgow, and seconded by the Rev. Andrew Marshall, Kirkintilloch. Irving began his address by declaring he could not agree with the Chairman's views, and proceeded to deliver an earnest address on the duties of Christians to send the Gospel to lands in pagan darkness. The Chairman demurred to some of his glowing periods. The interruption roused Irving, his eyes flashed, he grasped his stick nervously, and declared that the man did not exist on earth who would deter him from uttering what he believed to be the truth. He closed an earnest and impressive address with a passionate appeal on behalf of missions, and so deeply impressed was one of his hearers, the late Rev. Dr. Edwards, that after a lapse of seventy years the whole incident remained engraven on his memory—the looks, action, and words.

DISCIPLINE—HOW FINES WERE DISBURSED.

Under him the rigid discipline of previous times was relaxed. About 1791 a money payment for the poor of the parish was accepted in lieu of standing two days in church, and there is an entry under date of 13th August, 1807, to the effect that ————, eldest son of ————, in ————, paid a fine of five pounds sterling to the poor, being the sum required by the Kirk-Session in lieu of his undergoing public discipline by standing two days in church, being the alternative allowed by the Session about sixteen years ago, and in which already several of the parishioners had acquiesced, receiving a Sessional rebuke at the time they paid the fine. The money thus paid at first to the poor was soon diverted to other purposes. On 14th January, 1810, a fine of five guineas was levied. The session, for particular reasons, agreed to return two. Two were given to Mr. Lapslie in part payment of the balance due to him for the winter's sacrament, the other guinea was ordered to be distributed among the regular poor. On 19th January, 1812, a 15/ fine, levied for irregular marriage, was devoted to buying a new pulpit Bible. A very intelligent member of his church had frequently counted the number of worshippers. On three several occasions the enumeration was 37, 40, and 50, all told. The church was very small, and there was a very short space between the pulpit and the gallery. It was no unusual occurrence for Mr Lapslie, as soon as he had pronounced the benediction, to accost a hearer thus:— "Jamie, ye'll bring a cart o' coals the morn." The late Rev. Dr.

Edwards has told how he was admitted a member of the Parish Church. He went along to the manse to see the minister, with a view to his joining the church. The minister was out walking in his glebe. He was dressed carelessly in knee-breeches, and one of his stockings had slipped down, leaving his leg partially bare. He accosted his visitor—" Well, my man, what do you want? " " I want to join. I want a token." "What's your name? " " John Edwards." " Who are you? who is your father? " " Edwards, the mason." " Oh, a very decent man. Here, take your token." This was all the enquiry. Because his father was a very decent man—" Here, take your token ! "

ANECDOTES.

Allusion had been made in Kay's Portraits to his dreichness in paying accounts. He was always hard up and in debt, and in his straits for money tried begging and borrowing in the parish, where his credit was soon gone. In his impecuniosity he actually tried to borrow from Laird Reid, Hayston. The response came promptly—" I say, lad, I canna gie ye ony siller," but in order to compensate somewhat for the refusal of money which he could well have given, he stuffed Lapslie's pockets with bread and cheese, till they had the appearance of meal pocks. Mr. Lapslie's impecuniosity made him disagreeably familiar with duns, and he acquired a wonderful dexterity in eluding their pursuit. Constant practice developed fertility of resources, plausibility of excuses, and soft sawder. It is said that a grocer, seeing him about to pass his shop door when the street was quiet, thought it was a capital opportunity to remind him of his account, and accosted him. Mr. Lapslie enquired for himself and for his family, and passed on before the grocer could get a word in. But the minister turned back and cried out—" Oh, Mrs. Lapslie was just saying the cheese was done ; you might just send a cheese the same as the last. Good-bye." One story as to his borrowing is that he called on Mr. David Fleming, who, when he went away, came laughing into the weaving shop, where his brother, John Brown, and others were employed. He said—" The minister's very anxious to get a loan of ten pounds, and says, ' Ye maun lend me the ten pounds and I'll mak' ye an elder.' " Mr. Fleming lent the money and was made an elder, and at his death the ten pounds were still standing at Mr. Lapslie's debit—an undoubted bad debt. An eldership in Campsie cannot now be obtained for ten pounds.

Mr Baird, draper and merchant, Kirkintilloch, was an active member of Dr. Marshall's church. He wrote to Mr. Lapslie and asked him to preach a special sermon on behalf of some undenominational object. Mr. Lapslie complied readily with the request and preached an excellent sermon. Shortly afterwards he called at Mr. Baird's shop, and said he wished some cloth to make up into a suit of clothes for himself. He saw what suited him exactly, and having selected what he required he had it put up into a parcel, which, he said, he would just take with him. Then came the question—" Will you pay for it just now or will I mark it down ? " " Oh," said Lapslie, " I gied ye a sermon lately, this'll just do fine for the sermon," and away he went with his parcel under his arm.

Lapslie often obtained the loan of a horse to ride to Glasgow to attend meetings of one kind or another. On such occasions he generally contrived to evade payment of the Balquharrage Toll. He always made some excuse or another, generally that he had no small change and would pay next journey. He sometimes went into the toll-house to admire the young toll-keeper's live birds, and the cages he had made for them, then he would pat him on the head and say he was a very clever boy, and thus try to please him for the loss of his toll money.

When, in the autumn of 1824, the Rev. David Gemmell, formerly of Gourock, but then Bailie Gemmell, Kirkintilloch, asked him if he would marry him, he consented to do so upon one or other of these conditions. As his suit of clothes was very shabby the Rev. Bailie would either require to give him a new suit or come to the Clachan and repair his old ones. Rather a shabby reminder that in his early days at Milton the bailie had worked as a tailor.

James Dennistoun of Golfhill, Glasgow, the famous banker, and founder of the great mercantile house of J. & A. Dennistoun, was born in a thatched cottage that once stood near the Clousy Firs. His father afterwards became tenant of New Mill of Glorat, and James started for Glasgow to push his way in life, crossing the Glazert opposite New Mill with the proverbial half-crown in his pocket. He continued to take an interest in Campsie, and was very kind to the minister. Lapslie, who latterly was most slovenly and careless in the matter of dress, had called on him one day, when he said, " Excuse me, Mr. Lapslie, but that hat of yours is very shabby. Just step down to———, mentioning a well known hatter, and get a new hat, and tell him to put it down to me." " If you call that shabby," replied Lapslie, " I wonder what ye would say to my boys' hats." " Well, well," said Mr. Dennistoun, " take a new hat out to your boys also."

MR. LAPSLIE AND THE MINISTER OF THE RELIEF.

Mr. Lapslie regarded the minister of the Relief Kirk with no friendly eye; they had occasion to meet sometimes at funerals, and there is a story told of a funeral procession proceeding westwards by the old road to the Clachan, and when going over the Cumroch Brae, which was a very rough road, Mr. Colquhoun stumbled and fell, his head coming into contact with a large stone at the side of the road. When he had regained his feet, he put his hand up and exclaimed, " Oh, my head; it's ringin'."

" Ringin'," said Lapslie superciliously, "ringin', then it must be empty. Only empty vessels ring." "Well," said Colquhoun, "yours would not ring, at any rate, Lapslie." "Why not?" "Man, it's crackit, and no crackit pot 'll ring."

THE CREAM OF THE PARISH AND THE BUTTER.

The feelings of sectarian rivalry displayed by the pastors were also shown by their respective flocks. The Reliefs often assumed an air of superior sanctity, but carried things a little too far, when they alleged that all that were worth anything had forsaken the Auld Kirk, in fact, that in the Relief Kirk was to be found the cream of the parish. This came to be rather a popular phrase. It was used by a farmer one day, who sent his butter to Glasgow for sale. Shortly before this his butter had been stopped and weighed by the Glasgow authorities, and being found too light had been taken to the police office and confiscated. Dryburgh retorted, "So! so! the cream o' the parish gangs tae the Relief Kirk, and the butter, Broon, gangs tae the polis office in Glasgow." But the keenness of feeling had greatly abated on both sides before Lapslie's death.

THE AGRICULTURAL SOCIETY PLOUGH THE GLEBE.

One evening, on his way home, Mr. Lapslie went into a public-house to obtain an orange for Gloriana. The public-house was then kept by a sister of the late Laird Buchanan of Crosshouse. In the wee room off the kitchen there was a number of farmers assembled in connection with their Agricultural Society. Recognizing the minister, Stevenson of Alton called out they "had no secrets, would he no' come ben?" He complied and joined them. Laird Buchanan asked him if he would not join their society. When he did not respond, the laird offered on behalf of the members that if he would join their society the members would put his glebe right for him. He asked what membership cost. He was told it was only five shillings a year. He thereupon became a member, and Laird Buchanan was authorised to make arrangements for giving him a day's ploughing of the glebe. Seven or eight farmers united and made a somewhat better job of it than the bowed furrows they found on it.

---

* The Rev. James Colquhoun was the first minister of the Relief. After a successful pastorate of ten years, he was obliged to resign in consequence of a *fama*. He had gone to attend a Fair in the western part of the county. Here three young men proposed to put the Relief minister "on the fuddle." He seems to have been of a frank and sociable nature and fell into the trap set for him. He was put on his horse facing the tail and led in this state to the Relief Manse of Kilmaronock. When this became known in Campsie he resigned. It is said of the three young men who for a bit of amusement made him tipsy, that not one of them died in his bed. All came to sudden or violent deaths; and this was popularly regarded as a "judgment" for their tempting Mr Colquhoun.

THE RELIEF FARMERS PLOUGH IT.

On another occasion, when he had not been getting on very well with his farmers, he applied to Malcolm Brown for some assistance in working the glebe, and complained to Brown that his own folk, with one or two exceptions, would not give him a helping hand. Brown replied, " Weel, weel, ye whiles speak gey an' hard aboot us wee bodies in the Relief Kirk, but provided ye'll no' ask any o' your ain folks, I think I can get as many ploughs frae elders in the Relief as 'ill soon put the manse glebe in order." The minister gladly acceded to the conditions, so Brown went on, " Weel, we'll dae this for you the noo, and, tak my word for it, ye'll never be ill off again to get your glebe ploughed. Your ain folk will no' like to see the Reliefs at the job." The Relief ploughs duly turned out, and soon accomplished the work. There was abundance of refreshment provided, both meat and drink, and Mr. Lapslie was most effuse with his thanks. The farmers were highly pleased with their treatment, and before the meeting had broken up the Reliefs were getting rather boisterous in their hilarity. One of those who held a plough on this occasion is still spared to enjoy a green old age, and Mr. William Craig, late of Balglass, is now perhaps the sole survivor of that day's ploughing. This was the last occasion Mr. Lapslie ever required to have his glebe sorted, as he died before the end of that year.

TAKES OUT HIS TEETH AT BIRDSTON.

Calling at Birdston one day, Mrs. Forrest mentioned she remembered Mr. Lapslie coming to her father's house on his pastoral visits. Mrs. Forrest's reminiscences were very interesting. She said, " Mr. Lapslie was a real plain man. He wisna like ministers now-a-days ; he had nae airs. I mind o' him comin' to our house, and as we keepit cows my mither set down bread and milk before him. My sister and me were in the house, so he cried out, ' Come here, my little lassies, an' I'll gie ye a bawbee if ye can do this.' So he put his finger and thumb to his mouth ; there was a click ; wi' that his teeth cam' oot in his haun'. Putting the teeth upon the table before him he said to us, ' Noo, a bawbee to ye baith, if ye tak' oot your teeth like that.' " This act produced such astonishment at the time that the little girl never forgot it, and she narrated the incident in 1889, nearly sixty-one years after its occurrence, with all the freshness of recollection of an incident that had just happened.

FEATS AS A TEA-DRINKER.

He partook heartily of his friends' hospitality, but his performances as a tea-drinker were wonderful. In a farm-house, while drinking tea, he happened to remark that he never took more than three cups of tea. This astounding statement completely took his hostess aback. She exclaimed, "Never tak' mair than three cups! Ye are at your twelfth cup the noo." A similar story is still current as having happened in The Cottage, when he was enjoying Provost Dalglish's hospitality. "Will ye no' have another cup, Mr. Lapslie?" "No, I think I'll no' have any more." "Do ye know how many cups ye have had already?" "Well, no, I didna count them." "Well, that's your thirteenth ye are at now."

HIS SUDDEN DEATH IN GLASGOW.

Lapslie's death was a very sudden one. He was in the enjoyment of excellent health and was walking to Glasgow to attend a meeting of Presbytery. On the way he called at Hayston, where he saw a daughter of Mr. Reid, afterwards Mrs. Weir of Barrochan. Miss Reid, in her kind-hearted hospitality, went to the churn and took out a large bowlful of cream, which she offered to Mr. Lapslie. He was heated with walking, but he relished the excellent fare and drank heartily. He went on to Glasgow, where he was suddenly seized with severe inflammation and died the same day, in the Star Inn, Glasgow, in the very place where on 3rd Oct., 1792, the Society of the Friends of the Constitution was formed, of which Thomas Muir of Huntershill was vice-president.

CORPSE ARRESTED AT GRAVE.

After his death a coffin which was believed then to contain his body was laid to rest in the Clachan Churchyard. His wife died at Campsie in 1825, and she too was buried in the Clachan, but strange to say, their graves are marked neither by a tombstone of their own nor by any inscription on any other tomb. This strange fact may be accounted for by two reasons. On the day of the funeral the body was arrested at the mouth of the open grave, and further procedure barred by some legal process, until the arresting creditor had satisfaction given him for the payment of debt owing by the deceased. Sir Samuel Stirling, sixth baronet, became surety to the arresting creditor, and the body was then consigned to the grave. This incident greatly annoyed his friends. Shortly after the funeral a keen controversy broke out whether his body had ever been brought back to the parish at all, the statement made being that, within twenty-four hours after his death in the Star Inn, Glasgow, his corpse was recognised on the dissecting tables in the College, having been sold for ten pounds, and the coffin in which it was supposed his remains were brought back to Campsie for burial contained only a dummy and stones. It was currently rumoured that a Campsie student, recognising the corpse as Lapslie's, went out shocked, and said to some fellow-students, "I think that is the body of Lapslie, the minister of Campsie. I cannot look at it myself, but Lapslihad false teeth." These were described by him in detail. The report brought back was to the effect that the corpse had false teeth exactly as had been described, which satisfied the student as to the accuracy of his conjecture. To allay the disquieting doubts on the subject, the Rev. Norman Macleod caused the grave to be opened. The coffin was forced. It contained a corpse which had a set of false teeth, which were taken out in witness of the fact. This was held to set the matter at rest, but many doubted how the teeth got there. These teeth got into Mr. Muir's possession, and then into Dr. Monro's. They were sometimes produced at the elder's dinner in the manse after the communion, and the old story re-told and discussed.

Lapslie's most enduring memorial is his account of the parish. His descendant's are quite unknown in the district. It is rather strange that we have now no descendants of any of the ministers resident or connected with the parish.

I sent this MS. to an old Campsonian, who in returning it wrote :—

" I have been delighted in reading your narrative of Lapslie. Where on earth have you got the materials to weave such a web? What a strange man, or rather what a strange minister, he must have been ! I remember him His figure and dress are stamped on my memory—his hat, and top-coat high up on his neck and reaching nearly to his feet. I was tired reading to-night, and your paper makes me feel as if living my young life over again, and my mind has been full of Lapslie. I sat down and tried to sketch from memory the 'old man eloquent.' I drew the full figure, but was dissatisfied with the production as a whole, as I failed to give the right proportion, and I have torn the lower half off. Perhaps some of your family may complete the figure, and bring the topcoat down nearly to the heels, place a staff in his right hand, and put his left in his pocket.

" I recollect accompanying my mother one night to Tammy M'Luckie's wright shop, which was cleared out and seats extemporised for a district meeting. Mr Lapslie, then an old man, came in and gave an address and catechised the young. I remember the scene well; the whole surroundings stand out most distinctly in my mind's eye to-night.

" Glasgow, 20th October, 1891."

The sketch is reserved for the illustrated edition of "The Parish of Campsie," &c.

NORMAN MACLEOD, D.D.,

AND

ROBERT LEE, D.D.,

MINISTERS IN CAMPSIE, 1825-1843.

*Lecture delivered on 10th October, 1891, to Campsie Young Men's
Association.*

NORMAN MACLEOD, D.D.

MINISTER OF CAMPSIE.

A SKETCH OF HIS LIFE AND TIMES.

AFTER the death of Mr. Lapslie, the parishioners, warned by what had occurred at the last vacancy, were resolved that the appointment of his successor should not be made without their voice being heard in the matter. To accomplish this end a committee was appointed, which included representatives from the heritors, kirk-session, and congregation, whose duty was to make enquiry and submit a recommendation as to the filling up of the vacancy. This committee appointed Mr A. Gartshore-Stirling of Craigbarnet, convener, and entered at once on its duties. In due course it submitted a report, in which it recommended that the Rev. Norman Macleod, then minister of Campbeltown, should be appointed. In supporting this recommendation Mr. Gartshore-Stirling mentioned that when they turned their thoughts towards the Rev. Mr. Macleod they made exhaustive enquiry concerning him and his antecedents. Amongst the pile of letters, all favourable, there was one with which he had been much struck. It impressed him favourably, although some people might not have considered it any recommendation at all. This communication was from a Campbeltown man, who, in replying to the queries addressed to him, prefaced his statement by frankly admitting that he was not very often at the kirk himself, and when he was there, maybe was not a great judge of a sermon; but he could testify that, throughout the whole of his parish, there was not a bung drawn from a cask of whisky, nor a cork from a bottle of wine, but Mr Macleod was aye a welcome guest at all their gatherings, be the occasion joyous or sad. As the writer associated wine with funerals, and whisky with festive enjoyment and hilarity, Mr. Stirling further stated, that he took that to imply that in his social and pastoral relations Mr. Macleod was eminently popular, that he seemed to have a sympathetic nature, and that he was held in the highest respect for his personal character and ministerial gifts. All the other letters seemed to corroborate this. The report was adopted, and the kirk-session, heritors, and male communicants presented a humble petition to the Crown to present the Rev. Mr. Macleod to the vacant benefice at Campsie, as the unanimous choice of the people of Campsie.

Norman Macleod was born in the manse of Morven on 2nd Dec., 1783. He was licensed by the Presbytery of Mull in 1806. In the same year he was appointed assistant in the parish of Kilbrandon. In 1808 he was ordained minister of Campbeltown, and in 1811 he married Agnes Maxwell, eldest daughter of Mr. James Maxwell, chamberlain to the Duke of Argyle. In 1824 he called the attention of the Church to the want of elementary education in the Highlands and Islands, and from this movement, then originated by him, arose the Education Scheme of the Church of Scotland. His connection with the education question brought him into prominence at the time, and it was probably partly owing to this that the Campsie parishioners were made acquainted with his existence. When their call reached him there were many reasons which induced him to consider favourably the offer of such a parish as Campsie. To a man whose increasing family required a greater expenditure, the larger stipend of Campsie was welcome, but another great point was its proximity to the University, where he could send his sons. He accordingly accepted Campsie, but found it a sore and trying struggle to break away from the many associations and friends in and around Campbeltown. But he never regretted the step he then took. The Crown issued the presentation on the 25th Jan., 1825, and the induction took place on the 11th August following. The settlement was a most harmonious one, and Mr. Macleod received a most hearty welcome from all classes in Campsie. In the Glasgow Presbytery, however, there was at first unusual coldness shown him. Referring to this afterwards, Mr. Macleod said, "The cold reception I met with from my brethren in the Presbytery only served to stir me up to greater activity in the work of the ministry. I knew that I had all the people on my side, and from none of them did I meet with greater sympathy than from the dissenters, the members of the Relief congregation."

In Campsie Mr. Macleod at once attained great popularity as a preacher. His style had been unconsciously modelled on that of his father. There was the same peculiar pleading of tender affection, simple, clear statement, touching pathos, with occasional bursts of fervid eloquence.

At the period of Mr. Macleod's induction the minister of the Relief Church was the Rev. James Brown. Mr. Brown had been a mason to trade, and began to study for the Church after having wrought as journeyman for some years.* He was ordained minister of the Relief in 1810, when about thirty-six years of age. He was a diligent and conscientious pastor, a true son of consola-

* There is a story told of his meeting a labourer in Lennoxtown one day who had formerly carried the hod to him. Noticing his changed dress, he said, "Gude preserve me, Jamack, what are ye daen noo?" "Wheesht, man, wheesht, I'm a preacher now," said Mr Brown.

tion, and as a comforter in sorrow or bereavement was gratefully remembered by many outside his own congregation. But he was an uninteresting preacher. I have heard the late Mr James Gray say of him, that he became eloquent only when speaking of the love of Christ on a communion Sabbath; he then glowed with an unwonted fervour.

The erection of the new Parish Church in Lennoxtown, especially with a minister possessing so many popular gifts as Mr. Macleod, had been a matter of deep concern to the Rev. Mr. Brown's people in the Relief Church. The office-bearers conferred, and came to the conclusion, that it was expedient that an assistant to Mr. Brown should be obtained. They suggested this to Mr. Brown, to whom the proposal was most obnoxious. He assured them his health was good; he was quite able to overtake the whole of the pastoral supervision, and regarding preaching, he could preach as well as ever. The proposal was not pressed at that time, but one candid office-bearer told his minister in regard to his preaching as well as ever, "Well, ye ken yoursel', Mr. Brown, ye were never very guid at it." Those who were desirous of forsaking the Relief Zion and returning to the "Bondage of Egypt" made Mr. Brown's refusal of an assistant their pretext for leaving.

A number of the smaller lairds, farmers, and others, whose families had left the Parish Church when Mr. Lapslie was, in their opinion, obtruded on the parish. or who, from various reasons, had left it during his ministry, now returned to the bosom of the mother church. Among the families who gradually returned about this time were:—Buchanan of Crosshouse; Robert Ferrie, North Balgrochan; Stevenson, Alton; Samson, Wetshod; Samson, Whitehill; Reids of Hayston and Carlston; Ferrie, Balgrochan Mill; Buckie, East Balgrochan; M'Pherson, Milton; M'Ouat, slater; Motherwell, smith.

Forsaking the Relief Kirk was a terrible wrench to old William Stevenson, Alton. His father had built the church and his early associations were all connected with it. As he wended his way past it the first Sunday he was going to the new church, he looked at it lovingly, and said, "Man, I min' the biggin' o't."

PREACHING VERSUS PRAYING.

The numerous secessions revived the old spirit of rivalry between the Parish Kirk and the Relief. Comparisons were freely made by the members of both congregations, in illustration of which the following characteristic anecdote may be mentioned. One day a stranger accosted a flesher named Neil Rankin, who was standing at what was then known as Bulloch's corner, where Crosshill Street strikes off the Main Street. Having obtained the information he sought regarding his road, conversation was continued, and happened to turn on the relative merits of the two ministers. Neil said, " They were both very good men. Macleod

was a braw man and a gran' preacher; a gran', gran' preacher."
As a preacher he liked him far the best; " but, faith," he added,
" if I was deein' I would rather hae Broon's prayin'."

WANT OF CHURCH ACCOMMODATION.

Under Mr. Macleod's ministry the people soon attended church
with far greater regularity, and there was also an accession to the
membership. These and other causes combined to raise again
the question of church accommodation, and make it a matter that
required immediate attention. The old church at the Clachan
had long been inadequate, even for those who were in the habit
of attending previous to Mr. Macleod's settlement, as we have
seen already, when dealing with Mr. Lapslie. In the divided
state of opinion on the question of a new church nothing was being done by the heritors in the way of necessary maintenance and
repairs, and the fabric of the church had got into a most dilapidated state. Mr. Macleod ascertained what were the wishes of
all classes of his parishioners in the various districts, and determined to take up the matter and act resolutely. He first broached
it in the Session, stated his views, met objections, explained his
reasons, and soon got all his Session on his side. Then, with
singular tact and prudence. he approached the principal heritors,
and succeeded in enlisting their sympathy and securing their
co-operation. When the question was formally taken into consideration by the heritors, it was agreed that the Clachan Church
was very much out of repair, and that it was simply impossible by
any alterations to suit it to modern requirements. It was far too
small, yet to enlarge it would infringe vested rights, and disturb
the graveyard, around which so many hallowed and endearing
associations clung. The heritors had unanimously agreed at their
meeting, in 1821, to build a new church at the Clachan, but that
resolution had been overturned by a surprise vote at a subsequent
meeting, on the motion of Mr Buchanan of Carbeth and Auchinreoch. If a new church was to be erected, public opinion was
now strongly in favour of abandoning the site at the Clachan,
and selecting another in a more central situation. Miss Lennox
of Woodhead wished the church retained in some site at the
Clachan, and she strongly opposed the proposal to have it further
eastward, when it was demonstrated that it was impossible to
enlarge the old church. She then advocated erecting the new
church in the centre of a large square which she would form.
The Inn was to be in the line of the north side, and she caused a
new building line to be laid down for the west side of the square.
Her idea was that the Lennoxtown people, and the residents in
the eastern and southern portions of the parish, if they grudged
to walk to the Clachan, might have a new church, but it would
have to be a *quoad sacra* one, and the sacred site of the edifices in
which the parishioners had worshipped since the introduction of

Christianity must still be preserved as a place of worship. When the heritors resolved to abandon the original kirk and graveyard site, and build a new parish church with a graveyard around it at Lennoxtown, Miss Lennox's heart was like to break. She, however, acquiesced reluctantly in the decision, yielding to the numbers opposed to her views. Having done so, she put no factious obstruction in the way afterwards. but quietly resigned herself and fell in with the majority. This simplified matters. A careful consideration of the most suitable situation led to the selection of the Quarry Brae at Lennoxtown as in every way the most convenient and central. By skilful diplomacy Mr. Macleod at last overcame all scruples and prejudices, and the opposition of a few heritors and some other malcontents. " He's a pawkie, clever, cunnin' Hielan'man," was the verdict of one of his opponents on this question. Miss Lennox sold the site for a sum of £480, as fixed by arbiters.

Mr. David Hamilton, architect, Glasgow, was called on to inspect the new site and submit a suitable plan. Mr. Hamilton in course submitted a plan, which met with general approval. It shewed a Gothic building, estimated to accommodate 1550 and to cost about £5000. The stone was specified to be freestone from the quarries at Possil, which was to be conveyed by canal to Hillhead of Kirkintilloch and thence carted to Lennoxtown. Mr. Hamilton received instructions to issue specifications and invite offers for the execution of the work. The heritors met on the 10th April, 1827, to open the tenders and accept offers.

The freestone from the quarries near Bishopbriggs is decaying under the exposure to the weather. The local sandstone, which was rejected for this, is a little coarser in the grain, yet exposure to the weather only makes it whiter and harder, as may be seen in the lower masonry courses of Lennox Castle.

The architect's plan was to level the conical crest of the broom-covered knoll sufficiently to prepare the ground for the erection of the church there, and to place the church in such a position as that the door sill could be seen by a person standing on the turnpike road. The heritors employed a Mr. Scott, Strathblane, to act as civil engineer; to take the levels and give a section of the ground to the contractor—Mr. Alexander Stevenson of Schoolfield, Bishopbriggs. Mr Scott will be remembered by many, as he had a wooden leg, and rode from Strathblane on a white horse. Mr. Stevenson accordingly met Mr. Scott on the ground to receive his plan and section, and obtain his instructions. But Mr. Scott had neither plan nor levelling instruments. He declared he did not need to have recourse to levels; " he had a capital eye, and could depend on that." An eye-witness has described what then occurred. Mr. Scott proceeded to take the levels with his " eye." He walked round and round. Joshua only marched seven times round Jericho, but at the seventh round Scott was still " eyeing " the knoll. After having been round and round fully a dozen times he came to a halt. Raising his wooden leg he brought it down with a thump—" Put in a peg here. That's the level. I think you should hae sax feet o' cutting at the top " As it was he had entirely miscalculated the level. Instead of taking six feet off the top he took off about fourteen, and thereby placed the foundation about six feet too low, thus doing much to spoil the site. This caused a portion of the ground behind to be higher than the church and greatly increased the expenses attendant on levelling, on building retaining walls, forming the graveyard, &c. These, mainly owing to this mistake, amounted to about £3000, a far larger sum than anyone had anticipated. Mr Scott about this time was consulted by the factor on the Woodhead estate, who wished to have some improvement effected on the road leading to Woodhead. After examining the ground he had an interview with Miss Lennox at Woodhead. Disdaining the use of pen or paper, in order to explain his plan to Miss Lennox, he spat on the table, and with his finger and spittle drew a plan on the dining-room table! Mr. Scott was never consulted by Miss Lennox after that.

The best way of getting access to the brae on which the church was to be built was keenly contested, but Mr. David Fleming, one of the elders, and father of Mr. John T. Fleming, soon solved the difficulty. Taking up his bellows one day he expounded his plan. Pointing to one of the handles, he said, there you have your church. Drawing his hands round both sides of the bellows, here you have two winding roadways leading from the church and uniting in one main way—the nozzle, which would join the public road. The hint was taken, the ground was laid out, and the roads formed after David Fleming's bellows.

The Lennoxtown people and others throughout the parish hailed the project with enthusiasm, and arrangements were made for having a grand demonstration on the occasion of laying the foundation stone on the 21st June, 1827. The parish masonic lodges attended with a band of music. The minister and kirk-session, the heritors, schoolmasters, and gentlemen connected in various ways with the parish assembled, and walked in procession to the site of the proposed edifice, where they were saluted by thousands who had assembled to witness the ceremonies of the day. After the procession had taken the ground assigned to it the Rev. Norman Macleod, as minister of the parish, engaged in prayer, supplicating Almighty God in favour of the undertaking. Then John Lennox Kincaid, younger of Kincaid, as Grand Master of the Lennox Kilwinning Lodge, deposited in the foundation stone a glass bottle, hermetically sealed, containing coins, medals, Edinburgh and Glasgow newspapers, an almanac, calendar, &c., and a list of the clergymen who had served the cure since 1581. John M'Farlan of Ballancleroch then read the inscription plate laid on the foundation stone, after which Mr. J. L. Kincaid laid the stone with all the ceremonial usual on such occasions, closing with the Masonic benediction :—"May the Grand Architect of the universe enable us successfully to carry on and finish the work of which we have now laid the foundation stone, and every other undertaking which may tend to the advantage of the parish of Campsie and its inhabitants, and may this Church be long preserved from peril and decay." The spectators then gave three cheers, after which Mr. Kincaid addressed the meeting. Sir Samuel Stirling of Glorat then made an excellent speech, dwelling on the lessons taught by the occasion. and thanked the Right Worshipful Grand Master, the other Worthy Masters, office-bearers, and brethren of the lodges present, the pastor for all his exertions, and concluded by requesting that Mr. Kincaid would convey to his most worthy relative, Miss Lennox of Wood-head, the obligation which they felt they had come under to her for her consent to remove the Parish Church to its present situa-tion. "If," he said, "in yielding to the wishes of a numerous population she made a sacrifice of feeling, I trust that while she surveys a religious multitude enclosed within the walls of this building, the consciousness of having performed her duty will be its own reward, and that that reward will be in heaven." Up-wards of a hundred parishioners were entertained to dinner by the direction of Mr. Lennox Kincaid, some dining in the Clachan and some at Lennoxtown, and the evening was spent in harmony and real happiness.

MR. DENNISTOUN PRESENTS COMMUNION PLATE.

The church when erected was worthy of the parish. It was large and commodious, and although built nearly two miles away from the manse, still was where it should be, in the centre of the most populous portion of the parish, in the very midst of the people. Mr. Dennistoun of Golfhill, a native of the parish, who had become one of the leading merchants of Glasgow, took the opportunity of the erection of the church to present communion cups and flagon, thus following the excellent example of Mr. Graham of Gartmore, who, in 1790, presented two solid silver communion cups to the parish of Kippen, "in testimony of his veneration for the religion of his country, of his respect for the present pastor, and of his regard for the inhabitants of the parish." I was in the church when the stained-glass windows behind the pulpit were inaugurated, when several members of Dr. Macleod's family were present.

The custom of making gifts to churches, such as stained-glass memorial windows, harmoniums, organs, baptismal fonts, com-munion plate, &c., is an excellent one. Will some public-spirited parishioner defray the expense of having the church lighted by gas, so that evening services may be conducted when con-venient ? I remember when tallow candles, on the autumn communion Sabbath, made the darkness visible at the afternoon sermon, and I always considered it was not creditable to those concerned that a system of lighting the church should have been so long in being introduced. However, this is a digression. We must return to the new church.

THE FORMAL OPENING.

The formal opening was looked upon as a great event, and it was proposed that some great gun should be asked to preach on the occasion, and as Principal Baird of Edinburgh University was known to be a great friend, it was suggested that he might be asked. Dr Macleod had the greatest respect for the worthy Principal, after whom he named one of his sons—George Husband Baird—but he demurred to the proposal. No one, he declared, would enter his new pulpit to preach in it before himself, and he carried his point. He preached the first sermon in it, and there are those who recollect the stillness that pervaded the crowded assembly as he rose to give out the opening psalm. He gave the 84th, which he read out with feeling singularly appropriate to the new place of worship.

" How lovely is thy dwelling place,
O, Lord of Hosts, to me!
The tabernacles of Thy grace
How pleasant, Lord, they be!

Within his new church the minister found himself addressing a larger and more enthusiastic congregation than had ever been known in Campsie. His elders were devoted to him, and his new people were soon as friendly and loyal as those he had left at Campbeltown. There are still many surviving who remember the great demonstration at laying the foundation stone, and the opening of the church in 1828. After an interval of sixty-three years, I am informed there are a few still worshipping in it who saw it opened—Messrs. Buchanan, Shields, Robert Buchanan, Lennoxtown; Mrs. John Houston and her sister, Mrs. Blair, may be mentioned. There may be more of whose names I am not aware.

CHOLERA—DR. MACLEOD PROTECTS A POOR STRANGER'S BODY.

In this year (1827), the same year in which the new Parish Church was erected, the University of Edinburgh conferred on Mr. Macleod the degree of D.D., mainly in recognition of his services on behalf of education. While he was in Campsie the first outbreak of cholera which occured in this country made its appearance in the parish. It is as difficult now as it was to reflective people then to comprehend the strange feelings which it excited among the more ignorant of the people. They became the slaves of what might be called hysterical delusions. A spirit of wild fear and unreasoning panic was abroad. In some places they even accused the physicians of poisoning the wells.

A death had occurred in the parish, whereupon a crowd of ignorant and excited people gathered and threatened to oppose the removal of the dead body. Dr. Macleod went to the scene of the disturbance, entered the house, assisted to get out the coffin, placed it in a cart, and when a formidable line was formed across the road to obstruct the funeral, and the rein of the horse was seized, he commanded silence, and addressed the people. He said that this was the body of a poor stranger, an Irishman; that he himself, as a Highlander, was equally a stranger; that as such he would protect his poor brother, and he warned them that if any man dared to hinder his burial, he would give orders that the coffin should be left at that man's door. I need not add that the funeral was allowed to proceed, and that no mob ever afterwards assembled to interfere with the burial of the dead.

NO. 1 LAIR PRESENTED TO DR. MACLEOD.

A few years after the church had been opened it was resolved to have the ground that was to form the new graveyard laid out in lots for sale. On 7th Nov., 1833, the following committee was appointed to have this carried out:—Mr. M'Farlan of Kirkton, Mr. Lennox of Woodhead, Mr. A. G. Stirling of Craigbarnet, Mr. M'Laren (factor for Sir Archd. Edmonstone), Dr. Macleod, Mr. William Buchanan (Crosshouse), Mr. John Buckie, and Mr. David Dunn. This committee resolved to allocate No. 1 lair to Dr. Macleod, who expressed his willingness to pay the regular price for it; but it occurred to the committee that, considering Dr. Macleod's public services, especially in the matter of the new church and churchyard, it would not be becoming in the heritors to accept of any price from him. In accepting this gift from the heritors, Dr. Macleod promised to make it the burying-place of his family, and that his own remains should be brought back to Campsie.

COLLAPSE OF "TENT."

Mr. Stevenson of Beechmount occasionally accompanied the Maitlands of Balgrochan to the church at the Clachan. On sacramental occasions a "tent" was placed outside the church, usually just a little inside the entrance gate. It was here the ministers who were assisting preached. In the summer of 1826, the summer of the drought, Mr. Stevenson and the late Mr. James Maitland were both in the churchyard. It was a beautiful day, and the concourse of people was so large that Dr. Macleod came outside and preached the action sermon from the "tent." He then engaged in prayer, during which he was quoting from the 139th Psalm—"Whither shall I go from Thy spirit, or whither shall I flee from Thy presence? If I ascend up into heaven, Thou art there: if I make my bed in hell, behold"——

when he suddenly disappeared from sight, and there was silence. The platform on which he had been standing had given way, and the minister was thrown down but not injured. It was speedily put right again, when the minister remounted it, and having said, with calm dignity, "Let us solemnize our minds," he continued his sentence where it had been interrupted, and the service proceeded. Both Mr. Stevenson and the late Laird Maitland were agreed that the incident happened to the Doctor himself, and Mr. Stevenson is positive that, as he was never inside the church at all, and yet heard Dr. Macleod preach, he cannot be mistaken. He thinks Mr. M'Naughton preached afterwards in the "tent." *

Dr. Macleod's life in Campsie was a very busy one. A son of the manse, he had been accustomed in his native parish to familiar and hearty intercourse with all classes. When he came to Campsie he cultivated the acquaintance of his people, in whose personal and family concerns he took the liveliest interest. He was always ready to promote their prosperity, grudging neither time nor labour if he could thereby advance their interests. Besides discharging all the ordinary parochial duties he worked hard at establishing and carrying on the new Educational Scheme of the Church of Scotland. During all the ten years he was in Campsie he was also steadily working on the Gaelic Dictionary which he published in conjunction with Dr. Dewar. For the instruction and amusement of his countrymen he edited a Gaelic monthly magazine, of which he was also chief contributor. The name of Campsie became endeared to Highlanders as the place from which emanated his contributions to the *Teachdaire Gaelltachd* and to the *Cuartair nan Gleann*. He was also deeply interested in the Celtic population of Ireland. He went to Ulster to lend his aid to the Presbyterian Church to form and extend churches in the synod of Ulster. At the request of the Synod of Ulster he made a metrical version of the Psalms in Irish Gaelic, for use in the Irish Presbyterian Church. Though Dr. Macleod was in a lowland parish, his heart was in the Highlands; or, as Lord Cockburn once said of him, "If his heart was seen, I am sure it would be dressed in a kilt!" During Dr. Macleod's ministry in Campsie, Turkey-red dyeing and printing were carried on extensively in

---

* Before putting this MS. into the printer's hands, I took the precaution to send it to a gentleman who, I was assured, knew more of Dr. Macleod's life in Campsie than anyone now living. He writes me in reply :—" I have perused with pleasure your account of Dr. Macleod's life in Campsie, and its people. Nothing can be related of that dear old parish and its inhabitants but is full of interest to me. I have carefully read your paper, and have found nothing worthy of correction. I never heard the anecdote of the Campbeltown recommendation. Old Craigbarnet was a bit of a 'wag,' and probably the anecdote was improved on by 'Craigie.' I quite remember the breakdown of the 'tent,' but am not so sure of the quotation of the Psalm. It was, however, Mr. M'Naughton, afterwards Dr. M'Naughton, of Lesmahagow, who was in the tent, not Dr. Macleod, who, as the parish minister, was preaching *in* the old church, the tent outside being occupied by the ministers assisting. However, that is a small matter.'

Lennox Mill. Those in charge of these departments—Mr. M'Bean in the Turkey-reds and Sandy M'Lean the dyer—employed Highlanders by preference, and were instrumental in bringing many of these to Campsie, who were at first unable to speak English, but who quickly picked it up. Besides those employed in the public works there were, at that time, many others in the parish following various occupations. In the Highlanders of Campsie and surrounding districts Dr. Macleod took the liveliest interest. On several occasions he arranged for special services in Gaelic on summer Sabbath afternoons. At these musterings of the clans he was always in his best form, while those for whom the services were intended felt it a great privilege to be present.

Dr. Macleod's good humour and unfailing tact enabled him to overcome successfully many difficulties. There is an anecdote told of him before he came to Campsie how he managed to quiet the scruples of an old elder. This worthy felt aggrieved at the dial of a clock having been painted in the space reserved for a real one in the steeple of the Gaelic church. He expressed very great regret at his being compelled by his conscience to bring the matter before the kirk-session, on the ground that nothing false should ever be connected with a church. The minister made no objections to his proposed motion, but in the course of conversation which ensued took the opportunity of complimenting his old elder on the youthfulness of his looks, especially on the fine dark head of hair which adorned his venerable head. "Hoot, toot!" replied the elder, "you are going too far, sir, for you know it is a new wig." "A wig," exclaimed the minister, "you, an elder, to wear a wig! Is not false hair on the head of an elder of the church worse than a false clock on the steeple of a church?" "Aweel, aweel," said the old elder, "ye hae me there, minister, and I think we'll let baith alane!" Although this story may be regarded as a "chesnut," yet it does duty yet, and a few years ago was told by Dr. Donald Macleod, of Park Church, Glasgow, at a soiree of St. George's-in-the-Fields, Glasgow. His point was the misnomer of a city church being called "In-the-Fields;" and he narrated the story of his father and the old elder in the hearing of my old Campsie friend, Mr. Rowland Hill Eadie.

It was during the ministry of Dr. Macleod that the worship of the Roman Catholic Church was revived in Campsie. The first Irishman who settled in Campsie, about the beginning of this century, was named Felix M'Kewn, but he married a Haughhead woman and the family grew up Protestants. Shortly after the battle of Waterloo an Irishman, whose name was Loughrey, found employment about Torrance, where he took up his residence. In conjunction with a man named Hume he took some contracts connected with working minerals, and in course of time, as he required labourers, he brought them over from his own county in Ireland. When he came first to Torrance he was an object of curiosity and something like aversion. On Saturday or Sunday afternoons parties would be formed in the Newtown, as Lennoxtown was then called, to walk down and stare at this stranger and hear him speak in his native brogue. Year after year the number of Irish immigrants steadily increased. About 1830 they sent a petition to Dr. Paterson, the Vicar Apostolic of this district, representing that they were entirely without any spiritual provision, and praying for the appointment of a resident priest. Dr. M'Pherson was selected to visit the district, make enquiry, and report, and it was while he was carrying out this mission that he had the Irish residents in and around Torrance collected in a private house, where, on the 23rd January, 1831, he celebrated Mass in the parish for the first time since the Reformation. At the same time he baptized three children. On the 10th September of that year the late Monsignor M'Lachlan, of Stirling, was sent to take permanent charge of the Roman Catholics in Campsie and a wide district around it, embracing Milngavie, Strathblane, Balfron, Kilsyth, and Kirkintilloch. On his arrival in Campsie Dr. M'Lachlan found religious prejudices so strong against a Papist priest that he was refused a night's lodgings in the inn. It is said that in the district specified he had about a thousand souls under his pastoral care.

The subsequent history of the Roman Catholic Church may be here briefly summarized. Dr. M'Lachlan, appointed priest in 1831, was replaced in 1840 by Father Green, who was promoted in 1844. It is said, as illustrative of the strong animus against Roman Catholic priests, that a prominent man in the parish, on meeting Father Green, called out—"Oh! thou deceiver of souls." Rev. John Gillon was appointed in 1845, and was transferred in 1866. Died at Falkirk in 1871. The late Rev. John H. Magini was appointed in 1866. Provost M'Kerrell is now in charge. The Roman Catholic Chapel was built by Dr. Carruthers, Vicar Apostolic of the Eastern Division, and was opened in 1846, in Father Gillon's time. It was originally named St. Paul's, but when Father Magini became acquainted with the early ecclesiastical history of the parish he obtained the sanction of the late Archbishop Strain, and had the name altered to St. Machan's, in honour of the old patron saint of the parish, after whom the old church at the Clachan had been named.

In 1835 Dr. Macleod received the appointment to St. Columba's Church, in the City of Glasgow, and the same reasons which induced him to leave Campbeltown now led him to accept the city charge. When he was leaving for Glasgow, a subscription was got up to present him with a testimonial expressive of the respect and affection with which he was regarded in Campsie. He had maintained the traditional hospitality of the Scottish manse, while at the same time feeding, clothing, and educating a large family. His removal to the city entailed on him considerable expense, especially in furnishing a larger house. The result

of the appeal for subscriptions was that a large sum was raised.
I have heard the sum put as high as £1200. When this was
presented to him he said he would at least leave his bones with
them in Campsie. His testimony on leaving the parish was—
" That by one and all of the heritors both he and his family were
ever treated with the greatest kindness." In 1837, shortly after
leaving Campsie, he was Moderator of the General Assembly, and
he afterwards went to England to collect funds for the distress
then existing. As the result of his eloquent appeals the sum of
£100,000 was raised. He was in this connection brought into
contact with the prominent statesmen of the day. Sir Robert Peel
had a great regard for Dr. Macleod, and showed it in a way that
speaks volumes for his kindness of heart. One of the oldest
members of Parliament was sitting beside Sir Robert on the
opposition side of the house, when he turned round to him and
said, " Your friend Dr. Macleod dines with me to-morrow; will
you come and meet him? He is a noble character, and is in
my opinion the very beau-ideal of what a clergyman ought to be."
From a sketch of Dr. Macleod, privately printed as a small
pamphlet, I have gleaned the following particulars of his life in
Glasgow:—With his transference to Glasgow his connection with
the parish may be said to have ceased, and we cannot follow his subsequent history with the same detail we have given to his ministry
in Campsie. But I may be allowed to add that his position in
Glasgow became an unique one. Not only was he minister of St.
Columba, Glasgow, but the whole Highlands seemed to claim him
as their own. Every forenoon filled his lobby with innocent con-
fiding souls from distant glens and islands, who seemed to think
that he had only to "speak" and whatever they asked was done,
more especially as they "had never asked a favour before" and
had brought letters to him from laird, factor, schoolmaster, minister, or old friend of his own. The requests made were as varied
as their wants—strong men to get into the police; infirm men or
women to get into the hospital; parents with their boy looking
for a situation, or their daughter for service; crofters or farmers
evicted from their holdings, and wishing to emigrate, but when
and how? seekers after relatives at home and abroad, lost in unknown recesses among the wynds of Glasgow or woods of Canada;
the poverty-stricken stranger, solitary as a stray sheep in the
great city, and craving assistance to get back to the hills, or to
obtain as his last resource legal charity and relief from the poor's
boards, who had paid no heed to his complaints; old soldiers and
sailors anxious for an increase of their pensions; hundreds seeking "lines" to get work; eager hunters after fabulous legacies,
whose heirs among M'Leans, Camerons, or Campbells, &c., had,
as they were told, been advertised for—all and sundry came to
him to tell their long stories and obtain his aid. It was more
than flesh and blood could stand! It was enough to wear out the
most patient spirit, for it was itself a severe labour to convince

many that he had neither the time nor the power to help them; while the number that he did aid was verily not small! It is such nameless and endless details as these that are never known and that leave no visible trace behind, which make the life of a city minister so distracting and wearying, especially one so well known as he was, and with his peculiar relationship to the Celtic population in Glasgow and in the Highlands.

On one occasion a sick Highlander, who applied to him to procure medical advice, was offered by him a bed in the hospital. The invalid refused, on the ground that the doctors would kill him for the sake of obtaining his body, make " saw " (salve) of his bones, &c. But his scruples were overcome by Dr. Macleod promising to visit him regularly. He at last brought the patient the good news of his being convalescent, and able to return home. The Highlander seemed much cast down by the intelligence, and taking him aside, whispered to him that since he had got him in, he hoped he would be able to keep him in until the term day, as he had such good meat and drink and was so extraordinary comfortable.

Dr. Macleod died at Glasgow on Tuesday, 25th Nov., 1862. A Highland woman one night came to the door of his house when he was lying in his coffin. She implored the Highland servant who received her, with most earnest accent, to see him, and rapidly following her, she embraced his coffin, kissed his face, and disappeared. Who she was the family knew not. A correspondent writes :—

"I can have no doubt whatever as to the identity of the Highland woman who so earnestly entreated to be allowed a look at Dr. Macleod's corpse, and who, when this was allowed, looked at him with love and reverence, passionately, kissed him, and, overcome with emotion, so abruptly rushed out. This would be Kate Macintyre, who lived at centre of the Doddle Row and was employed at sewing what was termed flowering webs. She was the most expert sewer I have ever seen. You are aware that I was an exceedingly delicate child and required at one time constant nursing. Kate was a kind-hearted woman, who many a time relieved my dear mother, and nursed me. Kate was passionately attached to Dr. Macleod, for whom she had a reverence akin to superstition. I remember Kate and her brother John— Sugar Jock as he was called—quite distinctly, both were blind fair. Kate had white eyelashes, white hair, and was very shortsighted. When Dr. Macleod removed to Glasgow, so strongly was she attached to him, she walked in to Glasgow on the Saturday evening. For her kindness to me my mother gave her a bed. She attended her dear Doctor wherever he was preaching, and then walked out to Campsie on the Sabbath evening. Hers was the most ardent case of hero-worship I ever knew."

I give my friend's letter, but it could not possibly have been Kate, as she died in 1838. Her burying-place is quite near the Doctor's. She looked forward with pleasure to lying so near him, declaring it would be heartsome to be so near the Doctor. The road leading from Dr. Macleod's grave crosses the burial-place, and although the stone bears " This burial-place is ever to remain sacred to the memory of Colin Macintyre and Susan M'Gregor, his wife," the heritors have encroached on it so far as to allow it to be used as a pathway.

Dr. Macleod's funeral was a public one; but there was one feature in it which those who noticed will never forget—one which, to the members of his family, was more touching than even the long line of carriages in which leading citizens and men of every party kindly followed him to the grave—and that was the number of poor Highland men and women who accompanied the procession until it left the city, very many tottering in their weakness, helped along by those stronger than themselves, and weeping as they went for their pastor and their friend. He was buried in Campsie beside the new church, which he had been the chief means of erecting, and beside more than one dear child and relative, and in ground which itself was a mark of love, because given by the heritors to himself and family. When the funeral reached Campsie the spectacle was remarkable. It was twenty-five years since he left the parish, and yet in a town of two thousand every shop was shut spontaneously. "There we laid him and returned to my beloved mother," is what his son Norman writes in his diary. His funeral sermon, in Gaelic, was preached by his old and valued friend, Dr. M'Farlan, of Arrochar; and in English by another highly-valued friend, the son of his most attached elder in Campsie, the Rev. Dr. Mathieson, of Montreal, and brother of Mrs. Tagg, for long postmistress in Campsie.

In the north-east corner of the grave-yard, a tall, graceful Ionic cross has been erected to the memory of the two Doctor Norman Macleods, father and son, and their relatives. Architecturally it is not well-suited to the position; if it had a background of trees it would look better. It has the following inscription :—

IN MEMORY OF
NORMAN MACLEOD, D.D.,
ONE OF HER MAJESTY'S CHAPLAINS,
DEAN OF THE CHAPEL-ROYAL;
BORN 2ND DEC., 1783; DIED 25TH NOV., 1862.
AND OF HIS WIFE
AGNES MAXWELL,
BORN 5TH AUG., 1785; DIED 6TH APRIL, 1879.
ALSO OF THEIR SON
NORMAN MACLEOD, D.D.,
ONE OF HER MAJESTY'S CHAPLAINS,
DEAN OF THE CHAPEL-ROYAL,
DEAN OF THE MOST ANCIENT AND NOBLE ORDER OF THE THISTLE
BORN 3RD JUNE, 1812; DIED 16TH JUNE, 1872.

And on a recumbent stone there is inscribed—

HERE LIES NORMAN MACLEOD, D.D.,
MINISTER OF ST. COLUMBA'S PARISH, GLASGOW;
BORN 2ND DEC., 1783; DIED 25TH NOV., 1862.

It is not perhaps generally known that in Aug., 1872, the Queen intended to visit the grave of Dr. Macleod's more distinguished son, and had ordered Mr. Walker to have a carriage on the 15th Aug. at Lenzie Junction, to convey Her Majesty to Lennoxtown. The visit was only prevented by the weather proving unfavourable.

Since reading the paper I have learned that among the families who left the Relief and returned to the Parish Church when Dr. Macleod came were John Stevenson, farmer, Craigend, father of the late R. H. Stevenson, D.D., of St. George's, Edinburgh; Robert Morrison, feuar, North Birbiston; and James Goldie, Lennoxtown, &c.

ROBERT LEE, D.D.,

MINISTER OF CAMPSIE.

A SKETCH OF HIS LIFE AND TIMES.

THE transference of Dr. Macleod to St. Columba's, Glasgow, causing a vacancy in Campsie, the usual course was followed, and a committee was appointed to look out for a suitable minister. The late Rev. Dr. Stevenson, of Dalry, had preached for Dr. Macleod shortly before this, when he made such a favourable impression on his hearers that, on the vacancy occurring, they turned at once to him. He, however, had a choice of parishes, and declined Campsie. The committee then had their attention directed to the Rev. Robert Lee, then minister of the chapel-of-ease of Inverbrothick. A deputation was sent to hear him preach, and ascertain in what estimation he was held among his own people. It is recorded in the " Life and Remains of Robert Lee, D.D.," by R. H. Story, D.D., that the deputation from Campsie " was greatly influenced in his favour by the impressive manner and well-chosen language of his prayers." Their report was favourable, and it was adopted. In due course, on the petition of the parishioners, the advisers of the Crown issued a presentation to the benefice in his favour.

Mr. Robert Lee, who had thus been so harmoniously appointed to Campsie parish, was born in Tweedmouth, in 1804. His parents gave him the best education they could afford, sending him to Berwick Grammar School. They lacked the means to send him to college, so he commenced work in a boat-building yard, where he remained employed till he was about 20 years of age. When he had determined to study for the ministry young Lee occupied his leisure time in building a boat. This he sold, and with the price of it in his pockets he set off to College in 1824. He selected St. Andrew's, where living was cheap, the fees small, and bursaries were within the reach of the clever student. His biographer tells us how the young Tweedmouth boatbuilder became an ardent and successful student. With many things against him and no exceptional circumstances in his favour we find that in classics he eclipsed all rivals, taking first prize in the Senior Greek class, while in Latin classes he was uniformly the first scholar. We learn the secret of his success from the pages of his private journal. In his fourth year at college his time is planned methodically—the hours of rising, meals, exercise, college, study. He lays down that he is always to return home at eight o'clock, wherever he may be, "then study mathematics for two hours, till ten. Then the study of natural philosophy till twelve. After that, always read a chapter of the bible and pray, *Deus adsit*." Through years of severe manual toil he had looked forward to the opportunities of study he now enjoyed, and he applied himself unremittingly to take advantage of them all.

When he had completed his university curriculum Dr. Haldane, the principal of St. Mary's College, wrote concerning him—"This University has not for many years sent forth a more distinguished student. He has gained, during a succession of years, the highest honours which the University can award." While at College he maintained himself by teaching, and during his later sessions he became tutor at Mount Melville, near St. Andrews, having under his care the well-known Mr. G. J. Whyte-Melville, the author of many society novels, "Kate Coventry," "The Gladiators," &c.

Mr. Lee was licensed in 1832, and in the following year he was elected minister of the Inverbrothick Chapel. Here he worked hard for two years. As the results of his ministry were most successful, the managers of the Chapel shewed their appreciation of his labours by raising his stipend from £150 to £175. The young Tweedmouth boatbuilder, the St. Andrews student, and Arbroath minister had no personal influence or connections in the West, and he might have remained longer in the comparative obscurity of the Inverbrothick Chapel had he not gained the affections of a lady whose brother was rising into great influence in Glasgow. It was probably owing to the Rev. Robert Buchanan, then of the Tron Church, Glasgow, using his influence with Dr. Macleod, that the Campsie committee took his qualifications into their consideration at all. But when they had done so they found his own merits to be such that they sent the deputation to his chapel, with the result which has been already mentioned.

While near Arbroath he had for his neighbour the Rev. Thomas Guthrie, then minister of Arbirlot, afterwards the famous Dr. Guthrie of the Free Church. When Lee had decided to leave and go to Campsie, Guthrie wrote him the following characteristic letter:—

"Many thanks for all your kindness to me. I have enjoyed much pleasure in your friendship, and am sensible of no little profit from it, and you carry my respect, my affection, and my best wishes along with you. I could almost play the woman while I write this farewell note. Fare-thee-well, my good friend; again I say, fare-thee-well. May the Lord bless you, and make you a blessing; and I have now only to say, that at the very sight of you my door shall swing wide open on its hinges, and that I am, and ever will be, your most affectionate friend,   "THOMAS GUTHRIE.

"MANSE OF ARBIRLOT, *April 18, 1836.*"

The date of Mr Lee's presentation to Campsie was 5th Feb., 1836. His induction took place on the 5th May, and in the June following he was married to Miss Buchanan, a sister of the Rev. Dr. Robert Buchanan, the historian of the " Ten Years' Conflict." His biographer says his marriage was a most happy one, and he delighted in his children. His heart rejoiced in his home, and his life at Campsie " was singularly active, bright and happy—shining with a clear light of heart and intellect—full of well-done work and of kindly affection and friendship, with the sacredness, then as ever, of a real and quiet piety pervading all." Mr. Lee commenced his ministry in Campsie under favourable circumstances. He had always carefully thought out the subject matter of his prayers, and his preaching was both interesting and edifying. He carried on his studies with the ardour of a keen student, at the same time throwing himself heartily into his parochial work. This, by some considered a drudgery, to him was a labour of love, as he delighted in visiting and going among his people.

Shortly after his honeymoon he commenced a thorough and systematic visitation, resolving to call on every family in the parish, irrespective of their church connections, or whether they belonged nominally to any church at all. Calling one day at a house on his rounds in Lennoxtown he found the wife at home. Her husband was at his usual calling. What was that? A nailer. That reminded him of his old boatbuilding days, and he told that, when a young man, he had worked both in wood and iron, had tried his hand at smith and joiner work, and other allied handicrafts, but the most difficult thing he had ever attempted was to make a nail. Anything that recalled his Tweedmouth home was of interest. The sight of a toy boat sailing on the Whitefield pond stopped him one day as he was riding past. The boy owner was sheltering himself on the road from the strong north wind, but Lee accosted him and asked the details about his boat, and who had made it—he watched its progress for some time as it crossed the pond in the strong breeze, and then rode on, his thoughts away back to his own boyish days. When engaged in pastoral visitation he had a special aversion to married women standing in little knots idly talking on the pavement, and to their assembling in each other's houses, and passing the time in idleness or gossip. He entered a house one day, when he found a number of neighbours idly talking, when he thought they should have been attending to their household duties. He declined to sit down and " intrude " on them ; but, in going out, he turned and asked the assembled matrons if they knew what Abraham had replied when the Lord asked him where Sarah was ? None of them knew, so he told them that Abraham said Sarah was in her tent, or own house, where every good wife should be.

In conjunction with his assistant, Mr. Marshall, in 1842, he commenced a prayer meeting. Referring to one of these Campsie prayer meetings, he writes :—" I had not time to compose the second prayer, but I think the service was edifying. It is useful to feel that prayer and praise are the main matters for which people assemble." In this sentence we have a key-note showing that even in his Campsie ministry, while according to the sermon its due place in the public service of the sanctuary, he was seeking even then to raise the services of praise and prayer to that importance in worship which he thought they deserved, restoring to the public services in church the character which our Saviour ascribed to His Father's house, as a house of prayer, and not of preaching.

His reading of the scriptures was impressive, not from its mere elocution but from the impression he conveyed that he had a message to deliver, which it was important they should all hear and for which he claimed their closest attention. "I never heard the scriptures read with the same interest, I was young and his sermons were often above my comprehension, but I always enjoyed his reading," is the testimony of one of his hearers.

When the fierce "Ten Years' Conflict" was at its hottest, he kept nearly aloof from the strife. On the first page of his common-place book, written shortly after he had been inducted to Campsie, he writes:—"Let this be my ambition, to be known *in* my parish, to be unknown out of it, *i.e.*, to be known for use and edification, to be unknown to fame and men's speeches."

The Non-Intrusion question was taken up in Campsie and discussed, as it was then the burning question in Scotland. Lee's position was rather a peculiar one. A Liberal in politics, with strong popular sympathies, we learn from Dr. Cunningham's Lecture * that he appears to have sympathised with the Non-Intrusionists in their desire to give the people a voice in the choice of their minister, but he failed to see that patronage was anti-scriptural or sinful; and he derided the idea that Church courts could override statute law, under the name of spiritual independence. Dr. Cunningham says:—"He was not a great preacher: he was too cold, too purely intellectual for that. He had no graphic power, little imagination, no passion, lacking the power either to melt his audience to tears or rouse enthusiasm. But he could state facts clearly, reasoning on them convincingly. He could interest, instruct, persuade." I have heard it remarked that Mr. Lee was never so popular with his female parishioners as his predecessor and successor. He was too coldly intellectual in preaching, appealing to the understanding and rarely touching the feelings. In this respect he was a great contrast to the fervid appeals of Dr. Macleod and the polished rhetoric of Dr. Monro. Notwithstanding this drawback, if it was one, he made his position not only perfectly clear to his people at Campsie, but he seems also to have been successful in persuading them to follow his example. In after years he did the same with his people in Old Greyfriar's. He made his views known to them,

* *Scottish Divines. St. Giles' Lectures.* Third Series.

secured their concurrence in the changes he was about to introduce, and retained their individual support when assailed in the
Church courts. He was a vigilant pastor, and looked sharply
after members who were irregular in their attendance at church.
He was ready also to visit any parishioner, whether a hearer or
not. Asked if he would call and see a dying person, who, however, had no connection with the church, he replied—" Willingly;
that is all the more reason why I should go at once."

Under Macleod and Lee there were two diets of worship,
forenoon and afternoon. It was reserved to Mr. Munro to roll
these into one. When Lee was returning from church one
Sabbath afternoon he met John Brown and Robert Sloss, who
had been taking a walk to the Clachan. Sloss was able to inform
him he had attended church in the forenoon, so he turned to
Brown, who was one of the Relief, and presumed he had been at
his own church in the forenoon also. Brown was disposed to
be argumentative. Which was the true church was a question.
Whether was it the Moderates, Evangelicals, or Seceders. Brown
would like to know from Mr. Lee which of them was the true
Church of Scotland. Without attempting a reply, he said :—
" Well, its quite true, sir, these controversies are most lament-
able in their effects," and walked away. On another Sabbath
afternoon he saw Sandy L.—— coming home tipsy. The public-
houses were not then closed by a Forbes Mackenzie Act,
and Sandy and his cronies had partaken rather freely of the
refreshment which Johnnie Gray provided. Lee was vexed,
but went up and spoke kindly. Sandy thanked him for his
advice, but said he would be muckle more obliged if he would
lend him a shilling. Lee was grieved, and walked sadly
away. He had a quick eye in the pulpit. One day he saw a
prominent member fast asleep in the front of the gallery. He
paused, and, looking straight at the sleeper's pew, said—" I am
now coming to an important point, so I hope those who are asleep
will awake, and those who are awake will pay attention." There
can be little doubt that he excelled in exposition of scriptural
truth. I can recall how often Mr. James Gray used to quote his
opinions, which he must have put always with clearness and
precision, for his hearers were in no uncertainty as to his views.

He did not confine his teaching to his pulpit appearances. He
got up courses of lectures in his own church at a time when these
were not so common. But he had to have his lectures in summer,
as there was no provision for having the church lighted in winter.
This defect has not been remedied yet. The minister of the
parish of Campsie is compelled, in the year 1891, to go to the
Town Hall if he wishes to give a lecture on a Sabbath evening !
A parishioner, who greatly admired a course of his lectures,
suggested to him that he should publish them. He was told they
had never been written out, but preached from notes, and that he
could not now re-write them, as he had forgotten much both of

the matter and sequence. "Oh, Mr. Lee, that's a pity; if you had published these lectures they would have immortaleezed ye." An old member of the Y.M.A. has written to me, as follows:

"I have noted one or two incidents in connection with Dr. Lee's ministry in Campsie that may be of use to you. In your lecture you referred to his methodical habits as a student. He was also a most punctual man. One evening as he entered he saw the meeting had evidently been waiting for him. He stated that by his watch it was just the hour, but he apologised if he had kept them waiting. It was afterwards found that the church clock had been wrong. He was also an early riser. I had occasion to be sent a message to the manse early one morning, and I reached it shortly after 6 o'clock. I met him going out to the garden with a book in his hand. He was in the habit of walking and reading aloud in the open air. Many years afterwards he was on a visit at Glorat House. I happened to be taking a walk, and had turned up past Glorat, when I heard the sound of a voice over by the waterfall, as you enter the garden. I listened and soon discovered an elderly, pale-faced, and grey-headed man, in whom I at once recognised Dr. Lee, walking up and down, reading at the pitch of his voice, as if he were a student just going into training. Apparently he never thought he had arrived at such a state of perfection as that he could dispense with careful preparation.

The Chartist movement was at its greatest activity during his ministry. He had no sympathy with it or the Latter-Day-Saint movement which followed it. One of his people, Thomas Shields, joined the latter movement, and Dr. Story gives a letter addressed to "Dear Thomas" on this subject by Mr. Lee. This letter had not the effect Mr. Lee intended. Thomas had a twisted foot, and the Apostles of the Latter-Day Saints led Tom to hope that if he had faith, their power of working miracles or faith-healing might cure him of his lameness. In his expectation Tom was disappointed, owing, as the Latter-Day Saints alleged, to his want of faith. He determined to sever his connection, but did not like to return to the Parish Church, so when he got the appointment of precentor in the Relief he, with some of his relatives, joined it. Thomas Shields was an enthusiastic musician and an accomplished player on the flute. Tom had a kindly, genial nature, and was always ready to assist a young musician in every way he could.

Lee, as we have seen, was only licensed in 1832, yet eight years afterwards he boldly enrolled himself as a candidate for the Chair of Theology vacant in the Glasgow University in 1840. This action on his part shows that not only was he diligently labouring in his parish work, but he was also reading and thinking while his mind was maturing and developing and becoming fitted for exercising influence in a wider sphere of usefulness, such as in a chair of the University or in one of the city charges of Edinburgh. Two candidates for the Glasgow chair soon came to the front, and became the champions of their respective parties. The "Evangelicals" rallied in support of Dr. Chalmers, and the "Moderates" threw all the influence of their party into the support of Dr. Hill. Lee, who had sympathies with certain points on both sides, had never any chance of success. As it was pointedly put, "The University which had refused the Chair of Logic to Edmund Burke now refused that of theology to Dr. Chalmers."

The Disruption of the Church of Scotland occurred in May, 1843. The Edinburgh city churches were then vacated by Chalmers, Cunningham, Welsh, Gordon, Candlish, Guthrie, &c. It fell to the Edinburgh Town Council to fill these vacancies. Amongst their best selections was the minister of Campsie, and on the 29th Aug., 1843, they appointed Mr. Robert Lee to the church and parish of Old Greyfriar's, vacant by the secession of the Rev. John Sym. On the 5th Nov., Lee preached his last sermon in Campsie from the text, "Work out your own salvation." In the course of it he tells his people, with a frank honesty, that one of his reasons for leaving them is that with his growing family he cannot afford to live among them as a minister should. Mr. Lee left Campsie amid many expressions of his parishioners' affection and respect, one of these taking the form of a cheque for £110, forwarded by Mr. J. L. Kincaid Lennox, at the request of the subscribers, as a mark of their esteem and regard. Lee wrote the account of the parish in the New Statistical Account. On special subjects he had the assistance of some of his parishioners. Mr. Galloway, for instance, wrote on Agriculture, and the note on Nisbet's Heraldry, &c. Mr. Clark, Alum Works, also took a section, and one or two others assisted. This account is meagre compared with Lapslie's in Sir John Sinclair's *Account*.

There is a most interesting letter from the Rev. W. G. Smith, then of Ashkirk, but formerly minister of Fintry, given in his Life, from which I take the following :—" My intercourse with Dr. Lee began soon after my settlement at Fintry, in the end of 1840. He was then in the prime of life and full of vigour and activity. . . . I found him uniformly anxious, even then, to impress upon his younger brethren the necessity both of diligent study and of careful attention to all parish work. . . . He was at the same time very earnest in his searching after truth. With pains and prayers he strove to find it, and to hold it for himself. In his influence with his people there was something very striking. It was shewn very notably at the time of the Secession. . . . Every effort was of course made from Glasgow and elsewhere to persuade them to withdraw from the Church of their fathers, but in vain. In that large parish of some 6000 people, to the end of his incumbency, and for several years thereafter, there was not only no Free Church, but scarcely even a Free Churchman. I question much if such a case occurred throughout all Scotland, and the result was mainly due to the ability and honesty and the manliness with which our friend explained the points at issue. " It certainly was very remarkable, and formed one of the outstanding features of his ministry in Campsie that his large congregation should have so loyally supported him with unbroken ranks. Free Church people at the time considered that he was a good deal indebted to the friendly influence of his brother-in-law, Dr.

E

Robert Buchanan, who gently restrained all aggressive measures of Non-Intrusion propagandists, so far as Campsie was concerned.*
Lee had the degree of D.D. conferred on him in 1844 by his *Alma Mater*, St. Andrews. On the 19th January, 1845, his church was burned down. The congregation was accommodated in the Assembly Hall till 1857, when Old Greyfriars was restored. In 1847, Dr. Lee was appointed to the chair of Biblical Criticism in the University of Edinburgh. He was at the same time made Dean of the Chapel-Royal, and appointed one of Her Majesty's Chaplains. From an entry in his diary I observe that he re-visited Campsie on 3rd March, 1853. He says:—" Having dined at the Manse, I lectured at Lennoxtown to the Mechanics' Institute, and, having escaped suffocation, I slept in the room (in the Manse) where dear Jane was born and baptised." Regarding his lecture to the members of the Campsie Mechanics' Institution, Mr. John Young of the Hunterian Museum, Glasgow University, has kindly furnished the following memorandum. For a member to sit down, after an interval of 38 years, and give the substance of a lecture, is creditable both to the lecturer and his hearer. Mr. Young writes:—

"I was present at the lecture by Dr. Lee to the Mechanics' Institution to which you make reference. He had a large audience, and the lecture interested us all very much. He took for his subject, 'The Good connected with the so-called Evil of the present world.' In the course of his remarks, he stated that the organisation of man clearly showed that his present body was never intended by the Creator to live forever. Therefore death came in, through the operation of organic law, as a necessary evil, its function in

* Although Mr. Lee succeeded in preventing the Free Church obtaining a sympathiser in Campsie prior to 1843, yet that denomination made a successful raid seventeen years afterwards. In 1860, when Mr. Monro was absent in South America, the Glasgow Wynd Church, under the Rev. Mr. M'Coll, was a centre of evangelistic work and aggressive denominationalism. Not content with the wide sphere afforded in Glasgow, this Church's band of Christian workers organized revival meetings in surrounding towns, notably in Busby and Campsie. These meetings were attended with a certain measure of success in Campsie, and resulted in the nucleus being formed of a Free Church Mission. I remember a newspaper controversy on the subject and an amusing leader in the *Glasgow Bulletin* newspaper headed " Who saved the Sinners in Campsie?" This denied that the Revivalists were entitled to all the credit of the good work, which it was contended should be shared with the other Churches, the Parish and the U. P. Campsie was considered a promising field for a forward denominational movement, and it was decided to form a mission station in connection with the Free Church. The Rev. Archibald Henderson, the son of Dr. Henderson of Glasgow, and son-in-law of Dr. Candlish, was sent out by the Presbytery in 1861 as Missionary. The success which attended his efforts seemed to warrant recognition, and he was ordained in 1862. The following year he was translated to Crieff. He was succeeded, in 1864, by the Rev. Wm. Scott, who was translated in 1867 to Queen's Park, Glasgow. From 1867 till 1872 the Rev. D. Macleod was minister. In the latter year Mr. Macleod went to America. Mr. Dewar was then appointed as a Student Missionary. He was ordained in 1874, and translated to Aberdeen in 1879. In 1879 the Rev. John Duke was translated from Wellgate Free Church, Dundee. Mr. Duke is the present incumbent.

Nature being to remove the aged and infirm from the scene ; the further life of the world, as it rolled on through the centuries, being carried on by the young and active races. In further illustration of his views he clearly pointed out that all the so-called evils that arise through the operation of natural laws, exist for good in the long run, although in their operation they often bring afflictions and dire calamities on mankind throughout the world. It was a lecture based very much on the same kind of reasoning and illus· trating the same principles as Combe's ' Constitution of Man,' and upon much the same lines of thought as that which the late Lord Gifford has indicated in his will, that he wishes the Courses of Lectures on Natural Theology that he has founded should be conducted. I had been reading Combe previously and Dr. Lee's lecture impressed me very much as advancing the same views. There were, however, some present who considered that since he went to Edinburgh, Dr. Lee had become less orthodox than he was when in Campsie. These shook their heads at his setting aside many of those evils, which they considered had been brought on all races, through the temptation and fall of man."

Mr John Cowan, Wycliffe House, Anlaby Road, Hull, also favours me with some reminiscences. He writes :—

" Mr. Lee once delivered a lecture to young men which pleased me very much at the time, and I have always remembered what he said about exercising the body to promote health—" To walk for exercise is good, but to dig for the same is better." On another occasion, when on a visit from Edinburgh, he delivered a lecture in the School-house, Milton, on ' Eating, Drinking, &c.," and the point that struck me most was this. Over-eating and drinking were far worse for us than hunger. Gluttony brought about diseases which all the skill of man could not cure, whereas one pennyworth of bread could cure the pangs of hunger."

There were many causes which kept him from throwing himself with all his heart into the controversies which ended in the Disruption of 1843. He was a loyal son of the Church, and he was willing to devote his talents in any field of usefulness for which it appeared he was best adapted. Mrs. Oliphant says of him, in her introductory chapter to Dr. Story's life :—" He was not a missionary. His talents were administrative and constructive. When he turned his quick eye within the Church to mark what most wanted doing inside, instead of without, his gaze lighted on the weakest point of Scotch religion, its worship. Nowhere is there more true piety, nowhere more scripture knowledge ; but Scotland still says her prayers as she was compelled to do when she said them on the hill-sides, with the Covenanter sentinel ready to warn her of the approach of the red coats. John Knox's severe and solemn order had been cast aside in the hurry of flight and extremity of danger. It was too new to be carried in the bosom of the hunted minister, whose Bible was enough for him to carry, and with an incredible fond faithfulness the whole country has clung to the sketch of *ex tempore*, hurried, irregular worship, of which Claverhouse's troopers were the grand promoters." In a chapter on Innovations (1859), it is stated that Dr. Lee considered that of all the evils afflicting the Church an unimpressive and ill-ordered worship was the worst—that an ill-ordered, slovenly, uncertain service either blunted all reverential feeling, or drove devotion and culture from the sanctuary. The following description is given of the manner in which an average country congregation assembles :—"Coming into church with hardly any show of reverence for the sacred place, and sitting down without any sign of prayer or blessing asked. The minister enters the too often ugly and ungainly pulpit . . . . the singing led by some discordant or bull-throated precentor. A long, often doctrinal and historical and undevotional prayer is uttered by the minister, the people standing listlessly the while, most of them staring at the minister or their neighbours. and a benediction, during which the men get their hats ready, and the women gather up their bibles, and draw their shawls and cloaks into most becoming drape. and as soon as the last word is uttered they are all charging out of the kirk as if for their dear lives." This picture is no exaggeration : you and I have seen it a hundred times. Now, a service of such a nature as this is very remote from the ideal of true Christian worship. George Herbert, in his poem, " The Church Porch," refers to an unedifying service, in which case he says—

> " God takes a text and preaches patience.
> He that gets patience and the blessing which
> Preachers conclude with hath not lost his pains."

He attached importance to a reverent reception of the closing " blessing which preachers conclude with," as though it were truly the blessing of the Lord, and not a mere license to quit the place of worship. He admitted that the Presbyterian service was impressive when reverently performed by a clergyman of piety and eloquence, but was apt under some to be irksome when these were wanting. What Dr. Lee considered a faulty church service was, in his opinion, year after year sending people, especially among the aristocracy and educated classes, away from the Presbyterian churches to Episcopal chapels. Such secessions were especially active among the young. He desired to stop the process of depletion, and in the interest of the Church and for the glory of God he set himself to the task of reforming the Church's worship. His own people were ready to adopt the changes he suggested and to support him in carrying them out. In June, 1857, he took the opportunity of the re-opening of his church after restoration to introduce his earliest innovations. A large sum had been raised by the congregation in order that a restoration might be effected in a style worthy of the historical renown of the church. All the windows were filled with stained glass; some of them presented as memorials of departed friends, then quite a novelty in Scotch churches. At the opening service, in June, 1857, he requested his people to kneel at prayer and stand up to sing. He read his prayers from a book, which was printed and in the hands of the congregation, that they might be enabled to take a part in the service and join audibly in the responses and the Amens. He altered the first act of the worship, beginning with prayer instead of the psalm, as enjoined by the Directory,

which states, " The congregation being assembled, the minister is
to begin with prayer." He sought by his printed prayers to give
the blessing of common prayer to his own congregation in their
common worship. He had restored the order of deacons which
had been maintained in his church till 1834, when it was discontinued. These changes were fiercely denounced as "innovations."
He was able to point out that such a term was a misnomer for
resuming disused practices which had been in some cases recommended in the Directory of Public Worship, that the prayers of
Knox's Liturgy had been read, and that it had been customary to
render the responses in the Reformed Scottish Churches. In
1863 instrumental music was introduced, and a harmonium was
used till 1865, when he had it replaced by an organ. The
Directory enjoins regarding " The Solemnization of Matrimony "
that the minister is " publicly to solemnise it in the place
appointed by authority for public worship, before a competent
number of credible witnesses," &c. On the 6th Dec., 1865,
Lee was the first to revert to the ancient usage, when he celebrated a marriage in the church of Old Greyfriars, using the
marriage service as printed in his book.

This reform of the Church's worship was only one of the subjects which engaged his thoughts, as he mused on what abuses to
select for his pruning knife or the axe. Dr. Cunningham tells us
how he saw with concern that while the effect of the abolition of
the Corn Laws was to cheapen bread and greatly benefit the general
community, yet, as the parochial clergy were paid stipends calculated on the price of grain, their incomes were being reduced. It
did not affect himself, but he started a scheme for the augmentation
of the smaller livings, and advocated pew rents as a source of
revenue. He asked why a full church should only bring increased toil, anxiety, and outlay to the minister, and no increase
of stipend. He thought that where his labours were successful he
should have a right to participate in material benefits. Lee gave
a great impulse to the movement for the abolition of patronage,
although he did not live to see it abolished. He took the deepest
interest in a reform of the Church's faith. He considered that in
too many cases the ministers were only serving up theological
husks. He gave utterance to the striking thought,* that while it
was well that individuals, in matters of morality, should walk in
the narrow and not in the broad way, Churches, in matters of
faith, must walk in the broad and not in the narrow way, if they
would not go to destruction. All his lectures and sermons were
therefore cast in the Broad Church mould. The drift of his
Edinburgh sermons was to show that the laws of nature are uni-
form and irreversible, that the age of miracles is past, and that it
was our duty to study and obey these laws, as in this way only
can we escape the punishment of disobedience. When he

*St. Giles' Lectures, p. 416

preached before the Queen, he took for his text, " Glorify God in your body," 1 Cor. vi. 20. These are what he taught in Campsie, as the interesting reminiscences of Messrs. Young and Cowan show to us. In his college lectures, by enlightened and liberal teaching, he attracted thoughtful students to himself, and reared a race of ministers who are now the light of the Church. We have not only got familiar with, but have practically accepted many of the views which he was among the first to enunciate, and which caused himself and those who agreed with him to be regarded with horror, as revolutionists and rationalists, by sincere but mistaken people.

Lee was denounced as a latitudinarian, and even suspected to be a heretic. Dr. Cunningham summarises his life work thus— " He deserves to be ranked among the reformers of the Church, and no doubt in time he will. What a prodigious improvement has taken place in our Church services during the last twenty years. It is Robert Lee that is doing it, for all the evil passion was buried in his grave, and his influence is present and powerful everywhere, like an all-pervading spirit."

Lee was an occasional contributor to the *Scotsman* newspaper. Here he manifested his sharp incisive style, his love of liberty and detestation of bigotry. In his comments on Essays and Reviews and on Bishop Colenso's writings, he wrote that—" While he admired the comprehensiveness of the English Church, he pointed out that it was owing in a large measure to the impartial judgments given by the lay judges who had jurisdiction in ecclesiastical affairs, and who were able to deal with theological questions unbiassed by polemical feeling. He recognised the fact, almost lost sight of in Scotland, that justice is justice, and truth is truth, from whatever quarter, lay or clerical, it comes."

Another matter in which he took great interest was the movement for relaxation of the formulas of her faith which the Church required her office-bearers to sign. As a result of his bold and independent course of action, he felt himself almost entirely isolated from the most of his clerical brethren in Edinburgh. They considered him rash, and had no sympathy for his objects, which they never clearly understood.

His procedure in Old Greyfriars caused him to be engaged in frequent controversies in the Church Courts. Anyone reading the reports in the *Scotsman* of the debates, say on " Innovations," and then perusing the entries in his private journal, would hardly think it was the same individual. Dr. Story, in his Life, quotes a remark regarding him — " How little did those who called him cynical and bitter, who knew nothing more of him than what they saw and read, as disclosed in passages of arms on the floor of an angry Presbytery or hostile Assembly, understand what a fire of passionate affection was kindled under that calm exterior, what love and sorrow lay concealed beneath the cold, pale countenance."

We cannot enter on the conflict in the Church Courts regarding his innovations. The case was decided against him, in 1867, by the Presbytery of Edinburgh. He appealed to the Synod, who affirmed the decision of the lower Court. He appealed to the Assembly; but before it met he was seized with palsy, when riding one day in Princes Street, Edinburgh, and on account of the condition in which he then lay the case was not called in the Assembly. There is little doubt that had it been taken up the decision would have gone against him.

He died at Torquay in the following spring, 14th March, 1868, in the 64th year of his age and 35th of his ministry. The cause which he had so much at heart, when apparently on the eve of being stamped out, in reality became triumphant by his death. A reaction in his favour followed. Some who had been most bitterly opposed to him were now seen to be trimming their sails to the changing wind. The innovations which he introduced are now the usage of the churches, and standing at singing and kneeling at prayer have long since been introduced into his old church at Campsie. But when Lee asked his people to kneel he did not mean them to "hunker" and remain seated while bowing the head. Harmoniums have been introduced in both the Parish and U. P. Churches in Campsie, and the solemnization of matrimony in church will likely soon follow.

In the good old times Campsie ministers were sometimes taken to fill Edinburgh pulpits. The parish gave Edinburgh a Law in 1687, a Warden in 1755, and a Lee in 1843. Things are all changed now, when both Established and U. P. Churches have ministers taken from Edinburgh charges.

Lee's acceptance of the Edinburgh charge caused the parish of Campsie to be again vacant. Lee himself said he should like very much if he could "pawn" a minister upon the parish in the person of the Rev. Mr. Paisley, whom he strongly recommended. A congregational meeting was held in the church, over which Mr. J. L. K. Lennox was called to preside. Two names were proposed—the Rev. Norman Macleod, minister of the parish of Loudon, and the Rev. Mr. Paisley, Mr. Lee's nominee. After debate the chairman proposed they should take the sense of the meeting by dividing, Mr. Macleod's supporters going to one side and Mr. Paisley's to the other. All went to Macleod's side except three, namely, Mr. Macfarlan of Ballancleroch, Mr. M'Kinlay, Glenmill; and Mr. Thomas Stark, Keirhill. Mr. Macfarlan was so much disappointed at this result that he walked out of the church. In his Life, by his brother, Norman writes:—"Since the Disruption I have been offered the first charge of Cupar, Fife; Maybole; Campsie, by all the male communicants; St. John's, Edinburgh; St. Ninian's, Stirlingshire; Tolbooth, Edinburgh; and the elders and others in West Church, Greenock, have petitioned for me. When I nearly accepted Campsie I found many whom I had thought rocks sending forth tears, and gathered fruit from what appeared stony ground. God has, I believe, blessed my ministry. Now, all this and ten times more than I can mention, occurred just as I had made up my mind not to go to Campsie." Some of Norman's supporters had been confident that he would have accepted Campsie, and were deeply disappointed. On Norman's refusal, the public sentiment turned towards a Mr. Johnston, then in Fifeshire, who had at that time proposals from several parishes. He seemed to have a preference for Campsie, if he should like the locality when he saw it. He came privately and inspected the land, but did not like the manse. He wrote that he had made up his mind to accept Logie, where there was a nice one.

When Norman Macleod was inducted to Dalkeith parish, on 15th Dec., 1843, in the usual rotation the duty of presiding and preaching fell on that occasion to the Rev. Thos. Monro, minister of Fala. Mr. Macleod's father (Dr. Macleod of St. Columba's) and Dr. Black of the Barony were attracted to Dalkeith by their personal interest in the newly-ordained minister. They were seated together, and at the conclusion of the sermon, Dr. Black remarked of Mr. Monro, the preacher, "That's the man for St. John's." "No," said Dr. Macleod, "that's the man for Campsie." When Dr. Macleod came home he told some of the Campsie people how highly he and Dr. Black had been pleased, and in consequence of his recommendation it was arranged to send a deputation to have an interview with him and hear him preach, the members being— for the Kirk-Session, Mr. James Horn, New Mill; for the heritors, Mr. Alexander Galloway ; and for the male communicants, Mr. Robert Clark, manager, Alum Works. Instead of going to Fala it had been arranged that the deputation should hear Mr. Monro in the neighbourhood of Dunfermline. In the same train travelled Mr. Gordon Wilson and Mr. Ebenezer Brown, who were also bound for Dunfermline. Mr. Wilson was naturally curious to learn what impression had been produced, and called at the hotel in the evening where the deputation was staying overnight. The result had been highly satisfactory, and the members were prepared to give a favourable report. Dr. Black of the Barony Church, Glasgow, was Mr Horn's cousin, and it was arranged that Mr. Monro should preach in the Barony, where a number went and heard him. Mr. Monro was now asked to preach in Campsie, which he did on two Sabbaths. The people were unanimously in his favour, and the presentation came in due time. The election was a harmonious one, not a voice being raised against it. Mr. Monro had been a student in the universities of Aberdeen and Edinburgh. He was five years Governor of Watson's Hospital, Edinburgh, when he was presented by the Town Council of Edinburgh to the parish of Fala. With Mr. Monro's induction I draw my lecture to a close.

Erratum.—On page 43, for "north-east corner" read "north-west corner."

THE

CLACHAN OF CAMPSIE

AND DISTRICT.

Lecture delivered on 14th November, 1891, to Campsie Young Men's

Association.

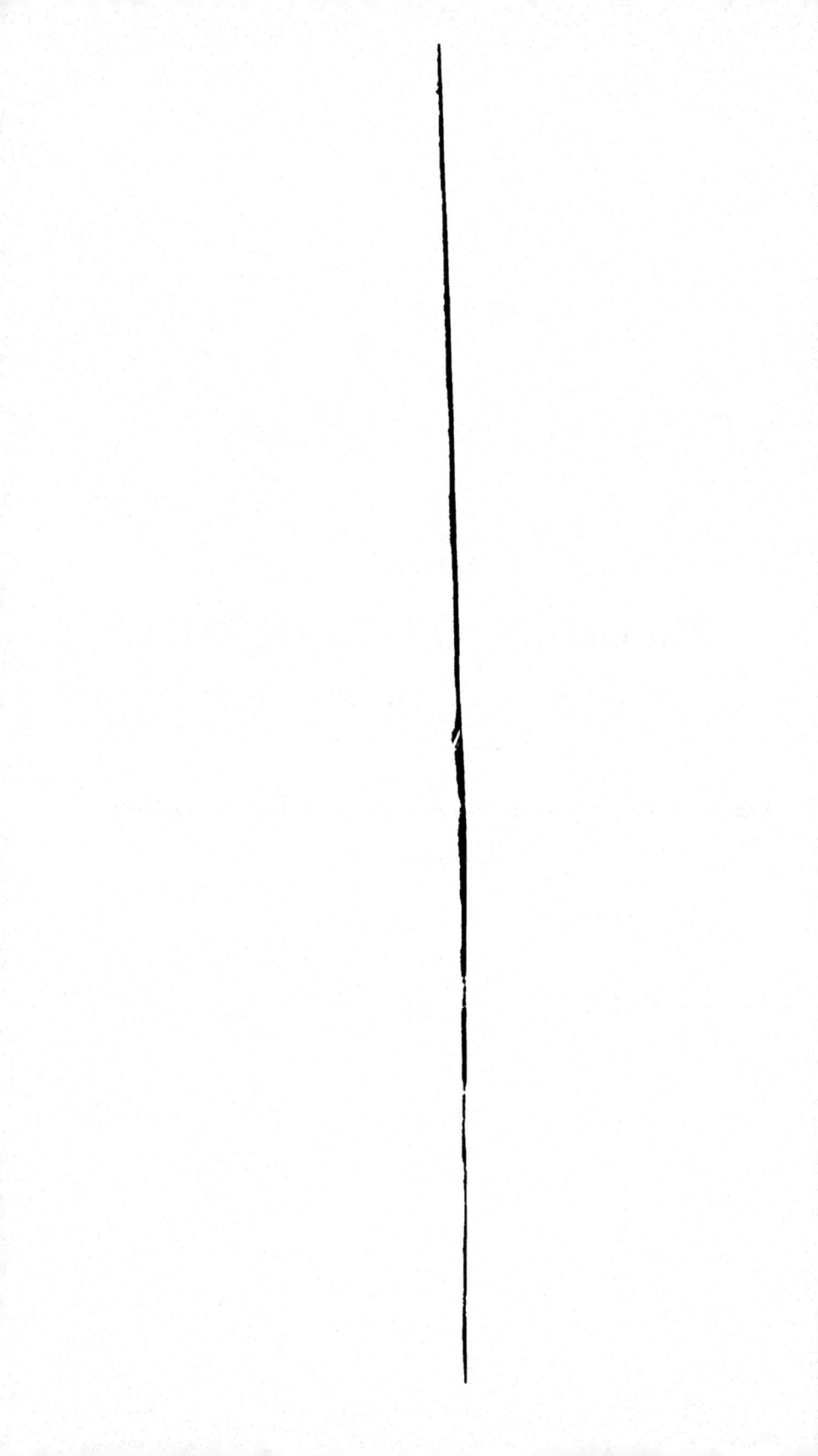

THE CLACHAN OF CAMPSIE.

In a lecture delivered by me in 1885, under the auspices of the Campsie Mechanics' Institution, I gave an account of the Ecclesiastical history of the parish. I do not intend to repeat to-night what I then stated regarding the introduction of Christianity by St. Machan, suffice it to say, that to a native born Scotchman called Machan belongs the credit of having been the first evangelist who proclaimed here the tidings of the gospel. He took up his abode at the foot of the glen, and erected there a little oratory, cill, or chapel as we would now call it. This building, rudely constructed of turf and wattles, and covered with brackens and branches of trees, was the first place of Christian worship in the parish. When Machan died, according to the custom of the ninth century, he would be buried within his little church. In the troubled times which followed, Scotland lost much of the Christianity taught by its earliest apostles ; but the memory of Machan was never forgotten, When more settled times came round and Scotland was being divided into parishes, in which churches were everywhere being built and endowed, it was found that in selecting the sites for these churches a preference was given to the grave of a martyr, or venerated saint. No place in Campsie seemed more suitable for the erection of its first parish church than over the grave of its earliest missionary. In Forbes' Calendar there is mentioned St. Adamnan's Acre in Campsie, but the Campsie referred to by Bishop Forbes is in Perthshire, where there was a croft called St. Adamnan's Acre. Accordingly, in the latter half of the twelfth century the church was built over the grave in which Machan's remains had been buried. The building was small and of the simplest construction, being oblong in form, with the nave running east and west. Near the eastern or innermost end were *cancelli*, or lattices, railing this part off from the rest of the nave, which was assigned to the faithful worshippers, while from the remaining space thus railed off the laity were strictly excluded. From the *cancelli*, this was ultimately called the chancel. It contained the altar at the eastern end, and the altar made it to be regarded as *sanctum*, *sacrarium*, or place of sanctuary, from the holiness supposed to be conferred upon it by the altar. There would be near this end a little recess for vestments—a vestry, and an entrance for the clergy and choir. The main entrance was from the west end, where there would be a little portico. Here, near the entrance, stood the baptismal font, its situation near the door being symbolical of the admission of the newly-baptized children into the Church Catholic. We find that this position of the font came to be regarded with disfavour, and at the Westminster Assembly of Divines, in 1643, the six Scotch members pleaded hard to have the font removed from the church door or portico, and to have it placed beside the pulpit. On a vote, the Scotch members or delegates carried their point, and the meeting decided " that the superstitious place of the font should be altered."

When the church had been erected, it would then be solemnly consecrated. In ancient times churches were dedicated to God and not to saints. They came in later times to be distinguished by the names of holy men and women, as memorials of them. The founders of the Campsie church desired to preserve the memory of Machan in the scene of his labours, so when this church was consecrated the dedication was to Saint Machan, who became the patron saint of the parish. His festival was on the 28th Sept. Presbyterians recognise neither the consecration of churches nor the building of their churches east and west, in order that the worshippers should always be looking towards the east; nor do they consider one part more sacred than another, and know nothing of their altars being sanctuaries or places of refuge. I mention these details, as we are apt to forget that the worship was conducted from 1175 till 1560, a long period of 385 years, according to the ritual of the Roman Catholic Church.

All remains of the original church of the twelfth century have disappeared long ago, in the re-buildings and repairs that time has rendered necessary. The last time the church was re-built, it seems to have been badly proportioned, being far too long for the width. The west gable was therefore taken down and rebuilt. The body of the church was thus shortened, but in order to maintain the same space for accommodating worshippers, it was at the same time resolved to form a transept to the north. Transepts thrown out at right angles from the nave give a church a cruciform arrangement, such as we see in the Parish Church of Kirkintilloch. In Campsie church only a north transept was formed. The position of the pulpit was also altered, and it was placed at the centre of the south wall, facing the north transept. The west gable just referred to, which is therefore the portion of least antiquity, and a portion of the north wall adjoining it are all that remain of the old structure. My earliest recollections of it recall more masonry than is now to be seen; indeed, in my boyhood the west gable, I think, was entire, with the belfry and bell. There were also standing considerable portions of the north and south walls and of the east gable. In my own recollection, therefore, many square yards of masonry of the side walls and east gable have tumbled down and been carried away. The old stones of the church have been taken to build the dyke round the kirk-yard,

and they may be seen in the boundary walls and the dykes enclos-
ing policies and fields of adjoining proprietors. The old church
building seems to have been regarded as a free quarry, where
anyone could take away what they wanted. The stones have
been used freely in the erection of houses, in which they can be
easily identified as having been at one time parts of an ecclesiastical building. The church bell was used not only on Sundays to
summon to public worship, but was tolled for all funerals. This
custom of tolling the bell on the occasion of funerals was continued long after the church had been abandoned. It was discontinued ostensibly as a matter of precaution when the gable was
alleged to be insecure. There were those who wished to have the
old practice continued, and they retorted that the gable had been
perfectly safe until Dr. Monro wished the bell to be removed to
Oswald School, Lennoxtown. There were those who thought
that this was something like sacrilege—taking a "consecrated"
bell and using it for a purely secular purpose, and that it rung
the Oswald School empty! It is a step in the right direction
placing it again in a church, to which we hope it will bring good
luck.

Formerly there used to be what seemed a pillar, just outside
the wall, to the right, at the gate, as you enter the church-yard.
Some considered it to have been the shaft of the old baptismal
font removed outside, and through ignorance or inadvertence
turned upside down. Others have thought it was intended for
a gargoyle, but the shaft of the font is the more plausible conjecture. At all events, it has been removed to the vestibule
of the Parish Church, in order to be preserved from injury or
being broken up and carried away to mend a dyke or cover
a drain.

In Lapslie's and Macleod's times the elm trees, which rather
overshadowed the church to the eastward, on a windy day "rattled
their branches against the east winnock." I examined the walls
one day this summer, and was pleased to see that the joints were
carefully pointed with cement, and that they appeared to be now
well cared for by the heritors. I measured the thickness of the
latest erected west gable, and found it to be 3 feet 9 inches at
bottom, and 3 feet 6 inches above the plinth. A little attention
from time to time by the heritors should preserve what remains of
this old sacred edifice. The gable, overshadowed by trees, and
covered with ivy, looks beautiful in its ruin. It is melancholy,
however, to see the state of neglect which has befallen the interior
(with the exception of the Craigbarnet tomb, which is beautifully
kept). The Auchinreoch tomb is dismal; an elm tree has grown
up from it, and its brushwood renders close access almost impossible. The north-west corner of the interior should be cleared
of rubbish and everything out of keeping with so sacred an
edifice. Something more might be done for the churchyard.
Two old burying-grounds in Kirkintilloch have quite recently

been greatly improved—the ground levelled, the tombstones relaid, and the amenity much enhanced. The rank growth of nettles and general state of neglect and disorder give the Clachan kirkyard an uncared-for look. There are many Campsonians, whose relatives have been interred here, who might be willing to take measures for improving the graveyard, repairing or re-erecting some of the stones, and having the inscriptions cleared of the moss, &c., which makes many of them illegible. *Verb. sap.*

The late Mr. Alex. Galloway, in a letter to Mr. Wm. Brown, Johnstone, says—" I have examined more than once every tomb and gravestone in the old kirk-yard that appeared to bear a date prior to the present century. I offered the heritors to make an exact drawing of everything within the boundary walls of this graveyard, giving each stone its proper place and size on ground plan, and writing on it its full inscription, for £10, which would have been needed to cover the expense of assistants, &c. Finding them hesitate, I backed out, and would not renew my offer." It is a great pity that such an offer as Mr. Galloway's was not accepted at once. Those who were formerly intimately acquainted with the graveyard—Donald Blair's family and the M'Lennans, father and son—are no longer in the Clachan, and there is hardly one to be seen who knows anything of the old families who used to reside in the parish, or can direct a stranger to where their tombstones are to be found in the graveyard. In this connection I must observe that I have always found Mr. Robert Blair, the Session-Clerk, most obliging and willing to afford every information in his power.

As early as the fourth century the enclosures round churches were used as cemeteries—sleeping grounds for the Christian dead. A century or two later they were consecrated, and in the ninth century we find burials taking place within churches. After the Reformation public opinion changed on this question, for on 24th Oct., 1576, the General Assembly had the question propounded to them, " Qwither if buriallis sould be in the kirk or not? Ansuerit not: and that the contraveiners be suspendid from ye benefites of the kirk, quhill they make public repentance." The question was again raised in 1588. The Assembly re-affirmed the decision of 1576, and ordained, " The minister that gives his consent to burials in his church and discharges not his conscience in opposing them thereto sal be suspended from his function of the ministrie." Notwithstanding this decision of the highest ecclesiastical court we find that exceptions were made in favour of families of local influence who desired sepulture within the church walls. In such cases the coffins of the deceased were not placed in this church in vaults under the church, but were merely put into the ground, generally just beneath the pew occupied by the surviving members of the family, who thus worshipped on the graves of their ancestors. Three landed families had burying-places within Clachan church—the Stirlings of Craigbarnet and

Glorat, and the lairds of Auchinreoch. Within an enclosure of dwarf wall, surmounted by a cast-iron railing, about 5 ft. 6 ins. high, stands within the old church a monument to the memory of the late Mr. and Mrs. Gartshore Stirling. Strange to say, there are no other tombstones belonging to this family to be seen at first, but on carefully examining the inside of the enclosure an old thruch stone can be made out in front, between the stone ark and dwarf wall. On further investigation, the existence of another thruch stone is discovered to the right, in great part covered with the stone ark which rests on it. There used to be a third one here, but it was removed in 1852, without permission being asked or obtained, and placed over the graves of a family named Allan, who had long been in the service of the Craigbarnet family. This stone may be seen; it is situated near the entrance to the right, quite close to the tombstone of the Buchanans of Cross-house. It may be identified by the Craigbarnet armorial bearings, the crest of which is a demi-angel couped, ensigned on the head with a cross proper, and the motto is " *Semper fidelis.*" While the bearings on the shields differ, the Glorat motto is also " *Semper fidelis* "; but the Glorat crest is a lion *passant gules.* The angel indicates the Craigbarnet family and is easily remembered.

Immediately behind the Craigbarnet tomb is the Glorat one. Like the other, it is enclosed by a dwarf wall and high railing, the upper portion of which somewhat resembles the battle axe, which is held in the right hand of one of the " heroes in armour" which support the Glorat arms. This tomb has rather a gloomy appearance, being thrown into the shade by the tomb in front and having a northern aspect. When looking at it lately, it was just after the fall of the leaf, and the recently fallen leaves lay thickly within the enclosure and completely covered the stones. Had the leaves been swept away some stones would have been discovered, but the moss would have to be cleared from the inscriptions before these could have been legible.

The lands of Auchinreoch formed at one time a part of the barony of Antermony, and thereafter were part of the Earldom of Wigton and lordship and barony of Cumbernauld. The rights of superiority passed from the Earl of Wigton to the M'Dowals, Castle Semple and Garthland; thence to Robert Dunmore of Ballindalloch, who, in 1788, disposed of them to John Lennox of Antermony. The lands themselves belonged at one time to the Kincaids, and passed from them by marriage, as I understand, to the Buchanans of Carbeth, who in respect of this call themselves Buchanan Kincaid. The old mansion house of Auchinreoch is beautifully situated, but in the early part of this century it was allowed to fall into decay, and it also got the character of being " haunted." It is called yet " the haunted house." The last Laird Buchanan who inhabited it had Woodburn House built for himself, when Auchinreoch was abandoned as a residence. The old laird, who died about 1823, was, I think,

buried at Killearn, and the old family burying-place at Clachan
has been utterly forgotten and neglected. Auchinreoch was sold
by a later laird to a Mr. James M'Innes, whose daughter, Lady
Gordon, is the present proprietrix. When we get outside the
church the Lennox mausoleum is the most striking object in the
church-yard. This is a square two-storied building, with dome-
shaped slated roof. No way of access to the upper storey is
visible till you get to the boundary wall, when you see a little
iron gate, and outside the wall, in the inn garden, there is an outside stair. When first built, in 1715, the building was only of
one storey, but during Miss Lennox's ownership of the estate she
caused a second storey to be added to it. This room she used as
a place of retreat when attending the church. Miss Lennox set
an excellent example, and attended church with great regularity.
She used to drive from Woodhead by the old road, over the
Laird's Brig and the Haughhead. She had her horses put into
the inn stables. She then walked through the inn garden to the
stairs which gave access to the upper room in the mausoleum,
where she had a fire in winter. In this room she removed any
wraps, or adjusted her dress before she proceeded to her seat in
the " Woodhead Loft," where the pew formerly was. In those
days there were both forenoon and afternoon diets, and Miss Lennox generally passed the interval between these in this room,
either reading a religious book or chatting with friends. I believe that the earlier interments of the Lennox family were made
in the ground now covered by the mausoleum. After 1715 the
coffins were laid on stone shelves, crypt-wise. This practice was,
however, discontinued, and I have it from eye-witnesses that the
coffins containing the remains of both Mr. and Mrs. Kincaid
Lennox were lowered into the ground. Within the building the
soil is so fine and so dry that it was necessary to shore up the
grave with wood to prevent the sides falling in at the last two
interments. Wood was sent down from the saw mill at the
Netherton for this purpose, and in 1859 the late Mr. John Prentice had charge of carrying out the arrangements at the grave for
Mr. Kincaid Lennox's funeral. I understand that all the stone
shelves have now been removed and all the coffins that had rested
on them have been buried. The crypt interior was entirely cleared
out when the mausoleum was opened to receive the remains of
Mrs. Kincaid Lennox, who was buried there on Friday, 15th
September, 1876. I shall quote three of the inscriptions set into
walls in the upper room. On a white marble tablet we find it
stated that—" This marble is raised in deep love and affection by
Frances Maxwell Kincaid Lennox, widow of John Lennox Kincaid Lennox, and their three daughters, Margaret Cunninghame
Bateman-Hanbury Kincaid-Lennox, Cecilia Peareth, Frances
Oakes, in memory of John Lennox Kincaid Lennox, laird of
Woodhead, Antermony, and Kincaid; born 8th Oct., 1802; died
6th March, 1859; and of John Kincaid Lennox, captain in the

12th Lancers; born 14th Oct., 1830; died 28th Feb., 1857; buried at Thebes, in Upper Egypt; only son of John Lennox Kincaid Lennox and Frances Maxwell Kincaid Lennox, his wife.

> " Let us praise and join the chorus
> Of the saints enthroned on high;
> Here they trusted God before us,
> Now their praises fill the sky.
> Thou hast washed us with Thy blood,
> Thou art worthy, Lamb of God."

That in memory of Mrs. Lennox has the following:—" This tablet is placed here by her three daughters, in loving memory of Frances Maxwell Cunninghame; born 28th April, 1807; died 10th Sept., 1876; third daughter of John Cunninghame, Esq., of Craigends, Renfrewshire, and widow of John Lennox Kincaid Lennox, Esq. ' Her children arise up and call her blessed.'— Proverbs xxxi. 28. ' And shall be Mine, said the Lord of Hosts, in that day when I make up my jewels.'—Mal. iii. 17. ' Blessed are the dead which die in the Lord.'—Rev. xiv. 13." On a black marble tablet there is a memorial of Mrs. Oakes' baby, with this inscribed on it—" In the bright hope of a glorious resurrection are laid the mortal remains of Rosa Oakes; born 2nd August, 1865; died 24th Nov., 1866; the beloved child of Col. Oakes, C.B., 12th Royal Lancers, and Frances Kincaid Lennox, his wife."

The graveyard has long been so fully occupied that interments could hardly be made without disturbing the coffins and remains of the departed. Sometimes the quantity of old coffins and human remains that were taken out and laid aside was so large as to be a shocking sight. In the interests of decency, the expediency of having this put a stop to and the graveyard declared closed, has been frequently mooted. A report was got one year but no formal proceedings have ever been taken, by which all future interments can be legally prevented, except, perhaps, exceptions in favour of particular survivors, where the other members of the family have all been buried here. Burials are now limited as much as possible to surviving members of families, but this year there have been about a dozen interments, while for some years back they have averaged from twelve to fifteen. In order to set a good example the Lennox mausoleum was finally closed in 1884, and I understand a vault was built in the ground in front of the church at Lennoxtown, where it is intended that all future interments of the Lennox family shall be made. The method adopted of closing the mausoleum was rather unusual. The obvious way would have been to have merely built up the doorway, but, instead of doing it in this fashion, two tombstones of the Kincaids of that Ilk, that had rested on dwarf-stone pillars for upwards of two hundred years, were lifted, and, being set closely together, were found to completely fill up the doorway. They were therefore built in, and so carefully have they been placed together and cemented that they appear at first to be one stone. The removal has deprived their record of strict accuracy when they testify that "Heir lyis," &c. The inscriptions and the Kincaid armorial bearings are quite legible, as follows :—" Heir lyis ane Honorabil man James Kinkaid of that Ilk quha desisit ye 13 of Febrovar Anno 1604." The other stone is almost identical, differing only in the name and date ; the name being " John quha decisit ye 9 of Janvar Anno 1606 "; and lower down are the initials of one who " desisit 18 Jan. 1645." These two tombstones are all that now can be seen here, in memoriam of a family who have been landowners in the parish since 1280. It does seem strange that there should be no other tombstone records here of the long line of lairds who have lived and died on their ancestral lands of Kincaid. The Lennoxes and Kincaids had their rivalries and bickerings in the old times, but all these were healed when the two families were united by the Laird of Kincaid marrying a Lennox of Woodhead and their son succeeding to both the united estates.

On another occasion I have told the story, so far as it is known, of William Boick, whose tombstone here is popularly styled " The Martyr's Stone." The inscription is—" Erected in memory of William Boick, who suffered at Glasgow, June XIV., MDCLXXIII, for his adherence to the Word of God and Scotland's Covenanted Work of Reformation.

> " Underneath this stone doth lie
> Dust sacrificed to tyrannie,
> Yet precious in Immanuel's sight
> Shines, martyered for His Kingly right."

There is a tradition in the parish that this stone has received the personal attentions of Richard Paterson, the prototype of Sir Walter Scott's " Old Mortality," who, as is well known, occupied himself in caring for the tombstones of the Covenanters, renewing the letterings, and clearing these of moss, so that the inscriptions should remain legible. Immediately adjacent to the stone of William Boick, the martyr, and to the north, there are two stones, with the letters " E. B." inscribed on them, and a symbol which to some appears to be a cross, while others regard it as a sword. Just beyond these with this symbol there are other three flat stones, alike in shape and lettering, evidently marking the last resting-place of family connections of the Boicks. No trace of such a family can now be found in the parish.

The stone erected to commemorate the late Mr. John M'Far-lan of Ballancleroch is evidently well cared for ; it looks as if new, and the inscription is perfectly distinct. This inscription is said to have been either written or revised by one or other of his distinguished friends, Lord Brougham or Lord Cockburn. It is —" In memory of John M'Farlan, Esq., Ballenglerach ; born 12th Jan., 1767 ; died 18th Dec., 1846. The prime of his life was spent in the practice of the law and in the ardent promotion of the cause of civil and religious liberty. In his later years, but in the vigour of his intellectual power, he retired from the bar, without wealth or worldly advancement, to spend his life in doing good by his writings, his counsel, and his example. He loved mercy and walked humbly with his God. Finally, possessing the esteem of all who knew him, the love of his neighbours, the affection and veneration of his numerous descendants, he passed from this world, rejoicing in the blessed hope of everlasting life, through our Lord Jesus Christ." All Campsonians are under obligation to Mr. M'Farlan, who so long ago as 1785 generously threw open to the public his side of the glen, in which he formed walks. He made no charge for admission, and his successors have continued this boon. It was with deep regret I saw in the *Glasgow Herald*, June, 1890, that Col. M'Farlan had occasion to complain of the injury to his fences and the damage done to his property by thoughtless excursionists, one of whom demanded of the policeman who was endeavouring to keep order and maintain the peace, why any restrictions should be put there *when the glen was public property!* Conduct like that of this senseless excursionist has caused owners to exclude the public from their picture galleries, gardens, and pleasure grounds, but Col. M'Farlan has never thought of closing the Glen. Mr. John M'Farlan passed as advocate in 1787, and he attended the Western Circuit with his friend, Thos. Muir, of Huntershill. The following lines, written by him, were posted for many a day on the old gates of Huntershill :—

> " Doomed from this mansion and his native land
>   To spend the days of gay and sprightly youth,
> And all for sowing, with a liberal hand,
>   The seeds of that seditious libel, Truth."

When it was not only unpopular but almost amounted to being professionally ostracised Mr. M'Farlan was a strong and advanced Liberal. When his party came into power on the passing of the Reform Bill, there was an expectation in some quarters that the Government of Earl Grey would have acknowledged his long and consistent services, in the times of adversity, and have raised him to the bench, under the title of Lord Campsie. He was silently passed over ; it may be, because he had retired by that time from the active duties of his profession, and was too retiring to press any claims he might have had on the Liberal party. It is said of him, that at a certain hour, on stated days of the week, he took his seat on the balcony of Ballancleroch, to give the benefit of his legal lore, gratuitously, to all who chose to consult him, and he was never better pleased than when as a peacemaker he was successful in adjusting disputes without recourse to litigation. All honour to his memory; the natives of Campsie should never forget him, when they think of their Glen. Had he been illiberal in his views he could have excluded them from his lands and made the Glen a sealed book.

Alongside the southern boundary wall is the walled-in burial place of the Bells of Auchtermony or Antermony. Patrick Bell was minister of Port-of-Menteith. He married Annabel, daughter of John, the IX. of Craigbarnet, and their son John became the distinguished traveller. Patrick acquired Antermony from the Earl of Wigton, soon after 1700. A tablet on the wall, with a perfectly legible inscription, commemorates Mary Peters, the wife of the great traveller, of whom it says:—"She was a faithful wife, an affectionate sister, and a kind friend; she was beloved while she lived, and died lamented."

On another marble tablet an inscription commemorates Mrs. Bell's half-sister, Jane Vigors, Countess of Hyndford, who died at Antermony, 13th May, 1802, aged 86 years. Two flat tombstones, with the armorial bearings of the Bell family, have inscriptions which cannot be well read by anyone outside the railings. I understand that the one is in memory of John Bell, the celebrated traveller, and author of "Travels from St. Petersburg to various parts of Asia," and the other is for the traveller's father, Rev. Patrick Bell.

Before passing from the old ruins of the church I should have mentioned that there were a number of marble memorial tablets in it. It is not easy now to ascertain exactly what these were, or what has become of them, but one of them, of beautiful white marble, was to Jean Maria, second daughter of Sir John Stirling, fifth baronet, born 7th January, 1773; married John Mackenzie of Garnkirk; and died 30th October, 1797, in her twenty-fifth year. When the old church was abandoned, the proprietor of Glorat was non-resident, but in order to preserve it, Andrew Motherwell, farmer, Baldorran, and acting factor on the estate, had this tablet taken to Baldorran Farm, and set up in the milkhouse there. It fell one day against a souring boat, and two pieces were broken off. These his son, James Motherwell, gave to a little girl who came then every day to Baldorran for milk. Her father had them ground, one round and the other oval, and they have served two generations as "peevers" or "peeveralls," and are still carefully preserved in the Mount of Glorat by Mrs. James Buchanan. Another tablet was in memory of some one residing about Balmore, who had left some money to the parish.

I have already incidentally mentioned that the tombstone to the memory of Mr. and Mrs. Gartshore-Stirling is beautifully kept, but I omitted to mention that her husband's grave was periodically visited by the late Mrs. Gartshore-Stirling. Latterly she became stone blind, but once a year at least she went to the grave. I have been informed that among the last times she went her coachman took her arm and led her to the grave, while her maid accompanied her. The sight of the venerable and blind lady in her pious pilgrimage awed even the children, who hushed their sports till her carriage had driven off.

To the north of the Lennox mausoleum there is a flat tombstone with armorial bearings and a marginal inscription, which is in some places quite illegible. What can be made out is, " Ane

Honorabil Ladie Hainan, who was both good and virtuous, who decessed at Craigbarnet." No one now can obtain any information regarding this "Honorabil Ladie."

The following ministers have died and been buried in the Clachan:— Stoddart, 1580; Stewart, 1622; Collins, 1648; Dennistoun, 1679; Govan, 1729; Forrester, 1731; Bell, 1783; Lapslie, 1824. In the gloomy and dilapidated enclosure known as the "Ministers' Tomb," only Messrs. Govan and Forrester are interred. This structure was rebuilt by the late Miss Lennox in 1818, and stands greatly in need of repair now. Two stones had originally been placed on dwarf pillars, to commemorate the two ministers, but these flat tombstones have now been set vertically against the western wall, and the pillars have been carefully lifted and set in the corners. When I was there lately the iron gate was open, and I went inside the enclosure, where there was a rank growth of nettles. Owing to the stones being covered with moss and lichens the armorial bearings only could be made out. The lettering was quite illegible, but I am indebted to the kindness of Mr Blair, Session-Clerk of the parish, who has furnished me with copies. The inscriptions are both in Latin, but I give you a free translation, as follows:—" This is the tomb of Mr. John Govean, for upwards of —— years a Herald of the Divine Word, viz., from 5th December, 1688, to 19th September, 1729; aged 79 years." On the other stone the inscription is—" In this Tomb is deposited the body of the Rev. John Forrester, born 14th December, 1705; ordained pastor of this parish 23rd September, 1730; died 15th August, 1731, aged 26 years." This Mr. Forrester was a nephew of the Rev. Mr. Govean.

Nearer the glen than the old church there is a tombstone erected to the memory of a man, who, for many years, as superintendent of an unsectarian Sabbath school, carried on with great success a good work in Lennoxtown. There are many old Campsonians who will recall now, with mingled feelings, the great demonstrations that attended Jamie Gray's May-milk, which used to be held on the third Saturday in June, the Saturday after the Summer Sacrament. His stone, near the north-east corner, records that James Gray died 20th Aug., 1871, aged 61. I cannot pass his tombstone without expressing the respect I felt for him, and my appreciation of his abundant labours in the Sabbath School, in his visitation of the sick and dying, and his eagerness to point out the way of salvation to those who were asking, "What must I do to be saved?"

In walking through the kirkyard I read many of the inscriptions with great interest, and can recall memories of great numbers who are silently resting in it. Here is the stone of the Rev. William James, who died 2nd April, 1867, aged 31 years, a man whom I remember well. Before studying for the ministry, he had served an apprenticeship in Lennoxmill as a block-cutter. He belonged to a pious family of Methodists, but studied fo the ministry of the U.P. Church, and was pastor of a chapel in Leeds when he died, in early manhood, full of enthusiasm and successful in his work. I was present at his marriage, and at a few minutes' notice had to act as his groomsman, owing to the "best man" having been unable to be present.

There is a stone erected by friends and admirers of Wm. Muir, the Birdston poet, who was born in 1766 and died in 1817. His poems on various subjects were published in 1818, and are now known to very few, either in Campsie or Kirkintilloch. It is strange the associations of ideas. Mr. William Craig told me he had been employed to cart the stones from the sculptors in Glasgow. The funds subscribed were rather short and Willie was never paid. He said he would not have minded that so much, but not even to get his outlays on tolls, &c., was too bad.

There are few quaint or striking epitaphs to be seen here. There is one on W. Brown's grave, in these words—

"Eternity is a wheel that turns,
A wheel that turneth ever;
A wheel that turns
And will leave turning never."

There are seven stones beside one another, very much alike, and without inscription of any kind. They are popularly known as "The seven brothers." These "brothers" seem to have been Highlanders who either had fled from their home in the North, or had strayed into the parish after the '45 and remained here. The traditions concerning them are vague and contradictory. Before the erection of the Muckcroft bridge over the Glazert there were large stepping stones at the ford there. Tradition associates the placing of these stepping stones with the seven brothers, who were very strong men. The seven unlettered stones commemorate these brethren.

Near them is a curious stone, resembling a boat turned keel uppermost. Though there is neither emblem nor inscription of any kind, the local tradition has it that it is the grave of a sailor. A gentleman, who has seen this stone in the Clachan, was one day in Abercorn graveyard, when he saw an almost exact *fac-simile*, but twice the size. There was the keel of the boat, the bow, and the stern. Upon asking the sexton, he was told nothing more was known about it except that it was said to cover the remains of a sailor, and that strangers visiting the churchyard asked to see this stone.

I have been informed that out of some of the graves two cartloads of stones have had to be taken before another interment could be made. There is reason to believe that this portion of the graveyard formed at one time part of the old channel of the Glen Burn—hence the quantity of large, gravelly stones. While digging graves these were carefully collected and replaced over the coffin. The stones were put there to ensure the graves being left inviolate in the resurrectionist times. Those who enclosed their graves with wall or iron railings little dreamt that the body-snatchers did not go down vertically but obliquely, and they often got the body without disturbing the surface of that grave at all.

Between the Lennox mausoleum and the boundary wall, just behind the Crown Inn, there is a horizontal stone, which formerly was quite close to the Kincaid stones, before they were removed to close the Lennox tomb. It is in memory of Miss Christina Dow, who died, Nov., 1830; aged 52 years. Miss Dow was housekeeper at Kincaid House, and in her lifetime was much attached to the family. Like the old domestic mentioned by Dean Ramsay, whose last request was, "Laird, will ye tell them to bury me whaur I'll be at your feet," Miss Dow wished to be laid beside the Kincaid family burying-place, so that her body would lie across the feet of the Laird. With the exception of some charitable bequests she bequeathed all her effects to Mr Kincaid. She had some fine rings, which she greatly valued, and which she had requested should remain on her fingers after death, and be buried with her. All her wishes were complied with, but her body was lifted the very night of her burial. Mr. Kincaid had the grave opened, to ascertain whether this was actually the case, when it was found that not only had the body been taken away but the coffin had disappeared likewise.

Anatomy and physiology have been called the basis on which rests the science of medicine. From the first we learn the structure of the human body, and from the latter the functions of the various organs. These require to be studied both in health and disease, and, in order to effect this, our great medical schools require a supply of dead bodies. They formerly obtained their supply of these in the shape of bodies of criminals or unclaimed paupers, granted for this purpose by the authorities of jails, &c. Between 1820 and 1832, owing to the greater attention being given to the study of anatomy, the supply of dead bodies to the medical schools, for the purpose of dissection, fell far short of the demand. What could not be obtained in a legitimate way was accomplished by unscrupulous people in an illegal way. Students and medical apprentices went out at night to the sepulchres of the dead in large cities and rifled them of their contents. Dr. Knox of Edinburgh was paying sums of from £8 to £14 for dead bodies, which Burke and Hare made it for a time their business to supply. The graveyards of Ireland were plundered, and a cargo actually arrived at Glasgow, consisting of human bodies, concealed in what appeared to be bales or bundles of some soft stuff. The freight and charges were made payable by the consignee. whose letter of advice not having arrived in time, he declined to pay the freight and charges. The bales lay meantime on the wharf till the stench drew attention and caused the discovery of what the consignment really consisted of. In Scotland respect, almost amounting to superstitious feeling, is paid to the dead. Robert the Bruce's request that his heart should be taken out of his body, and taken to Jerusalem by his friend the good Sir James Douglas. appeared to the Pope such a shocking request that it called for his malediction. The inscription on Shakespere's tomb may be taken as illustrating the feeling that generally prevailed—

> " Good friends for Jesus' sake forbear
> To dig the dust enclosed here ;
> Blest be the man that spares these stones,
> And curst be he that moves my bones."

Few criminal trials have excited such deep and widespread interest as the Burke and Hare trial. Hare turned King's evidence ; Burke was convicted and hanged 29th Jan., 1829. In consequence of the shocking revelations at this trial, Parliament passed an Act in 1832 making legal provision for the supply of bodies for scientific purposes. This made the violation of graves not only unnecessary but quite inexcusable ; and, as connected with the kirk and kirkyard, we shall now recall the period of the

RESURRECTIONISTS IN CAMPSIE.

> " Be honours which to kings we give
> To doctors also paid.
> We're the king's subjects while we live,
> The doctors when we're dead."

When body-lifting became dangerous in university cities, then country graveyards were resorted to, and there are many stories of the exciting adventures of those engaged in this unlawful quest. People became at length alarmed, and sought to prevent the violation of their burying-places by the erection of those huge, unsightly iron cages or high railings, to be seen both in the Clachan and Auld Aisle graveyards. Beside these, householders were detailed to watch in turn. This custom obtained in Campsie. Lists of watchers who took their turn in the Clachan churchyard were regularly made up. The list began at the one end of Lennoxtown and came on to the other, making no exceptions, all householders having to take their turn. Three neighbours were on the roll for each night to watch the graveyard. Fire-arms were kept at the guard-house at the Clachan, for use by the watch, if required. It was customary to lay in a stock of refreshments, especially whisky, to keep up their courage and dispel the eerie feeling that crept over many of them as they sat thinking of ghosts, wandering spirits, and reckless resurrectionists. Some householders pled guilty to being great cowards and to be frightened, and pled for exemption on this score, but they had to take their turn with the rest or pay for a substitute.

There was a man, a poacher and a hanger-on about the Clachan, by name Robert Brown, or " Scuffy " as he was called. " Scuffy " made it his business to know the names and characters for vigilance of those forming the watch. He favoured them with his company to keep them from wearying, and of course partook of any refreshing that was needed. In this way it could be known by the resurrectionists whether the watch was only nominal or real, and measures could be taken accordingly, if they wished to make a raid on a fresh " corpse." There can be little doubt that graves were frequently rifled, both in Campsie and in Kirkintilloch.

There was another man, named Robin M'H——, who was occasionally employed in the parish to kill a pig or a calf. He kept an old horse and a conveyance, and was considered a useless body, who managed somehow or other to earn money very easily; by body-lifting, it was generally supposed. He was driving one dark night with a companion, who was wrapped up in a large greatcoat, seated alongside of him. Robin stopped at Strathblane toll for a dram, which when handed to him he tossed off without a remark. As he returned the glass, the toll-keeper said—" Man, are ye no' gaun to gie a drink to your neebor?" " Oh," replied he, " this man drinks nane," and then he applied the whip to the old horse.

There is another story that Robin and another had lifted a body in the Clachan and gone to Torrance to meet the buyers there, and hand over their bargain. To their disgust they were only offered £3, instead of the current rate of from £7 to £10 for a good subject. " Hout, fie!" said his companion, " £3 only for a big, strong, fresh Irishman. What do you say to this, Robin?" " Oh," replied Robin, " it'll no' dae ava; a big man like this for £3! Before I'd sell him for that, I'll tak' him back and bury him in the Clachan mools."

In the Orchard graveyard, attached to the old Marshall Church, Kirkintilloch, similar scenes were enacted. Here a Campsie man came to grief. Will Monach was at one time tenant of Easter Crosshouse Farm, now standing in ruins, having been joined to Balcorrach. Will in his young days had been a handsome man, although he was a " coorse beggar" in his later days. He was married to one of the handsomest women in the parish, on whose family he latterly sponged. He kept a public-house near Lockhart's Loan, now occupied by Mr. M'Cahill. Will did a little in the resurrectionist line. Learning that a Mrs. Dickson in Kirkintilloch had died, he made arrangements to lift the body a night or two after her burial. Her son was Bailie Dickson, a flesher in Kirkintilloch, and her friends, as was then customary, watched the grave and kept a vigilant look out that no one disturbed it. Those on watch heard the resurrectionist operations commence, and at once rushed out. One of the watch, lifting a hook with which he had been cutting a hedge, came upon an intruder in the act of leaping the wall. Grasping his hedgebill with both his hands, he struck out with all his might, and he knew he had hit the body-lifter, but the man rolled over the wall and disappeared. The watchers then returned to examine the grave and were pleased to find they had been in time to preserve it inviolate. After a period of seclusion, Will Monach reappeared in Campsie, having mysteriously lost a leg, and now wearing a wooden one. At the sale of his effects after his death, Henry Daisley, a cobbler in Lennoxtown, bought Will's pin leg. When asked what use he could have for a wooden leg, he replied that it made a "capital heel stock," and as Henry Daisley's heel stock the wooden leg was used for many years. Henry was well known in Lennoxtown thirty years ago.

What happened occasionally at the Clachan prevailed all around. Parishioners at Torrance, who buried in Cadder, being nearer to Glasgow, had even greater risks. One case I have authentic information about. There were two brothers, Duncan and Daniel C——, who were well known at Torrance fifty or more years ago. The wife of one of the brothers died and was buried in Cadder Churchyard. As usual the grave was watched as long as there was any danger of it being violated. This churchyard was quiet and sequestered, yet near a good road, and was a most likely spot for the resurrectionist. The body snatchers actually lifted the body while the watch were supposed to be guarding the churchyard. The guard had been caught napping, but they were not altogether careless, so when they discovered what had been done, they set off in hot pursuit. They got on the scent and overtook the resurrectionists near Glasgow, but they had got rid of the corpse, which was found next day roughly concealed in a stable dungstead and covered with straw. The body was taken back and decently reinterred.

There was a great turnout in Kirkintilloch on the Queen's Jubilee, a neighbour then told me he had only once seen a crowd like it in Kirkintilloch, that was when Janet Scobbie was lifted at the Auld Aisle, and one of the three men was caught.

The late Mr. Alexander Galloway, in his lecture, entitled, "Historical notes regarding Campsie, Part II.," delivered to the Campsie Mechanics' Institution, on 9th March, 1864, stated that the parish school of Campsie was erected in 1661 by John, Archbishop of Glasgow. The salary of the teacher was to be £100 Scots. The deed of erection contains an express clause declaring that the schoolmaster shall in all times coming teach Latin, and that the school shall be constantly held at the Clachan of Campsie. The population of the parish at this time was estimated at 1500. It is to be hoped that none of the Haughhead ratepayers will heckle the candidates for the School Board on this point at the next election. For a long succession of years the Parochial schoolmasters have had the reputation of being excellent teachers and good Latin and Greek scholars. In my young days, Mr. Gilchrist, a native of Carluke, Lanarkshire, was Parochial schoolmaster and session-clerk. As a teacher, he had the reputation of being one of the best of his day, and was said to be an excellent classical scholar. He took an interest in his old pupils and did all he could to assist them in preparing for college. He was old when I recollect him, and was indisposed for any exertion or being put off his usual routine. I remember he used to come into church very late, having waited to count the collection. His sister, who was quite a character in her way, kept his house. When she came to church she had on her best dress, but this was taken off the moment she got home, and a shortgown and petticoat resumed, which she always wore, even when the minister or a laird was calling. The brother and sister lived affectionately together. At twelve o'clock, when the country scholars swarmed into her kitchen for the "pieces" they had brought from home, her first care in her affectionate solicitude was to have her brother Willie's pipe ready. She was herself very fond of tobacco, and as smoking by a female was a thing almost unheard of then, it caused her to be regarded as peculiar. She was a great believer in buttermilk, especially the "gran' sour milk frae Crosshouse," and attributed the good health enjoyed by her brother and herself to the copious potations they both heartily relished.

Robert Lindsay of Pitscottie, in his "History of Scotland from 1436 to 1604," mentions that in the year 1439 a great host of Highlanders raided the district between Lochlomond and Stirling, swept the Lennox hills and Strathblane, Campsie, and Kilsyth of nearly all the cattle, and committed many most cruel murders. Campsie kirk and its clachan village and many of its people were sufferers by this incursion.

The hamlet of the Clachan of Campsie, as it existed during the first quarter of the present century, has now almost entirely passed away. The meal mill and kiln of the olden times gave place to the bleachfield of modern days, but a few roofless walls are all that remain of this once thriving field. Printfields, smithy, cottages, and loomshops are now all things of the past, only one of the old houses remains standing, and in this the pedestrian may obtain lemonade or a cup of tea. The ruins of the houses below the "Kirkstyle" are almost all that remain of a once thriving little village, that seventy years ago was full of life. It had been the religious centre of the parish for hundreds of years. Hither all classes had come in joy and sorrow. The removal of the church to Lennoxtown was the first deadly blow to its importance. The opening of the new graveyard soon followed. Since that time the place decayed, even after a weaving factory had been successfully commenced at Haughhead, which might have given employment to its inhabitants and been the precursor of other factories on the Finglen burn. Unfortunately, the sight of it being disagreeable to the land owner, the mill owner has had to betake himself and his enterprise elsewhere. There used to be about 100 people employed at Mr Gardiner's, afterwards Mr Cunningham's bleachfield. A smithy stood to the east of the Crown Inn, in which a blacksmith named Cassells hammered away cheerfully. Houses and loomshops extended from the smithy down the eastern side of the road and right round for some distance into the old road to the east by Cumroch Brae. At one time 50 looms were actively employed here. The most of the weavers worked to Glasgow manufacturers. A Haughhead weaver, working for a Glasgow house, Gibson & Macnee, took in some work, which was said to be defective, and five per cent. was deducted on this account. Charlie expected a sum which he did not get. " Gie me the price o' my web," said he. "Ye've got it there, less five per cent." " Gie me the price o' my web." " Ye have it less the per centage." " Hang your per cent. ; gie me the siller for my web." Charlie declared he could never in his life understand "these confounded per cents." Others, such as Brown, whose loom-shop was at the upper corner of the old road, did what was called a " customer trade," weaving the materials which were brought to him for this purpose. At the opposite corner, where there is now a two-storey villa, formerly stood a four-loom shop, while " Deacon " Gilchrist's loomshop occupied the site of Mrs. Jamie-son Provan's cottage. The Clachan folks of these days were intelligent, simple-minded, and of rather primitive habits and customs. Many of them were better known by nicknames than by their own baptismal names. They affected style in these names, and it happened that quite a lot of titled personages were living here whose names were not to be found in Peerage or Baronetage. As specimens of these names I may mention " Prince Charlie," " Royal Stewart," " Whistle Wull," " The Old Shirra " and " The Young Shirra." All these were Stewarts. The best known was David Ferguson, " the Earl," as he was always called. There was " Lord John," " Lady Marget," " Sir Donald Grant," " The Deacon," " Cooper John," " Snip Wull," "Bauchle Jock," " Beagle Rab," and " Scuffy Brown." Saunders Norie, the Relief precentor, resided here, and to him the com-munity were greatly indebted for any musical training they re-ceived ; and there was also a weaver named James Morrison, with the reputation of dabbling in poetry. Concerning " Bauchle Jock," it is said he never made any profession of religion When very ill the parish minister called on him, and after some conver-sation the minister offered to engage in prayer with him. " Na, na," replied Jock ; I'll never get tae heaven wi' borrowed wings." Poor man, he had come to this conclusion when it was too late to " tak' a thocht an' men'."

The Inn used to be as you enter the glen. Here, in the early years of the present century, came William Muir, who, for some time, worked at his trade of block printer in Lennoxmill, while his wife attended to the business. Muir was born and brought up in the farm adjoining Mossgiel, where the Burnses were tenants. He remembered seeing the poet at work in the fields, and has been in his company at festive gatherings in the farm barns in the winter evenings. Muir became rather a favourite with Miss Lennox, and as his house, with 1661 cut on the lintel, and still to be seen as you approach the glen, was too small, she built larger premises for him in 1818, with greater accommodation for stabling.

As the public worship was then conducted in the old church, Sunday was a busy day in the Clachan. Those who came long distances required some refreshment. Friends and acquaintances, who rarely met except at church, had to enquire about one another's welfare, and adjourned to the inn for a "crack." Forbes Mackenzie's Act, closing public houses on Sundays, was not passed till long afterwards. But the greatest event in the Clachan was the Sacramental occasions, when great numbers used to attend from neighbouring parishes, and provision had to be made for giving the visitors food and liquor. To hit the happy medium of what quantity of refreshments to have ready was a matter of deep concern to all who provided entertainment for man and beast in the Clachan and Haughhead. If the weather proved fine large crowds might be expected; if unpropitious, the attendance of strangers might be very small. On one occasion, on the Saturday preceding the communion Sabbath, the clouds were dark and lowering, and rain was expected. That Saturday afternoon and evening Mallie was frequently coming out and intently scanning the clouds for some signs of clearing; but the outlook got worse and worse, and, realising this, and despairing of the good harvest on the morrow, she had prepared for and expected, she turned sadly to re-enter, muttering to herself, "I think the morn'H no be worth a snuff." The Muirs conducted their business in the new inn with great enterprise, and the public soon found out that they could get better accommodation and service in the Clachan for dinners, suppers, balls, or public meetings than anywhere else in the parish. This branch developed, for on great occasions they arranged to obtain the use of a large apartment in the Bleach Field, which was capable of holding more people than any other hall then to be had. The yeomanry ball was perhaps the greatest festive event of the year. The " Field " was obtained for dancing and supper, and the rooms were gaily decorated with evergreens and draperies. The Stirlingshire Yeomanry Cavalry consisted of five troops—(1) Stirling, (2) Falkirk, (3) Strathendrick, (4) Kilsyth and eastwards, and (5) Campsie, Strathblane, and Baldernock. The lairds, principal farmers, or their sons, the doctors, a few shopkeepers, &c.. formed the Campsie troop. The regiment met at Stirling annually for eight days' training and rode home through Campsie Muir, by the Craw Road, and down the Ward Brae to the Clachan Inn, at which they halted and partook of a parting cup before separating for their homes. I have become acquainted with an incident that happened at a Yeomanry ball in 1836, which I shall narrate. Of the many handsome young ladies present three by common consent were pre-eminently beautiful, and who was the belle of the ball was being keenly discussed by several groups. It had narrowed down to three—a farmer's daughter from the eastern end and two sisters from Lennoxtown. Mr. Robert Dalglish, afterwards M.P., was present, and was appealed to to give his verdict

as referee. After consideration, his award was in favour of the
two sisters dressed in blue. These young ladies, then the Misses
Brown, still survive, and as Mrs. Walker and Mrs. Archibald are
known to me. Mrs. Walker still retains many of the good looks
which made her the belle of the Clachan ball in 1836. The
other young lady was Miss Jane Buchanan of the Shields. In
the opinion of others she was undoubtedly the belle. This was
certainly the opinion of Mr. Brown, the parochial schoolmaster,
for he came up to the late Mr. Alexander Galloway, then a
sprightly young bachelor who had recently become factor on the
Woodhead estate. Addressing Mr. Galloway, Mr. Brown pointed
out Miss Jane Buchanan to him, declaring that he considered her
the prettiest girl in the parish. Not only was she pretty, he added,
she was good and clever withal, and would be sure to make him an
excellent wife if he were contemplating matrimony. Mr. Galloway jocularly declared he was not thinking of matrimony, but
was obliged to Mr. Brown all the same. The famous Tibby
Fowler o' the Glen was not in it with Miss Buchanan of Shields.
In Tibby's case,

> " Ten cam' east and ten cam' west,
> Ten cam' rowin' o'er the water,
> Twa cam' doon the lang dyke side:
> There's twa-and-thirty wooin' at her."

But then

> " it was for her pelf
> That a' the lads were wooin' at her."

Local gossip in the Milton reckoned the number of Miss Buchanan's
admirers at 42. She became the wife of Mr. James Bowman,
farmer and miller at Cadder. In these times it was a common
practice for farmers to ride to church, carrying their wives or
daughters on a pillion behind. For their convenience there was
a loupin'-on stone almost opposite the old inn, and near the
corner of the School-house garden, where it may still be seen,
being used to guard the wall at the corner as you turn into the
glen. It is about 2½ feet high, rounded at top, and has been
used as a seat by the younger generation, who never saw it put to
its original use. It was also very common for females to walk
barefooted to the church. Young women who did not do this
were considered by their neighbours as " wasterfu', extravagant
jades." Some of the householders at the Clachan used to set out
in their gardens a boyne filled with water for the convenience of
their friends and acquaintances. There was then a little burn
which used to flow past the School-house and past the " Dean's
House," where two stone steps gave access to the old Shirra's.
It flowed into the glen burn just below Ballancleroch. The little
burnie was the favourite resort of these thrifty females. Here they
bathed their feet before putting on shoes and stockings, here curl
papers would be taken out and the finishing touches given to toilets
that had not been quite completed before leaving home. The shoes

and stockings were taken off when they came out of church, and
the homeward journey was made barefoot. The house commonly
called the Dean's House has now been entirely removed. It stood
below the School-house. It was probably erected as a manse or
parsonage for the incumbent. In after times this house being
too small, a larger one was built, which now forms part of the
offices of the existing manse. It is the two-storey building on
the north side of the court.

Localities were clearly defined. On the old road from the
ruined farmhouse of Easter Crosshouse to the end of the road at
the green was the Ha'-end. From the green to the Haughhead
bridge was the Howe Loan. Clashmore was in the Ballancleroch grounds. Near the foot of the glen the little streamlet
formed the Heron's Glen. Just above this the brae was called
" The Dinnins," where a little higher still was " Maggie Lapslie's
Knowe." Maggie had no connection with the parish minister of
that name, but at one time occupied a little cottage here. She
came to a tragic end. She was in the act of stealing a sheep,
and had tied its feet and swung the animal on to her back, and
was in this way carrying it home. Getting over a dyke quite
close to her house she seems to have lost her hold of the animal,
and when she got down on one side the sheep remained on the
other, and its feet being round her neck, she died by stran-
gulation almost at her own door. Mr John M'Farlane had made
a new plantation up the glen. Addressing Felix M'Kewn, who
had been engaged in planting it he said, " Well, Felix, what shall
we call this plantation? " " Well, sir, to-morrow is St. Patrick's
day; won't you just call it St. Patrick's plantin'? " " St. Patrick's
be it, Felix," and so in the Clachan it came to be called. Donald
Levenax, the son of Duncan, Earl of Lennox, had his house of
Ballecorrach, north of the old road and almost opposite Mrs.
Provan's cottage. The trees on the slope of the hill would be
part of the ornamental grounds above his mansion house.

In Sketches of Manners, Customs, and Scenery of Scotland,
published in 1811, we find Miss Spence the authoress, who was
on a visit at Craigbarnet in 1810, mentioning that when going
to the Church at the Clachan, she observed the door of the house
covered with large spots of white paint. Asking the meaning of
this she was informed that the head of the house had died recently
and that these white spots symbolised the tears shed by the be-
reaved family. Referring to the superstitious observance of freits
and omens as affecting luck, Miss Spence mentions that even the
Laird of Craigbarnet gave heed to them. For having been warned
by the fairies to the effect that having commenced a journey he was
on no account to turn back. One day the Laird was thrown from
his horse into a burn after he had set out. He would not return
himself for dry clothes, but waited till his servant returned with
them. One day James Provan galloped from Craigbarnet to the
Smiddy at the Clachan and called for Cassels the Smith to " get

his fleams and come awa' this minit." The Smith complied, got the instrument he used for bleeding a horse and was well down the Howe Loan when Provan began to explain that his callant had tried to execute himself on the tree in "Murray's grove," close by the march between Craigbarnet and Crosshouse lands. "It's no a beast, it's a bodie, then?" "Aye, my callant." "I must go back for a lancet, then; these won't do to bleed a laddie." The boy had been enjoined by his mother to "mind the wean." Rather than obey, in a fit of passion the boy got a rope and attempted to hang himself on the tree. He was seen and cut down before he had effected his purpose. In the excitement of the moment old James Provan could think of nothing else than getting the smith to restore him to animation but by bleeding him, and bled he was, and survived, notwithstanding this treatment. Old Provan used to go down to the Court Hill and look around "just to hae a look at the world." This is the old servant of whom it is said that having exasperated the Laird of Craigbarnet he said, "Well, James, we must part." "Where are you gaun, Laird?" When he was told he must go away he refused. "If the Laird didna ken a guid servant, he kent a guid master." James Rankin in the Haughhead was one of the most superstitious of men. If he had started to go anywhere, and met or saw anything that he considered of evil omen or unlucky, he would turn at once; of course he had a horse shoe nailed outside his door, and rowan tree and red thread hung up inside, these being considered as specifics against witchcraft.

> "Rowan tree and red thread
> Put the witches to their speed."

The rowan tree was frequently fixed above the byre door to prevent mischief from witchcraft. In Norse mythology, the rowan was associated with stealing fire from heaven, the rowan having sprung from a feather of the bird that stole the fire. According to ancient custom, the people wore on the eve of May-day a slip of rowan tree tied with red thread, the red berries and thread being typical of fire, and they were considered a charm against ill luck, with the power of averting evil from their cattle. It used to be told of a prominent man on the Woodhead property, a most estimable individual in every respect, that when going about on the Lennox estates, if a hare happened to cross his path he at once turned back to the Netherton and did not go on his journey that day. The brother of the James Rankin just referred to, John Rankin, was a mill-wright in Lennoxmill at one time, but he retired when his wife succeeded to her fortune, and he lived quietly at the Clachan. He was considered to be a great authority on cattle and their diseases, more especially where these were supposed to be affected by witchcraft, &c. He was often called upon to advise farmers and others, not only in Campsie but also in the neighbouring parishes of Fintry, Kippen, and Buchlyvie.

He was sent for by a Fintry farmer to see his cows, as something had gone wrong with the milk. The farmer's household had great faith in his skill, but a maid servant was sceptical and rather jeered at his methods. He stopped at once, declared he saw a woman here in whose presence he could not proceed. She must be put out of the way. She was thereupon put into a box-bed, the doors were tied and chairs put up in front to make sure. Rankin then went to the byre, had all the cows' tails tied to a rope, and then he belaboured the poor frightened animals with a stick to exorcise the evil spirit. In departing, he left instructions that they were not to be released till he was round the Craw Road on his way home, when the cure would have been effected. The minister of Fintry on another occasion called in his services for some cow that was ill. The minister expected he was calling in a vet., who would ascertain by examination what was the matter and prescribe accordingly. Rankin, however, declared it was witchcraft, and commenced his usual formula. The minister could not stand that. "Here's a half-crown and take the road, my man." Rankin expressed his great regret at the result as, he said, "when ye had the minister ye got the whole parish," and this unceremonious dismissal meant a loss to him of prestige in that district. Robert Mitchell, Balgrochan, had great faith in Rankin and consulted him often. On one occasion he declared somebody had "cuissen an ill e'e on the kye," and enquired whether Mitchell had not seen anyone keeking about? He said he had seen a farmer prowling about one night, but as Rabbie's failing was the lasses he never thought of any harm to the kye. "That's the man," said Rankin, "that has cast the bad e'e." Mr. William Craig, now of Crosshill, Lennoxtown, but whose family were long tenants of Balglass farm, has many stories of Rankin's experiences in curing witchcraft. Dr. Robertson, who was Rankin's brother-in-law, and knew all his cattle-curing and milk-healing tricks, was on one occasion professionally visiting at the Mains Farm. He opened the milk-house door by mistake, and was surprised to see on the floor a row of milk dishes, each one almost filled with fresh earth, and a branch of newly-pulled broom laid across each dish. He retired and entered by the kitchen door, and addressed the farmer's wife thus:—"I see ye've been consulting Johnnie Rankin." "Wheest! Wheest!" says she, speaking low; "dinna mention it. Our milk has been gaun a' wrang for some time past, and yon's what we are recommended to try to cure it." The fresh earth was for the purpose of seasoning and afterwards scouring the wood of the milk dishes, and the branch of broom had some supposed charm.

I remember Mr. Samson, who, when I was a boy, was proprietor and occupier of Wetshod. He very much astonished and amused a visitor one day by informing him that one of his horses had died that morning, notwithstanding his utmost care during its illness, and his use of a specific cure which he had been taught to regard as infallible, which he had never known to fail before This cure was the taking an old horse-shoe off another horse, boiling it for several hours in water, and then making the ailing horse drink of this horse-shoe tea or bree.

A Haughhead woman, in a court of justice, was called upon to take an oath. This she did, and then gave evidence. A neighbour knew her witness was false, and asked her how she could say that on oath. "Oh, woman," she replied, "did ye no' see I kept my hand below my breath," referring to some superstitious belief that if the right hand was not held above the mouth when taking the oath, it was not binding.

In the year 1804, a young woman named Bennie, residing either at the Netherton, or at Calside, or at Cloch Core, I am not certain which, became unwell. She had previously enjoyed robust health, but now was evidently drooping; her appetite was gone, and her spirits were depressed. The cause of her illness could not at first be discovered by the collective wisdom of the wise-women of the Netherton and Cloch Core. Not to be baffled, they agreed to lay aside their own theories in favour of one who was inclined to believe that the girl had been bewitched by some evil-disposed person, perhaps a neighbour! This seemed the likeliest cause. So the people living in the hamlet agreed to assemble in one of the houses and have a witch-finder called in to see what he would recommend, after hearing all the circumstances. One of the women who assembled at this strange gathering was the mother of the late John Brown, Crosshill Street. Another has her great-grandson still living in Lennoxtown. A third was a woman whose maiden name was Martha Cassels and whose married name was Mrs. Baird. The witchcraft expert was brought from Kilmaronock, and his arrival being notified, he was introduced to the meeting and solemnly proceeded with his investigation. He called on each person present to repeat the Lord's Prayer. This had been successfully accomplished by one or two, when it came to Mrs. Baird's turn. She, it would appear, had rather a peculiar expression or pronunciation. She commenced briskly, and was understood to say—"Our Father which wert in heaven." "Stop! 'which wert in heaven.' Ah! who was in heaven at one time and was put out?" "Why, the Devil!!" "Why," said the witchfinder, "the woman's saying the prayer to the Evil Ane!" On this ground alone he declared this woman was the cause of the girl's ill health. This strange award, which had no bearing or effect on the invalid, on her relations, or on her neighbours, was declared in all seriousness to a number of married women, by a so-called man of skill, in the parish of Campsie, within the present century.

The minister's man, church beadle, and gravedigger is an important personage in a clachan. The beadle was for the first quarter of the century Nicol Hunter, who must have succeeded well, for he built the public-house at the Haughhead bridge. It was then customary for large towns to board out their poor waifs and orphans in country hamlets and villages, and some of them were boarded in the Clachan. Nicol had two, and when his daughters married one of them kept his house. She identified herself with his interests, and expressed her regret at the healthiness of the parish, as "no' a rib had crossed the kirk-style for a month."

About the time that Dr. Norman Macleod came to Campsie Nicol was succeeded in his post by Donald Blair. Many queer stories were long current about Donald's sayings and doings, but they have now nearly all passed into oblivion, and the number of persons who recollect having seen Donald are very few now. Like his predecessor, Donald complained of the healthiness of the parish. In reply to an enquiry how he was getting on, he declared he was na getting on at all. He had not buried a leevin' soul for sax weeks. Donald had not the consideration of a Dunfermline beadle, who, when he was among his cronies, used to say—"'Deed, man, I'm feared to speir at onybody how they are, in case they micht think I was wearyin' on them." For the some reason, when he was taking a dram, he never dared say— "My services tae you." To a young man, evidently dying, who, although very weak and feeble, was occasionally taking a walk to the church-yard, Donald volunteered the comforting assurance, that he would gie him a nice place in the graveyard, a canny place near the yett, where he widna be jostled and hurt by the rush of the outcoming crowd at the Last Day! It was complained that the scale of charges for grave-digging was very elastic with Donald. There was no fixed tariff, but the price depended on the ability of the customer to pay. Strange to say, he had often difficulty in obtaining payment of his fees for opening the graves, and he complained most of the Irish in this respect. Being irritated one day at not being paid for his work, he declared that he "would never bury another leevin' soul o' an Irishman." He was fussy and officious when lowering the coffin, and having it laid straight and solid. On one occasion, when he had been showing off, making his assistants move it an "aught" east or west, a relative of deceased, getting exasperated, exclaimed, "Ye auld Hielan' reiver, what do ye ken about an aught part." He was always made very angry when the boys got into the churchyard and commenced ringing the bell. This ringing of the kirk bell, from the danger and excitement attendant upon it, became a great sport for the wilder spirits amongst the Clachan youths. There is a song to be found amongst Sir Walter Scott's miscellaneous poems, entitled, "Donald Caird's come again." This song was parodied by a local poet named Morrison, and sung at Clachan concerts by one Livingstone, then a very popular comic singer, who came from Glasgow. Livingstone became a great favourite in Campsie. When disabled by rheumatism from going out to concerts, he lay in a bed in the Bush Tavern, Glasgow, where he was always glad to see and sing to his old patrons, and was a source of attracting guests to the tavern to see and hear him. Donald and his family always resented the singing of the song, and this led occasionally to quarrels. It was sung well by old Jock Shand, who went to Glasgow to sing it at one of the earlier Campsie re-unions. Shand sang it with all the spoken asides and local hits. I give a few quotations from this once well-known song:—

> Whiles he's glooming, whiles he's civil,
> Whiles he's raging like a devil;
> Gin you want to please him, tryst a lair,
> That's the nick for Donald Blair.
> > Donald Blair's come again,
> > Donald Blair's come again;
> > Tell the news in Campsie Glen,
> > Donald Blair's come again.

> Donald Blair can ring the bell
> Maist as weel's the Earl himsel';
> But the body canna gie't the richt girt jow,   ...
> > (Imitation of the bell ringing.)
> To Nicol's notes of lint and tow, lint and tow,
> Yet the body fain would bring
> Notes out o' the auld cracked thing;
> But instead o' its auld ancient air.
> > (Imitation of bell.)

Spoken.—As true as I'm standing here, if he's no learning the bell to sing "Donald Blair."

> Donald cries when nane are deein',
> "Save us, mun, it's a trade no worth ha'en,
> There's naething made o't noo at a',"
> But faith he winna fling't awa.

Spoken.—There was ae day there was a neibour speer'd at Donald how business was getting on wi' him. Business! quo' he, to tell you the truth, I haena buried a living soul this sax week.

> So kintra folks be good to Donald,
> For he's come aff the great clan Ronald
> He'll watch your kirkyards after ten.

Spoken.—Aye, and when the sorrows of Resurrection men that come about the kirkyaird at night, ye ken, Donald can slip in ahint a tombstone gey an cannie, wi' a spade shaft in his han', till ance he sees the fallows beginning to their work, then Donald slips out an' says:—I'm saying, callans, what's t'at you're about; it's a confounded thing that the dead canna get leave to lie for a set o' scoundrels. I suppose you wasna expecting—(striking at the Resurrection men)—

> That Donald Blair's come again.
> Tell the Resurrection men,
> Donald Blair's come back again.

There was a family named Ferguson who used to live at the Clachan, all of whom were silly and in receipt of parochial relief. There were Sandy, John, David, Meg, and Janet. Their father had been a cousin or other relation of D—— of G——, who was exceedingly kind to them, to David especially. John was quiet and attended church, and it was no unusual thing for him to express his satisfaction when the minister had been in his best form— "Man, ye preached prime the day, Lapslie." John was said to have had a most retentive memory. After the tent preaching in the Glen he could get up among his cronies and reproduce the sermon, imitating both manner and speech of the preacher. I do not recollect having ever seen him. I have heard he was in the habit of wearing a petticoat. I only recollect David, "the Earl," who was a regular attender at the parish church in my boyish days. David entered the church from the vestry door, and took his seat in the front pew of the area. In those days Mr. Monro had a lecture and a sermon at the one diet of worship. David generally sat out the lecture patiently, but soon became tired with the sermon. He wore a toy penny watch and when he first began to weary this was pulled out with increasing frequency; then he would stand up, and, looking long at his watch, endeavoured to catch the minister's eye, in a mute appeal. Sometimes he remained till the last psalm; or if he got too wearied he walked out by the vestry door, no one taking any notice of him. His movements, yawning, nose-blowing, and watch-pulling were taken as matters of course, and did not cause any distraction. Mr. D—— is said to have provided him with a suit of clothes every year. This was of dark moleskin, with brass buttons.

I have already mentioned that the old church bell was tolled for all funerals. In Davie's time this was his special duty. As soon as the funeral procession entered the Howe Loan he commenced, and continued tolling until it arrived at the churchyard. For this he always expected a little remuneration or a dram, which was seldom refused. David Wilkie was the best fisher in this part of the country, and Wilkie was kind to the Earl, who, unable to make him any other return, prayed for Wilkie. The late Robert S. Muir of the Clachan has informed me that he had heard the Earl praying in all seriousness for Wilkie in these terms:—"Lord, hae mercy on that poor d——d thief Wilkie." This was said without any idea of incongruity or irreverence in the expression. Indeed, in all Davie's prayers there was always an oath or two. Donald Blair's wife Bell had also been kind to the Earl. When she died, a few neighbours came into the house to the coffining of Bell. Davie felt solemnized, and was greatly touched in his feelings. There was no minister or elder present, reading and prayer being quite unknown then and there as a service at coffining. The body of Bell having been coffined, and those present were rising to depart, when Davie, seeking relief to his feelings in a religious rite, suddenly exclaimed—"Stay, bodies, bide a wee; we micht hae a word." Then reverently folding his hands and closing his eyes he exclaimed—"God bless puir auld Bell. May the Lord receive her." The devoutness, the pathos of poor Davie, whose mind was so clouded, brought tears to the eyes of one who was present on this occasion, and who herself told me she could never forget the incident, or the lesson it was calculated to teach. The Earl was attacked with cholera in 1854, and died after eight hours' illness. Before he died he turned to Donald Blair's daughter, then the wife of Alex. M'Lennan, and exclaimed—" Lord hae mercy on me, Marget." He was buried in the churchyard at Lennoxtown in the part where all cholera victims were interred.

My recollections extend over a pretty long period. It is only according to nature that a generation should have now almost passed away since I knew it first, but the striking feature to me is that so many families of tenant farmers, for instance, after sojourning for longer or shorter periods, should have passed away, and so few have left any descendants who are now either resident or connected otherwise with the parish. I can recollect Dunns in Ballagan; Cowans and Coubroughs in Blairtummach; Meikle, Craigend; Buchanan, Crosshouse; Muirs and Hamiltons in Lukeston; M'Kinlays and, later, Reid and M'Neilage in Glenmill; Galbraiths and Stevensons in Kilwinnet; Foyer of Knowehead; Jacks and Slimmons in Balcorrach; Robin Alexander, in The Hole; Simpsons in Capieston; Cunningham in Hole and Capieston conjoined; Mitchell and Black in Balgrochan; and so on, over almost all the parish. The only exceptions that occur to me are the Hornes in New Mill and Buchanans in Shields. Not only has the old clachan passed away, but the name will now likely fall into disuse. The postal district is now Campsie Glen; all the associations connected with the term " clachan," the kirk, and kirkyard are now disappearing. The manse alone remains—the last link. I have before me an extract of a letter dated March, 1877. The writer mentions there had been at the clachan that day a great Masonic demonstration, with bands and flags. The occasion of it was, he says, the laying of the foundation stone of a house for the stationmaster at the Glen station. What gave importance to this event was the expectation that this was the first of a large number of villas which, it was expected, would be erected there according to a feuing plan, and which would in time entirely replace the old clachan cottages by the modern villa, and convert the locality into a residential suburb of Glasgow !

As the large landed proprietors held their lands on condition of rendering feudal service when called up to muster with their retainers for the purposes of war, or a peaceful demonstration in honour of a royal wedding, they were compelled to attend the call under pain of forfeiture of their estates. In their turn they called on the farmers, cottars, and retainers to accompany them under pain of the gallows, so that there was a fair turnout from Campsie at times. At the Battle of Flodden the Campsie men were on the right wing, under the Earl of Lennox, and on other occasions they did their duty to their king and country. They were not as well drilled and equipped as our modern volunteers, but they were animated by the same spirit of loyalty and patriotism.

The great natural beauties of Campsie Glen have been a source of pleasure and enjoyment to the natives of the parish, who have been wont, especially since the beginning of the century, to make it a favourite resort every day of the week, but particularly on Sundays. Numbers of the worshippers in the old Parish Church went into the Glen between the forenoon and afternoon services, but on the Sabbath evenings it was a favourite walk from all quarters. Mr. John M'Farlan, of Ballancleroch, said he had three courses open to him in connection with these trespasses on his lands—(1) To wink at the trespass, as he did for a number of years; (2) to prevent it by the arm of the law; and (3) to give his consent in express terms. This last he resolved to do, and he published a notice making all the world welcome every day of the week, except during the hours of divine service on Sundays. His reason for this limitation was that people could not pass and repass from the Glen without in some measure disturbing the congregation in the old church. In acknowledgment of the privilege conceded to them in common with others, a handsome piece of silver-plate was subscribed for, and Mr. Robert Barclay was commissioned to present it. It bore the following inscription:— " Presented by the operatives of Lennoxmill Printfield, in testimony of their gratitude for the privilege of having access to the romantic Glen of Kirktoun. 1825." This expression of feeling, Mr. M'Farlan declared, made him very proud. Mr. John Brown, Whitefield, Lennoxtown, was present at the public meeting at which it was decided to get up this presentation. He is perhaps now the only survivor. This privilege was regarded with mixed feelings, for, in 1833, a petition was presented to the proprietors of the Glen—Mr. M'Farlan and Mr. J. L. K. Lennox—in which the petitioners begged " leave to bring before your notice the advantage which is taken by many, and particularly by persons from Glasgow and other places at a distance, of resorting to your glens on Sabbath for purposes of mere amusement, by which your petitioners conceive that the holy day is profaned, and an example highly prejudicial to the morals of the young and inconsiderate of their neighbourhood, is held out. But your petitioners would more especially beg leave to advert to a circumstance resulting from the advantage so taken by some of resorting to the glens on Sabbath, which is that such persons are seen, in very many instances, returning to their places of abode in a state of intoxication; that rioting and quarrelling frequently take place between them on the roads; that fields are trampled down, cattle disturbed, and the inhabitants of farm-houses and cottages on the road frequently annoyed." The petitioners submit that " by prohibiting all access to the glens on that day there would be less resort to their neighbourhood by strangers from a distance, and that the parish would be spared in a great degree the contagious influence of a profane and licentious example so injurious to the morals of all, particularly of the young, on that holy day, whilst the inhabitants at large would be rid of what they cannot but feel as a constant grievance and an annoyance." The signatures attached were those of well-known parishioners:—Malcolm Brown,

John Alexander, Robt. Ferrie, Wm. Simpson, John M'Pherson. John M'Adam, Robt. Fergus, John Buckie, John Angus, Ebenr. Brown, Andw. Brown, Geo. Brown, Alex. Fergus, Archd. Craig, John Milne, Alex. Ewing, Jas. Maitland, John M'Kellar, John Service, Robt. Brown, Jas. Maitland, Andw. Motherwell, Wm. Stevenson, sen., Wm. Stevenson, jun., Wm. Stevenson (elder), Wm. Brown, Wm. Reid, Thomson M'Naught, Adam M'Luckie, Geo. Matthison (elder), John Menzies, Jas. Brown (minister), Robt. Barclay, John Brown, Norman Macleod (minister), John Turnbull, Jas. Ferrie, Robt. Towers, Matthew M'Culloch, Peter Stirling, Robert. Clarke, Alexander Fraser, Wm. Buchanan, Jas. M'Kinlay, Wm. Gardiner, John M'Lean, Wm. Malcolm.

Messrs. Robert Clarke, Alexander Fraser, and James M'Kinlay were appointed on behalf of the subscribers to present the petition. They waited, in the first instance, on Mr. Lennox, by whom they reported they were politely and courteously received. He declared himself willing to have the glen shut on Sabbath, provided Mr. M'Farlan would co-operate with him in any measure that might be deemed effectual for the purpose. They then waited on Mr. M'Farlan. They reported—" Here their reception was not such as they considered themselves, either individually or as the representatives of a respectable class of persons in the parish, entitled to expect, and their communication was cut short by Mr. M'Farlan turning on his heel, and in affected obeisance taking leave of them." Some definite answer, however, being requested to the petition, he promised this should be sent to one of the party in the course of two days after; but instead of this, a placard was observed on the following day (being Sabbath) to have been posted on the gate of the parish church and other public places, a copy of which is as follows :—" Mr. M'Farlan has received a petition, craving that all access to the glens may be prohibited on Sundays. So far as he is acquainted with the signatures, it contains but five tradesmen. The host of worthy men in that predicament who have refused to join in it may rest assured that Mr M'Farlan will never dishonour himself nor the religion to which he belongs by interfering with their enjoyments. Ballancleroch, 15th June." In a letter afterwards, Mr. M'Farlan said, " You go into particulars and complain of intemperate and licentious behaviour, of practices improper and reprehensible, of pedestrians and noisy vehicles. I am sometimes in the glen on Sunday evening. I see a happy world. I meet good humour and good manners, and I think unaffected good will. Drunkenness I never saw, nor levity of any description. I have again and again seen company taking their carriages at the Inn, and I never saw one drunken or noisy scene. I wish I could say as much of the funerals I have seen there, or of communion days, or of pay-nights in Lennoxtown. Surely you do not mean to abolish all these institutions." He mentions that the most of the signatures are landed proprietors or farmers, in the open air all week ; but that all men were not so blest. An angry correspondence ensued, into which the Rev. Mr Macleod was ultimately dragged, and the whole controversy got into print. A statement of proceedings relative to the Petition for shutting the Campsie Glen on Sabbath was published by a committee of the petitioners. This was an octavo pamphlet of 21 pages. Although I had heard of the controversy I had never seen the pamphlet till last week, when Mr. Malcolm Baird kindly posted it to me. I take this opportunity of thanking Mr. Baird for this and for having on many other occasions given me great assistance in ascertaining historical facts about parish matters.

THE RIGHT-OF-WAY CASE.

The road from the eastern parts of the parish to the western, and especially to the Parish Church, had been *via* Crosshill and an old road passing over the Cumroch Brae. This road had been in use from the erection of the church in the twelfth century until it was finally closed, as a result of an action of declarator in the Court of Session, by the late Mr. J. L. K. Lennox. When the new road past the Whitefield was constructed, the Road Trustees gave over to the Woodhead estate the ground occupied by the Cumroch Brae Road, in lieu of the land required for the broader and more level road then formed. While the wheel traffic, in course of time, preferred this new road, the conservative instincts of the people long preferred to use the old one, and for many years after the new road had been opened all funerals passed along the old Cumroch Brae Road. But this old road fell gradually into disuse, the traffic taking the better and more level road. About 1837 Mr. Lennox was led to understand that the people of the village of Lennoxtown were using this old clachan road for the purpose of poaching, and were setting snares for his game. It was considered a short cut to the clachan, where the parish registrar was then resident, where all the " cries " had to be put in, and births and deaths recorded. Lads and lasses strolled along the old highway in the summer evenings, and some people represented to the Laird of Woodhead that, under pretence of walking for pleasure or of a short cut to the clachan, the road was used, especially after dark, for worse purposes; so he willingly availed himself of these excuses as a reason for having it shut up altogether. Accordingly, availing himself of the grant of the solum by the Road Trustees, Mr. J. L. K. Lennox, acting under the advice of his factor, Mr. Alex. Galloway, had a fence drawn across the Crosshill end of the road and a notice put up, warning trespassers of the terrors of the law. This was found quite insufficient. The people continued to use the old road, and disregarded the notices to trespassers. Mr. Galloway, the factor, having once entered on the prohibition path, was determined not to be beaten. He therefore built a strong stone and lime dyke, forming at the entrance a recess for breaking road metal. This, however, was still insufficient. A deep ditch was then cut in front of the dyke. This led to an adjoining part of the field fence being broken for a passage. This persistence on the part of the people seems to have thoroughly riled the factor, who now had men employed at 2s 6d per day and 2s 6d per night to watch and take the names of persons insisting on using the old road. Prosecutions were raised against individuals in the Sheriff Courts. The people of Lennoxtown, who had no idea that the Road Trustees had given over the land of the old road in exchange for the new road, rose up in defence of what they considered their rights—for rights to a highway that the parishioners had used to go to the kirk, and by which all funerals had gone to the graveyard, from time immemorial. Meetings were held to protest against the supposed arbitrary proceedings. At the public meeting called to consider what steps should be taken to maintain the right-of-way, a prudent counsellor suggested that every effort should be exhausted before going to law. This was not in unison with the feeling of the meeting. One man brought down the house by calling out, "No molligrants, but DEMAND our RIGHTS" The meeting resolved to defend what they believed their rights in a court of law. It was a matter to be deeply regretted that they did not send a deputation to Mr. Lennox and endeavour to settle the matter amicably. Printed statements were now circulated and appeals made for funds. The case was called, and Mr. Lennox established his rights to the satisfaction of the Court of Session, who thereupon gave judgment in his favour, with expenses against the opponents. The champions of the public rights were now saddled with the expenses in the court, and they appealed to the public of Campsie to come forward and relieve them of the personal liabilities they had incurred. Thomas Davidson, now of Busby, William Craighead, and —— Lochead, were perhaps the leading spirits in this case. When gathering the material for this lecture I wrote to Mr. Davidson, telling him I intended to refer to the case to-night, and he replied to me :—

" JAMES PLACE,
" BUSBY, 7th Nov., 1891.

" DEAR SIR,—It is now forty years since interdict was granted to shut up the old road to the Clachan. I was one of the parties to a long and troublesome battle to maintain the Right-of-Way. We had to raise the funds to carry on the law-suit. For a number of years in succession we got up concerts, lectures, and subscriptions, but the people got tired and left us in the lurch, with a heavy balance to pay to the law-agents. At the time, I sold all my household effects to prevent them coming down on myself personally. I left Campsie in 1882, and since then have been very seldom back to talk over early days and old times, and the incidents of our fight. But I believed then, and my conviction is still unshaken, that the law-agents sold the case in favour of the Lennox claims. William Craighead and I went several times to Edinburgh, and with difficulty got our travelling expenses paid. I hope you will be able to condemn strongly the action of Mr. Lennox in shutting up the old road to the Auld Clachan Kirk, and his entering into a law-suit against the inhabitants of Lennoxtown and the district.—I am, yours sincerely,   THOS. DAVIDSON."

As popular opinion had been in favour of a legal defence a fair response was made to appeals for money; public subscriptions were opened; concerts to raise funds were organized and well patronized; and in course of time the more pressing liabilities were liquidated. Mr. Lennox must have spent a lot of money on the case, besides incurring a good deal of unpopularity in Lennoxtown, which was also extended to his factor, Mr. Galloway, who was generally regarded as the prime mover in the whole affair.

OLD PARISH ROADS.

There is reason to believe that the mansion house of Craig-barnet, which King James the IV. visited in 1508, stood nearly on the site of the present house, and the public road then would pass behind Wellbank, by Lukeston, Crosshouse, Craigbarnet House and out by the West Lodge. A new mansion house was built in 1660, leaving the public road undisturbed. When this house was abandoned and the present Craigbarnet built, in order to give greater privacy, the Laird, "Old Burry," had the road altered. A new road was made through the soft, boggy land to the south of the house, and this was very imperfectly bottomed, so much so that a loaded cart would sink deep in the ruts, some-times even up to the nave of the wheels. People disliked it there-fore, and persisted in taking the old road past his new mansion, which greatly annoyed Old Burry, who was then old and easily irritated. Burry caught the late Jamieson Provan's father on the forbidden ground and on being challenged for trespassing and threatened with a stick which the Laird held in his hand, Provan manfully retorted, "Well, Laird, if you are to stop this road ye must make a better one than the road down bye, where the loaded cart'll sink to the naves." The last laird found parties using the old road to pass from Blairtummach to Crosshouse, but he had this stopped by a high fence and a notice to beware of mantraps. The centre of the new road is now fairly bottomed, but the sides have room for improvement. A good many years ago a boiler was being brought from Blanefield. Near Craigbarnet it was taken to one side to allow something to pass, and the wheels sunk at once in the soft ground.

DIVERSION OF ROAD BETWEEN WHITEFIELD AND HAUGHHEAD.

It is not perhaps generally known that when the Blane Valley Railway was proposed the original plan of the railway was to have level crossings on the road I have been referring to, which superseded the old road to the Clachan. They were to have been just beyond Whitefield, and again near Balcorrach Farm, where the line passed under the Woodhead. This was the cheaper route for the railway company, and they secured the support of Mr. Hanbury Lennox to their scheme. It was necessary, however, to obtain the sanction of the Road Trustees, and a meeting of that body was called to consider the question. The case for the railway company was put, the question of expense to the promoters was enlarged upon, and the Road Trustees were asked by the railway company to concede level crossings between Whitefield and Haughhead. The late Sir Archibald Edmonstone led the opposition to this proposal. He had carefully considered the matter and had come to the conclusion that two level crossings on this road would involve risk to the public. He feared lest some one would be injured by a train, and the safety of the people, in his estimation, was not to be placed for a single instant in jeopardy, to save a little expense to the railway company, even when they had the assent of the landed proprietor, as the Blane Valley company had in that of Mr. Hanbury Lennox. He declared against a level crossing therefore, and carried a majority of the Road Trustees with him, with the result that the level crossing was refused, and the railway company had accordingly to make an expensive alteration of the road from a little beyond Whitefield to Campsie Glen station, whereby crossing the road was altogether avoided, but at great expense to the railway company. Everyone will admit that his counsel was the wiser, and perhaps few people are aware to whom they owe the result.

HAUGHHEAD.

The hamlet of Haughhead is not a very old one. The feus for the buildings in that village began to be taken off about 1735, and were continued till about 1785 or 1795. In an advertisement of a house for sale in 1818 it is stated that the lease was for 99 years from Whitsunday 1735, that on the ground then leased there had been erected two substantial tenements, also a four-loom shop, cellars, &c. The tack duty was trifling, and the setter was bound by the terms of the original tack to renew the same at the end of the 99 years, or to pay the value of all buildings erected or to be erected on the ground. All the building leases in Lennox-town contained such a clause; but when Mr. Galloway became factor of the Lennox estate, in 1836, he refused to insert a clause of that kind in the new tacks. He very much surprised the owners of the existing buildings, who were relying on this clause to have their tacks renewed, or that their value should be paid by the proprietor, by informing them that such a clause was ineffec-tual and worthless to them, for it was only personal, not heritable, and that they would find it useless at the end of 99 years to call upon a proprietor of an entailed estate for fulfilment.

SERMONS TO PEOPLE IN WORKING CLOTHES.

There were a number of the residenters in Haughhead who dropped away from church attendance altogether when the new church was built at Lennoxtown. When the Rev. Robert Lee became minister, his visiting at every house in the parish soon revealed the state of matters to him. Despite his entreaties and expostulations he could not get these people to go to church. They "hadna claes to gang to the kirk;" they "were tired and it was far awa'." So Lee arranged to get the use of the largest room in Ferguson's public-house. He had service there on the Sabbath evenings and invited them to come in their working clothes. Mr. Lee's determined importunity carried the day, and he had a great measure of success in these meetings, at which the gospel was preached for the first time in the Haughhead. Mr. Lee was not content till he had got his Sabbath evening flock to resume attendance at the parish church, for he found that when once they began to attend his evening services a Sunday suit of clothes soon followed, and they found their way then to the parish church.

LAIRD BUCHANAN AND THE CORSHOUSE KIRN.

The late William Buchanan of Crosshouse was a well-known man in Campsie. He was a quiet, unassuming, sober, industrious, well-living. respectable man, a good specimen of the Presbyterian elder and small laird. He was content to occupy all his life the house, steading, and farm which he owned. Taking rank as a farmer-laird, he made himself very useful as an heritor, convener of parish committees, secretary of Farmers' Society, and for two or three years after the passing of the Poor Law Act he was the Parochial Board's Inspector. The laird was sometimes prevailed upon to recite a metrical description of a Scottish harvest home festival, entitled, "The Laird of Corshouse's Kirn, on Friday, 15th Oct., 1790." The poem, if I may call it so, is too long for insertion here, but it truly describes a festive gathering at a harvest home in 1790. This annual kirn came to have quite a local celebrity. It was frequently attended by the minister, the lairds of Craigbarnet and Ballancleroch, their families, and visitors. The narrator has ridden out from Glasgow to be present, and describes his ride and his call at Downie's in the Newtown, where he "primed himself well before joining the ball." Having reached the Corshouse, as Crosshouse was then called,

"On our arrival did meet with dames plenty,
All deck'd for the ploy—I am sure more than twenty.
In the house, 'mongst the gentry, I sat down to tea,
Where a throng of braw damsels ranged round in full glee;
Whilst the clowns and their lasses made the barn joyfully ring.
Well pleased, undismayed, to begin the said kirn,
Where whooping and capering to fiddle and pipe,
And whirling their partners in frenzied delight
Soon brought ben the gentry, to join in the whoop,
Which caused for a time each rustic to droop;
Till, warmed by the dance, no distinction was seen—
Man, mistress, and maid mingling in the blyth scene.

There were reels, Highland flings, and other such capers—
All danced in the barn, both the clowns and their betters.
Taking turns at the jig, the liveliest of all,
And bab-at-the-bowster, which ended the ball.

. . . .

How grieved when we're ordered to the house all to run,
Being warmed up by the dancing we wanted more fun.
But the orders of Corshouse we had to obey,
For the pies and the milk were set out for the fray.
And now to have seen us all placed round the table,
Some lads to their sweethearts love stories did gabble ;
While others plyed keenly at pies and sweet cream,
And some ben the kitchen with songs made a din.
This pleased rural medlay would have yielded rare sport
To those who had never been absent from court.
For what doth the prince or the statesman ere know
Of the harmless glad mirth that a kirn doth bestow.
Worn out with this harvest home's annual diversion
Each to their respective homes took their direction.
And I with Miss Brown, a fair damsel, went home.
About three in the morning we trudged along.

. . . .

But when to her dad's dwelling safely we came,
In boldly I entered to yield up my dame,
And down near a clear blazing fireside did sit."

After bolting a bumper of spirit of malt, our Glasgow visitor
took his leave. He started up next morning, after having slept
at Corshouse, moralising—

"How oft, in blythe moments, are some called from earth
To appear before God, who at first gave them birth.
Then, thanks to Him who presides o'er each ploy,
For the health I was blessed with, the kirn to enjoy."

What strikes one here is, while there was an abundant tea,
dancing, and fun, and plenty of pies, sweet cream, &c., to supper,
there is no indication of drinking to excess at the kirn. The visitor " primes himself " by a dram in passing through the Newton,
and the lady he has taken home gives him a " nightcap." The
festive gatherings of the yeomanry were accompanied with more
conviviality. Returning from one of these the tenant of Kilwinnet saw the sign of a highlander in full dress above Roger
Sinclair's public in the Haughhead. This dress was associated
in his mind with Mr. Leckie Ewing, of Stirling, Gordon, & Co.,
Glasgow, who was a very frequent visitor at Ballancleroch, and
who, on the 28th June, 1826, married Eleanora, the eldest
daughter of John M'Farlan, advocate, to whom I have already
referred in the course of this lecture. Mr. Leckie Ewing was a
handsome man, and the kilt, which he frequently wore, showed
his well-proportioned figure to advantage. On his way home
from the yeomanry ball in rather an elevated condition, the
Kilwinnet farmer, at the sight of Roger Sinclair's sign, called
out, " Set to Leckie Ewing, Jenny," and proceeded to set and go

through the figure of a Scotch reel on the road, winding up with a vigorous "Hooch!".

PARISH MILLS.

The feudal charters gave other privileges, jurisdictions, and rights besides the land. Mills were a part of nearly every grant. The feudal baron had power to compel all the inhabitants of the barony to grind all their grain at the barony mill, and he could exact certain dues from his tenants who were thirled to his mill, This is not the place to describe the multures, knaveships, lock, and gowpen, &c., as these dues were called. Brisbane of Bishopton was proprietor of the lands of " Balnacleroch " (Ballancleroch is the modern name) before these were acquired by Patrick M'Farlan of Keithtoun, in 1642. In 1637, in an old charter, I find these lands referred to as the " said lands of Balnacleroch, with miln, miln lands, and pertinents." Balnacleroch Miln was formerly at the foot of the glen. It was in later times converted into a bleachfield. To this mill the tenants on the Balnacleroch lands were bound to send their grain. Glenmiln was the mill to which the Craigbarnet tenants were thirled and bound to send their grain. The Antermony estate had Lochmill. Bencloich had The Mill or Bencloich Mill. Glorat had its own mill, so had Kincaid at French Mill; while that for the Woodhead estate was the Lennox Mill, which before the calico printwork was commenced, stood in what is now the garden of " The Cottage."

Dougal Graham, the author of many Scottish chap books, and also of the metrical account of the rebellion of 1745, and who, about 1770, became skellat bellman of the city of Glasgow, was born at Raploch, near Stirling. When about three years of age he came to reside with an uncle in Campsie parish. Miss Spence, in the " Sketches " I have already quoted, writing in 1811, says :— " It is said that on the side of the hill above the old village of Campsie (the clachan) are to be seen traces of a turf cottage, the early residence of Dougal Graham."

James Bell, born in 1769, in Jedburgh, where his father was Relief minister, the author of " A System of Geography " and other works, came to live at Lukeston about 1821. He spent the last twelve years of his life in domestic comfort and tranquility, and died 3rd May, 1833, in his sixty-fourth year. He was buried in the Clachan churchyard.

Since this was read, I have learned that the late Mr. John Barclay, a son of Mr. Robert Barclay, whose name is mentioned in this paper, visited Thebes, and paid a visit to the little British cemetery where Capt. Lennox was buried. He found everything about it in very nice condition. The air is so pure that stone-work retains its new look for ages. He found, for instance, the ancient stone columns at Thebes looking as if they had just left the hands of the masons. In this little cemetery there were only two graves when Captain Lennox's remains were interred there. In 1889 there were then six in all, and all about it was in perfect order. A plain granite slab marks his resting-place. On this is inscribed :—

HERE LIES
TILL THE RETURN OF
OUR LORD
THE BELOVED REMAINS
OF
JOHN KINCAID LENNOX,
YOUNGER, OF
LENNOX CASTLE, SCOTLAND,
WHO DIED AT THEBES,
FEB. 28TH, 1857;
AGED 26 YEARS.

"Blessed are the dead which die in the Lord."—REV. xiv., 13.

I have also learned that the proprietor of Ballancleroch is said to have had and still claims to retain the right of sepulture within the Clachan Kirk.

It would further appear that Keithtoun was the name which the M'Farlan who married a Keith wished to give his seat of Balnacleroch, as it used to be spelt in old documents.

JOTTINGS ABOUT

LENNOXTOWN AND DISTRICT.

707577

H

LENNOXTOWN AND DISTRICT.

In the lecture on "The Clachan and District" I dealt almost exclusively with the western portion of the parish. In the present paper the village of Lennoxtown will be the centre with which my notes will be chiefly concerned, but when referring to matters of a more general character I shall have to include the whole parish. I propose to narrate some of the village annals, in so far as these may be of interest to the natives of the parish, not merely to those now resident within its bounds, but to the many who are scattered over all the world. It was very interesting to observe from a letter published in the *Kirkintilloch Herald* of 23rd September, 1891, that Mr. Gordon Wilson, jun., found a small colony of Campsonians in Salt Lake City. He was introduced to an old worker in the field as the son of Mr. Gordon Wilson of Lennoxmill. Old Campbell said, with pleased astonishment, "You are not a son of Gordon Wilson! Well, well! and from Campsie too!" When he heard the name of his native village mentioned, he actually broke down, tears filling his eyes. The last time the late Mr. John Macleod was in Kirkintilloch, very shortly before his death, meeting him by chance, I asked him how my old schoolmates the Maclays were getting on in Australia. He told me how a wayfarer turned aside one day to a comfortable homestead, and asked for a drink. The lady of the house was a hospitable Scotchwoman. The traveller noticed something which, he said, reminded him of Campsie. "Campsie!" said the lady, "what do you know about Campsie?" "Oh!" replied the traveller, "I was born and brought up there." "So was I," remarked the lady; my maiden name was Maclay, and we lived at Rowantreefauld." James M'Gilchrist, while travelling on the top of an omnibus in a town in Portugal, one day heard, "Hilloa, —— breeks!" This salutation, he thought, must be from some Campsie person, so he came off and looked about, to find he had been recognised by another native, a sojourner in Lusitania. The lecture on "Calico Printing in Campsie," published last year, has been scattered all over the globe, and in foreign lands has been passed from hand to hand, as recalling associations of the old homes. Like auld Scotia's sangs, reminiscences are more highly valued the further we get away from our native land.

> "They're twined wi' mony lovely thochts, wi' mony lo'esome themes,
> They gar the glass o' memorie glint back wi' brichter shine
> On far off scenes and far off friends—and Auld Lang Syne."

FREEMASONRY.

Freemasonry early obtained an introduction to the parish. The charter of "Lennox (Kilwinning)" Lodge, No. 74, is dated 24th June, 1772, and "St. John's Caledonian R.A." No. 195, commenced about 1796. "Lennox (Kilwinning)" had its head quarters in the Clachan; indeed it used to be called "The Clachan Lodge." It was originated by the farming class, and was the lodge of the rural community, just as the "St. John's R.A." drew its membership mainly from the printfields. The " Lennox (Kilwinning)" Lodge is now defunct but the " St. John's " still exists. Its membership at present is not numerous, but the brethren are enthusiastic, and the good time coming may see their numbers largely reinforced. The charter of No. 74 is as follows:—

"LENNOX (KILWINNING) LODGE, NO. 74.

" KILWINNING, 24th June, 1772.

" Which day a petition of sundry Masons from Campsie, county of Lennox or Dumbarton, craving a decree of constitution by the name and title of Lennox (Kilwinning) Lodge having been presented to the Mother Lodge, the Brethren, after due consideration, unanimously grant the request thereof.

" We, Robert Reid, Deputy Grand Master of the Mother Lodge of Kilwinning, having taken into consideration the request of certain Masons at Campsie, praying our authority to be formed into a regular Lodge or Society; being well assured of their moral character and of their inclination to promote the good of masonry, we, with the consent of our Wardens and other Brethren, do constitute and erect them into a regular Lodge, by the name of Lennox (Kilwinning) Lodge, and we grant them all powers and privileges which now are, or for any time past may have been, legally enjoyed by any other Lodge of our creating. The same to be always holden of the Worshipful Grand Master of the Mother Lodge of Kilwinning, and his successors in office, upon the yearly payment of one Merk Scots money, at the anniversary meeting of the Mother Lodge, in December, and upon attendance of one of their members, if required, at said meetings. Given at Kilwinning, 24th June, 1772."

A young man named William Morrison, a son of the tenant of Shields Farm, went to London, to learn the trade of coach building. Having done so, Morrison resolved to go abroad to push his fortune. He sailed for India, but the vessel had the misfortune to be captured by pirates, and all on board were taken into captivity. Of the passengers and crew, Morrison alone got away, not only with the whole of his own effects, but it was said, also with money that had belonged to others of the same ill-fated vessel, who either perished when captured or had died in slavery. He was a member of the Campsie "Lennox Kilwinning" Lodge No. 74, and it was reported that he had saved his life by making some Masonic Signs, which his captors understood. They acknowledged a principle of brotherhood, and in consequence preserved his life and assisted him to get on board a British ship outward bound for the Indies. He succeeded in business in Calcutta, and on his return found his parents had left the Shields and that they were then residing in a thatched cottage, with a byre at the end of it, on Balgrochan Farm, about one hundred yards from the road to the west of Meadowbank. This was called the Damhead. Wishing to settle in Campsie, he intended to erect a suitable residence, and he had planned to have Meadowbank built for his own occupation. He fell one morning at his own door in Campsie, having slipped on a frozen step. A few days afterwards he had occasion to return to London on business, and while there he died suddenly, on 22nd July, 1818. The immediate cause of death was the rupture of a blood vessel, and it is considered this was the result of the injuries received when he fell on the doorstep in Campsie. Meadowbank was built afterwards and occupied by his parents and his sisters. In his will Mr. William Morrison bequeathed £100 to his native parish.

HAND-LOOM WEAVING. CARRIERS.

The Newton of Campsie, as Lennoxtown was at first called, owed its being mainly to Lennoxmill. Besides the employment afforded at the printfields and secret works, at the commencement of the present century, there was a good deal of handloom weaving carried on, for when Lennoxmill was stopped, owing to the failure of Lindsay, Smith, & Co., the inhabitants had recourse to handloom weaving for employment. This was followed in two branches, viz., the customer trade (weaving the wool which had been spun on the spinning-wheel at home into blankets and cloth, a variety of which was known in the district as "Campsie grey"), and working to manufacturers in Glasgow, who supplied materials and paid for the workmanship. "The swish of the shuttle and the monotonous thud of the lay" are sounds which have long ceased to be heard in our streets. At the end of the first decade of this century there were four hundred weavers in Campsie, the great bulk of whom wrought to Glasgow houses. In those days Auld Jamie Maitland was carter in the village, and on Wednesdays and Saturdays he went to Glasgow as carrier. He took in the finished webs and brought out the money paid for the labour, and also the warp, wheep, coops, &c., the materials to be worked into the new web. Maitland was succeeded by Jamie Adams, who besides being carrier filled other important offices. He was precentor in the Parish Church at the Clachan and also acted as an auctioneer. Mr. James Millar has told me that he once heard Adams officiating at a sale of furniture in Lockhart's Loan. He could get no bid for a spinning-wheel, which he declared was 200 years old. In despair, he said, "Will ye no gie me a bid just for the *iniquity* of the thing?" It was a common occurrence for those weavers awaiting money or work to gather at Luckie Callender's public, a one-storeyed house, still standing opposite the Alum Work road. Here they awaited the arrival of each successive carrier. When the worthy had handed over his money, and delivered his messages concerning work, a dram was not uncommon; but there was no drinking to excess on the part of the weavers, similar to what obtained at the west end of the village, when the block printers had a spree. Hand-loom weaving died a natural death, owing to the more remunerative employment to be had in Lennoxmill. John Jack and Daniel M'Kenzie were probably the last of the old Campsie weavers. The former died in 1875, and the latter in 1883. Bennie succeeded Maitland as Glasgow carrier, and was in turn succeeded by Andrew M'Farlane, who had a sort of caravan, where he could give passengers " a lift." There was also a carrier, John M'Farlan, who came from the Haughhead. Andrew M'Farlane's sons were at Mr. Taylor's school with me. The whole family went to Canada. Robert Younger was next carrier, in succession to Andrew M'Farlane.

JAMIE FOYER.

All natives of Campsie have heard of young Jamie Foyer. Jamie's father had been employed at Sculliongour limeworks. He was bellman in Campsie when public intimations were made in that primitive fashion, and I have heard of some very amusing intimations of his. He was also a barber. Jamie became a weaver, was drawn for the militia, and, being unable to pay for a substitute, had no alternative but serve his time. From the militia he volunteered into the 42nd regiment, always a popular one with Campsie recruits. In 1812 this fine regiment was sent to Portugal, where, on 22nd July, it took part in the battle of Salamanca. On 19th September it took part in the assault and capture of Fort St. Michael, Burgos, where its loss was 228 officers and men. When storming this fort, Foyer had ascended to the top of a scaling ladder, when he received a bullet in his breast, and fell off the ladder mortally wounded. When dying, he wished for a drink of water from a well-known well in Campsie. This incident was referred to in a song, of which I quote the following stanzas :—

> " Oh! if I had a drink of Baker Brown's well,
>   My thirst it would quench, and my fever would quell;"
> But life's purple current was ebbing so fast
> That young Jamie Foyer soon breathed his last.
>
> They took for a winding sheet his tartan plaid,
>   And in the cold grave his body was laid;
> With hearts full of sorrow, they covered his clay,
> And, muttering " Poor Foyer," marched slowly away.

This song used to be sung frequently in the streets of Campsie, and especially in front of the shop of Mr. James Jack, who could never hear it without rewarding the singer. The authorship of the song seems to be unknown. Jamie Foyer's wish for the drink from Baker Brown's well is not yet forgotten. Mr. James Jack has mentioned to me that in the summer of 1887 two strangers called on him to ascertain where this well was. They wished to fill two bottles of water from it, as they were about to start for Spain, and intended to drink the water as near the spot at Burgos where poor Jamie fell as it was possible now to ascertain it. They had come out to Lennoxtown that day for the express purpose of procuring the water, in order to carry out their strange whim.

DISTILLERIES.

During the first quarter of the present century there was a number of distilleries in Campsie and Kirkintilloch. These have now all been given up, owing to the impossibility of small concerns competing with distilleries as carried on nowadays. At Milton Mr. John Forrest had a distillery on the Glazert, near the railway station. Some of the building may still be seen in ruins. Lillyburn was a distillery till about 1831. Mr. George Brown had a distillery at the Mains of Bencloich. A Campsie man who worked here told my informant that, while he was employed there, he was drunk every day for two years (Sundays excepted.) In Kirkintilloch there were distilleries at the Loch (Alexander's), at Duntiblae, at the Holm, at Habbie's How, on Luggie (opposite the Old Foundry); and there was Freeland's (near Oswald School), besides two breweries, Jaffrey's and Wood's. In connection with this, the supervisors and other Excise officers were nearly all Englishmen, and their graves are to be seen in a portion of the old burying-ground at the Auld Aisle, Kirkintilloch. This corner pathetically records the last resting-places of these strangers and sojourners in the service of the Excise, nearly all of whom hailed from the South of England.

SMUGGLING.

It is said that a good deal of smuggling used to be carried on at Campsie, as indeed it extensively prevailed all over the country. Previous to 1823 the duty on spirits was 6s 2d per gallon. It was reduced to 2s 4¾d, with the rather surprising result that, whereas only 2,225,124 gallons were charged duty for home consumption in 1822, the quantity in 1825 was 5,981,549 gallons. The consumption had not increased much, but with the reduction of duty the smuggling had diminished. While smuggling was illegal, few had scruples in buying smuggled goods, the smuggler regarding his calling as innocent, and defending, even with violence, what he considered his own. The people were in sympathy, and espoused his cause to the extent that no information was given that would betray him into the hands of the Excise. The knowledge that it had been smuggled imparted an additional recommendation to the mountain dew, over and above that which had the legal "permit." Finglen was a great resort of smugglers. It is reported that at one time there could be detected by the smoke seven illicit stills working there at the same time. Smuggling was carried on also up the Back Burn, the burn which rises behind the Fells and comes down at Alnwick bridge. There is a plantation below the Ferrets, called in my young days "The Smugglers' Plantin'." Their materials were conveyed to these places on horseback. Smuggling was also carried on at Mount of Glorat. Within the last 25 years one ingenious individual is said to have carried on a brisk trade at the Mount, having erected a regular still in a dwelling-house there. When the Macgregors, under their assumed name of Colquhouns, were on one occasion harrying the Campsie valley, and driving off the cattle, they discovered a smugglers' still on the hill. When they had got the "lifted" cattle secured in the level field between Easter Muckcroft and New Mill of Glorat, they brought down the whisky they had unexpectedly discovered, and went in for a regular jollification. The Campsie farmers, who had been spoiled of their cattle, had watched the marauders carrying these off, but owing to the number of the raiders, the farmers' households, including shepherds and men and maid servants, could not offer effective resistance. But when they saw the whisky being taken to the encampment, their hopes rose. They were advised to wait, and when the reivers were asleep, many of them drunk, then to attack them. There was no watch, and the Campsie farmers made "siccar" and spared not, and the cattle were back at their own pastures in course of the following day. The field is now marked on the Ordnance Survey map as "The Field of Blood."

Some Milton smugglers used to have a still on the hill above Keirhill. When they were afraid of any gauger they brought their utensils down to Keirhill Farm, where Mr. Gray was then tenant, and they concealed them carefully in the heart of a hay-stack. In this way a copper worm was left, and long lay in Mr. Gray's steading. It was probably taken down to the Smithy in Milton, where Mr. Gray's son still carries on his calling as "village blacksmith." Here the revenue officers tried, with very indifferent success it must be admitted, to keep a watch on illicit distillation. They had two courses open, to discover if possible the still, or endeavour to seize the whisky in transit. On their part the smugglers and their sympathisers kept a vigilant look out for gaugers, and warnings were conveyed sometimes by very ingenious ruses. When the revenue officers had reason to suspect that a quantity of whisky was to be sent to Glasgow, they would set a watch, sometimes on the bridge over the Kelvin at Torrance, or at similar easily watched localities, but the smugglers were immediately made aware of any increased vigilance, so the Campsie blockade-runners went over the Southhill by Barraston and crossed the Kelvin at the stepping-stones below Balmore. There is a story told of a large quantity of whisky having been brought over Campsie Muir from the north by smugglers, who had it in kegs slung on ponies. The smugglers passed the night at Kinkell farm, where they heard that there was a watch at Torrance bridge. One of their number arrived in advance, and having obtained two old naves at the wheel wright's shop in Torrance, he put them into a sack, which he then put on his pony and proceeded towards Glasgow. When the guagers had seen him, he appeared to start off in flight, but was pursued and overtaken near Kirkintilloch. When they took what appeared to be kegs out of his sack they were sold to find the wheel naves. Of course he had gone off in the opposite direction and his confederates ran their cargo safely into Glasgow, via Balmore. When the contraband liquor had to be carried by a pedestrian, it was put into tin vessels, which were strapped round the body, and could be concealed from observation. At other times it was conveyed in carts, often under various disguises; at other times in a jar covered over with some agricultural produce. A once well-known man in Lennoxtown, long employed in Lennoxmill, used to tell this story, in which he himself was an actor. In the first decade of the present century his father carried on business as a wright, and in addition he had a grocer's shop with a spirit license in Torrance. Early one morning a cart stopped at the shop door and several articles were taken out and left in the shop. Amongst these there was a jar, containing about five gallons of smuggled whisky. After breakfast one of the gaugers called and came as usual into the kitchen. He was well known to the goodwife, who was busily engaged in folding blankets, which she was putting into a large chest, standing open just behind him. While engaged with her blankets, she was chatting cheerily, when he began to make enquiry about a cart that had passed early that morning, and which, he had ascertained, had stopped at her door, where it had delivered some goods. The thought of the jar with the smuggled whisky, standing almost openly under his eyes, flashed through her mind. Instead of replying to the query, she proceeded to make some jocular remarks, which set the gauger laughing; the blanket she had in her arms she now threw over the gauger, and tipped him over into the chest. She got the lid down and kept him there, while she signed to her litttle boy to take the jar she pointed to away and hide it out of sight. The boy acted promptly and she then released the gauger, who was by this time in a towering passion. But she kept her good humour, and she laughed so heartily at her own successful trick, that he gradually mollified. When he left the house he did not know whether it was done purely in fun or whether he had been sold. The clever goodwife got a lesson and never tried the same game again.

DOUGAL THE RANGER.

About the years 1820-22 a serious riot and uproar occurred in Lennoxtown, for which two of the ringleaders, Malcolm M'Gre-

gor and — Shannon, were convicted, and sentenced to eighteen
months' imprisonment. Bulloch, the prime mover of the whole
affair, fled, and remained in hiding till the excitement had calmed
down and the authorities had ceased to look out for him. He then
returned to Lennoxtown. About this time the smugglers solicited
orders for their manufactures, and delivered these more or less
openly, just like other traders. For a funeral at Maryhill a
supply of whisky had been ordered, and an old man named
Macintosh was as usual conveying it to the destination. The
whisky was in tin cans, which were strapped around him. He had
gone by Haughhead, past Woodhead, and was near Newlands, or
Cock-ma-lane, when he encountered Dougal, the Ranger, who
faithfully discharged his duty. Dougal was employed to scour
the country in search of illicit stills or smuggled whisky. He
took the whisky from old 'Tosh, and in doing so was perhaps
rather rough on the old man. The smugglers determined to have
their revenge. Observing Dougal enter Lennoxtown one Saturday,
they collected their friends and sympathisers. My informant, Mr
John Brown, Whitefield, Lennoxtown, had been sent from the
Burnhouse, where he then resided, into the village a message.
Coming opposite the Relief Church, he saw a crowd in front of
Robertson's Inn. Then a man came out, whom the crowd assailed with stones, mud, and missiles of various kinds. With
these the man was struck, and his face was cut. Bleeding and
frightened, he made his way westwards as quickly as possible,
with the crowd in full pursuit. At the bottom of School Loan he
ran for shelter into Bennie, the flesher's. He was, however, dragged
out, and on emerging was received with a shower of stones. He fled
west and took refuge in the Tontine, then kept by Malcolm Watters.
The landlord at once closed his doors against the infuriated
crowd, and protected the refugee. The attack was organised by
local smugglers in revenge for Dougal's faithful discharge of duty.
The riot had assumed so large proportions, and the Ranger was so
severely injured, that the authorities were aroused and took measures to bring the promoters to trial. Some few months afterwards Dougal disappeared—no one knew where. One day a
shepherd on the old Craw Road, just above Jamie Wright's well,
threw himself down on the grass. His dog went at once to a
heap of stones and commenced scraping vigorously. He recollected that he had seen the dog at that heap before, and his curiosity being aroused he went to ascertain the cause. Throwing
aside some stones, he noticed the tail of a coat, then the body of a
man. He went to the Clachan and obtained the assistance of
Cassels the smith, and some others, and had the body conveyed
to the Clachan. Here it was identified as that of Dougal, the
Ranger, who had been murdered by smugglers, and his body hidden beneath a heap of stones. The murderers were never discovered. Very shortly after this incident Cassels was called over
to Fintry. He started homewards, but never reached the Clachan.

His body was found about 400 yards from the spot where the Ranger had been found. The cause of Cassels' death could only be conjectured. A cairn was erected where his body was found. There are other stories of revenue officers being attacked and maltreated by smugglers in the surrounding districts.

CAMPSIE BIBLE, MISSIONARY, AND SCHOOL SOCIETY.

At a public meeting of the inhabitants in the Schoolhouse on 30th Jan., 1819, it was resolved to form a society, whose principal objects should be :—1. To discover whether all the poor possessed bibles; if not, to supply them either gratis or at a reduced rate. 2. To assist School Societies, Missionary, and Bible Societies throughout the country. Miss Lennox was requested to become patroness, and the landed proprietors and partners of the public works in the parish were elected vice-presidents; John Lockhart and Robert Brown, students in divinity, were joint secretaries; William Duncan was appointed depositary; Mr John M'Farlane, preacher, was treasurer. The parish was divided into 28 districts, which were allocated among the directors. The directors were to employ every prudent exertion to obtain subscribers, personally wait on these when their subscriptions became due, discover, record, and report those who had not bibles, and what they would be willing to pay, to meet monthly, &c. I find the following names among the directors :—Eastern district—W. Stevenson, Alton; Wm. M'Laws, John Forrest, James Heddleston, Hugh Cameron, John Gray, Milton; John M'Pherson, David Buchanan, Wm. Forrest; Birdston—John Gray, David Calder, David Muir. The names of nearly all the farmers are to be found, and in Lennoxtown, Robert Barclay, James Glen, James Fergus, George Mathieson, David Kinghorn, James Fairlie, Duncan Morrison, James M'Pherson, James and John Downie, James Maitland, John Kincaid, Robert Morrison, Moses M'Lay, James Davidson, John King, &c.

The minutes are rather amusing reading. The secretaries had requested Sir Samuel Stirling and Patrick Falconer and others to accept the office of vice-presidents. Both of these gentlemen declined. Sir Samuel intimated a donation of £5, and Mr. Falconer would either give £5 as a donation or in five-yearly subscriptions. The minutes record the matter thus :—

" Resolved, ' That the generous and obliging manner in which Sir Samuel Stirling has become a donor to this society, and his interesting expression of attachment to its objects, merit the warmest thanks of this committee, that this be communicated to him, ... and in similar terms to Mr. Falconer. That this meeting declines dictating to Mr. Falconer the mode of his contribution, confident that he shall adopt such mode as shall be suitable to the state of the society.' "

Mr. M'Farlan of Ballancleroch, wishing the Society to distribute some testaments in Haughhead, proceeds by this petition :—

" The petition of John M'Farlan of Ballancleroch, Esq., humbly sheweth,

That the petitioner finds that among many families in the Haughhead a disposition to cultivate religious knowledge, combined with great poverty and a total want of books, particularly in the families of (here six names are given), that your petitioner has furnished testaments to a considerable number of other families, still more numerous than those now mentioned, but not enough to supply the wants of such families. May it therefore please the Society to authorise their Depositary to furnish your petitioner with such a number of testaments or other books as the Society may find it expedient to bestow on these families, and your petitioner will see them distributed to the best of his discretion, and remain ever grateful to the Society.

"JOHN M'FARLAN.

"Ballancleroch, 25th Oct., 1821."

The Society not only granted the prayer of the petition, but minuted that at all times coming Mr. M'Farlan's demands for bibles and catechisms be promptly furnished. The Society had a fairly good income for many years, and was assisted by legacies. At the ninety-second quarterly meeting, on 20th May, 1842, it was intimated that Mr. John M'Farlane, Lennoxtown, had left a legacy of £150 to the Society. After deducting legacy duty (£15) and for discharge (£1), £134 were at the disposal of the directors. The minutes state :—

"Mr. James M'Kinlay moved and Mr. Wylie seconded—'That this legacy be invested permanently in such a manner as shall be satisfactory to the Directors of this Society, the proceeds to be placed annually at their disposal.' Mr William Munro moved and Mr P. Stirling seconded—'That said legacy be at present divided amongst the different societies which stand mostly in need of it. Upon being put to the vote, Mr. Munro's amendment was carried by a majority of 2. And there was then voted:—To Glasgow Missionary Society, £20; Glasgow African, £20; Campsie Educational, £40; Colonial, £20; Campsie Tract, £5; Bible Society, £5; Hibernian School, £5; Gaelic School, £5; leaving the balance in the hands of the treasurer in the meantime.'"

The final meeting was held on 3rd May, 1853, when there were present:—Rev. James Brown, who presided; James M'Kinlay, Glenmill; Peter Stirling; William Taylor, teacher. The funds in hand (£2) were voted—£1 to the Tract Society, the remainder for the purchase of bibles. It was considered that the objects which the Society had in view when first instituted being now nearly superseded by the various schemes in the churches, it was unnecessary to urge its claims any longer upon the parish. It was accordingly dissolved and the minute book lodged with the Rev. Mr. Brown. The minute book afterwards passed into the custody of the Rev. W. Wood. When leaving Lennoxtown, Mrs. Wood handed it over to Mr. Robert Davidson, merchant, Lennoxtown, who is the present custodian, and to whom I am indebted for a perusal of its contents.

SABBATH SCHOOLS AND CHRISTIAN WORKERS.

Lennoxtown has always been fortunate in having a number of earnest laymen devoting themselves to active Christian work.

There used to be a Sabbath School held in the Tar Row. James M'Pherson, James Davidson, Rab Logan, and others were the teachers. The boys were very mischievous. It was great fun to them to aggravate Rab, as he swore at them when he got angry. When, by going out one after another during class hours, and leaving the door open, till Rab, who had risen and shut it half-a-dozen times, called out, with an oath, " Come back and shut the door "—a bit of the old Adam that made James Davidson hold up his hands. Another Sabbath School was held in the Old School in the Loan. Here Mr Downie was a leading spirit. I only recollect him as an aged man coming occasionally to Mr. James Gray's Sabbath School. Those who remember him speak of his prayers as impressing his hearers with the singularly devout and guileless character of the man. His short addresses were very impressive. Co-operating with him in the school were Mr. Archibald Duncan, Mr. Goldie, &c. Another man taking an interest in Sabbath Schools was Mr. Mackie. David Mackie was a cooper to trade, and in his younger days had gone several voyages to the Coast of Africa, engaged in bringing home oil. He had some peculiarities of his own, but his experience at sea and adventures in Africa enriched his teaching with illustrations and anecdotes which could arouse and sustain the interest and attention of the wildest boys. As Mr Archibald Duncan was coming down one day he saw Mr James Gray passing, and invited him to come and assist. James was diffident, but ultimately agreed. The school in the Loan was transferred about 1840 to the New Subscription School, where I remember it. Mr Downie fell out at the transfer owing to age. The teaching staff that I recollect when I went to it as a scholar was James Gray, John Young, Andrew Motherwell, John Cowan, Rowland Eadie, Miss Williams, Miss Drysdale, Betsy Brown, &c., &c. Alexander Fraser had a Sabbath School class in the Doddle Row which was largely attended, and through which he exercised a great influence for good. He was assisted in his labours here by William Malcolm and Robert (Bob.) Stewart, a son of Auld John or Greenbreeks, as he was called. When I was a boy Stewart lived beside James Glen's workshop. A Sabbath morning prayer meeting was held in Mr Fraser's school, in which Mr William Gardiner, engraver, was a leading spirit. My friend Mr James Millar used to attend this, and it was here in 1832 he made his *debut* as a Christian worker. Like many a young man's first address, it made an indelible impression on his own mind, and he still remembers that his text was from Romans xl. 20—" Be not high-minded, but fear."

In the lecture on Calico Printing I referred to the abounding labours of Alexander Fraser and James M'Pherson in promoting Temperance and social reform. After Mr. M'Pherson went to England he visited the parish occasionally. He was well liked, and public meetings were held at which he told his old friends about his work in the South. He had a sweet voice and was an excellent singer. At his meetings he began by singing some songs with attractive and catching airs and chorus. One of his hearers could remember a part of one, rarely if ever heard now:

" The whale, the whale, the whale I'll sing,
The ocean's pride and the fishes' king."

Having put his audience in good humour with his songs, he then gave interesting descriptions of his work, and enlisted their sympathies on behalf of temperance and religious work.

There were two men who were in great request for praying at sick beds and conversing on religious topics. These were Moses M'Lay, block-printer, to whom I have made reference in another paper, and James Buchanan, a labourer employed in Lennoxmill. Buchanan's pronunciation was very primitive and the grammatical construction of his sentences was open to criticism, but he was earnest and devout, and there was undoubted unction in his prayers. It often happened that neither the parish minister nor the minister of the Relief could be present at funerals and some layman had to officiate. One decent man had carefully committed to memory a prayer for such a contingency. Beginning at the Creation the whole scheme of redemption was elaborated in detail, so that it was rather tedious. He was called on to pray at a funeral where the room was filled; those who could not get into the room remained in the trance which was also full, and those who could not get into the trance had to remain outside. The day was cold, and those outside became impatient. " Is he nearly done?" asked one of the outsiders. The reply was whispered back—" No, no, he is only paidling through Jordan yet." Those who had heard the prayer knew that much had to follow the " paidling." At another funeral, when, I think, Mr. Peter M'Lintock was engaging in prayer, the company were standing reverently when suddenly Brechin, the flesher, who had fallen asleep on his feet, fell heavily against the one who was praying, knocking the wind out of him. As Brechin could not be awakened without stopping the prayer, he was brought to the perpendicular and buttressed on all sides till the amen was reached.

Profane swearing was very common and was frequently quite unconsciously used. There was a decent man Sawney Ronald, a block printer in his early years, who used to be a great discusser of doctrinal points. One Sabbath morning Sawney was engaged in family worship. During prayer his son Rab was intently watching a tame sparrow flitting about the room. The window was down from the top. The sparrow alighted on the top sash and flew out. Rab could not stand this, but sprang to his feet while his father was still praying, exclaiming with an oath, " Oh faither, my sparrow's oot," and with that he bolted out after it. Sawney was a strict disciplinarian and Rab was made aware of the heinousness of his conduct, and dealt with in a manner likely to impress the lesson on his memory.

READING-ROOM.

Mainly through the instrumentality of Alexander Fraser and James M'Pherson, a reading-room was opened about 1830. A room and kitchen was converted into a single apartment, very neatly got up, with two tables well supplied with the Edinburgh and Glasgow newspapers, and several of the magazines and other periodicals were also taken in. This room was next door to Mr. Fleming's drapery shop.

CIRCULATING LIBRARY.

A stationer and bookseller named Robertson, who had a shop in Drysdale's Land, was the first to start a circulating library, which had began to be well patronized when Robertson left the village to go to Kirkintilloch. He ultimately emigrated to America. There was no general diffusion of healthy literature. Chap books and sensational stories of rather loose morality had been the popular pabulum, but novels, such as Sir Walter Scott's, and magazines like Chambers' soon drove the chap rubbish out of the market. Mrs. Tagg, postmistress, Crosshill, also kept a circulating library.

Although newspapers were dear, a few found their way to Campsie and were eagerly read. Sometimes those interested assembled in a loomshop or a private house, one reading aloud to a number of attentive listeners. In this way the folks knew what was going on in the world. It was quite common, when the price of a newspaper was sevenpence, for six or seven persons to club together; each one got a full day for perusal, the last reader retaining the paper.

There was a general illumination for Waterloo by putting candles in the windows, sometimes as many as a dozen candles being employed for a victory like Waterloo or the passing of the Reform Bill. After the trial of Queen Caroline the illumination was not so general. When the candles in Mr. Fraser's windows were almost flickering in their sockets, a passer-by remarked, "Oh, you're loyal, I see." "You see my loyalty is nearly extinguished."

At weddings, before the passing of the Poor Law Act, it was customary for the minister to put round the hat, and the money collected in this way was distributed among the poor. When a child was taken to church to be baptised, the mother was generally accompanied by a young female who was honoured to carry the baby. A christening piece was always carried, and was presented to the first person they met, who had to take it and turn back a short distance with the christening party. There was a gratuity to the beadle, who exercised great care that all the boys were baptised before the girls. Had a girl been baptized before a boy, the superstition was that she would have the beard and the boy would be effeminate.

CAMPSIE FAIR.

The Fair day in the olden times would be on St. Machan's festival. This became both a religious and social event, the whole country side turned out, and traders soon took advantage of the numbers assembled to sell their goods. In this way the religious festival gradually became the local Fair. I have heard that in olden times there used to be two fairs in the parish—one held at the Clachan, which would probably be the original one, on St. Machan's festival; the other held at Roitfair at the east end of the parish. This fair became notorious for brawling and quarrelling between the parishioners of Campsie, Kirkintilloch, and Kilsyth, and representations were made to the Sheriff of the county concerning this. The old fair at the Clachan had almost died a natural death at the end of the century, so it would appear that the Sheriff had suggested transferring the Roitfair to the Newtown, as the centre of population, which was accordingly acted on; and this, becoming more popular, gave the *coup de grace* to the older one at the Clachan. The fair in Lennoxtown was therefore held on the date of the Roitfair instead of St. Machan's, hence the change from September to October. There are many who will remember the time when the Fair was held in due form. Horses and cattle stood in the Main Street, adjoining the Tontine, while numerous barrows with sweetmeats, toys, and fairin's were ranged along the street between the Field Road and the School Loan. After the establishment of the weekly cattle markets in Glasgow, the local Fairs gradually disappeared. Long after the Fair had ceased to be held, the Fair night was remembered, and was a favourite date for social and convivial gatherings. I can recollect when it was quite common for young women to ask their male friends "if they were not going to give them their fairin' the night." The Fair day was at one time impressed in the memory of the young folks by another custom. Those who, from motives of economy, had gone barefooted all spring and summer, were allowed at the Fair to don their shoes and stockings. But when the month of March came round, they were required to go barefoot again.

I have known people who remembered the Torrance and Balgrochan Fair, which was held on the 5th of November, in a field beside Wester Balgrochan. At this Torrance Fair many cattle were exposed for sale. This Fair fell into disuse fully twenty-five years before the one at Lennoxtown was discontinued.

PENNY REELS.

Penny Reels were an institution at one time. A fiddler took the room and supplied the music, and young men and young women resorted thither, paying a penny a reel. There was often a good deal of fun, and it was not considered discreditable in any way to have a night's fun at these.

MUSIC.

Music was at a very low ebb in Campsie in the earlier decades of this century. If the people were pleased with the preaching they would tolerate almost any kind of singing. Alexander Norris, a weaver at the Clachan, did a great deal in his day to promote the cultivation of music. He could read music at sight and he played the violin. He had a class on Saturday night to teach singing to the Sabbath School scholars. He sang and played over the tune and the scholars learned it by the ear, he leading with his violin. He was appointed precentor in the Relief, where he soon made his mark. The congregation were accustomed to sing in very slow time, so Norris's quicker time gave great offence to the older members of the congregation. The introduction of the newer tunes was objected to, and when "St. George's Edinburgh" was first sung in the Relief Church, a worthy couple, Mr. and Mrs. Wallace, rose and walked out. They were displeased at singing so fast and at the repetitions, and declared, "Siclike singing was like a theatre, no' like a kirk ava." An old woman named Mrs. Malcolm complained bitterly of the innovations in the singing in the Relief. "Indeed," she said, "Sawney Norris sings that quick that I am aye a dooble verse behin'." Norris's singing was slow compared to that of the present time. When the new parish church was opened in 1828, a precentor, named William Cuddie, was appointed, who had an excellent tenor voice, and was a very fine, sweet singer. Cuddie formed a small but very efficient choir, gave the members a little training, and then boldly introduced them into the church, where their appearance caused quite a sensation. Cuddie gave an impetus to the study of music while he was in Campsie. He followed Dr. Macleod to Glasgow, and was long precentor in St. Columba's. The leading singer in his Campsie choir was a young woman named Maggie Hill, who belonged to the village and was employed in Lennoxmill for some years. Maggie's powerful contralto voice was distinctly heard all over the new church. Cuddie used to get up concerts in Lennoxtown and neighbourhood. In all these he was accompanied by his prima donna, Maggie, who was everywhere a great favourite. Mr. James Drummond succeeded Cuddie. After a few years in Campsie he became precentor in the High Church, Paisley, and afterwards in St. George's, Glasgow. He in turn was succeeded by Archibald Fyfe, who was the precentor in my time.

When Cuddie had started his choir, Norris followed up by instituting a musical club, the members of which were mostly connected with Lennoxmill This club for a number of years gave an annual concert, and the knowledge of the science of music began to be diffused more generally in the village. I have heard a rather amusing anecdote of Sawney Norris. One day the Rev. Mr. Murdoch of Kilmaronock was preaching in the

Relief. At the conclusion of the sermon he gave out a psalm and sat down. The precentor was motionless. No one had noticed that he was sound asleep, and now every eye was directed at him, while he, quite unconscious, slept soundly on. Mr. Murdoch now began to wonder why the precentor was not beginning. When he had realised the situation, he seized the pulpit Bible, by which he reached Norris. Giving him a vigorous push, he called out, "Sing, sir, sing!" Norris awoke, started to his feet, looked all around and then commenced singing. My informant was young at the time, and says he was so confounded at the precentor singing away when he did not even know the psalm that he sat staring at Norris the whole time. A similar feat was accomplished also in the Relief church by a Mr. Christie, whom I recollect very well. Christie failed to hear what the psalm was which the minister gave out, so he rose and "hum-ha'd" through a common metre tune, and nobody noticed anything unusual.

In 1817 and 1818 Alexander Rodger, a Glasgow poet and song writer, started a class in Torrance once a week. It was conducted in Mr. J. Young's large room. Sandy Rodger's object was to earn money by teaching the art of music, and in this he was fairly successful, but he also succeeded in diffusing a taste for it, and many pleasant associations are connected with Sandy's music class. Songs and duets were chiefly taught.

CHARTIST MOVEMENT IN LENNOXTOWN.

The Chartist movement had many ardent supporters in Campsie, during the ten years this agitation lasted, from 1838 to 1848. The demands in the People's Charter were for (1) universal suffrage; (2) vote by ballot; (3) annual parliaments; (4) no property qualification; (5) equal electoral districts and (6) payment of Members of Parliament. Some of these reforms have been attained, yet their advocates in 1838-48 were regarded by most people as revolutionary zealots. In 1839 the Chartists throughout the country presented a monster petition in favour of their six points. This was signed by 1,200,000 persons. The prayer was rejected, whereupon the working classes in many parts of the country became riotous. In Monmouthshire, for instance, four or five thousand rioters, armed with various weapons, and headed by John Frost, a magistrate, attacked the town of Newport, but they were soon and easily dispersed. John Frost was deprived of his magistracy and banished, and as he thus became a martyr to the cause, he became the popular Chartist idol. It was suggested that petitions to be effectual should be presented with "pens of steel" and "ink of red."

Among the most enthusiastic Chartist advocates in Campsie Robert Wingate stands pre-eminent. A decent, intelligent, God-fearing man, Wingate had been brought up in the Relief Church, and was a member of Mr. Harvie's congregation in Calton,

Glasgow. One Sabbath in 1832, Mr Harvie preached a sermon against the extreme political agitation then prevalent all over the country, and he denounced some of the views as being extreme. In consequence of his strong expression of opinion 49 members left his church that day and never returned to it. Wingate was one of these. This happened all over the country, men of extreme opinions perhaps, but yet of strong convictions had their most cherished opinions denounced in the pulpits. They came to regard the clergy, both Established and Dissenting, as unsympathetic and hostile, and this feeling gradually intensified. In 1834 Wingate removed from Glasgow to Milton of Campsie, to a house in Mr. John Russell's land, and he obtained employment as a "nob" block-printer in Kincaid Field. Here he soon came to the front, being a man of great intelligence, and possessing a natural eloquence, which impressed from the transparent honesty and earnestness of the man. The local leaders of the Radical reformers of that day were mostly connected with the Relief Church in Lennoxtown or the Secession Church in Kirkintilloch, of which the well-known Dr. Andrew Marshall was then the minister. The Radicals approached the Relief and Secession Church Courts, requesting them, by petition, to assist them in obtaining the objects they were agitating to obtain, which they described as obtaining civil liberty. The Synod, however, declined to interfere, and refused their petition. About this time (1841), Dr. Marshall showed hostility to the movement, and preached against it. This brought matters to a crisis. Wingate, Cowan, and others quitted the Relief Church at Lennoxtown, and Davie and others forsook the Secession Church in Kirkintilloch. These, meeting and conferring on the situation, resolved to do in Lennoxtown what had been done in other places, such as Glasgow, Kilbarchan, &c. This was the formation of a new congregation, called "The Christian Brotherhood." Its members met, and, after due deliberation, resolved to act according to the precedents of the Apostolic Church, and "call" two elders to spiritual office, with power to administer the sacrament of baptism, and administer the ordinance of the Lord's Supper. After prayer, Mr. Robert Wingate, block-printer, and James Cowan, weaver, were appointed to the office of elders without any imposition of hands.

The hall of Robertson's Inn was engaged for the meetings on Sabbaths. Services were held there regularly at 11 and 2 o'clock, the same hours at which the services in the Relief Church were held. Many a good Gospel sermon was preached here by earnest laymen. The services were conducted in the same fashion as in the Relief Church. Occasionally the addresses were only ostensibly sermons, based on scripture texts, but partaking rather of the nature of political harangues, proving the righteousness of their cause and expounding their new gospel. There was a regular communion-roll kept. The admission of members was as carefully safe-guarded as in the Relief Church itself, and the attendance at these Sabbath services averaged from 150 to 250. One of the principles of the Christian Brotherhood was that of the ministry being unpaid. They had elders from other districts frequently addressing the meetings. Amongst those were Malcolm M'Farlane, cabinetmaker, Glasgow; and Matthew Cullen, a power-loom dresser, who were the elders of the Christian Brotherhood in Glasgow; William Symington Brown, a doctor of medicine, who afterwards went to America, where he became a professor; and James Jenkins, nailer, St. Ninians, who came frequently. He was a very intelligent man and a ready and effective speaker. He was a popular favourite, and whenever it was known he was to speak many strangers flocked to hear him. James Moir, the well-known tea merchant in Glasgow, was a member of the Christian Brotherhood, and frequently came to Lennoxtown to week-night meetings. Another who came frequently was Abram Duncan, from Falkirk.

In the year 1841, a labourer named Raggs, who was employed in Kincaid, was a member of the Christian Brotherhood, and desired his child to be named "John Frost," after the banished magistrate. Wingate, in performing the baptismal rite, named the boy accordingly, "John Frost Raggs." Mr. Inglis heard of this the following day, and he sent for Wingate to the counting-house, to whom he expressed his opinions on the transaction in rather strong language. He told the foreman he had decided to dismiss Wingate, and to "give him the slip." Mr. Heys, the manager, entered at this moment, and Mr. Inglis told him what he had just done. Said he, "You're wrong, Mr. Inglis; you're wrong. Do you think Wingate'll let that pass?. It'll be blazing in the *Glasgow Herald* and will raise a great outcry against you for your tyranny. Don't do it; at least don't do it just now, Mr. Inglis." At Heys' intercession, the matter was passed over, and Wingate continued for three years. Owing to his abilities as a preacher, he was well known in Glasgow, and a sympathetic employer or manager offered him work in Clydebank Printworks, Glasgow, where he wrought at his trade for a number of years, and his connection with the parish ceased. He removed to Paisley, where he was for twenty years the keeper of a reading and coffee room. Cataract compelled him to resign this appointment, and for the last fifteen years he has lived retired. After he left Campsie the Christian Brotherhood church languished, and then became extinguished, its members being absorbed into other denominations. Cowan and his family joined the Latter-Day Saints, and went to America. The Glasgow church ended similarly, and the last to be given up was the church in Kilbarchan. When Bailie "Jeems" Martin was working as a "nob" at Milton he lodged in Wingate's house.

A hand-loom weaver, named John Stevenson, who belonged to the district of the Cathkin Braes, held extreme opinions in politics, which led him into overt acts of sedition. In particular he had taken a prominent part in a rising against the Government of the day at Strathaven. To escape prosecution he left the Cathkin district, and turned up at Clachan, where "Deacon" Gilchrist gave him a web. Shortly afterwards the Deacon's young daughter, the late Mrs. Jamieson Provan, saw some troopers coming along the old Clachan road, and she called in at the loom-shop "to come and see the sodgers." Stevenson bolted at once, and concealed himself in the glen, until his acquaintances went and discovered him and told him the soldiers were away. It transpired they had come out in connection with smuggling at Finglen, and the officer had instructions to wait on Mr Gartshore Stirling, the nearest resident magistrate, confer with him, but act on his own discretion. The officer was satisfied that smuggling prevailed to a great extent, and surmised that the smugglers had the tacit sympathy of the farmers, shepherds, and cottars, who would not betray them. He was satisfied that he had not force to make a raid on the glen, as his troopers would have to dismount, so, having gleaned information, he returned and reported, but no further action followed. The appearance of the red-coats made Stevenson very cautious. He got employment at Lennoxmill at the time of the strike. When the Chartist movement commenced its partizans at first looked to Stevenson as a veteran reformer to lead them, but he subjected them and their scheme to his very caustic, almost vitriolic, criticism. Stevenson was a sly, pawky, secretive man, of unsociable disposition. His action caused division in the extreme party, and this led to embittered personalities. The Chartists had a song composed on one whom they considered as a sort of renegade. Two strong men were got to sing it through the village. It had a popular air, copies were sold, and it took the public ear, was sung very generally, and even now old Field hands remember its stanzas. It extinguished Stevenson as a political force. Two verses, repeated from memory by contemporaries, I now quote, as Stevenson is dead long ago, and there is no one who might be annoyed by their reproduction.

" Ye'll a' hae heard tell o' oor great Cathkinite,
Ye'll a' hae heard tell o' oor great Cathkinite,
They'll mak' him an elder—at the plate he'll look bright—
For he's braw muckle pouches, oor great Cathkinite.

" Ye'll a' hae heard tell o' oor great Cathkinite,
Ye'll a' hae heard tell o' oor great Cathkinite,
To please the kirk bigots he'll baith bark and bite—
He's a true son of Belial, the great Cathkinite."

Feeling himself in rather an isolated position Stevenson went to Australia. He had obtained possession of a famous old Radical flag that had seen service at the Strathaven rising, and when he went off to Australia, shortly after the discovery of the gold-fields there, he took it with him. When he died it was, by his own request, used as his winding-sheet.

THE RELIEF CHURCH.

The old Relief Meeting-House of 1784 was replaced in 1872 by a handsome new church, the entire cost of which, amounting to £3750, was defrayed within six years. A new U. P. manse had previously been erected in 1855. In 1884 the Church celebrated its centenary, and instrumental music was then introduced, Mr. Ritchie of Viewpark having presented a harmonium. The following gives the line of ministers for over a century:—

1786-1796—Rev. James Colquhoun; resigned.
1796-1798—Vacancy.
1798-1808—Rev. James Thomson; called to Thread Street Church, Paisley; elected Moderator of Relief Synod, 1818; first Professor of Theology of Relief Church, 1824-1841; had degree of D.D. conferred by University of Glasgow.
1808-1810—Vacancy.
1810-1854—Rev. James Brown; died at Wellbank Cottage, in the 80th year of his age and the 44th of his ministry.
1845-1854—Rev. William Wood, as colleague and successor.
1854-1883— Do., as sole pastor; died suddenly at Carradale, 1883, in the 65th year of his age and the 38th of his ministry.
1884—Rev. W. B. Y. Davidson, the present pastor, inducted.

THE ROBERTSON ARMS INN.

The Inn adjoining the Relief Church was the principal one in the district at the beginning of the century. The host and hostess were connected with the Relief Church, and the first minister, Mr Colquhoun, used to drop in when passing. The country members were very kind to their pastor, when he visited them and used to send him away laden with butter, cheese, eggs, and farm produce of various kinds. When making a pastoral visit at a farmhouse one day Mr. Colquhoun received a roll of butter, which he put carefully into his coat pocket. He dropped in to the Robertson Arms before getting home. Here in the cheerful kitchen, standing before the blazing fire, he got into animated discussion. The butter in the meantime was melted by the heat, and was running down to the floor, oozing out of his pocket like jelly from a straining bag. When noticed by the bystanders it caused laughter at the expense of the minister, and it was too good a joke to pass soon into oblivion. The host and proprietor was a joiner, and was engaged in this business, leaving his better half to attend to the house. She seems to have been an energetic, capable woman, prompt in action. Coming in from the garden one day with a cabbage in one arm and the knife with which she had cut it in the other, she found her domestic barring the egress of a man whom she had served with refreshment and who had then coolly declared that he had nothing to pay for it. Indignant at being swindled, the hostess demanded payment, failing which she declared she would have satisfaction, even if she had to rump him before he got out. No payment being forthcoming, she seized one of his coat-tails and cut it off, leaving the astonished defaulter to go through the town with his coat with one tail. The story got wind and was the occasion of her getting "Rump him" for a nickname. She was very proud of her three handsome daughters, whom she commended as likely to make excellent wives. She declared that they were "wind tight and water free," which passed into a proverbial saying. One of the daughters was married in very strange circumstances. Her intended husband had become bankrupt; the daughter was likely to be well dowered by and bye, so, in order that the creditors might not seize his wife's money in payment of his debts, he divested himself of his all and was married clothed with a barrel. The idea of an ante-nuptial contract, in which the husband's *jus mariti* was excluded and her own money settled upon herself, never occurred to any of these simple-minded folks.

I recollect the Inn in the "fifties." The Robertson Arms were blazoned in all their details as a sign above the door. On the shield three wolves heads erased ar, a man in chains lying under the escutcheon, the crest a dexter hand holding a regal crown. The supporters were a serpent balancing itself on its tail, and a dove of immense size, for it was as long as the serpent. I remember shortly after beginning Latin trying to make out the motto, *Virtutis gloria merces*; *virtutis* I knew, *gloria* I knew, but *merces!* I would have to turn up my Ainsworth for that when I got home. I learned in after years how James II. had granted to the family of Robertson of Struan the crest supporting the regal crown, and for motto, "Glory the recompense of valour." I look back on this sign as my first lesson in heraldry; it was more complicated and difficult to understand than the Lennox Arms, the supporters of which were two savages, wreathed head and middle with oak, holding in the hands clubs erect. The motto, "I'll defend," being in English, was not a hard nut for a boy to crack, like a Latin motto. There was a dancing school held in the hall of the Robertson Arms by a Mr. Brocklebank, and of those who attended that class there are very few now resident in the parish—many are dead, many I have lost sight of altogether. I look back on that class in the Robertson Arms when the Kirkwoods were tenants as a very happy time. At the ball which wound it up, Willie Simpson, then of Capieston, Gavin Jack, then of Balcurroch, and myself danced the hornpipe of Jack Tar.

CHOLERA.

The parish suffered from a visitation of cholera in 1833, 1849, and again in 1854. On the 22nd January, 1832, it broke out in Kirkintilloch. There was considerable difference of opinion as to whether it was introduced there by a sailor suffering from it, or through the medium of a cargo of horns, hoofs, woollen rags, etc., from the Baltic, which was discharged at Hillhead for the Hurlet and Campsie Alum Company's works at Campsie, for the manufacture of their prussiates. It raged in Kirkintilloch with terrible virulence, about forty deaths having taken place in the square formed by Moodie's Land, Townhead, Freeland Place, and the Canal Bank or Luggie Bank Road. It was attempted to draw a sanitary cordon round Campsie, the roads were watched, and tramps or vagrants were not permitted to enter, in case of bringing infection. So rigidly was this carried out that some families residing in Kirkintilloch, but employed in Kincaid Printfield, were compelled either to flit into Milton or be excluded from entering the parish, and they removed their dwelling-places accordingly. Notwithstanding all these precautions, cholera broke out in Lennoxtown, but was confined to the east end of the village. The frightful suddenness of the attack, the celerity with which it ran its course, the helplessness of man in the midst of a pestilence which walked in darkness, and a destruction that wasted at noon day, were sources of terror by day and by night. Neighbours were too frightened to perform the most common offices of humanity. In no country perhaps is there such a strong feeling of reverence and respect for the dead as in Scotland; yet, here in Lennoxtown, people living on the same stairhead could not be got to assist in carrying out the coffin of a departed neighbour, or to help in any way. Even in 1854, M'Luckie's apprentice joiners, in several instances, carried the coffin to the door and left it there, refusing either to put in the corpse or go in to carry out the coffin. The foreman, Mr. Shearer, said this was scandalous, and with the assistance of W. Kelly had it done himself.

On the occasion of the first outbreak in 1833, a Mrs. Smith was seized on the Sunday, and was dead on Monday morning. Her acquaintances and neighbours were in terror, so her son procured a coffin, into which he placed the corpse. He then got a two-wheeled barrow, and he managed unaided to carry his mother's coffin and place it on the barrow. Unaccompanied, he wheeled his burden towards the new Parish Church, the graveyard around which had only been laid off in 1831, the first interment being that of William M'Laws, who died 3rd February, 1833, aged 87. His burial-place is in the north-east corner; Dr. Macleod's is in the north-west corner; M'Law's at the opposite end. In pushing his load up the steep brae, in front of the church, he became exhausted, and was compelled to stop. Two sons of John Glen, shoemaker, had been watching this unusual sight, admiring the filial devotion, and, prompted by feelings of humanity, they now walked up towards him, accosting him with the words, "Your case is a hard one; we have come to give you a helping hand." James M'Pherson had learned of the circumstance, and he, too, hastened up to assist, and Mrs. Smith was buried by her son and his three volunteer helps. Funerals caused the village to have a deserted look. No person was to be seen in the streets, the doors were shut, and blinds, screens, or shutters were closed to hide the awe-inspiring processions from sight. On one occasion James Kincaid was one of four carrying a coffin shoulder high. There were a number of people following at a greater distance than usual. Kincaid became exhausted with the burden, but there was none of the usual readiness to relieve the pall-bearers, and he had to stop. " Men," he exclaimed, " do you mean us to carry all the road? We're fairly exhausted." Some came forward on this appeal and relieved the bearers.

In the 1833 attack Dr. Robertson was the principal medical man. Dr. Finlayson was also in practice. To assist them Mr. R. Dalglish, the Provost, sent a German medical man, who had the reputation of being very clever. Mr. Robert Dalglish, late M.P., showed an excellent example at this time. When people were paralysed with fear he took measures to have the bedding, &c., fumigated in the houses where deaths had taken place. Clothes were disinfected by steeping in large boynes. The late James Kincaid, long of the madder colour dye-house, and for many years beadle in the U. P. Church, was his right-hand man in carrying out this work. Taking the precaution to have a half-glass of whisky the first thing in the morning, Kincaid then lighted his pipe and took a smoke, thus fortifying himself for his disagreeable and dangerous but most essential duties. Kincaid was three weeks engaged at this work in the village, during which he had his full wages at Lennoxmill, although absent from his own proper work. Provost Dalglish came out from Glasgow, and brought a quantity of adherent plaster cloths—like a batter. The substance making it adhere was warmed and stuck on the breast and belly. Thomas Young, the joiner in Lennoxmill, was instructed to have a number of wooden shapes made for cutting out these plasters, so as to suit all ages and sizes. Camphor, worn round the neck in a little woollen bag, was also used as a disinfectant. The mortality from cholera in 1833 was about 20 or 30.

In 1849 the Parochial Board, as the Local Authority, set about measures to improve the sanitary state of the parish, in view of a possible outbreak. Dr. Eadie was then the principal village doctor. As Inspector of Nuisances, he examined every ashpit in Lennoxtown, Mount of Glorat, Milton, and Torrance. Protective measures were adopted when cholera did break out. Those affected were isolated, and, mainly owing to the carrying out of greatly improved sanitary arrangements, only five fatal cases occurred at this time. James Thomson, engraver, died 31st December, 1848, and Mrs. Gourlay on 28th January, 1849.

The outbreak in 1854 raged with great virulence. The local doctors were overwhelmed with work, and two medical men had to be got from Glasgow to assist. One of these was sent by Mr. Dalglish, the other was obtained by the Local Authority. Before the epidemic had spent itself, nurses had also to be obtained from

Glasgow. Its appearance was sudden. The first case was that of Wm. Gilmour, farmer, Bencloich Mill, and grocer, Lennoxtown. He was in Glasgow on Fair Saturday in his usual robust health, and was dead before Monday morning. The disease spread rapidly, and a great depression rested on and oppressed the whole community. On the annual holiday at the end of July there were five corpses in the village, all cholera victims, yet the trip to Ediuburgh by railway went on as usual. On a fine Sabbath evening four acquaintances had a walk. As they bade each other good-night they wondered what would be the news in the morning —whom would it be next? Before morning, Peter M'Kindlay, one of the four, was dead. In the beginning of August 1854, at the Easter Lodge to Lennox Castle, immediately adjoining the present Railway Station, Bob M'Callum's son John and an inmate of the house, Leezie Anderson, an elderly woman, had been attacked, and both died. When the friends came to bury the two dead, they found the father and his son Wee Bob had also been attacked. It was a distressed household. The relations who had come to bury the two dead hesitated to touch the coffins iu order to screw on the lids. Rab Torrance and Kelly did this, and carried out the bodies. In another case, Mrs. M'Intyre had died at Whitefield. The old husband was unable to coffin his wife, and the daughters were unable to lift their mother into the coffin, which had been left at the door for her, so they appealed for assistance from the open window. Here again Torrance and Kelly offered their services and a terrible job they had to get the body down the narrow winding stair, as Mrs. Macintyre was very stout and very heavy.

In some families there were two deaths, notably Mrs. Downie, grocer, and her daughter, and the two M'Callums. When the gloom was resting heavily on the village and at its blackest, when burning tar barrels were being carried through the streets at night, some one suggested that the excellent brass band might march through the town, playing their most inspiriting music, to help to break the melancholy spell. The band, at that time most efficient, promptly responded to the suggestion, and played through all the streets. The music roused and cheered the drooping spirits of the community, and as the epidemic had by that time spent its virulence, the performances of the band got a share of the credit of having done good work, which put the villagers under obligation to assist them when they next appealed for pecuniary help for new instruments, etc.

One family removed or rather fled to a house at Aberfoyle while the pestilence raged in Campsie. When it had entirely ceased, and all seemed well again, they returned to Campsie. Mrs.—— very soon afterwards took violent cramp in the stomach, and died very suddenly. In one case in Lennoxtown the Inspector, Mr. Johnston, wished to remove the other inmates and put them into an unoccupied building on the Finglen Burn at

Haughhead. This was the old printfield, afterwards a weaving factory, which was to have been turned for a time into a temporary hospital. Some bundles of straw had been got from Mr. Galbraith, the farmer in Kilwinnet, but the Haughhead people rose in a kind of riot as a protest against this. The crowd tore out the straw and scattered it, and owing to the strong opposition, which was mainly headed by a Mrs. Dearie and her two sons, the idea of carrying out the proposed hospital at Haughhead was abandoned. It was a strange fancy, but Robert Torrance, the late keeper of Campsie bowling green, attended nearly every cholera funeral, at all events all west of Lockhart's Loan. He only once had a momentary fear. In going to M'Intyre's, at Whitefield, some woman in terror asked if he was not afraid. "Not a bit," said he. "Do you never take a glass of whisky before you go in?" "Never a drop." He took a shiver and came back and asked his wife for a glass of whisky. To her remonstrances against his going to all these funerals he replied, "I canna help it; I must go." Ultimately, on the application of the Local Authority, two nurses were got from Glasgow, but by this time things were improving.

In making enquiries on this subject it occurred to me to write to my old friend Dr. Wilson, then residing at Kirn, who favoured me with the following reply, which I give *in extenso*:—

" EAST VIEW BANK,
" CRIEFF, *15th July, 1889.*

" DEAR MR. CAMERON,

" Your note was forwarded to me here about a fortnight ago, and I have been thinking on the subject of it since, but so long a time has elapsed since the epidemic you referred to occurred, and at the time, and since, in Campsie, I led such a busy life, that I retain but a very general impression of the events that occurred during its course.

" The outbreak of cholera in Campsie commenced in the early part of the summer—I think of 1854—but not having any books here I cannot speak positively as to the date. In anticipation of it we had for some months previously been endeavouring to set our house in order, by getting dung-steads and pig-styes cleaned out, and, when too close to dwelling-houses, removed to a distance. In this work we were considerably obstructed by the unwillingness of some people to obey instructions, for as you are probably aware, at that time, it was a common belief among country people that such things were not hurtful but positively wholesome!

" The first case of cholera I saw in the epidemic was the case of Dr. Taylor, of Kirkintilloch, who was then the only practitioner there. On hearing, casually, that he had been seized, I rode over to see him, and found him collapsed and pulseless, and evidently dying. I waited and did what I could for him. He died during the night. His was the first case in Kirkintilloch. A day or two afterwards, the first case occurred in Campsie, ending in death in about 24 hours, and for a period of about three months fresh cases occurred almost daily. The number of cases during that time was, I think, about 120 of genuine cholera, apart from those of diarrhoea, which were innumerable, and which, being treated in time, were probably prevented from running into the collapsed stage. The Parochial Board engaged an assistant for me, and Mr. Dalglish sent out another, so that, with Messrs. Baird and Marshall, there were five of us engaged in fighting the enemy, and yet we were all kept busy—so much so in my case that I am safe to say that for three months I scarcely ever had a whole night in bed, and was compelled, in order to get some needful rest, to get a friend to give me a bed in his house occasionally, and thereby enable my housekeeper to say truthfully that I was not in. Of course, the long-continued strain told upon me, and towards the end of the epidemic I had a sharp attack of the preliminary symptoms, by which I was laid up for a few days, and which I rather welcomed as an opportunity for getting some rest. I may mention that during my illness almost the only person who called to sympathise with me was the Rev. Father Gillon, Catholic priest; and to show the devotion of the Catholic priesthood to their duties I may mention that he also had a smart attack of the preliminary symptoms one Saturday night. On being called to see him, I told him he must keep his bed next day or he would run great risk, but he said he could not do so, if he were able to be up at all, that he had mass to perform both at Kilsyth and Kirkintilloch, and must go. I then advised him that before leaving (which he had to do at six o'clock in the morning), he should take a cup of coffee and some toast; but this also he said he could not do, as, according to the rules of his Church, he dare not take food or drink before saying mass at both places, so as it would be two o'clock before his duties were over you may fancy the risk he ran. I said to him I thought that taking it under medical advice would exonerate him, but he said, ' No, I could take meat on a Friday, or on any of the ordinary fast days of our Church, by your advice, but I cannot do so on this occasion without a special dispensation from the Pope.' It is worthy of mention, too, that he was equally strict and assiduous in his attendance on those of his flock who were attacked, both by night and day. I have pleasure in recalling these reminiscences of a good and worthy man. I am sorry that I cannot say that our Protestant clergymen were equally assiduous in visiting those who were attacked. Indeed, one of them went to reside at the coast, coming up on Saturday nights for his duties next day, and going away again on the Mondays; and I was very much amused, and, at the same time, sorry at such an exhibition of the lack of faith, to observe that if I met him in the village, and held out my hand to shake hands, he carefully avoided seeing it. Indeed, he never once shook hands with me during the epidemic, although I, rather mischeviously, always offered to do so when we met.

" With regard to your query, ' Was there a panic in Campsie, and were people afraid to perform the last offices for the dead, as in 1833? ' I do not think that such was the case. There were, I believe, two or three isolated instances of such disinclination, but the feeling was not at all general. As a rule, too, the sufferers were faithfully attended to by their relatives. Albeit I met with one instance of apparent desertion of a patient who was *in extremis*. One night, during a round of late visits, I called to see a patient, whose case I had given up as hopeless some hours previously, and found him tossing in the agonies of death, and deserted by his relatives. This, however, was the only instance of such inhumanity, caused by fear, I have no doubt, that I met with. There was fear of the disease very generally, doubtless, but I do not think there was any general fear of *infection*, and the reason for this was because it was held and inculcated by medical men that the disease was not infectious. And from my experience of a former epidemic at Coatbridge, in 1849, I was very strongly of that opinion, and, therefore, lost no opportunity of impressing it upon the people. Largely, no doubt, in consequence of this, the sufferers, as a rule, were assiduously attended by their relatives; and for those who had no relatives able to perform these duties nurses were provided by the Parochial Board. In addition to providing nurses and medical attendance, the Board also issued instructions as to checking the first symptoms of the disease, and I was instructed to have supplies of medicine for that purpose at Torrance, Lillyburn, Kincaidfield, Lennoxmill, and Clachan and Glenmill Bleachfields. The mention of the last place reminds me that the only case of cholera (?) that occurred there was rather a ludicrous one, which served to relieve somewhat the grim horrors of the period. The proprietor of Glenmill was, as you will remember, Mr. M'Kinlay, a very worthy man, and who took great interest in the spiritual as well as the physical condition of his workers. These were chiefly women, and resided in the works—a large flat being fitted up as a dormitory for their use, which was called the woman-house, and Mr M'Kinlay was naturally anxious in case the disease should break out there. One morning early I got a message from him saying that one of the girls in the woman-house had been attacked during the night, and that he had regularly administered the medicine I had left him, but that she seemed no better. Of course I hurried up at once and saw the patient; but at a glance I saw it was not a case of cholera. Mr M'Kinlay said she had been vomiting, and suffering much pain nearly the whole night, and he had done all he could to relieve her. Thinking she must have taken something that had caused a fit of indigestion I ordered a mustard poultice, and turned to leave when she was seized with a paroxysm of pain which stopped me, and aroused certain suspicions. I then made a closer examination, and found that she was about to increase the population of the woman-house, which she did in about an hour in the shape of a fine boy. Imagine the horror of poor Mr. M'Kinlay when told of the cause of his case of cholera.

" With regard to any Campsie incidents outside of my profession, I do not remember any worth recording. There may have been, but I was so absorbed in my professional duties that if there were I have retained no recollection of them. If, however, there is any incident you may have heard of, on which you think I could throw any light, I will be glad to do so, if I can. I trust you will be able to read the foregoing rambling and meagre reminiscences (medical men, as you know, are proverbially bad penmen), of a time, alas! now long ago (nearly 40 years), when you were a very small stripling, and your worthy father, of whose friendship I still retain a warm appreciation, was alive. I, too, was then a young man, beginning the battle of life. How much has happened since then! But I must not get into a moralising vein, or you will be thinking I am getting doited as well as old. Do you intend to publish the results of your labours, or is it for a lecture you are working? If the former, I will be glad to see a copy. By the way, it occurs to me that your neighbour, Mr. Gordon Wilson, might be able to give you some information about Campsie. Any statistical information, such as the number of cholera cases, number of deaths, &c., you could easily get from the Parochial Board books of the period.—With kindest regards, believe me, sincerely yours,

" A. T. WILSON.

" J. CAMERON, Esq."

Dr. Wilson's letter is very interesting, but in contrasting the conduct of Father Gillon with that of the parish clergyman he unintentionally rather omits to do justice to the Rev. William Wood of the U. P. Church. Mr. Wood did his pastoral duties most faithfully at that trying period, and was not afraid to visit at the houses where there was cholera, or where there had been deaths from that disease. He became so worn out with his labours, especially after having had a slight attack of the cholera himself, that he was obliged to go away for a few weeks' rest after the epidemic was over.

THE LENNOXTOWN FRIENDLY VICTUALLING SOCIETY.

This Co-operative Society was founded in 1812 and is now, I believe, either the second or third oldest Co-operative Society in Scotland.

JAMES DENNISTOUN OF GOLFHILL.

James Dennistoun, the well-known banker and merchant in Glasgow, was born in Campsie in 1752, at Clousey Firs, I have been led to understand; but in 1756 his father was tenant of New Mill of Glorat, where he was factor for Glorat and also to his kinsman, Dennistoun of Colgrain. His brother John succeeded his father in New Mill, and died there in 1813. In 1782, in conjunction with his brother Archibald, he established the great mercantile house of J. & A. Dennistoun, which in time became one of the largest firms in Glasgow, having branches at London, Liverpool, New Orleans, Havre, New York, and Melbourne. He also founded the Glasgow Bank, in which adventure there were sixteen partners. This bank joined "The Ship," and afterwards "The Thistle," and is now represented by the Union Bank. During Dennistoun's management the bank maintained a very high reputation. He retired from active life in 1829, when his fellow-citizens entertained him at a great public dinner, "in testimony of their respect for him not only as a banker, but as a man of liberal political views and principles." In 1832 he was offered a baronetcy by Lord Grey, but he declined this honour. He purchased Golfhill estate in 1802. He died in 1834, and was buried in the Ram's Horn churchyard in Ingram Street, but his body was afterwards transferred to the family vault in the Necropolis, Glasgow. His eldest son, Alexander, was member of Parliament for Dumbartonshire, and his young son, John, was M.P. for Glasgow from 1837-47. There is a tradition in the parish that when he left New Mill for Glasgow to push his way in the world he crossed the Glazert opposite New Mill with only a half-crown in his pocket.

The Lennoxtown folks, during the first quarter of the century, were many of them simple-minded people, with very primitive notions. When in the Sabbath school at Tar Row, some mischievous boys ignited a peeoy while old James Davidson was engaged in prayer. Feeling the smell of gunpowder he remarked, " Surely the devil is in this place and I knew it not." At the Burnhouse a hot bread and milk poultice was to be applied to B——. The poultice disappeared while the preparations for putting it on were being made. The invalid was the culprit; it looked inviting, so he admitted having supped it, and he added, " Let the saw (salve) seek the sair." Once old Robert Baird (" Auld Whey ") was having a visit from his elder, who was dealing very pointedly and faithfully with him, in view of his serious illness and the apparent near approach of death. This he disliked, and, instead of replying to the query whether he was at peace in Christ, he turned round at bay and said, " Man, Tummas, fu' muckle will Willie Craig pay for Baglass?" On another occasion, when Robert Reid, Clousey Firs, was on his death-bed, his wife, Babbie Allan, a good woman, was reading the account of our

Saviour walking on the sea towards the boat in which His disciples were being tossed by the waves. His commentary did not take a personal application. It was, "Losh! Babbie, He wasna a fear'd ane; my certy, Babbie, He wud 'a made a gran' sailor!" There were a family of Bairds, miners, who did not go to any church, but rambled over the hillsides on the Sunday. During one of these excursions, old "Muchty" Baird was standing leaning on the wooden paling which fenced an old pit, when the railing suddenly gave way and he fell in. Fortunately the pit was not very deep, and had some water at the bottom, but Baird had on his Sunday surtout coat, the tails of which greatly broke his fall. When he was got out he remarked to one of his brothers, "Man, Jimmack, wisna it the Lord's wull that I had on ma Sunday coat the day, or I micht hae been shivered a' tae spunks."

Robin Stirling, Crosshill, I remember as rather a queer one. He was of superior intelligence, shrewd and logical, and delighted in disquisitions on Scottish Law, and when tired of that he would descant on original sin. The houses in Crosshill were at one time called Stirling's Dandy Raw. The first of these, at the higher end, were commenced by Saunders Service, the grandfather of the D.D., but Robin bought this and had the remainder built. He was at one time the Field carter. When he suddenly and unexpectedly became an owner of house property, people said he must have found a purse, but while going with the Field cart he had been obliging in executing commissions in Glasgow and his own industry and frugality laid the foundation of his competency. He had a great dislike to Mr. Joseph Kay, and would come out and bow with mock humility as Mr. Kay was passing and repassing to his work. One day before some spectators he came out and taking off his hat he bowed before Kay almost to the ground. Kay affected not to understand his object, putting his hand into his pocket he tossed a copper into the hat and walked on. The laugh at Robin's expense cured the salaaming, and Kay was not further troubled in this respect.

Thomas M'Luckie received an order from Mr. Cunningham for a wooden gate. This gate Tammy could not make to fit in between the posts, "Haud yer wheesht; it'll wear till't," he always said; and "It'll wear till't like Tammy's yett" became proverbial, and is quoted by Dr. Service in his novel of "Novantia," which appeared in *Good Words*.

THE GLAZERT COACH COMPANY.

In Pigot's Directory of Scotland, published about 1825, it is stated that a noddy leaves Lennoxtown for Glasgow each Wednesday morning, being market day, and returns in the evening. This was, however, quite inadequate to the requirements of the village of Lennoxtown and surrounding districts. Accordingly, a meeting of those interested was held on the 20th September, 1825,

at the Robertson Arms Inn, when it was resolved to established a
stage coach to run between Campsie and Glasgow three times a
week, or as much oftener as circumstances seemed to require.
The articles of agreement provided that the style of the co-partnery
should be The Glazert Coach Company, trading as William Ross
& Company.

1. That the number of subscribers to the new venture should be limited
to sixty, and that all these should be resident in the parish.

2. That the amount of each subscription should be Five Pounds, and
that no member have more than one share.

.   .   .   .   .   .

6. The business to be managed by a committee of directors, who were to
have the assistance of a special committee in the first instance to purchase
the horses and the coach, but they were to provide provender, maintain the
coach in good repair, appoint the driver, pay tolls, &c.

The committee of directors chosen at the first meeting, held on
20th September, 1825, when the company was floated, was—
Robert Clarke, president; Robert Brown, treasurer; William
Ross, clerk; Robert Barclay, John Leckie, James Robertson,
James Buchanan, James Ronald, Malcolm Buchanan. The
directors agreed with Robert Ferrie to supply the horses with hay
and litter for a year. On 29th September, 1825, William Nelson
was appointed driver at 16s. per week, for which he was to do all
the work of the stable, etc. On 17th October, the contract for
shoeing was given to Alexander Cassels, at 19s. each horse per
annum. Advertisements were inserted in *Glasgow Herald* and
Chronicle that the coach was to commence on 19th October,
starting from the Robertson Arms Inn at eight o'clock morning,
and leaving M'Kerracher's King's Head Inn, Glasgow, at five
o'clock evening; fares to and from Glasgow, 3s. 6d. inside,
2s. 6d. outside; single journey, 2s. and 1s. 6d; to Kirkintilloch,
9d. inside and 6d. outside; Kirkintilloch to Glasgow, 1s. 6d. and
1s.; any intermediate place, 9d. and 6d. On 22nd June. 1826,
it was agreed that any days when not running to Glasgow
members of the coach society could have the use of the coach on
applying to the president, but distance must not exceed twelve
miles from Lennoxtown. On 21st August the coach arrived,
having sustained damages. It had been racing with the Stirling
coach. The driver of the Stirling coach was considered entirely
to blame for collision, but the Campsie driver was cautioned not
to strive on the road with any other coach. In October it was
agreed that the coach run daily, leaving during winter at 8.30,
returning from Mein's Blackfriar's Inn at four o'clock. On 28th
March, 1827, the coach was attacked by James Lawrence, jun.,
James Adam, jun., and William Nelson (late driver), who
attempted to overturn it. It was agreed that a complaint be
lodged, and the minute to this effect was signed and handed over
to Robert Millar, messenger-at-arms, for execution.

Like a great many other joint stock concerns, the Glazert
Coach Co. was not a financial success, and on 25th April, 1831,

at a general meeting of the proprietors it was resolved to take in offers for the coach, horses, harness, &c. The offer of John Gray, Tontine, was accepted, being £106 for coach, horses, and harness. On 3rd Nov., 1831, the proprietors received £2 4s. 9d. for their five pound shares and the concern was finally wound up. The tenant of the Tontine or Lennox Arms continued to run the coach as a private undertaking, but the opening of the railway caused the Campsie Coach to be withdrawn about 1848.

The Tontine, or Lennox Arms, took the lead as the principal inn. after the opening of the new church in 1828. It was rather enterprising to take the coach away from the Robertson Arms, as this brought custom from passengers. The Robertson Arms then fell into a secondary place. The passengers by the Tontine coach had sometimes a little zest added to the journey by accident. One day an axle suddenly broke. All on the top were thrown off, except Major Graham Stirling, then a youth, who held on to the seat. Among the passengers were the late Mr. William Cunningham and Miss Isabella Ewing, Arngomery. One lady had an arm broken. Gilroy was the driver, but no blame attached to him.

MISS OSWALD, FOUNDER OF THE OSWALD SCHOOLS.

The laird of Kincaid had a son and two daughters. One daughter was married to Mr. Oswald, writer, Glasgow, who became connected with the parish on being appointed clerk to the Woodhead Baron-Bailie court in 1775, and they had two daughters. On Mr. Oswald's death his widow came to reside in Kirkintilloch, in a two-storey thatched house at the foot of the Crofts, popularly known as the "Old Phœnix," from the insurance label on it. After having resided here for a number of years, she returned to Glasgow, and had the house in Kirkintilloch taken down and rebuilt. It is now the property of Mr. James Wood, who resides in it. Mr. Wood's mother, Jean Dollar, was for many years Mrs. Oswald's faithful and devoted attendant. Mrs. Oswald and her daughters afterwards removed to Viewfield Cottage, above Kincaid House, which the laird had built for his sister. After the death of her sister and mother, Miss Oswald made a will, bequeathing all her means to build schools in Campsie and Kirkintilloch, which in due time were built and named after Miss Oswald. After erecting these buildings there was not enough left to endow them. They have now been handed over to the respective School Boards of Campsie and Kirkintilloch (burgh). In the latter case, the Kirk-Sessions made certain reservations in their own favour, in order that they might have the use of them whenever they wished. when not required for educational purposes. Many who are familiar with the name Oswald School know nothing of the kind-hearted lady who founded them to promote the educational interests of the two parishes she was connected with.

K

CENSUS OF CHURCH ATTENDANCE IN 1876.

The *North British Daily Mail* took a census of Church attendance in and around Glasgow in 1876. The census in Campsie was taken on 30th April of that year, and in my scrap book I have the following particulars:—

Church.		Minister.		On Roll.		Attendance.
Established,	...	Rev. T. Monro,	...	1053	...	840
Free,	... ...	Rev. J Dewar,	...	120	...	178
Torrance Free,...		Rev. Mr. Brown,	...	—	...	78
U. P.,	... ...	Rev. W. Wood,	...	295	...	333
Summary of Attendance—Established,		...	...	...		840
	Dissenting,	...	...	...		589
						1429

MINISTERS BELONGING TO CAMPSIE.

A friend has suggested including in this paper a list of the natives of the parish, or those belonging to families closely connected or identified with the parish, who have been ordained to the Ministry of the Gospel, or licensed to preach it, during the present century. The following list has been compiled to show this, and unless where otherwise stated the charges are those of the Church of Scotland :—

JAMES LAPSLIE, son of the tenant of Bencloich Mill. — Campsie.

JAMES ADAM, son of the tenant of Clousey Farm, on Bencloich estate. — Assistant at Kilbirnie, where he wrote the new *Statistical Account*; presented by the Earl of Glasgow to parish of Cumbrae.

JAMES ANDERSON, son of — Anderson, joiner and farmer, Lukeston. — Relief Church, Beith.

PATRICK M'FARLAN, D.D., younger brother of John M'Farlan of Ballancleroch. — St. John's, Glasgow; West Parish, Greenock; latterly of Free Church, Greenock.

THOMAS GORDON; father a printfield worker, Lennoxtown—attended Orig. Secess. Church, Kirkintilloch. — Original Secession Church, Falkirk; Established Church, latterly of Free Church.

ALEXANDER MATHIESON, D.D., son of George Mathieson, calico press printer, Lennoxmill. — Montreal.

JOHN STEVENSON, D.D., son of Wm. Stevenson, Birdston, who died in 1844. — Teacher at Rowantreefauld; Church of Scotland, Bombay; afterwards of Ladykirk.

JOHN LOCKHART, D.D., son of John Lockhart, feuar and Sheriff-officer, Lockhart's Loan, Lennoxtown. — Teacher in School Loan; Scotch Church, Newcastle-on-Tyne; afterwards of Fraserburgh (resigned).

JOHN EDWARDS, D.D., son of Wm. Edwards, mason, Alum Works. — Greenhead U.P. Church, Glasgow.

JAMES M'FARLAN, son of John M'Farlan of Ballancleroch. — Muiravonside.

ALEXANDER FRASER, son of James Fraser, teacher, at one time foreman engraver in Lennoxmill. — Congregational Churches in Edinburgh and Colchester; Ewing Chapel, Waterloo St., Glasgow; went in 1863 to Australia, owing to health failing.

ALEXANDER STEVENSON, son of the tenant of Birdston. — Berbice, British Guiana; Ruthwell Parish.

ROBERT STEVENSON, son of the tenant of Birdston. — Airdrie and Forfar.

MATTHEW R. BATTERSBY, son of M. Battersby, block printer, Lennoxmill. — U. P. Church, Hamilton.

ROBERT H. STEVENSON, D.D.; his father was joint-tenant of Shields with his cousin, then tenant of Craigend, and latterly Netherinch. — Crieff; St. George's, Edinburgh; Moderator in 1871.

JOHN SHEARER, son of Wm. Shearer, tenant of Sterriqua farm. — U. P. Church, Larkhall.

GEORGE STEVENSON, brother of late W. Stevenson, Alton farm, son of tenant of Birdston. — Free Church, Tullibody; Wick.

ALEXANDER B. SCLANDERS, son of Robert Sclanders, baker, Torrance. — U. P. Churches, Bathgate and Musselburgh.

WILLIAM BROWN, grandson of Robt. Brown—"Baker Brown's Well"—son of William Brown, baker. — Independent minister, Middlesboro', Dorsetshire; Brisbane, Queensland.

DONALD MACLEOD, D.D., son of Dr. Macleod of Campsie. — Linlithgow; Park Church, Glasgow.

JOHN M'LUCKIE, sketch-maker in Lennoxmill, son of Adam M'Luckie, block printer. — U. P. Churches, Lanark and Uddingston (resigned).

WILLIAM F. STEVENSON, son of the tenant of Alton. — Rutherglen.

JOHN SERVICE, D.D., formerly in Lennoxmill, son of John Service, block cutter, Lennoxmill. — Hamilton; Melbourne, Australia; Inch, Wigtonshire; Hyndland Church, Glasgow. Author of *Sermons and Essays, Novantia,* &c.

WILLIAM JAMES, block cutter, son of Robert James, block printer. — U. P. Church, Leeds.

JAMES MOFFAT SCOTT, son of John Scott, Fingerpost, now of East-side and Ashwood, Kirkintilloch.	Free Church, Alloa; Arbroath. Author of *The Martyrs of Angus and Mearns*.
PETER MACLEOD, son of Peter Mac-leod, Muckcroft and Alum Works.	St. Luke's, Dundee; Neilston.
THOMAS THOMSON, son of James Thomson, engraver, who died of cholera, stepson of Thomas Watson, grocer and farmer, with whom he went out to Canada.	Presb. Church, British Columbia; Hamilton, Ontario.
JOHN CONNOR, son of John Connor, block printer, Milton.	Fauldhouse (resigned).
JAMES W. HARPER, son of William Harper, Whitefield, block printer, Lennoxmill.	Free West, Alloa.
ROBERT FERGUS, son of Wm. Fergus, block cutter.	Presbyterian Church, Melbourne.

The following were licensed to preach in connection with the Church of Scotland, but were never ordained:—John M'Farlan, parochial teacher. Clachan; Joseph Stirling, son of Sir John, fifth baronet of Glorat; Robert Brown, Westerton of Glorat; Robert Horne, New Mill of Glorat; Charles A. Monro, Manse of Campsie. It has been remarked of the Hornes and Stevensons that both families evidently belonged to the tribe of Levi, as they found their vocation in the Church. A Mr. Stevenson of Boghead had three daughters who married three farmers, Horne, Ferrie, and Black, all of whom had sons who entered the Church. The first was Robert Horne, Braes o' Yetts (father of James Horne, New Mill), whose son David became minister of Corstorphine, whose son Robert succeeded him. He resigned owing to ill health, when Dr. Dodds, the present incumbent, succeeded. Ferrie's son (Gartclash) was Dr. Wm. Ferrie, professor of Civil History in the University of St. Andrews. Black's son (Kenmuir) was Dr. William Black of the Barony. George Horne, son of the Braes o' Yetts farmer, Cumbernauld, had two sons in the Church, one in Slamannan, the other at Port-Glasgow. Two cousins, Stevenson, were tenants of the Shields. John went to Craigend, afterwards to Netherinch. His son was Moderator of the Church of Scotland in 1871. His son became a minister, and, after being assistant to Dr. Mathieson, was lately ordained to Athel-staneford. Dr. Stevenson's successor in St. George's, Edinburgh, was Dr. Scott, a son of the tenant of Bogton, whose mother was a Brown of Balcorrach. William Stevenson, after separating from his cousin at Shields, took Alton, afterwards removing to Birdston, leaving his second son William as tenant in Alton. He had six sons, four of whom became ministers, and two farmers. After an exhibition in the Glasgow Presbytery, a leading Glasgow minister said of Lapslie, "The minister of Campsie should be tied in the pulpit and fed there with milk and brose meal over the side of it. He is a good man in the pulpit and a fool out of it."

CAMPSIE RE-UNIONS IN GLASGOW.

The Campsie Re-union in 1875 was presided over by Mr. Alex. Galloway, and the other speaker was the Rev. William Wood. In 1876 I had the honour of presiding, and the other speaker was the Rev. W. F. Stevenson of Rutherglen. The following year the chairman was James King, Esq., then Lord Dean of Guild of Glasgow, when the speakers were the Rev. Dr. Macleod of Park Church and the Rev. Dr. Monro. When I again presided, in 1885, I had a note from Mr. Jas. M'Lay, now of Bird & M'Lay, C.A., Glasgow, in which he said:—" It would oblige me much if in the course of your remarks as chairman you would urge upon the audience, and especially the Re-union committee, the necessity of taking up the dormant Benevolent Association. At present there is in Bank a sum of £54, and I should like much to see this sum increased to £100, the interest of which would help some indigent Campsonian. My own time is too much occupied to give the Benevolent Association any attention, but I shall be very pleased if some others can be got to do so."

A Glasgow Benevolent Association of Campsonians had been previously formed and office-bearers appointed. Mr. John Duff, 131 Annfield Street, was president; John Wotherspoon, 112 Parson Street, vice-president. Peter Connell, 272 Dalmarnock Road; William Hume, 295 Nuneaton Street; Andrew Faulds, 7 Grovebank Place; William Cooper, 25 Meuse Lane, Renfield Street; and T. Forrester, 178 Castle Street, St. Rollox, were directors. Mr. William Houston, 221 Gallowgate, was treasurer; and Mr. James M'Lay, 5 Grafton Square, was secretary. The following is the preface to the rules :—

" Considering the great number and steady increase of Campsie people in Glasgow, and that notwithstanding the numerous Charitable Institutions in the city there exists none at present of a local nature, where Campsonians in distress may lodge special claims to relief, and that cases frequently occur where no proper fund exists to alleviate the suffering; it is therefore resolved (by the Committee for the eighth Annual Re-Union of the Natives of Campsie in and around Glasgow), to form a Benevolent Association for behoof of honest and industrious but necessitous persons having connection with or interest in the parish, by nativity or adoption. The *chief* object of the Association, therefore, is to deal with exigent cases of distress arising from accident, disease, bereavement, or old age. The Association is further intended to serve as a medium to moral and social advancement, and to stablish or strengthen an agreeable disposition of brotherly unanimity, by instilling or fostering reciprocal feelings of regard among the members, and the maintaining of vivid and lively recollections of the companions, scenes, and associations connected with the parish and the past."

The re-unions have been discontinued for some years, although those I have seen were well attended. What has become of the Benevolent Association? It is a pity that it should be allowed to drop.

THE DESIGNATION "OF CAMPSIE."

I was not present at the Campsie Re-union in 1877, when Mr. (now Sir) James King presided. In some way a discussion had arisen over the words, "of Campsie," which generally followed the name of the chairman of that evening, and the Rev. Dr. Monro referred to this in the course of his soiree speech. Dr. Monro was essentially a courtier, and he referred to the chairman as "the proprietor of the barony of Campsie," and, as such, entitled to assume the very comprehensive title "of Campsie." From papers which have come under my notice subsequently I see that Dr. Monro's dictum has been called in question. I shall endeavour now to state the facts of the case. The lands of Torphin, Muckcroft, &c., were once portions of the estate of the Lairds of Woodhead. When the Laird had been almost ruined, owing to his have joined Montrose in the civil wars, he had recourse to borrowing. He obtained first a loan on Balglas, and then parted with this outright to Adam Cunningham of Boquhan, near Killearn. He borrowed money from Sir James Livingstone, in security for which he gave a wadset bond over his lands of Bencloich, part of Easter and Wester Muckra, Baldow, Carrower, Tamfin, Tambuy, &c. Being unable to redeem this bond within the prescribed time of twelve years, Sir James Livingstone became proprietor. Shortly before his death Sir James purchased from the Duke of Lennox, who had now possession of all the rights of the Earls of Lennox of the old line, the superiority of a great part of the lands in Campsie, which had come into the Darnley family and the Crown, after the death of Earl Duncan's daughter, Duchess of Albany and Countess of Lennox. In this purchase even the superiority of Balcorrach was included. Sir James also acquired part of the Antermony lands, viz., Inchbelly, Inchbreak, and Auchinririe, from Fleming of Wadilee, who had recently got these from the Laird of Kincaid, in whose family they had been since 1444. Sir James having obtained possession of the Woodhead Laird's lands of Bencloich, &c., which he had been in the occupation of for twelve years as security only, and having become superior of these lands and the portion of the Antermony lands, he got them erected into a Barony of Campsie, as distinguished from his Kilsyth lands, which formed the East and West Barony of Kilsyth. The original charter from the Crown in the time of Charles II., erecting the lands into a Barony of Campsie describes in the following manner the lands thus embraced :—

"All and haill the lands of Bencloich and Mains of the same, Over and Nether Colsay, with cottages, outsets, and pertinents thereunto belonging, the lands of Easter and Wester and Little Mockcrofts, Tamfin, Baldow, Carrower, Tambuy, with the privilege of Bancloich Mill, lands, multures, and sequels of the same, united and incorporated into a whole and free barony, called the Barony of Campsie, ordaining the place and tower of Bancloich to be the principal messuage of the said barony, and a sasine to be taken at said place, tower, or messuage of Bancloich to be a sufficient service for the whole said barony."

Sir James Livingstone was raised to the peerage shortly after the restoration of Charles II., as Viscount Kilsyth and Baron Campsie. He died in 1661. Viscount Kilsyth having "gone out" in 1715 had his estates forfeited for rebellion, and the superiority reverted to the Crown. By charter dated 29th November, 1716, the Crown bestowed the superiority on William Lennox of Balcorrach and Woodhead. The Campsie estates of Lord Kilsyth were afterwards acquired by the York Buildings Company, who sold them in 1784 to Sir Archibald Edmonstone of Duntreath. In 1834 Sir Archibald's grandson, also a Sir Archibald, sold the lands of Torphin and a small part of Bencloich to Mr. Charles Macintosh, of Crossbasket and Alum Works. The remainder of the estate was sold by Sir Archibald to Captain M'Farlane of Luggiebank, Kirkintilloch, whose trustees sold it to Sir Charles Stirling, Bart., of Glorat. Mr. Mackintosh's son, General Mackintosh, in 1856 sold his portion of Livingstone's forfeited estate to * Mr. John King of the Alum Company. The old barony having thus been broken up and some of the rights of superiority having reverted to the Crown, the question has arisen who is entitled to claim the designation, "of Campsie." I believe it is a rule in law that the owner of the major part of an estate is the custodier of the principal title deeds and is to be regarded as the chief of those who have acquired portions of the estate. But Livingstone's lands were but a small portion of Campsie, and were only a portion of the Woodhead estate. None of the old landed families who have held their lands for centuries ever assumed the designation, "of Campsie." If in virtue of their having been formed into a barony, and if the proprietor of Torfin has the larger portion of the old barony, he may technically have the right to assume the "of Campsie," notwithstanding that the charter ordained the place and tower of Bancloich to be the "principal messuage of the said barony." But it should also be remembered that the Earl of Lennox granted a charter of the "Castle and lands of Camsi" to his son Malcolm, and that the Stirlings of Craigbarnet and Glorat are the lineal descendents of Malcolm. If anyone has a right to the designation one would fancy it would be those deriving their descent from the Earl's son upon whom the lands and castle were originally bestowed. The proprietor of Ballagan, where the original castle of Camsi was situated, might have some claim, unless the right was conferred subsequently in some of Livingstone's charters and not forfeited by his rebellion.

* In 1869 Mr. King registered as armorial bearings :—Az. on a fess ar. betw. a lion's head erased in chief and two billets in base ; or., three round buckles of the field ; crest, a dexter hand prpr. ; motto, *Honos industriæ præmium.*

GREAT PUBLIC DEMONSTRATIONS.

In my lecture on " Calico Printing in Campsie," published last year, at page 16, I referred to one of the great popular demonstrations at Glasgow in favour of reform. The Lennoxtown people had among their leaders only one of the local landed proprietors, Mr. John M'Farlan of Ballancleroch, but Mr. Alexander Fraser, Mr. James M'Pherson, and others were the moving spirits, and they had their full share of the political meetings, gatherings, and commotions of that exciting period, when the country was on the eve of civil war, when dragoons were held in readiness to act promptly if any symptoms of revolution appeared; but the "people quietly took an attitude whose resolute meaning could not be mistaken."

One great local gathering assembled in the middle of the village to march across the muir to Fintry to take part in a great demonstration in which contingents were to meet from all parts of the county of Stirling, and at which Admiral Fleming and Captain Speirs of Culcreuch gave addresses. Fraser and M'Pherson from Campsie, when called on to speak, gave very telling speeches. The Campsie contingent had arranged to be accompanied by a brass band, but while the processionists were assembling a lot of strolling players, exhibiting mechanical figures or marionettes, paraded back and forward through the Main Street and proved a counter excitement to the procession. The players decided to attend the political demonstration, and headed the march across the muir to the appointed place of muster. The strolling bandsmen were experienced players, and fairly eclipsed the Campsie band by the excellence of the music they discoursed.

The Anti-Corn-Law League was originated in 1837 at a public dinner in Manchester. Two great reformers came prominently before the public agitating for free trade in bread. These were Richard Cobden and John Bright. The failure of the potato crop in Ireland in 1845 brought matters to a crisis and the Corn Laws were abolished the following year. This was made the occasion of great public rejoicing and accordingly the Lennoxtown people organised a demonstration, which took the form of a great procession, in the summer of 1846. With many banners displayed, and with a large loaf borne aloft on a pole, emblematic of the cheap bread which the abolition of the Corn Laws was expected to produce, they marched to the Clachan, and round Ballancleroch House, as a compliment to John M'Farlan, or " Old Kirkton," as he was then affectionately called. When we think now of the low wages and dear bread which the labouring classes had to put up with previous to this time we almost wonder how they could live and bring up their families.

The close of the war with Russia was celebrated by a great public gathering in the early summer of 1856. This again took the form of a procession to the Clachan and Ballancleroch, returning to the Field Park, where the day's performances were finished up with games and races.

A welcome-home reception to Major Graham Stirling of Craigbarnet, on his safe return from the Crimea, was the next occasion which caused a public demonstration. This took place on the 23rd August, 1856. Charles Campbell Graham, the heir-presumptive to the Craigbarnet estates under the entail,* in the event of Alex. Gartshore Stirling having no issue, entered the army in 1844, joining the 42nd Royal Highlanders. He had served in various parts of the world, including Malta, Bermuda, and Nova Scotia. The regiment was stationed at Portsea when it received orders to embark for the Eastern expedition. It sailed 21st May, 1854, and disembarked at Scutari 9th June. At the battle of Alma it formed the right wing of the Highland Brigade, the other regiments being the 79th and the 93rd. At this battle the regiment was thus addressed by Sir Colin Campbell—"Now, men, the army will watch us; make me proud of the Highland Brigade." He then gave the order, "Forward, Forty-Second." All through the trying period of the Crimean war the 42nd bore its full share of the trials, privations, and sickness endured in the camp and trenches before Sebastopol. This was shown by the fact of the command of the regiment having devolved on Major Graham Stirling when the final assault was made. For his gallantry on this occasion he was made Brevet-Major. The Major received the Crimean medal and clasp, the Turkish medal and Order of the Medjidie. At the conclusion of the war, having succeeded to the estates on the death of Mr. A. G. Stirling in 1852, and having assumed the surname of Stirling under the entail, he retired from the army on 1st May, 1857, and on his return to Campsie received a most enthusiastic reception from all classes in the parish. The local congratulations were on his accession to the estates, and also an expression of the satisfaction felt by the people of Campsie at his safe return from the war. His arrival was announced by a salute of 18 guns. Two bands were present— one played, "See the conquering hero comes," the other, "Welcome,

* Mungo Stirling, tenth of Craigbarnet, married Marjory Stirling, his cousin, daughter of Sir George, the first baronet of Glorat. Their only surviving son was James Stirling, the famous " Burry " who was " out " in 1715 and 1745. Their daughter Mary married George Graham in Shannochhill, a cadet of the Grahams of Airth, and great-grandfather of Charles Campbell Graham Stirling, the present laird. He is the only son of John Graham, who was second son of Robert Graham Burden, of Feddal, in Perthshire. The eldest son, Robert Graham, was for some time in the navy, and on the death of his father succeeded to Feddal. John Stirling, the twelfth laird of Craigbarnet, in 1799 executed an entail on which, after the heirs of his own body, he called to the succession the heirs of the body of his sister, Charlotte Stirling, and James Gartshore, her husband, whom failing, the heirs of the body of Robert Graham Burden of Feddal. Under this substitution the present laird has succeeded.

Royal Charlie." A beautiful floral arch was erected at the head of the Field Road, and another at the junction of the Craigbarnet and Ballancleroch estates. Craigbarnet House was beautifully decorated, with " Welcome, Thrice Welcome Home," above the door. Marching alongside his carriage was an escort of Campsie men who had served under him in the Crimea. I can now only recollect the names of Alexander Hosie, who had been wounded in the throat, and Muirhead the slater, generally called " The Slasher." An address of welcome and congratulation from the workers of Lennoxmill was read by George Norval, the foreman in the finished warehouse. The following was then read by one present :—

> Awake, ye proud sons of the heath-covered mountains,
> And welcome, thrice welcome, Brevet Major Graham.
> Come forth, let us meet him wi' pibroch's loud chanting
> His welcome return to the braes o' Strathblane.
>
> For brave did he march o'er the red field of danger,
> Where vengeance did fly on her dark crimson car,
> But ne'er did he flinch from the blood-thirsty stranger,
> Till peace was proclaimed in the land of the Czar.
>
> May glory attend him, and honour still crown him,
> And aye tae Auld Scotia and Colin prove true.
> May heaven still award him, where justice invites him
> To fight for his Queen 'mang the bonnets o' blue.

The Major replied in a brief, soldier-like speech, and three cheers were then given for the Major, for Mrs. Gartshore Stirling of Craigbarnet, for Sir Colin and the Highland Brigade. The procession was then formed four deep and marched back, every one intensely gratified at the manner in which the proceedings had gone off.

A public reception of Mr. Robert Dalglish in 1857, after his election to represent the City of Glasgow in Parliament, was the next occasion of a great public gathering. By arrangement, Mr Dalglish drove out from Glasgow, and was met between Muckcroft and Kinkell by the workers in Lennoxmill, headed by the manager and the foremen. He came out of his carriage and walked at the head of the procession. The brass band led the way, and the company marched through Lennoxtown to the Field Park where a platform had been erected. Here a congratulatory address from the workers was presented to Mr. Dalglish, which, after referring to the great interest his father had always taken, and the many good deeds he had done for Campsie, referred to Mr. Dalglish's own services to his people. This was read by Thomas Young, engraver, and Mr. Dalglish made a long speech in reply, thanking them for their good wishes and for the enthusiastic reception they had given him. He stated that in leaving to attend to his Parliamentary duties in London he had every confidence in leaving the management of the work in the capable hands of Mr. Gordon Wilson and those acting under him in charge of the various departments. When the proceedings in the Field Park were over the procession was reformed and marched westwards by Service Street. When clear of the village Mr. Dalglish entered his carriage and amid great cheering drove home to Kilmardinny by way of Strathblane.

These demonstrations I have attempted to describe briefly were almost entirely originated in Lennoxmill, where the details were worked out and all arrangements made, with great spirit and enthusiasm. For several weeks beforehand it was a busy time in Lennoxmill, where the employees were permitted to work at this on their own time in meal hours, or after work hours in the evening. On such occasions, and especially so in the reception of Mr. Dalglish, great numbers were actively engaged designing the devices of the various departments, printing or drawing them on the banners. There was one emblematic of the wright shop that had the merits of novelty of design and artistic effect. The motto was cut out of thin deal wood; so was the name of the handicraft whose emblem it was. This was hung round by festoons of long curled wood shavings, arranged most skilfully, and was much admired. Another flag showed Mr. Dalglish in a railway carriage, just starting for London. He was looking out of the window, waving his hand in token of farewell, while above was displayed in large letters, "Hurrah for St. Stephen's."

The other public reception that I can recall was the one in 1862, on the occasion of the home-coming of the Hon. Mr. and Mrs. Hanbury Lennox after their marriage. The newly-married couple were met at the railway station by the two local corps of rifle volunteers, with the brass band, a great many local gentry in carriages, the tenantry on the estate, many of whom were on horseback to form a mounted escort, and a great multitude of wellwishers. On emerging from the station they were received with a general salute, the band playing "The last Rose of Summer." Miss Annette Campbell then advanced and presented a beautiful bouquet from the school children. The crowd cheered heartily. A procession was then formed, and accompanied Mr. and Mrs. Lennox to the Castle, where refreshments were liberally provided to the tenantry, volunteers, &c.

The three public receptions accorded so spontaneously and enthusiastically were quite unique in their way. Nothing like them has occurred in Campsie since. The only occurrence that resembles them was the presentation to the Rev. Dr. Thomas Monro of a testimonial consisting of a silver salver, a timepiece, a musical box, several other valuable articles, and a purse of 300 guineas, the contributions of over 1200 subscribers. This meeting was held in the Town Hall about 1872, and was presided over by Sir Charles Stirling of Glorat, who, in presenting the testimonial, assured Dr. Monro that by it they wished to show the appreciation they felt for his faithful services to them, as pastor, friend, and adviser during the past 28 years. Dr. Monro, in replying, said this meeting was a great era in his life, a white stone in his existence, a joyful landmark in the afternoon, or perhaps he should say the evening, of his pilgrimage.

At a conversazione of the United Presbyterian Church, held in the Town Hall a few years ago, there was rather a novel exhibition among the objects of interest exhibited in the hall. This was a display of memorials of former ministers of the church. "The Unity of the Church," containing a reply to the Rev. James Lapslie, by Mr. Colquhoun, the first minister. There were portraits of Dr. Thomson, Mr. James Brown, and Mr. William Wood, the second, third, and fourth ministers. Mr. Davidson concluded his speech by observing that they saw before them a true and faithful likeness of their present minister in his own person. In the course of some remarks by Mr. John Barr, one of the elders, he said he remembered the time when he first came to Campsie, that even a soiree in those days was looked upon as a kind of innovation, and now the conversazione was an innovation on the soiree.

LIGHTING.

I can recollect when the illuminants were tallow candles and lamps in which "train" oil was burned; wax candles were rarely used, or only on great occasions. The properties of coal gas had been long known before it occurred to Mr. Murdoch, an engineer, to store the gas in a gasometer and use it for lighting purposes. Murdoch's first gasometer was fitted up in 1792. In 1798 he fitted up gas in Boulton & Watt's Soho Works, Birmingham. The front of these works was very brilliantly lighted up in 1802, and the effect produced quite a sensation throughout the country. After this the use of gas rapidly spread, in the manufacturing towns first, then in London. Gas was introduced into Lennoxmill about the year 1828-29. It was not till 1852 that it was adopted in Lennoxtown. A joint stock company was formed in that year, the original promoters of which were chiefly Messrs. James Bishop, banker; Gordon Wilson; Robert Clarke, Alum Works; and the Rev. William Wood. Neil M'Callum was the first secretary; Mr. Bishop was, I think, treasurer. When Mr. M'Callum left Lennoxtown, Mr. William White, banker, was appointed secretary and treasurer, the duties of which offices he has performed now for many years to the entire satisfaction of the shareholders. Mr. Gordon Wilson has been chairman of the company for upwards of twenty years. The company were exceedingly fortunate in many respects. Iron was then very cheap, and wages were low. For instance, the wages for mason work and excavations were at the rate of—masons, 18s to 20s per week; labourers, 11s and 12s per week. Had the works been erected a few years later they would have cost a great deal more, both for pipes and labour. The first site thought of for the gas works was the field between the U. P. Church and the Glazert, but the managers of the church objected; they thought there would be disagreeable smells and other drawbacks, so the present site was then chosen. Matthew Blair was the first manager, but he did not remain long. He was succeeded by James Inglis, who filled the situation with great satisfaction to all concerned for about 30 years. The company has been prudently managed, the works have increased in value, and as yet always paid a good dividend. Shortly after its introduction into the village, there being no legal power of assessing for lighting, a voluntary association was formed for lighting the streets. Lamp pillars were erected, and a wonderful improvement was effected by these lamps during the dark nights of winter. The use of gas was at one time almost universal. It is very likely it will be subjected to the competition of the excellent illuminating paraffin oils which afford now such brilliant light at small cost. Gas made from oil has been introduced into some of the mansion houses and larger villas, and this gives brilliant results.

WATER SUPPLY.

Lennoxtown used to be supplied with water from various sources—Crosshill had Craig's burn; the Main Street and streets abutting near Field Road had the Spout; further east there were the "Clash" well at Birbieston, and the famous "Baker Broon's well," while there were other private and less publicly known sources of supply. From these water for domestic purposes was carried in wooden stoups. In course of time it was proposed to have a supply by gravitation, and the agitation for this having convinced the Local Authority of its utility, they proceeded to have a water district formed. Over this a keen contest raged, mainly on the question of the boundaries—who were to be included and who excluded?—because, in the latter case, those denied the advantages were free from assessment. At first the Local Authority turned to the Glorat estate as the likeliest source of supply. Obstacles came in the way of prosecuting this scheme, and, after discussion, the Bencloich scheme was finally abandoned on the Local Authority becoming aware of others having prior claims on the water. After a lull the question was again raised. Various other sources of supply were mentioned and examined, such as the Shields burn, the Cress well on the North hill, and the Katie Crystal spring on the South brae, above the targets and lime works. All these having been considered, were set aside in favour of a scheme for taking a supply from the Glen or Clachan burn away up near Auldwick Bridge. An analysis of the water by Dr. Stevenson Macadam was considered very satisfactory. The supply was abundant, at a high level which permitted the formation of a storeage reservoir at a lower level, yet sufficiently high to give pressure over the whole of the water district. The land for this reservoir was acquired at a cost of £110, Mrs. Hanbury Lennox giving the supply of water free. The preliminaries having been arranged, the water works were formed at a total cost of £2900, which included preliminary expenses in some of the other schemes. Mrs. Hanbury Lennox was invited to turn on the water and thus formally open the works. This was done on 4th October, 1884. The Lennoxtown people assembled on the Field Park and marched in procession up to the reservoir. Here the engineer presented a silver key to Mrs. Lennox, who then turned on the water, after which the procession was re-formed and marched to a platform in front of the Town Hall, where the Campsie Horticultural Sciety presented Mrs. Lennox with a beautiful bouquet of choice flowers, and the contractor gave a silver cup. The Rev. John Duke opened the proceedings by asking the company to unite in singing Psalm C. He then engaged in prayer, after which speeches were delivered by the Chairman of the Local Authority, the Hon. Mr. Hanbury Lennox, Col. M'Farlan of Ballancleroch, and others. The supply has been a great success. Before the charge of the water supply was taken over by the County Council the rate of assessment by the Local Authority was only twopence per pound, which made it one of the cheapest as well as one of the best supplies in Scotland.

MUCKCROFT BRIDGE.

The road from Lennoxtown to Glasgow via Kinkell and Balquharrage was at one time a statute labour road. There was then no bridge over the Glazert at Muckcroft and when the Glazert was in flood there was no passage. An Act of Parliament made it a turnpike and enabled the Road Trustees to borrow money to build the bridge. It was built very shortly before the Relief Church, as the grandfather of the late Mr. Stevenson of Alton was the mason, and he had very shortly completed the bridge when he got the erection of the Relief Church. Some accident happened when just being completed. There was a sudden call to the workmen to "clear the brig," when a portion fell into the water. One tradition is that the seven brothers whose nameless graves are in the Clachan kirkyard were killed by its fall. This I do not think was the case.

THE LATE JAMES M. NEILSON.

On glancing over "Poems and Songs, chiefly in the Scottish Language," by James M. Neilson, a native of Campsie, I see a poem which will bring many recollections to Campsonian boys and girls, and recalls M'Namee, whose "bull's eyes" were considered then as something that could not be surpassed. The poem includes the following :—

> "It's as sure as the pay day comes, there comes the man
> Wi' his bull's eyes an' candy in sticks a lang span;
> An' as sune as the schule skails oor Willie skelters hame
> For his bawbee, on whilk he has surely a claim,—

For he's oot in the mornin's, an' a' the street redds
O' the kye an' horse drappin's for oor ingin beds ;
An' ye'd think that his faither had hooses an' lan',
As he struts proodly back tae the candyman's stan'.

Gin his mither aye settles wi' Rab in the store
For oor tauties an' meal, she gets sweeties galore ;
An' she's fain tae get Will tae buy oot o' her pock,
But he kens he aye gets them, Will's no' sic a gowk.
At the schule he's in coontin', an' writin' an' a',
Fills a copy a week, an' whiles three in the twa ;
But I doot it's no dune for improvin' his haun—
For auld copies are ta'en at the candy-man's stan'."

Mr. Neilson contributed a number of very interesting articles
to the *Glasgow Weekly Herald* on "The Auld Kirk at the
Clachan," &c. He died at Thornliebank at a comparatively
early age. I have cut out of the *Glasgow Weekly Herald* of 7th
July, 1888, an "In Memoriam" poem, signed "Caviare," and
I now quote the first and last stanzas of it, as follows :—

" Oh, friend, whose homely singing woke
    The first crude impulse of my pen
To imitate thy muse, that spoke
    Of simple themes to simple men.
Oh, genuine poet, thy pure soul,
    Burning with passionate love of song,
Chafed at the forces that control
    Life's fitful fever, and prolong
The weary routine and the strife
That warps a humble poet's life.

" Yet not in vain you lived awhile
    To die ere thou did'st reach thy prime ;
For still thy pleasing strains beguile,
    And linger o'er the fields of rhyme.
We weave a garland for thy lyre,
    Whose echoes softly sound again,
Imbued with the poetic fire
    That stirs the hearts of honest men—
And cheers the humble cottage hearth
With simple song and artless mirth."

THE BRASS BAND.

In these papers I have had occasion to mention the band
several times. A short notice of it may not be uninteresting. I
can recollect the starting of the band in 1850, and the praise-
worthy assiduity with which the members in meal hours and
evenings practised on their instruments, and the discordant sounds
they at first drew out of them. When they assembled for practice
in Miss Sloss's school I was sometimes there with my school-
fellows to listen, and I remember how pleased everyone was when
at length they ventured to march out, playing a few simple
melodies, quadrilles, &c. Mr. Edward B. Connor, a most
enthusiastic musician, was conductor and teacher, and he really
deserved the utmost credit for the rapid progress the bandsmen

made under his tuition. It occurred to me to call on Mr. Connor, at 12 Scotia Street, Glasgow, and get, if possible, a few particulars. Although I had not seen Mr. Connor, as far as I could recollect, since I left Lennoxtown in 1864, I knew him at once, and he was very pleased to see me. Apropos of the lecture on "Calico Printing," he said that although of a Milton family and in Kincaid field as boy and man till 1850, he had never rightly understood the history of it till he had read it there. He told me he recollected the first Campsie band, to which I had referred at page 31, as starring through the country at the time of the strike. His family were "Auld Lichts," and went to church at Kirkintilloch, but he remembers coming to the new Parish Church to hear Cuddie's choir, and the delight their singing afforded him; such singing opened a new world to him. He came to Lennoxmill in 1850.

When the movement to get up a brass band was started in 1850 it was favourably received by the public, who subscribed the funds to purchase the instruments, and the object aimed at was speedily accomplished. A reed band, numbering about 16 performers, was enrolled. Most of these were quite ignorant of music or instrumentation. Some did not want to be "fashed" or take much trouble to acquire the necessary training. At the end of the first three months, therefore, there were a number of resignations and changes. The members who then settled steadily to practice were:—4 clarionets, James Shand, James Stirling, John Hume, and Robert Taylor; flute, William Kincaid; cornet, George Dinwoodie and John Shields; French horns, William Morrison and Peter Blair; trumpet, Thomas Stones; ophicleide, M. Johnstone; trombones, W. M'Gilchrist and David Ross; big drum, James Purdon, &c.; drummers, triangle, &c. The first public appearance was at a concert on Campsie Fair Night, 1850, to raise funds for the right-of-way case over the old road to the Clachan. They also turned out to a Masonic torch-light procession in December, 1850. At this there was some unpleasantness, the band complaining about the quantity of refreshments. When the Freemasons next wished a band to accompany them to the laying of the foundation stone of the new bridge at the bottom of Stockwell Street, Glasgow, in 1851, they could not agree as to terms. The band were willing to play gratuitously if they were paid their day's wages. Rather than agree to this the Freemasons engaged the Kirkintilloch band and paid them more money. The band languished for want of public support. It was only taken out at long intervals, the funds got low, and it came to be disheartening work taking round the hat for subscriptions. Practice ceased about 1855, but by a great effort the old members were mustered to accompany the procession that was to meet Mr. Dalglish in 1857. This was the last time this band was out.

A new band was got up in 1857, the nucleus of this being formed of members of the now defunct reed band, but these, with

the exceptions of Dunwoodie' and Archie Wilson, did not remain
very long in it. The new band was of brass instruments only,
there were no reeds as in the last one. George Dunwoodie was
elected 1st E flat cornetta. Archie Wilson, a drummer in the old
band, got a cornet, and was ultimately solo cornet, a position he
was eminently qualified for. A number of willing and intelligent
members left the existing flute band and joined the brass band,
which caused a little ill feeling at the time. Mr. Conner was
asked to undertake the training, but he was at first most reluctant
to do so. The people in Lennoxtown were waking up to the importance of the culture of music in the family circle, and
pianos were becoming very common, and harmoniums were also
being introduced. Mr. Conner had formed a large connection
in private teaching of music. However, he was prevailed on to
give it a trial, and he soon ascertained that the members now
forming the band were of the right metal to make into a splendid
band.

In 1858, Mr. Dalglish invited his foremen in Lennoxmill and
a few others to an entertainment in the Crown Inn, Clachan, as a
return for their magnificent demonstration the previous year.
Mr. Gordon Wilson had always evinced a kindly interest in the
band, but had never shown any marked encouragement. It now
occurred to him to invite the band to play during the feast, and
they acquitted themselves so well that Mr. Conner was sent for
to come into the supper room, where he was highly complimented
on the efficiency of his pupils. Mr. Dalglish and Mr. Wilson
were both agreeably surprised, and the fate of the band as an
institution was at once secured. During the course of this evening, Mr. Begg, then factor on the Lennox estates, suggested to
Mr. Dalglish the desirability of raising a yeomanry cavalry
corps (he pronounced this corpse). The M.P., with great gravity
of mien, but with a merry twinkle in his eye, replied that for his
part he would prefer an infantry *corps* to a cavalry *corpse*. An
entertainer's little jokes are always well received, this one caused
tremendous hilarity. The band diligently went on with their
training, and when next year the volunteer movement overspread
the land a Lennoxmill corps was got up of 80 members, and the
band, consisting of 20, were incorporated with the volunteer corps.
The band was now established on a safer basis and set before it
the systematic study of music. Not content with the mere
average ability of a country band, such as playing marches or easy
dance music, Mr. Conner in 1859 had the overture to Guy
Mannering arranged for them. This was followed by selections
from the operas and choruses from the oratorios of the great
masters.

It was very cheering to the Conductor that when he called on
them for an effort, in preparing for a special occasion, the members would steadily practise for four or five nights a week without
a murmur, and never grudged the time required to keep them-

selves in good form. In a short time they had acquired a degree of proficiency they themselves never suspected. This was discovered unexpectedly in 1861, when they played at a Band Ridotto in Dumbarton, where some of the best volunteer bands of the West of Scotland were present. The bands of the 76th regiment and of H.M. guardship, then lying at the Tail of the Bank, were also present. They had travelled down from Glasgow in the same train with the band of the 76th, who rather affected to look down on a mere country band, what notice they did take was the reverse of complimentary, but a wonderful change came over them afterwards. The 76th played Masaniello. Campsie played Stradella, when they had finished their overture they were simply mobbed by the generous and appreciative bandsmen of the 76th and other rivals. Where did you get that overture? Your piano passages were magnificent! Invitations were showered on them to allow themselves to be treated to a glass of ale, &c. Mr. Conner however held his highly gratified men well in hand. He thanked those who wished to treat them, but they had another piece to play, and "business before pleasure, gentlemen." He said if their *piano* bits were so well played as to merit their approbation, there was little for them to fear in their *fortes*. Mr. Clark was there that day from the Vale of Leven, to choose the best band he could hear, for the Lochlomond Regatta on that day week. "Stradella" had settled that in their favour. When he offered them the engagement, they could not accept without previously asking and obtaining permission. " Whose permission?" Captain Wilson's, was the reply. Mr. Clark, "Oh, I'll make that all right, I know Mr. Wilson well," and it was made all right. It was said of the Campsie band that they were the only volunteer band that could play overture for overture with the army and navy bands. Mr. Conner had succeeded in infusing his own enthusiasm for music in his bandsmen, and they played *con amore.* The band was sometimes taken out to play at the Glasgow flower shows, and carried off a prize at a great competition at Perth.

I annex a list of the players, who in 1861 raised the reputation of the Campsie Brass Band so high in musical circles:—Cornets, G. Dunwoodie, A. Wilson, J. Herron, A. M'Intyre, J. Mulholland, G. Britton. M. Brown, and A. M'Sporran; trombones, E. M'Sporran and John James; bombardons, D. Gardner, Elphinstone Dalglish, and G. M'Kay; horns (various), M. Cameron, J. Stewart, and T. Shand; euphonian, E. B. Conner; drum, Tom Herron, afterwards Joe Brown; side-drum, H. Erskine. This band was occasionally asked to Lennox Castle to play during dinner, when there were distinguished visitors at the Castle. One day a party of the guests there were being shown through Lennoxmill. In passing through the machine-engraving shop the Hon. Mr. Hanbury Lennox recognised Mr. Conner, and came forward and spoke to him. The sight of him suggested the brass band, and Mr. Lennox mentioned that there was a large number of guests at the Castle.

"Why," said he, "that gentleman is the Duke of Leinster. This lady coming along is the Duchess of Montrose. I should be much obliged if your band would come up to-night and play your very best, for you will have a critical audience." When the Duchess of Montrose came to Mr. Conner's machine Mr. Lennox asked it to be stopped and the process explained to her Grace. This having been done Mr. Lennox mentioned that this was the conductor of the local brass band, which was to play to them that evening. The Duchess turned, looked at the machine-engraver, standing with his shirt-sleeves turned up and his white pinafore on, and showed unmistakeably that she did not look forward to much of a treat from the playing of the band. Her look and manner put Conner on his mettle; he made out his most attractive programme and called on the bandsmen to do their very best. The band never played better. Mr. Conner was extremely gratified when the Duchess of Montrose came up to him and said she had heard the best bands in London, but had never been more agreeably surprised and delighted than she had been that evening. From young men working hard at their daily work for ten hours a day, and only taking music up in their leisure, she could never have anticipated such proficiency in execution and such exquisite taste. She was very pleased to have the opportunity of telling him so.

Mr. Conner spoke very warmly in praise of Mr. Gordon Wilson, for many years the captain of the Lennoxmill corps. He said he proved a noble patron to the band. The amount of good he did in a quiet, unostentatious manner to the members individually and collectively was more than he could recapitulate. The history of the band after 1864 must fall into other hands than mine. I am sorry I have no particulars of the flute bands that existed for brief periods in Lennoxtown.

GAMES AND PASTIMES.

Forty years ago the games and amusements of boys were entirely different from those of the present day, when firstly cricket, and latterly football, have superseded almost entirely the old games. In my boyish days the handball was used in many ways. There were two kinds of ball, the tennis ball and the solid caoutchouc one. Some games were played against a wall, the ball being returned either before it touched the ground or in its first rebound. Another game was played by sides, who, when they got it to one end, claimed a "hail." "Rounders" and "house-ball" were favourite games. "Smugglers," or "smuggle the geg," was another favourite in the evenings. The "geg" was generally a penknife, and the outs had to get this to the "den," the "ins" capturing the smugglers; and when they caught the one having the "geg" they changed places. A favourite den was the high wall in front of John Allan's coal-ree,

where the Tea Rooms were built subsequently, near the head of
the Field Road. The den could be reached from front, rear, and
both flanks. Shinty was common. Boys looked carefully in the
hedges and woods for a bent branch suitable for their purpose ; in
other cases it was bent artificially. With an evenly-matched side,
a round, wooden knacket was started in the centre between the
goals, and each side tried to get it to their goal. It was a delightful game. Cricket was then only played at a single wicket,
a big stone generally serving as wicket. In its present form of
double wicket it was really introduced by a Mr. James Sowter, a
grocer, who was a great enthusiast in the game, and one of the
gentlest and most unassuming of men. Football was then the
" kickba'," and when played, which was not very frequently, was
a far more indiscriminate game than we are acquainted with now.
" Leap-frog, or "Foot-and-a-half," was a common game, played
both in the school playground and in the evenings. It continued
to be practised by lads long after they had left school. At the
New-Year there were formerly shooting raffles. A cheese or
some other prize was thus shot for with small shot, the winner
being the one who put the greatest number of pellets into a paper
mark. This custom appears also to have been discontinued.
There used to be a gathering in Mr. Taylor's school on New-
Year's Day, when a little present was given to Mrs. Hume, who
occupied the lodge at the end of the playground. This was a
sort of survival of what was usual in parts of the country where
the teacher got presents at Hansel Monday.

SNOWSTORMS.

Some very heavy falls of snow have taken place within living
memory. One of these snowstorms occurred in February, 1821,
and some individuals perished on Campsie Muir, having been
overtaken there while crossing, and having got bewildered and
lost their way. The snow on the roads between Lennoxtown and
Milton and Torrance was nearly level with the tops of the hedges.
There were then no snow ploughs, and the roads had to be cleared
by gangs of men, who were only provided with shovels, and whose
rate of progress was very slow. This fall was long of melting,
and very great hardships were experienced in many parts of the
parish that were situated any distance from the main roads.
These had been made passable, but it was almost impossible to
get coals, provisions, and farm produce conveyed to or from the
isolated farm houses or cottages. The roofs of Rowantreefauld
cottages were then lower than at present, and were literally a
tar-covered row, with four feet of snow on the flat roofs. The
row had the appearance of a long level ridge, and the
smoke of the concealed chimneys, rising out of the white expanse,
produced a very curious effect on the landscape.

FARMERS NINETY YEARS AGO.

The great changes that have taken place in the work of the farmers' households are illustrated by a comparison of then and now. The parish farmer then was a man of fair intelligence, of sturdy independence, who required to practise self-help in many things never dreamed of now. A Campsie farmer ninety years ago rarely if ever required to have recourse to butcher, baker, or draper. His own cattle, sheep, and pigs supplied the family requirements. The wool of his sheep—scoured, carded, and spun, dyed indigo blue and woven into cloth on the home loom, or by the local weaver—provided the outer garments for both men and women. Home-grown flax, cut, weathered, steeped for six weeks in the lint pond, then dried, heckled, brought back to the farm as lint or tow, was then spun into yarn, woven into cloth on hand-looms, bleached in the open-air for weeks, with frequent waterings, until it became as white as snow. Then under-garments for both sexes and mutches for the women were made from this, and the shroud for the inevitable end of all. The farmer's household was the scene of unceasing industry, of constant occupation. It is difficult for us of the present day, with everything made ready to our hands, to realise how they managed then to get along so well without the many aids which we enjoy.

A CONTRAST : 1798—1874.

I have seen somewhere a contrast of farmers in 1798 and 1874, which had reference to the East of Scotland :—

1798.

Farmer haudin' the plough,
Wife milkin' the coo,
Sons thrashing in the barn,
Dochters thrang spinnin' yarn ;
Ilk ane busy ; a' happy ;
The farm clear.

1874.

Farmer goes to Cattle Show,
His lady plays the piano ;
Sons at college studying Latin,
Daughters at home dressed in satin,
Style, carriage, hunting, coursing ;
The farm bonded.

THE CLOCHCORE PLOUGHMAN AND THE WISE MARE MAGGIE.

Then, as now, when a new tenant entered on the occupation of his farm, his neighbours all round, on a set day, sent ploughs, horses, and men, and gave him a day's ploughing. On the Baldernock side of the South Hill there was a great turn-out, and after the day's work was over the ploughmen and neighbours were hospitably entertained. A contingent had been there from Clochcore Farm, and as Bob the ploughman was riding home across Clochcore Moor, his legs lost all power of grip, and he was unable to keep his seat on the horse's back. He fell off softly and lay helpless. He was sufficiently conscious to observe the mare Maggie, who was greatly distressed on his account. She walked round and round him, put the chains as near his hand as she could, wishing him to catch hold, and she would lift him. Bob could just understand her good intentions, but was powerless to avail himself of her aid. When Maggie realised this she set off for human help. The farmer's household had meantime got uneasy, as it was now getting late, and many anxious looks had been directed across the moor. Then Maggie was seen coming briskly, but all alone. She would not enter her stable, but went to the house place, and whinnied again and again, and then made for going back to the moor again. The household were called out, and she was promptly followed. She led them to Bob lying helplessly drunk. He was then taken home, and when he sobered he was able to tell how wisely the animal had acted, and had in all probability saved his life.

A CHRISTENING PARTY LOSE THE BABY.

On the same South Hill, about a mile to the eastward of Clochcore Farm, stood then a small cothouse called Braehead. It was situated just above Baldow, a little west of the lime works. It was inhabited by Rabbie Baird, better known as Whey. He was one of four brothers, all of whom were well known in the parish. All of them had very limited vocabularies. All of them had phrases constantly on their lips which gave them their nicknames. Rabbie began his sentences with " Why," which he pronounced " Whey ; " hence his name. With Tam, everything he saw or heard was " a dainty bit," so he was dubbed " Dainty ; " Jock was " Forrit bye ; " Jammack was " Muchty," from his " sprosing " sometimes that he had two or three guid Muchties left yet of some paper currency or securities connected with Auchtermuchty. Rab, or " Whey," and his wife had taken their child to the Clachan church for baptism. The rite was duly performed, and after the kirk had skailed a number of relatives and friends were making kindly inquiries after the mother and child. The party turned into a field, where they sat down to have some refreshment before starting homewards. Eatables and drinkables having had justice done to them, the Braehead party started homewards, all very jolly. When they reached home, and were asked where the wean was, they were obliged to make the humiliating confession that they must have lost it on the road, and that they had forgotten all about it. Maternal instincts were now aroused, and caused the despatch of a search party, who discovered the baby lying in the field, where it had been deposited when the eating and drinking was commenced. If anyone wanted to have their little joke with a young anxious mother taking her first baby out to church, they advised her to be careful and not lose the wean on the road home.

In bringing this paper to a close I realise how many subjects have had to be omitted altogether, owing to my incomplete information, and I cannot help expressing my regret that so many of the old local traditions, legends, superstitious observances, freits, and obsolete usages should have been allowed to pass away without any effort having hitherto been made to preserve some record of them. Within my own recollection there has been a goodly number of very intelligent men, with retentive memories and quick observation, who had acquired a minute acquaintance with parish history, whose minds were stored with local knowledge of the best kind, obtained from older parishioners or the results of their own experience or observation. When coming into personal contact with some of these men, I see now that I had many opportunities of acquiring facts and obtaining information, but I was then too careless or indifferent or busy to give what I heard much attention, or make any note of it at the time. I also see where I could have obtained much local lore from individuals who would have been delighted to impart it, but who are now dead. I have myself, when a boy, listened spell-bound to the wonderful stories, which dealt with topics that I rarely hear referred to now. They dealt greatly in the supernatural, in apparitions from the other world, friends making solemn compacts that whoever died first should pay a visit to the survivor; sights, such as Hugh Miller describes, when as a boy, on his father being lost at sea, he saw at the open door, within a yard of his breast, as plainly as ever he saw anything, a dissevered hand and arm stretched towards him *; and as Mungo Park's appearance to his sister, when he had just perished in Africa. I have only a vague and confused recollection of stories of apparitions or wraiths, when a man who came by sudden death, such as drowning or murder, was seen by certain individuals almost at the exact moment when such must have happened. In one case I can condescend on names. A young man named Tamson served his apprenticeship as a wright with Robert Robertson, Drumfernhill, West Balgrochan, Torrance. Having completed his term, he went away to work in another part of the country. One winter evening it was reported to his former employer that Tamson had returned to his father's house at West Balgrochan. This was matter of great surprise to Mr. Robertson, and he closely interrogated his informant, who declared that he knew him quite well, and that he had passed him on the road close to " Markie " Tamson's house; he had not spoken to him, but he had no doubt as to his identity, and there was no mistake as regards having seen him. But, as Tamson had not been at his father's, and no one else had seen him, the

* *My Schools and Schoolmasters.* Chapter ii.

impression became common in the hamlet that it was a case of mistaken identity. A few days afterwards intelligence came that Tamson had been accidentally drowned, on the same evening and about the same time that he had been seen at Balgrochan. Robert Robertson, who has been referred to in these papers, carried on at one time a business as wright at West Balgrochan. He then removed to Glasgow, and after a few years again returned to West Balgrochan. When he did so he got as many as he required of his neighbours' carts placed at his disposal to remove his furniture and tools and plant. "Markie" Thomson was one of those assisting, and he had got all his load of furniture in his cart safely except a valuable grate. He was turning this over the edge of the cart, remarking, "It wis a guid thing thae yettlan' things didna break," when the grate slipped from his grasp, and, falling on the ground, was smashed to pieces. While at West Balgrochan, although it is not relevant, I may here record the following story. One of the wee Balgrochan lairds, old Laird Turner, lived to a very great age, to the great regret of his son Rab, who had many a time been heard to wish that his father were dead. Latterly the old man became so infirm that he was entirely confined to the house. One day, however, he was seen seated in a chair a little bit in front of the house, while his son stood in the doorway. A neighbour expressed his surprise at seeing Rab's father out there in front of the house, and asked what he was doing there. Rab replied, "The Lord has quite forgotten that ma faither's leevin' yet, and I've just brocht him oot that He micht just see him for His sel'." There also bulked largely in these stories recitals of remarkable dreams, foreshadowing future events or conveying warnings of danger or death, and singular realizations of such visions of the night; mysterious sounds, calls, knocks; the howling of dogs, the terror of animals, which it was supposed saw the angel of death or the departing spirits of the dead, all presaging death or other imminent disaster. They also told of scenes in varicus localities or ruins that were reputed to be haunted, such as Auchinreoch and old Bencloich Tower; fairies, omens of good and evil, what to do to secure luck and avert skaith, a lucky "first foot;" survivals of old pagan rites or sun worship, such as getting up early on May morning to wash with May dew, a thing which I have myself practised; also charms, salt being under certain conditions considered an effective one. Down to the end of last century, and even later, there were lingering legends of fairies and witches having once lived in the district. Bowbank Glen was reputed to be haunted by the former, while Craigenglen was the abode of the latter. Craigenglen was also known among the old people as witch-whorl glen, as the witches got the credit of manufacturing the numerous stems of fossil crinoids, called by them witch-whorls, which are to be found in the strata of the glen. I have seen men who believed they had seen fairies in Campsie

Moor. Seventy years ago there were one or two old women living
about West Balgrochan, who had some reputation of being witches,
but I have been unable to glean any particulars of their doings.

There was then a greater acquaintance with our native plants
than what appears to obtain now, and many of these were credited
with possessing great medicinal virtues. From our common
herbs, many laxatives and purgatives were obtained. There were
also carminatives, such as mint or peppermint water, to expel
wind ; diuretics, such as a decoction of broom tops, to promote
flow of urine. Diaphoretics and sudorifics, to induce perspiration
and sweating, were got from yarrow or sage. Anodynes, to allay
pain or procure sleep, were got from such a plant as henbane, which
in some respects resembles opium, without causing costiveness.
Tonics and bitters for stomach complaints were got from many of
our commonest plants, such as gentian, camomile, centaury, dandelion, &c. The flowers of camomile were used externally as a
fomentation, and the common wéed groundsel had wonderful
healing virtues when made into a poultice. Some of these plants
and roots were used for illegitimate purposes, such as to procure
abortion, &c. The infusion from centaury was considered to
be superior to the finest wine for strengthening, while the
dandelion or taraxacum root, leaves, and flowers, was considered to be a corrective for the liver and also a tonic for
the stomach. Meadow sweet, or queen of the meadow, was
believed to be a specific for stone and gravel, indeed it was
also called gravel root. There are people who are always treat-
ing themselves for real or often imaginary ailments. If these
simple decoctions, which the mother or neighbour had gathered
and "masked" themselves did no good, they could do little harm,
which is perhaps more than can be said of the numerous kinds of
pills, &c., which are swallowed in great quantities now-a-days by
the credulous. I can recollect collectors gathering herbs in the
proper season, which was generally when they were full of sap in
coming into full blossom. They were gathered on a dry day, tied
up in bunches, hung up to dry, and then either wrapped up in paper
or rubbed to a powder and put away carefully. Campsie florists are
famous for the perfection with which they grow herbaceous plants,
phloxes, penstemons, pansies, &c., but fifty years ago I think
there was more general acquaintance with our wild flowers and
plants and the virtues ascribed to them. A little attention devoted to these would greatly increase the interest of a summer
evening walk. Dr. Charles Mackay says of them* :

"My fair companions of the wood, who love the morning light—
Valerian, saffron, camomile, and rue and aconite ;

The golden mallow of the marsh, the hemlock, broad and rank ;
The nightshade, foxglove, meadow-sweet, and tansy on the bank,
And poppy with her sleepful eyes, and water iris, dank.

* *Under Green Leaves*, by Charles Mackay, page 53.

Are we not fair? Despise us not!—we soothe the couch of pain;
We bring divine forgetfulness to calm the stormy brain;
And through the languid pulse of life drop healing like the rain.

There's not a weed, however small, that peeps where rivers flow
Or in the bosom of the woods has privilege to grow,
But has some goodness in its breast, or bounty to bestow.

And if we poison; yours the fault.

Use us unwisely we may kill—use wisely, and we save.

Our virtues and our loveliness are none the less our own.

And if we're common, so is light, and every blessing known."

Since the paragraph " Freemasonry," on page 102, was printed,
I have obtained further information regarding William Morrison,
referred to there. It was in 1819 that Miss Lennox of Woodhead
granted a tack for 99 years of the ground of Damhead (now
Meadowbank) to John Morrison and Cecilia Lennox, his spouse.
At that time they had removed from the old thatched cottage of
Damhead, and were residing at Leddriegreen, Strathblane, while
Meadowbank was being built for their occupation. There is
another version of the Freemasonry story to this effect, that
Wm. Morrison, having learned the handicraft of a coachbuilder,
was going out to India in the same passenger ship as his relative,
Captain Lennox. While on her voyage the vessel was boarded by
a press-gang, and William Morrison was among those who were
seized. On his giving the Masonic sign he was liberated. There
seems no doubt of the fact that he was saved by giving the
Masonic sign. Afterwards, in a great storm, the crew, in order
to lighten the vessel, threw a lot of cargo overboard, and with it
many of William Morrison's tools. Morrison was in business in
Calcutta for about 20 years, and made a lot of money there. He
then came home to Campsie. He had gone up to London to see
a young man off to India, and when there he burst a blood-
vessel. His eldest sister, Miss Cecilia, went to London by coach.
He was in life when she arrived, but did not live long. Miss
Lennox of Woodhead took a great interest in the Morrison family,
sometimes calling and often sending fruit. The list of ministers
is as exhaustive as I have been able to make it—it does not
profess to be complete. Since it was printed I have heard of one
omission—James Allan, son of William Allan, long resident at
Easter Alton, and afterwards at Craighead of Milton. He went
to New South Wales when he was a minister.

POPULATION OF CAMPSIE PARISH IN 1881 AND 1891 (PUBLISHED BY PERMISSION OF THE REGISTRAR-GENERAL).

	Inhabited Houses.		Uninhabited Houses.		Houses Building.		Males.		Females.		Total.		Number of Rooms.	
	1881	1891	1881	1891	1881	1891	1881	1891	1881	1891	1881	1891	1881	1891
Lennoxtown, ...	693	636	96	106	...	...	1570	1391	1679	1447	3249	2838	1520	1401
Clachan, ...	9	10	2	3	...	...	19	12	24	38	43	45	52	45
Haughhead, ...	50	43	8	5	...	...	92	84	115	101	207	185	133	108
Glenmill, ...	20	13	...	7	...	...	19	21	54	45	73	66	57	48
Milton, ...	128	139	16	16	...	...	292	334	263	330	555	664	266	370
Mount of Glorat, ...	18	18	4	...	...	...	42	50	41	47	88	97	86	47
Birdston, ...	24	20	2	...	...	...	34	37	51	52	85	89	78	72
Torrance, .. .	113	95	13	27	...	...	230	191	266	189	496	380	227	216
East Balgrochan, ...	11	7	1	4	...	...	32	11	28	12	60	23	27	16
West Balgrochan, ...	24	19	1	10	3	...	64	48	64	48	128	86	58	45
Landward Districts, ...	162	155	14	21	1	...	409	399	485	466	894	865	900	905
Total, ...	1247	1155	157	199	4	...	2808	2573	3070	2765	5878	5338	3354	3808

VITAL STATISTICS OF CAMPSIE PARISH.

YEAR.	BIRTHS.			MARRIAGES.	DEATHS.	No. of Births in Excess of Deaths.
	Legitimate.	Illegitimate.	Total.			
1881, ...	162	15	177	35	108	69
1882, ...	165	11	176	32	120	56
1883, ...	170	12	182	35	117	65
1884, ...	168	13	181	28	101	80
1885, ...	156	16	172	30	121	51
1886, ...	165	15	180	45	121	59
1887, ...	184	16	200	30	108	92
1888, ...	167	8	175	33	111	64
1889, ...	132	13	145	24	98	47
1890, ...	154	13	167	26	107	60
1891, ...	141	17	158	32	121	37
Total for 11 years,	1764	149	1913	350	1233	680
Average each year,	160	13½	174	32	112	62

The average mortality per 1000 of population—

Basing on 5873 the census of 1881 is 19.07.

,, 5338 ,, 1891 is 20.98.

The percentage of illegitimate births on the total number of births averages 7.51 for the period of eleven years.

THE LENNOXES OF LENNOX CASTLE.

THE LENNOXES OF LENNOX CASTLE.

THE GENEALOGY.

THIS family are lineally descended from Duncan the eighth Earl of Lennox of the old line, who, when eighty years of age, was beheaded at Stirling, in May, 1425. The Earl, his son-in-law Murdoch Duke of Albany, and Murdoch's two sons, were all tried, condemned, and executed in one day. Some years before his death the Earl, by charter dated 22nd July, 1421, granted the lands of Ballyncorrauch, Ballyncloich, Thombuy, and others to his well-beloved son Donald of the Levenax, who, in 1423, acquired the lands of Ballegrochyr, formerly held by Sir William Graham of Kyncardine.

Donald Levenax married Elizabeth, daughter of Sir John Stewart of Girthon and Callie, and settled down at his castle of Ballecorrauch, the site of which was very close to the bottom of Campsie Glen, and traces of the pleasure grounds and also some of the trees therein can be seen on the hill slope opposite the present manse. He had two sons—John, who succeeded him, and William, who became first of the Callie line. Five Lennox lairds lived and died at Balcorrach. Duncan, the fifth laird, died childless, in 1572, and was succeeded by his brother John, who was sixth of Balcorrach, and first of Woodhead; for it was he who built the mansion house of Woodheid, as it was then designated.

Passing over eight generations, at the beginning of the present century, the fourteenth of Balcorrach was John Lennox, who died in 1811, and was succeeded in the family estates by his sister, Margaret Lennox, who then became the fifteenth of Balcorrach and tenth of Woodhead.

"THE CASE OF MARGARET LENNOX," &c.

Miss Lennox, being impressed with the conviction that her family had undoubted rights to the title and honours of the ancient earldom of the Lennox, at once put the matter into the hands of Mr. Robert Hamilton of Gilkerscleugh, a clever Edinburgh advocate, and some time Sheriff-Depute of Lanarkshire. He devoted himself for a considerable period to the careful preparation of the grounds upon which Miss Lennox of Woodhead based her claim to the Earldom. When Mr. Hamilton had completed his labours, Miss Lennox had them printed in 1818, by Alex. Lawrie & Co., Edinburgh. Hamilton's production is entitled, "The Case of Margaret Lennox of Woodhead, in relation to the Title, Honours, and Dignity of the ancient Earls of Levenax or Lennox." It was printed for private circulation among friends and others likely to be interested. It has been often referred to, and has been quoted by genealogists and history writers, and it is also a valuable historical record upon other points besides the history and genealogy of the Lennox family.

Miss Lennox was a most estimable lady, but her life and character were in no way remarkable, unless the strong desire to be recognised as nearest lawful heir of Duncan, eighth Earl and last of the old line of Lennox, or to have the title of Countess of Lennox conferred upon her. Miss Lennox enjoyed possession of the estates from 1811 until her death in 1833, when she was succeeded by her nephew, John Lennox Kincaid, son of John Kincaid of Kincaid and Cecilia Lennox her younger sister.

JOHN LENNOX KINCAID LENNOX.

John Lennox Kincaid then became John sixteenth of Balcorrach and eleventh of Woodhead. He at once assumed the name of Lennox, as required by the entail. Mr. Kincaid-Lennox was born in 1802. On 26th August, 1828, he was married at Craigends, Renfrewshire, to Frances Maxwell, third daughter of John Cunningham of Craigends. In 1836, when the Ship Bank was amalgamated with the Glasgow Bank, which was afterwards merged in the Union Bank, he and the late Michael Rowand were the only proprietors of the former establishment. In 1842 he was appointed convener of the County of Stirling. Mr. Lennox devoted much time and attention to the improvement of his estates. He understood well and delighted in observing the successful progress of such improvements. He was a considerate, judicious, and altogether an excellent landlord, a good, practical man of business, and strictly honourable in all his transactions. He took much interest in county and parochial concerns, anxiously endeavouring to promote the public welfare whenever it was in his power to do so. Shortly after becoming owner of the estate, in 1833, Mr. Lennox resolved upon making an extensive addition to the old mansion house of Woodhead, and he employed Mr. David Hamilton, architect, Glasgow, to prepare a plan giving effect to the wishes of Mrs. Lennox and himself in the matter.

PLAN TO ENLARGE THE OLD MANSION HOUSE.

Mr. Hamilton's instructions were to prepare a plan showing a large extension to the existing mansion house of Woodhead, as both Mr. and Mrs. Lennox were resolved to abide by the old ancestral home. Mr. Hamilton soon realised that the site and style of the old mansion presented great difficulties, and he ventured to suggest that Woodhead should be abandoned altogether and an

entirely new house built on the old site or on one to be selected
by Mr. Lennox. The architect's objections were overruled. Mr.
and Mrs. Lennox, at this time, clung like limpets to the old
Woodhead, which had been so long occupied by their family. The
plans were accordingly made out in conformity with their ideas ;
specifications of the work were prepared, and were about to be
issued to contractors. The plans had been passed to the newly-
appointed factor, Mr. Alexander Galloway, to have the lines of
the proposed buildings marked out, to show their extent, and the
ground that was to be taken in. This was done, and Mr. and
Mrs. Lennox were going over the ground with their professional
advisers, when these united in asking them to carefully reconsider
the matter of the site. Together they explained the difficulties of
the proposed plan and the inconvenience of the occupation. They
reminded them that Woodhead was not the first seat of the
family ; that had been Ballecorrauch, near the old church. and at
the foot of the Glen. This old site was not suitable now, but
Woodhead was not much more so. People do not select sites
now-a-days in inaccessible places or build mansions with thick
walls and small windows. What was wanted now was architec-
tural ornamentation, with comfort and all the elegancies and con-
veniences of the present day. Their relative, the late Miss Lennox,
had almost set her heart on regaining or attaining the ancient
title of Countess Lennox. In this both Mr. and Mrs. Lennox
heartily sympathised, and at that very time skilled experts had
been set to the task of studying the details of charters and other
documents stored away in Woodhead, Kincaid, and with the
Edinburgh agents of the family. All this labour was in continuation of Hamilton's "Case of Margaret Lennox of Woodhead."
It was then being zealously prosecuted, as both Mr. and Mrs.
Lennox cherished the intention of petitioning the House of Lords
to restore the ancient title of Earl of Lennox to Mr J. L. Kincaid Lennox. This being so, "Why not," it was asked, "go
back to the early origin of the family, in the period of the Norman
Conquest ? As they wished to renew these titles as Earls of
Lennox, why not abandon the old site, inconvenient and unsuit-
able in many respects? Why not adopt a Norman style of
architecture, build an entirely new house on a suitable site, and
call it Lennox Castle ? After consideration the plans for enlarg-
ing and reconstructing Woodhead were discarded, and the idea of
a new house, in the Norman style, to be called Lennox Castle,
found favour, and it was determined to have an entirely new
house on a suitable site.

A NEW LENNOX CASTLE TO BE BUILT.

Fresh plans were called for, the site was discussed and settled,
and the new plans were approved of, specifications were issued
and contracts for the work accepted. Then Mr. and Mrs. Lennox

M

went off to reside in France for two years, while the building operations were in progress. When these had all been completed, and the castle was being got ready for occupation, the question arose, what was to be done with the old mansion. Mr. Lennox would have had it removed entirely, but Mrs. Lennox's views and wishes were given effect to. These were to have Woodhead partially pulled down, but so much left standing as would represent and keep in mind the old structure as an interesting ruin. This was done. What was left standing was planted with ivy and climbing plants, and the arched apartments of the ground floor were to have been converted into an ice-house, but this part of the scheme miscarried through their having proceeded on a wrong method of construction for an ice-house. The house was stored with ice, but when opened for a supply, on the occasion of a large party, not a bit was to be seen. The ice-house was a total failure. These alterations were carried out in 1840-41.

Meantime, Mr. Lennox was reconsidering the matter of the petition to the House of Lords. The castle had swallowed up the stock formerly invested in the Ship Bank, and of course the dividends from that quarter would now cease. A moderate estimate of the expenses likely to follow prosecuting the petition placed it at not less than five thousand pounds. Then, even with the free income of the estate, was it prudent to undertake to maintain the dignity of a peerage? Mr. Lennox came reluctantly to the conclusion that he had better abandon the idea of going forward with the case. While Mrs. Lennox acquiesced this was understood to be a great disappointment to her.

The issue of the marriage was one son and three daughters. I can recall vividly the appearance of the family pew in the front of the gallery of Campsie Church. Mr. and Mrs. Lennox and their daughters, Miss Lennox, Miss Cecilia, and Miss Fanny. Frequent visitors were young William Cunningham, and another nephew of Mrs. Lennox named Duke. Mr. Lennox's cousin Mr. Pitcairn, and the late Captain Lennox, of 12th Lancers, &c. I remember the young laird, and recollect seeing his trunks being made at M'Luckie & Taylor's wright shop, when his regiment was ordered abroad. I watched his initials and regiment being painted on the boxes. Young Lennox joined the 12th Lancers, which was sent out to the Cape, to take part in the Caffre War, which this country had on hand then. Here " his lodging was on the cold ground " literally, and through exposure on night duty and the hardships incidental to a harassing campaign, he caught disease of the lungs and asthma. London doctors informed him that he could not live long in this climate, but that in the warmth and sunshine of the Nile valley his life might be prolonged. They could not give him any hope of ultimate recovery. He elected to spend what time he had to live in the sunshine. His mother and eldest sister accompanied him to Egypt, and they had ascended the Nile Valley when they were introduced to Viscount Strangford, who was in delicate health himself, and who had a boat of his own on the Nile, in which he was living. He invited the Lennox party to share its accommodation, and prevailed on them to proceed in it with him as far as the falls and back. While on this voyage young Lennox died, 28th Feb., 1857, and was buried at Thebes, in Upper Egypt. Born 14th Oct., 1830, heir to a fine estate, he passed away in his 27th year. The rest of the party returned at once to Cairo, and as soon as possible sailed for England. During this voyage Lord Strangford made himself most agreeable. He was of the greatest use to the ladies during the illness and after the death, and they were naturally very grateful for his kindness, hospitality, and sympathy. However, he wanted more than gratitude, and before they separated he had engaged Miss Lennox to marry him as soon after getting home as possible, as at that time he thought himself quite convalescent. But after being in this country for a short time he relapsed, and grew more and more of an invalid. Miss Lennox insisted on going to nurse him, and went. Lord Strangford and she had not been long beside each other till they resolved to marry. On 9th Nov., 1857, Margaret, eldest daughter of Mr. and Mrs. Kincaid Lennox, was married to George Augustus Frederick Percy Sydney Smythe, seventh Viscount Strangford, who was born 13th April, 1818, succeeded 29th May, 1855, and died 23rd Nov., 1857, just a fortnight after his marriage. His younger brother succeeded to the title, but he died 9th Jan., 1869, when the title of Viscount Strangford became extinct.

The death of his only son had been a great blow to Mr. Lennox. After it he was frequently ailing, and change of air and scene was tried first in Edinburgh and afterwards in the south of England. He continued to droop, and died in London on the 6th March, 1859, in the fifty-seventh year of his age, little more than two years after his son. After that for him the zest of his life was gone,

" For his heart in his grave was lying."

On the death of her father, Margaret Viscountess Strangford became seventeenth of Balcorrach, twelfth of Woodhead, and second of Lennox Castle. On 17th October, 1861, Viscountess Strangford was married to the Hon. Charles Spencer Bateman Hanbury, second son of William, first Lord Bateman, born 8th October, 1827, and who was at that time M.P. for Leominster. He assumed the name of Kincaid-Lennox. She waived her title of Viscountess, and elected to be styled the Hon. Mrs. Hanbury Kincaid Lennox. There has been no issue of this marriage, and the heir presumptive is her sister, Mrs. Peareth, and after her her eldest son, who also inherits extensive estates in England.

Mrs. Kincaid Lennox died on 10th September, 1876, aged 69 years. Mrs. Lennox had erected, in 1861, at her own expense, the Lennox Tea-Rooms, which she designed to be a workingmen's club, on temperance principles. This did well as long as it was a novelty, but the games and reading-room in time were deserted, and the building, which stands on the Main Street, opposite the head of the Field Road, was then converted into dwelling-houses. A Dorcas Society in Lennoxtown was commenced by her. She liberally supported and personally superintended this, and many of the poor have been greatly benefited by her considerate kindness during the winter time. When preaching her funeral sermon, the late Rev. Dr. Monro thus feelingly referred to her:—"During the thirty-two years of my incumbency no one has more earnestly or more generously, nay, let me say at once, so earnestly or so generously helped me in my ministry as the late Mrs. Lennox. In that lengthened period how many plans designed by her for the good of the parish, how many acts of thoughtful beneficence performed by her, how many instances of unostentatious liberality and genuine kindness exhibited by her rush into my memory, and not one angry word, not one ungenerous action. In some respects, indeed, her death seems to me almost like an epoch in my ministry. Perhaps in some departments I have leaned too much on her generous kindness, and I will need during what remains of my incumbency to appeal more earnestly to you, dear brethren, to hold up my hands in my work, that that work may not suffer."

Captain Peareth, who married Miss Cecilia, and Colonel Oakes, who married Miss Fanny, had both been brother officers of Captain Lennox in the 12th Lancers.

FEUDAL JURISDICTION AND COURTS.

Feudal charters, such as were granted by the old Earls of Lennox, besides the lands, gave privileges, jurisdictions, and rights which constituted the owner of the barony a most influential personage within his own baronial jurisdiction. King Malcolm gave feudal barons power to have a pit wherein women condemned for theft could be drowned, and gallows whereon men could be hanged. When the feudal superior had the power of pit and gallows he had as ample jurisdiction as the justiciar or the sheriff. The powers thus conferred on owners were exercised in the barony courts. Viscount Kilsyth was the last to exercise the power of life and death, held by him under his feudal tenure. In 1693, he condemned one of his own servants in Bencloich to be hanged for stealing silver-plate from the Tower of Bencloich, and the man was forthwith hanged on the gallows-knowe of Bencloich, which is just south of the N. B. Railway, between New Mill and Muckcroft, just beyond "The Field of Blood." Mr Galloway, in his lecture in 1864, referred to the institution of the Woodhead Barony Court, and he gave a list of the lands and tenants of the Woodhead estate in 1660. These were—The lands of Bin, 3 tenants; Baccorach, 10; Corshouse, 1; Champiestoune and Holl, 2; Balgrochan, 5; Parkestoune upper, 2; Parkestoune nether, 2 ; Birbestoune, 4 ; Boghous, 3 ; Invertedie, 10 ; also 4 cottars, one of whom, James Allan, was a weaver. The number of tenants on the estate as it then stood was 48.

While the Kirk-Session attended to the morals of the parish the Barony Courts were occupied with the affairs of their own estates—Souming and oversouming, encroachments on tackmen's rights, regulating the order and quantities of coals to be led to the baron's mansion house, &c.

The history of the Lennox estate and its farmers from the year 1660 is well brought out, almost month by month, in its barony court minutes. These minutes contain no notice of any blackmail having been payable by the tenants or by the laird, so that the tradition of Rob Roy's wife riding down to Wodheid and reminding the laird of his arrears finds no corroboration here, whereas, had blackmail been levied, we might have expected some reference to it. The payment of blackmail, generally about 4 per cent. on the rental, was a necessity of the times. In one respect it was superior to our police rates, for those who levied it undertook for the money to return the cattle stolen or their values. The farmer might not get back the identical cattle, but he asked no questions for conscience's sake.

The number of horses and cattle which the tenant might own were regulated according to the extent of his infield and of his liability for services ; it might be work in harvest, cartage or carriage of landowner's goods or chattels, labour on the roads in the barony, or provision payments for the mansion house. The tenants watched jealously and resented hotly any encroachments on their joint rights, and resorted to the barony court whenever they fancied they had ground of complaint. These courts were generally held on knolls, laws, or little hills, and were called Mute Hill, mote or mute meaning a plea or quarrel. Adjoining this court place was the pit and gallows hill, noted already. We have still remaining the "Law" at Balgrochan, the "Law Park" at Kincaid, the "Gallowhill" of Bencloich, and the "Courthill" of Craigbarnet, where King James the IV. held a court in 1507.

The Woodhead barony courts were held pretty regularly about twice a-year, and occasionally more or less frequently. They continued from 1660 to 1775. Other neighbouring baronies as well as all the important free baronies throughout the kingdom used such courts, and their records are to be found in the General Register House or the Advocates' Library.

WOODHEAD BARON BAILIES COURT.

The Records of the Court of the Baron Bailie of Woodhead contain much having a local interest.

The John Lennox who presided at the first Court, in 1660, had married Jean Cunninghame, the daughter and heiress of Adam Cunninghame the Laird of Balglass, who was said to have murdered

Collins, the minister, in 164?. Jean brought back the Balglass lands to Woodhead as her tocher. The first minute begins thus :—
" Ane Court of the lands of Woodheid, halden at the place of Woodheid be John Lennox, heritable proprietor, yr. of James Wallace of Bardrame his bailzie, upon the 23rd November, 1600 and three score yeris. Callit Court, &c., Walter Lennox was officer. John M'llhose, damster, and William Graham, clerk and writer to the court.

" The Bailzie did inquyre at ye officer if he knew of any bloods depriements, or break of arrestments. The officer declared on oath he knew none.

" Considering that the woods within the glen above the Kirk hath not been dressed and guydet as they ought in time past, it is statut and ordained that no person or persons within the land presume to cut any bit of greenwood in all time coming, and that under the penalty, &c.

The following is a list of the Baron Bailies :—

1660—James Wallace of Bardrame.
1661—John Stirling of Craigbarnet.
1663—James Wallace, chamberlain to the Viscount of Kilsyth.
1664—Edmonstone of Hurlehaven, now called Arlehaven.
1665—Archibald Edmonstone of Callean, who was likely tacksman of Colzium under the Viscount.
1666}
   to } Archibald Edmonstone of Ballewan, probably the same man.
1684}
1686—Archibald Edmonstone of Spittal.
1686—John Napier of Culcreuch, or Kilcroich, as he spelt it.
1715—Hugh M'Farlan of Kirktoune.
1720}
   to } James Napier of Culcreuch ; in his absence John Rankin of Green-
1728}   foot officiated.
1775—George Brown, tenant of Damhead, was appointed. He chose James Oswald, writer in Glasgow, as clerk.

The following cases illustrate the nature of the business coming before this court :—
Compeared Archd. Brown in Boghouse and John Blair in Capieston as to what soumes were wont to be kept by the Crosshouse tenants. Deponed they heard there were 26 soumes. Ordains them not to exceed the foresaid soumes, under the penalty of £5 Scots for each soume over.

On 24th Aug., 1721, at the Woodhead Court, the fiscal complained against Janet Brown, living in cottage in Auchenrossie, Netherton of Innertadie or Wodheid, was charged with cursing several persons in Woodhead. She pleaded *on her knees* that she had cursed none but those who took away her honest name. The Bailie fined her £20 Scots.

In 1716, John Rankin of Greenfoot, as *pro tempore* Bailie of Woodhead, ordained, at the instance of one of the tenants, named Brown, about the oversouming, they shall eat the grass and muir, conform to an Act dated 23rd June, 1661, and all subsequent

Acts made thereanent, viz., to be hirded upon the lands of Bin 6 score soumes of nolt, 24 heads of sheep, 12 heads of horse, and 9 score lambs, &c.

In 1730 the Bailie ordained the Clachan soumes in the mure to continue as formerly, under the penalty of £5 Scots for each soumin over.

Court of the Lands and Barony of Woodhead, holden at the Manor place of Woodhead, the 11th day of August, 1735, by Sir William Fleming of Ferm, Bailie—anent the complaint given in by Mr. Hugh Stewart, merchant in Glasgow, tacksman of the Lym Craig of Skulliongour, mentioning that certain individuals named wrought the said Lym Craig, notwithstanding the pursuer's tack. The Bailie having considered the complaint, finds that the Pursuer has right to the Lym Craig of Skulliongour, and that the defenders have not title to work therein, excepting for the use of their grounds, and ten chalder yearly to sell, each of them, therefore decerns the Defenders to desist from working the said Lym Craig in time coming, excepting as above, under the penalty of £12 Scots for each chalder they shall exceed the ten chalder mentioned yearly each of them. Signed, Wm. Fleming, Bailie.

Having quoted about the Lym (lime) Works, I should also quote about the coal, which is thus referred to—Court of the Lands and Barony of Woodhead, holden at Woodhead, the 16th day of January, 1744 years, by John Rankin in Kilwinnet, Bailie. The Bailie decerns and ordains the whole tenants to lead twelve loads of coals weekly to the House of Woodhead, in manner aftermentioned, viz.—Each plough to lead twelve loads weekly, eight of which loads to be brought from the coalpit at Drumlourick and four from Skulliongour coalpit, that Thursday every week be the day for leading the said twelve loads of coals, and that the plough of land of Balgrochan, begin on Thursday first, and so on weekly, under penalty of Twenty Shillings Scots for each transgression. Signed, J. Rankin.

In concluding these notes on the Lennox family and the barony rights, it may be of interest to give the following copy of the charter granted by Duncan, eighth Earl of Lennox, in favour of Donald de Levenax of Ballyncorrauch :—

"Be it kende till all men be yr prnt lers, us Duncane Erle of ye Levenax, with ye consent and ye assent of Walter Stewart, till haff giffine and till haff grantit And be this prnt writ gifes and grantis till my weil belufit sone laffwell Donald of ye Levenax All and Singlar my Landis of Ballyncorrauch wt. ye pertinas, all ye Landis of Ballyncloich and Thomboy wt. yair pertinas Lyand wtin ye parisching of Camsy and wtin ye Erledome of ye Levenax, Haldand and till Hald All and Singlar ye forsaid Landis of Ballyncorrauch, Ballyncloich, and Thomboy wt. yair ptinas of mie and myne ayris till ye forsaid Donald my laffwell sone and his ayris and assigns in fle and heritage for evirmair be all richt mkis ald and divisis in bushis planis in myrris and marrisies in vayis roddis in watteris stangis wt. mylnys & ye multuris of yaim and yair folowingis in medowis pasturis and lesowris with haukyne and huntyng and fysching wt. pettis and turfis with orichiardis and dowcottis wt. stane and lyme wt. collis wt. brewhousis and bakhousis wt. smythyis with aneragiis and carriagiis and dawerkis with tenand and tenandry with bludewittis herzeldis and merchettis of women wt. courtis and ye escheittis of yaim with all and uther singlar conmodities fredomis and aysiamentis and wt. all richwiss pertinas quhatsumever yat be als weil unnemyt as nemyt als weil under ye erd as abuffe als weil fer as ner yat till ye said (landis) wt. ye ptinans richtwysly ptenis or may pertene be ony maner of way in tyme to cum frely quytly fulily halyly honourabilly weill and in peiss in all & be all withoutyn ony gaynstandying—Giffand yairfor zerly ye forsaid Donald my laffwell son and his ayris and his assignaes till me myne ayris a peny of silwir in name of Blanche ferme at ye fest of Witsunday allanerly gif it be askit for all uther wardis relewis mariagis soyttis of courttis dupliacions ferme and for all oyir wont seryice secular exaccions or demaunde ye quhilk of ye forsaid Land with ye ptinans may be askit be mie or myne ayris or requiryt in tyme to cum. And we forsutht ye said Duncane and our ayris ye forsaid Land with yair ptinans till ye forsaid Donalde and till his ayris and till his assignaes agayne all erdely man and woman we sall warand mak quyt and for evirmair defende. In Witnes of ye quhilk thyng till ye put charter we haf hungyne to our Sell at Strablayn ye xxii day of ye monetht of Julij ye zere of our Lord a thousand four hunder twenty and a zer. Befoir yir Witness Yat is to say Walter Stewart and James Stewart his broyer William of Strevylling Lord of Cadar Alexander of ye Levenax Sir Robert Lang Prson of Inchecalzach Gilbon   of Galbrath Donald Clerk with oyr mony personis."

The Walter Stewart whose assent and consent is given in the above charter was the Earl's grandson, eldest son of his daughter Isabella Duchess of Albany. James Stewart, a witness, was a brother of Walter. Alexander was a younger brother of the Earl himself. In 1423 Donald acquired the lands of Ballegrochyr from Sir William Graham of Kyncardyne, and he is styled in the charter by Sir William—"*filius legitimus Duncani Comitis de Levenax.*" To this charter Earl Duncan, Donald's father, was a witness. This was confirmed in 1444 by Isabella Duchess of Albany. In her charter Donald is styled—"*Donaldo de Levenax filio legittime Dni Duncani quondam Comitis de Levenax.*" Hamilton's contention was that such an appellation could not have been applied to any one who was not *de jure* entitled to it. The heirs male of Earl Duncan lawfully begotten were entitled to the succession, and Donald being heir male by a second marriage, as alleged by Hamilton, should have succeeded to the Earldom of the Lennox. But, in 1423, Sir William de Grahame granted a charter to John Brisbane of a quarter of land in Campsy called Ballenclerach. In this the witnesses are the Earl Duncan himself and "*Malcolmo Thoma et Donaldo filiis suis naturalibus.*" (Malcolm, Thomas, and Donald his natural sons.) Sir William Fraser, in "The Lennox," vol. i., pp. 258-9, quotes a charter which had never before been brought to light proving that the spouse of Duncan, Countess Helen, mother of Isabella Duchess of Lennox, survived her husband for about 9 years, and died in or shortly before 1434. If Countess Helen survived her husband, that would effectually dispose of the theory of a second marriage.

GENEALOGIES AND OLD PARISH TOWERS.

In the chartulary of the Lennox Earls we see how the lands within their jurisdiction were from time to time apportioned among the members of the Earl's family, and other favoured individuals. Alwyn or Allan 2nd Earl of Lennox (1155-1217) had a large family of nine sons and one daughter. The sons were:—1, Maldwin; 2. Duffgall, or Dougal; 3, Malcolm; 4, Amelic (Auleth or Aulay are various forms of spelling the name of the Earl's fourth son); 5, Gilchrist; 6, Christinus; 7, Corc; 8, Duncan; 9, Henry. The daughter's name was Eva. Maldwin succeeded his father, and from his lineal descendant, Duncan, the eighth earl, sprang the Lennox family of Balcorrach and Woodhead. Duffgall the second son was a churchman, and Rector of Kilpatrick. The Earl, in 1199, gave Cochnach, Edeubaruet, Monach-Keneran, Drumleth, Climan, and Cultbuie, to the church of Kilpatrick of which his son was rector. Malcolm, the third son, obtained·from his father the " castle and lands of Camsi." Probably the castle was named after the parish church which had a few years previously been erected and endowed by Earl Allan and his predecessor Earl David. The " lands of Camsi " embraced portions of what are now included in the parishes of Strathblane and Baldernock, as well as Campsie. Amelic or Aulay, the fourth son, got as his portion the lands of Faslane and an extensive tract on both sides of the Gareloch, including Rosneath, Glenfruin and Luss. Gilchrist, the fifth son, got for his share the lands of Arother (Arrochar). He had a son Duncan, whom we find designated as Duncan Mac Gilchrist de Levenax. His son was Maldwin, whose son was Bartholomew or, in Gaelic, Parlan. His descendants were called M'Parlanes, and latterly MacFarlans. The Arrochar estate of the old M'Farlans was sold in 1785 for £28,000 to Ferguson of Raith, who sold it in 1821 to Sir James Colquhoun for £78,000. The M'Farlans of Arrochar ended in the person of Elizabeth Margaret, the daughter of the chief who had sold his patrimonial estate. This lady died 12th May, 1846. Before her death she pronounced Col. John Warden M'Farlan of Ballancleroch to be the Chief of the Clan M'Farlan, as the head of the oldest cadets of the old stock. The Colonel's ancestors had acquired in 1642 the lands of Balnacleroch, Keithtown, Kirktown or Ballancleroch, as this estate had been called at various times. The Earl's only daughter married Malcolm, son of Duncan, Thane of Callendar, in Stirlingshire. Her brother, Earl Maldwin, granted a charter to her and her husband, dated 10th August, 1217, of Glaskell, Brengoene, and a ploughgate and a half of Kilnasyde (Kilsyth), with the patronage of the church of Monybroch. Their descendant Patrick favoured the claims of Baliol, for which he paid the penalty of forfeiture of his lands. Patrick's daughter married Sir William Livingstone. She had the lands restored to her, and in this way the Livingstones became connected with Kilsyth. Omitting all reference to the other sons, we have seen how amply the Allan 2nd Earl had provided for his family, distributing amongst them a great portion of his earldom of the Lennox.

We now revert to the Earl of Lennox's third son, Malcolm. In all probability the Earl Allan had caused Camsi Castle to be built for this son. Until the beginning of the present century some of the remains of this old castle or peel were to be seen at Ballagan, on the opposite site of the Blane from the present house, but the materials were used as a quarry for stones for the present Ballagan House, and as only debris and rubbish were left, these were cleared away, and all trace above the surface of the old castle disappeared, the last stones having been built into the present garden wall. The north garden wall is said to be built on some of the ruins. A magnificent old yew tree, close to the site of the old castle, is now the sole memorial of the past. But there are still traces of the old foundations, which Mr. Galloway said he had had no difficulty in tracing. They showed that the buildings of Camsi had been much more extensive than those of Balcurroch, Bencloich, Glorat, Kyncade, or Craigmaddie. I have been favoured by Mr. William Brown, a son of George Brown, formerly tenant of the Mains of Bencloich Farm, with a perusal of some letters on this subject. My correspondent, Mr. William Brown, is one of the Browns of Westerton, but has long been resident in Renfrewshire. He takes the deepest interest in Campsie history, as many of the older residents can testify, his thirst for information being almost insatiable, especially in all that relates to the old Tower of Bencloich. He carried on a long correspondence with the late Mr. Alexander Galloway, extending from 1868 till 1883, the year of Mr. Galloway's death, and Mr. Galloway was in the habit of imparting to him in these letters anything interesting about Campsie. Concerning Camsi Castle Mr. Galloway became himself deeply interested, and detailed his labours from time to time in letters to Mr. Brown. The story, as gleaned from those letters, may be summarized as follows. Mr. Galloway, in the course of perusing some old charters, quite unexpectedly chanced on the discovery that Ballagan old castle, from its erection about 1190 till the year 1390, was called Camsi Castle, and he followed up this clue with great enthusiasm. He first proceeded to make a large plan of the ground. On this he laid down, as he believed, the site of the castle, with ground plan of the castle buildings, and offices, barns, stables, harness and store rooms. He laid down a moat with drawbridge, and showed. the principal approach to be from the west, with a secondary, one from the east. The large ordnance survey map was the basis of this plan. It was all to a regular scale, corresponded to the ordnance survey map where the parts coincided, and gave the minutest detail, even showing the arrangements for regulating the height of water in the moat. Mr. Galloway thus, described his plan :— .

"CAMSI CASTLE IN 1190.

"Sketch showing the probable construction, ground floor arrangements, and accesses of the original castle at Ballagan. .

"The main sketch shows what I assume to have been a ground plan of the buildings, that is in accordance with the practice of the time, the position, and the circumstances; the main building 140 feet square, outside measure, with walls 5 feet thick; internal bearing walls, 3 feet thick; in the centre an open court 82 by 72 feet; main entrance near centre of west side, and outer court entrance on north side; three circular stairs for access to the upper floors; a tower at each of the west corners; north court for barn, stables, and harness; a moat 14 wide by 11 feet deep round all these, with a drawbridge for main entrance and another for cart and horse entrance; a farmery in three sides of a square, placed nearly where the present mansion is; garden west from the castle a short way; principal approach road coming from the west of the public road at Broadgate, Bredgate, big gate; and a secondary approach from the east, outside the moat and the burn."

Malcolm, the occupier of Camsi Castle, had no male heir, and his daughter succeeded. She married Finli, son of Robert of Redheuch, Menteith. Surnames were then unknown, and the owners of estates took their names from the lands they occupied. Finli having married the heiress thereupon becomes Finli of Camsi, and his descendents were called Finlis or Finlays of Camsi. Finli appears to have had no sons, but three daughters : (1) Maria, wife of John de Wardrobe; (2) Elena, wife of Bernard de Erth of that Ilk; and (3) Forveleth, wife of Norrin de Monargrund of that Ilk in the shire of Perth. About 1390 the name of the owner's residence becomes changed from Camsi to Strathblayn. Duncan, eighth Earl of Lennox signed the charter to his son Donald de Levenax of Balcorrach, at Strath-blayn. The lands of the original charter, in so far as not in possession of the successors of Elena, a daughter and co-heiress of Finli, and in so far as they had not been sold or alienated, would appear to have reverted, from want of entered heirs or otherwise, to Earl Duncan about 1422. Earl Duncan was beheaded in 1425, and in this year the name would seem to have been changed from Strathblane Castle to Ballagan Castle, for reasons which cannot now be dis-covered. When King James I. had seized and beheaded Earl.

Duncan, he took possession of lands to which he had no legal right, and he gave these away to his friends. In this way, before 1434, he made over to his brother-in-law the lands of Duntreyve and others in Strathblane. Isabella, the daughter and heiress of Duncan, held out against this partition until 1445, when, in consideration most likely of her grand-daughter, Matilda Stewart, having married Sir William Edmonstone, she granted a charter to the Edmonstones, which was afterwards confirmed by a charter of James II. He bestowed the Earl's Duntreath lands on his brother-in-law, William Edmonstone of Culloden. Some of the Ballagan lands, according to Mr. Galloway, were given as hush money to the Bishop of Glasgow, who, had he represented to the Pope the manner in which the Earl's daughter had been unrighteously despoiled, might have made it very disagreeable to the king. Although Parliament decided that the Earl of Lennox had not committed any act which involved forfeiture of his estates, yet James I. seized and held as for the Crown the estates of his daughter and successor, Isabella, Duchess of Albany. After the reformation we find Ballagan lands divided among the lairds of Mugdock, Duntreath, Easter Ballewan, Craigbarnet, and Glorat, and the buildings of the old castle gradually disappeared, being applied in building farm-houses, building and repairing dykes, &c.

The present Ballagan House was erected early in this century. It is only in as far as Camsi castle was erected here, that I can take any cognisance of it in a paper on the parish of Campsie. Elena, the second daughter of Finli de Camsi had thus a third of the lands of Camsi, and of her estate. which was probably of much greater extent then than it is now Cragbernard, formed a portion. Elena married Bernard de Erth, from whom a part of her estate was called Crag Bernard. Nisbet on Ragman Roll says of Alexander de Erth (1296)—an ancient family in Stirlingshire, that had the baronies of Airth, Carnock, Playne (Plean), which in the reign of James I. came to heir's female, and by marriage to the Bruces, Drummonds, and Somervilles.

The succession was as follows :—Bernard de Erth (1271-1300) ; Elena, daughter of Finli had a son Bernard de Erth (1280-1340) ; this Bernard had a son, Malcolm de Erth (1320-1375) who married Annot Sproll. Their daughter, Alicia de Erth (1400) married Gilbert de Buquhanne or Buchquhanan. Their daughter and heiress married Gilbert de Strivelyn, a younger son or brother of William de Strivelyn, eighth lord of Cadder (1408-34). The Laird of Cadder was a man of great position, he had been one of the hostages chosen among the foremost men of Scotland for the ransom of James I. For his services in that capacity he might consider himself entitled to ask the hand of an heiress for a near relative, a son or brother, and Cragbernard was then in the hands of the Crown during the minority of the heiress. In this way a member of the Cadder Stirlings became the first

Stirling of Cragbernard.* Gilbert de Strivelyn the first of Craigbernard died a young man, before 1424, leaving a son and heir, who became John de Strivelyn of Cragbernard, who died about 26th July, 1497, and was succeeded by his son, Sir John Striveling third of Cragbernard. King James IV. visited Sir John at Cragbernard in 1507, as the accounts of the Lord High Treasurer for that year, 9th Feb., bear. "Item, that nycht in Craigbernard to the King to play at cartis xxiiij. s." The King is said to have held a Court at the place still known as the Court hill. Sir John acquired the lands of Glorat in 1507 and obtained a charter from the superior, Mathew Earl of Lennox, in 1508. He died in 1510. He divided his estates among his three sons, George, the eldest, inheriting Cragbernard; William the second, obtaining Glorat; and Walter, the third, getting Ballagan. There was another son, Robert, and there was a daughter, who was married to John Lennox, fourth of Balcurrach. I am indebted for most of these details to "The Stirlings of Craigbernard and Glorat," &c., by Joseph Bain, F.S.A. Scot.; privately printed for Sir Charles Elphinstone Fleming Stirling, the eighth and present Baronet of Glorat, who, in 1885, presented me with a copy; and also to "The Lennox," by Sir William Fraser.

It thus becomes evident that the Stirlings of Craigbarnet and Glorat and the M'Farlans of Ballancleroch have a common ancestor in Earl Allan, the second Earl of Lennox. The Woodhead family branched off the same stock about 200 years later, the Kincaids of that ilk obtained a charter for their lands in 1280, a fourth part of which, however, passed out of their family in 1350, and which was successively owned by Galbraiths and Hamiltons of Bardowie, and the Montrose family got their Torrance lands in 1400. It is no wonder, therefore, that the Rev. James Lapslie, in his statistical account, remarked on the little change that had taken place in the ownership of land in the parish, estates having been transmitted from generation to generation in the same families.

* The family of Stirlings of Cadder were a branch of the Comyn family who were hereditary Sheriffs of Stirling. William the Lion gifted the lands of Cadder to the Bishop of Glasgow, in order that prayers and masses might be said for the good of his soul, and for the souls of his relatives. Lands like Cadder piously dedicated to the church soon passed away into the hands of laymen and Sir Alexander de Striveling became first a feuar under the Bishop and ultimately proprietor of these church lands. Bruce, when he became King, caused Comyn's estates of Kirkintilloch, Cumbernauld and others to be forfeited, he could not interfere with church lands, and it has been conjectured that the Comyns who had been hereditary Sheriffs of Stirling, then for political reasons dropped the Comyn from the name and adopted Striveling. The Bishop of Glasgow's connection with these lands is commemorated in the name of Bishop's Brig, Bishop's burn, and Bishop's Moss, the bridge over the burn at Bishopbriggs having been erected by the Bishop of Glasgow. The Bishop's effigy used to stand at one end of this bridge. The effigy disappeared when the road was raised the first time.

Alicia, lady of Cragbernard, had for her residence a tower or castle, the exact site of which is now unknown. Judging from the old course of the turnpike road, the trees, and other landmarks, the site must have been in very close proximity to the present mansion house. It would be in this old tower that Sir John Striveling entertained King James IV. in 1507. When the building at last required to be renewed, owing to its age, John Striveling the ninth laird decided to erect for himself a new mansion, and he decided to change the site to one which he must have fancied to be more eligible. The spot he selected and where he commenced his building operations was nearer the Finglen Burn than the old house, on a mound or knoll known as Keir Hill. Miss Spence, in her sketches, tells how the building operations, as soon as they had been commenced, were interrupted by brownies, little fairy elves, who issued from their subterranean abodes and demolished in the night what had been built during the day. While this was going on, nothing could be seen, but frequently a warning voice was heard to repeat—

> " Burry, big your house in a bog,
> And you'll never want a fu' cog."

The laird listened to the admonition, and altered the site. Taking the hint from the fairies, he built it in the bog, on the opposite or south side of the turnpike road between Campsie and Strathblane. There is a clump of trees existing very near the old site. The new house was a substantial square building, with a pepper-box turret at each corner. It was surrounded by a wet ditch or moat, and defended by a drawbridge and gateway. The gables may have been corbel steps, called popularly now-a-days corbie or crow steps. Dressed stones, bearing the initials of the laird and his wife, Mary Stirling, youngest daughter of Sir Mungo Stirling of Glorat, whom he had married in 1656, have been removed when it was demolished in 1786, when the present mansion house was built. These stones now surmount the Mains of Craigbarnet, immediately to the west of the modern house. The initials and dates are—

> J. S.   M. S.
> 16.   62.

Whether the prophetic instinct of the fairies foresaw the fu' cog, or it was owing to good luck, the builder's descendants emerged triumphantly from the dark days which overwhelmed them in the following century, when the Laird like the Prince for whom he risked so much—

> On hills that are by right his ain,
> He roams a lonely stranger ;
> On ilka hand he's pressed by want,
> On ilka side by danger.

Good fortune again smiled upon them, what had been scattered and lost by their adherence to a failing cause was more than regained by commercial enterprise, and James Stirling the eleventh laird, the famous Burry of the '15 and '45, who had to convey his patrimony to his kinsmen when political troubles engulfed him, was enabled to clear off all the encumbrances and debts upon his patrimonial estate and was once more reinvested in it in 1768, having made a fortune in the tobacco trade. An incident of the '45 occurs to me now. Burry, in his desire to get arms wherewith to equip those who were about to join the rising under Prince Charlie, one day invaded the Manse of Campsie in search of these, intending to requisition whatever he could find. Mrs. Warden was displeased at his unceremonious raid, and said so. Burry was determined and not to be put off, and was perhaps rather brusque to the lady. Her husband was absent, but on his return he, a minister of the gospel, who had thrown himself with great enthusiasm into the great religious revival at Kilsyth, in his indignation at the treatment given to his wife in his absence, at once sent a challenge to the laird of Craigbarnet. Burry, however, had his scruples about fighting a duel with a minister. Had it only been a layman he would have given him satisfaction to his heart's content. So he apologised rather than accept. His remark was—"The deil tak' me if I meddle wi' ane of the Lord's corbies." Burry's son John, the twelfth laird, built the present Mansion House in 1786. He deserted the fairies' lucky site in the bog, for a more convenient one in every way, and nearly identical with that of the original castle or tower or Peel of Cragbernard. The mansion then erected is the one we are acquainted with as Craigbarnet.

Before concluding the notice of this family, let me revert to an old endowment in 1508:—Sir John Striveling of Cragbernard, on 6th June, 1508 (just ten days after he had acquired Glorat lands), founded a chaplainry in the church of Campsie. He had previously erected a private chapel at his place of Cragbernard, and he of this date granted to the ministering priest an annual rent of twelve marks and ten shillings Scots money; payable, six marks and ten shillings from his lands of Cragbernard, and six marks from his lands of Glorat,—until the founder or his heirs found a sacellum or chapel in honour of the Virgin Mary in said church, and in his chapel at Cragbernard.

Mathew, Earl of Levenax, &c. Greeting; has seen the following charter by his beloved Sir John Stirling of Cragbernard, knight, &c., whereby the said Sir John, for the glory and honour of Almighty God, . . . and for the safety of his [the said John Stirling's] own soul and that of his wife, Margaret Abirnethy, and of their fathers and mothers and their own offspring, and of all those to whom he was a debtor in this world and whom he had any ways injured. Gave and Granted to a chaplain, perpetually to serve God in the Parish Church of Campsy, and in his chapel, erected and founded in honour of the Most Blessed Virgin Mary, within his place and manor of Cragbernard, an annual rent of 12 marks and 10 shillings Scots money, at the terms of Pentecost and St.

Martin in winter, by equal portions, viz., six marks and ten shillings from his lands of Cragbernard, and six marks from his lands of Glorat; to be held by the said chaplin and his successors celebrating divine offices at the altar of Our Lady in the parish church of Campsy, always until the granter or his heirs found a " sacellum " or chapel in her honour in said church, and in his chapel of Cragbernard, in pure and perpetual alms. The granter binds the chaplain to continual residence, and should he absent himself fifteen days, he is to vacate his benefice ; and he is daily to celebrate as follows : viz., thrice in each week in the parish church, and four times in the chapel of Cragbernard each week, all the year for ever, and at the first " lavatorium," he shall be bound at each mass to exhort the people that they say a " Pater Noster,' with the angelic salutation " Ave Maria," for the aforesaid souls ; nor shall the said chaplain for the time have, or keep " continuously," a concubine or attendant [focaria] ; if this be " notourly " known, he shall vacate the chaplaincy and service ; the granter's heirs being bound within twenty days thereafter to nominate and institute a fit successor to him ; the said chaplain for the time further being bound every " Feria sexta " [Good Friday] each year for ever, to pray and say a " Placebo " and " Dirige " with the usual collects, for the foresaid souls, as he shall answer before the Supreme Judge. The granter further directs the foresaid 10 shillings to be expended on bread, wine, and wax candles, for the sustentation of the masses of said service.

In the Diocesan Registers of Glasgow (vol. ii., page 413), Sir John's successor had Sir George Mason, late Vicar of Drymen, inducted to the chaplainry in the Parish Church and in the private chapel of Cragbernard.   The Reformation came in 1560, and the chapel at Cragbernard seems to have fallen into disuse; for, when John, the ninth laird, was building his new house in the bog, he unceremoniously took the stones of this " consecrated " chapel, and used them in the new building; and thereby hangs a tale. These chapel stones would be brought back again in 1786; and thereby hangs a continuation of the tale.   Many clergymen of the Church of Rome are thoroughly conversant with the Scottish ecclesiastical history of pre-Reformation times.   The late Rev. John H. Magini, although an Italian by birth, was well acquainted with the early ecclesiastical history of the parish ; and one day he enquired at the present proprietor of Craigbarnet about the old endowment for the priest.   But the laird laughed good-naturedly, and told him that since the year 1560 a great many changes had taken place.

In my lecture to the Campsie Mechanics' Institution in 1886, I referred at some length to the relics of Prince Charlie, which are carefully treasured at Craigbarnet ; to the relics brought by Bell, the traveller, from Russia ; and to that distinguished soldier and native of the parish, General Stirling, who was in command of the 42nd in Egypt, where he captured the eagles of the French " Invincibles."

In the present paper, I confine myself to the genealogies and mansions of the old landed families.   On another occasion I may deal at greater length with their family histories.

GLORAT.

An early notice of Glorat is made in the Chamberlain's Rolls in H. M. Register House, Edinburgh.   This records that a precept

of sasine which had been issued from chancery for infefting the
heir of the lands of Glorat in the earldom of Lennox had not
been executed and the heir entered, though the relief duty had
been paid ; and that the old Countess of Lennox continued to
receive the farms of these lands, and not the King, in regard to
which his Majesty was to be consulted. · Isabella Countess of
Lennox died in 1460, and in the next notice in the chamberlain's
accounts his account is not charged with the farms of the earldom
of Lennox, inasmuch as the King had assigned them for the
building of Stirling Castle ; King James II. on the death of the
Countess having availed himself of his feudal casualty of non-entry.

Sir John Striveling of Cragbernard acquired the lands of
Glorat from Matthew Earl of Lennox by charter dated 27th May
1508, which was confirmed by James IV. by charter dated 31st
May, where he is styled the King's familiar knight. Sir John
Striveling married Margaret, eldest daughter of James third Lord
Abernethy of Saltoun, by whom he had at least four sons and one
daughter. As stated on page 177, he divided his estates among
his sons, William, the second son, getting Glorat as his portion.
Sir John died in 1510, when William would enter on possession
of Glorat, where he would find an old tower or peel then existing,
some remains of the foundations of which can still be traced to the
north-west of the present mansion house. This William Striveling
of Glorat seems to have been a man of energy and resource, for
on 3rd February, 1514, we find the Earl of Lennox acknowledging his services in the following abstract of obligation, quoted on
page 84 of *The Stirlings of Craigbernard and Glorat.* The
Earl in the narrative says, "that forsameikle as our traist cousyng
and familiar servitor William Strivelyng of Gloret has be his
labouris, travellis, costis and expensis, gotten and optenit to us
the Castale of Dunbertane," therefore, and for other faithful
services made and to be made by him, binds and obliges himself
within a year after the date of the letters, to infeft him by charter
and seisin of the £5 lands of Keppoch of old extent in the
earldom of Lennox and shire of Dumbarton," fre for a penny of
Bleachferme." This William Striveling first of Glorat was
married before 20th April, 1517, to Mariota Brisbane, a daughter
of Brisbane of Bishoptoun and Balnaclerroch. He again married,
before 1527, Margaret, a daughter of Houston of that Ilk, a
barony that was anciently called Kilpeter, from the church being
dedicated to St. Peter. In the middle of the twelfth century the
barony passed from Baldwin of Biggar to Hugh of Padvinan, and
came to be called Hugh's town, corrupted into Houston, well
known as a parish in Renfrewshire. The Houstons retained the
barony till 1740. William Striveling of Glorat was murdered on
Good Friday, 1534, when going from Striveling to Dumbarton,
on King's business.

Sir John Striveling of Cragbernard had obtained a grant from
James IV. on 26th July, 1497, for the keeping of Dumbarton.

Castle for nineteen years. William his son seems to have acted as his father's deputy in Dumbarton before 1510. William seems to have been a busy man, and his duties would require him to reside at Dumbarton. This explains why he was evidently quite content to inhabit the old peel at Glorat, which he would find there as when it came into the possession of his father.

William, the first laird of Glorat, was succeeded by his son George, who succeeded his father in the captaincy of Dumbarton Castle, having had that office continued to him by King James V. The ratification says :—

> "The king having consideration of the thankful and true service done to himself and his most faithful father, by the late William Stirling of Glorat, and his father; and that William was cruelly slain last Good Friday, acting in the king's service, ratifies to George Stirling, his son and heir, the assedation of the said office of constabulary and keeping the said castle and lands and emoluments thereof, given by him to the said William for the years contained therein. Subscribed at Stirling, 13th April, twenty-first year of the king's reign (1534).
>
> "JAMES R."

In the following month, King James V. in a letter writes :—

> "Wherefore we thank you greatly, praying you to continew in your dilligence and gud service in time coming."

The story of his keepership of the castle cannot be gone into here.

It was not until the time of John Striveling fourth of Glorat, that a more commodious residence was built. John succeeded to the estate about 1613, and died about 1642. In the tower of the present mansion house there has been built the old memorial stone of this building. It bears the initials, not of the Laird, but of his son, Sir Mungo—

M S
1 6 2 5
18 Rebuilt 79

There is also a stone bearing Sir Charles Stirling's monogram and the year 1869.

Sir George the sixth of Glorat, like his father Sir Mungo, was a strong Royalist, but the only reward they received was the dignity of knight baronet, and an honourable augmentation to their armorial bearings. Sir George, who was already a knight, was created a baronet of Nova Scotia, with limitation to the heirs male of his body, by patent dated at Whitehall, 30th April, 1666. It narrates :—

> "The good and faithful services, great sufferings, and losses, through several imprisonments, fynes, and other prejudices sustained be Sir Mungo Stirling of Glorat, and Sir George Stirling, his sone, for and in His Majestie's service, and his Majesty being no less sensible thereof, as desyrous for there encouragement in the future, to put ane mark of His Majestie's favour upon that family,"

Sir George married Marjory, a daughter of Sir William Purves of Woodhouselee, Baronet, who was the prototype of Allan Ramsay's "Sir William Worthy" in the *Gentle Shepherd*. Sir George's third son, John, married Elizabeth, eldest daughter of Sir Alexander Home of Renton, Baronet, and his son eventually succeeded to the estate of Renton, and transmitted with it to his descendants the representation of the historic houses—Hepburns, Earls of Bothwell, and their successors, the Stewarts of Coldinghame; and also George Home, Earl of Dunbar, the trusted councillor of James VI.*

Sir Samuel Home Stirling, seventh baronet, died on 18th September, 1861, without male issue, but left two daughters. The elder, under the entail of Renton, by her great-grandfather, succeeded to the Renton estate, while under the entail of Glorat by the third baronet in 1765, her uncle, Sir Charles, succeeded his elder brother in it, as also in the baronetcy under the patent.

Sir Charles Elphinstone Fleming Stirling, the eighth and present baronet, has rebuilt the mansion house of Glorat, which is now a handsome building in the Scottish domestic baronial style of architecture. It is beautifully situated at the bottom of the Campsie Fells, with a southern exposure, sheltered by fine old timber and surrounded by thriving young plantations. Glorat was rebuilt in 1869, and the tower was added in 1879.

KYNCADES (LATTERLY KINCAIDS) OF THAT ILK.

In 1230, when Alexander III. was king, Earl Maldwin, by charter, granted to Maurice Galbret, son of his senescallus, Gilespie Galbret, the lands of Cartenbenach. We first hear of Kyncade in 1238, when a Galbraith got a charter of these lands. The Galbraiths were at one time a very powerful family in the Lennox, and proprietors of Mains, Garscadden, Balvie, Gartconnel, Craigmaddie, Bardowie, &c. Their principal castle was originally at Craigmaddie. The name disappeared owing to the failure of male heirs, and the estate was partitioned as tochers amongst three sisters, co-heiresses. In 1381 one of these, Janet Keith, married John Hamilton of Cadzow, from whom are descended the Hamiltons of Bardowie, &c., and brought with her the lands of Easter and Wester Bathernock, &c. Another co-heiress married Nicholas Douglas, and brought him the estate of Mains. The third married a Logan, and brought with her the lands of Balvie, then a large estate. The Galbraiths parted with their Kyncade lands after having possessed them for forty-two years, and we next find that another family then acquired them by a charter from Maldwin, fourth Earl of Lennox, in 1280, and this family then took their surname from their property. These Kyncade lands extended from the Glazert to the Kelvin. Considerable portions have been parted with from time to time,

*The Stirlings of Craigbarnet and Glorat, pages 29-30.

the family, while respectable, having never been affluent. Miss Lennox's claim to the ancient earldom of Lennox brought this family into prominence, owing to a Kincaid being heir presumptive to the Woodhead estate, and genealogists such as Burke and others applied to them for their family tree and history. It then transpired that many of their family papers had been destroyed by a fire at Cannerton, where they had been stowed away while tradesmen were in possession of Kincaid House, engaged in the building of the new mansion.

This family have not made any great mark in history, but one of them distinguished himself for gallant conduct against the English, and for his valiant services in recovering Edinburgh Castle from the English in the time of Edward I. the then laird of Kincaid was made Constable of Edinburgh Castle, and his posterity enjoyed that office for a considerable period. He had the castle on the Kincaid shield granted as an honourable augmentation to his armorial bearings. These were—Gu. a fess. erm. betw. two mullets in chief. or., and a castle triple towered in base ar. masoned sa. Crest—A castle, as in the arms, and issuing therefrom a dexter arm embowed, grasping a sword ppr. Supporters—Two Highlanders, armed with cuirasses, each grasping a Lochaber axe, all ppr. Motto—I'll defend. This shield may be seen on the tombstones at Clachan churchyard, and above the Lennox Arms Inn, Lennoxtown, where it is quartered with the Lennox arms, which are—Ar. a saltire gu. between four roses of of the last, barbed vert. Crest—Two broadswords in saltire behind an imperial crown all ppr. Supporters—Two savages, wreathed head and middle with oak, holding in their hands clubs. Motto—I'll defend. In Nimmo's History of Stirlingshire there is mention made of an old broadsword belonging to a branch of the family, upon which are the Kincaid arms as given, with these words—

> " Wha will pursew, I will defend
> My life and honour to the end."

The Kincaids appear in the parochial records through squabbling with the Lennoxes and Stirlings. The parish landowners were not a very harmonious lot, and the Kincaids and Lennoxes, Kincaids and Stirlings, and Stirlings and M'Farlans wrangled and quarrelled and fought with each other to the effusion of blood and even the taking of life. There is one amusing instance in which they took the law into their own hands, and surprised the laird of Wodheid while he was engaged saying his prayers, treated him very roughly, and finally carried him off with them to Kyncade, where he was kept for some time a prisoner. The case as quoted is taken from the Register of Privy Council, vol. ii., page 82, where there is a complaint at the instance of the kin and friends of Johnne Levenax of Woodheid makand mentioun—That quhairupon the seventene day of September instant, he being solitar at his prayers beside his dwelling-place of Woodheid, belevit na evill of ony person, but to have levit under Godis peax and the King's, nottheles the sounes and brethir of James Kincaid of that Ilk, upon set purpois, cruellie invadit the said Johnne, and woundit and hurt him in diverse partis of his body, to the effusioun of his blude in great quantitie, and maister-fullie and per force tuke him with thame to the place of Kincaid, quhair they detene him captive as yit in hie contemption of our Soverane Lord and his auchoritie. The Stirlings attacked the Kincaids in June, 1581, when Malcolm Kincaid, a son of the laird was slain. This brought the Stirlings into trouble. In the local feuds this family stood by one another shoulder to shoulder, and the whole clan of them are included in the charge of murdering young Kincaid. The case is mentioned in Pitcairn's Criminal Trials, December 9, 1581:—Johnne Striveling of Glorat, Johnne Striveling younger of Craigbernat, Walter Striveling of Ballagane, Louke Striveling of Baldorane, Alex. Abernethie in Strablane, and John Striveling servitor to Glorat, dilatit of airt and pairt of the crewall slauchter of vnigle Malcum Kincaid, sone to (James) Kincaid of that Ilk, committed in Jun ij last bypast. The pannell askit instrumentis, that young Kincaid, being requyrit gif he wald persew thame of thaer lyfis; ansueris that he wald. Replegiated the pannell to the Regality of Lennox and assigned 24th March following for administration of Justice.

In 1604 James Kincaid of that Ilk and James Kincaid his son were bound in 500 merks not to slay salmon in the waters of the Clyd, Lewin, Blanis, Kalvin, or branches thereof.

When the Kincaids obtained their lands in 1280 they would have to get a suitable residence, and they seem shortly afterwards to have built

KYNCADE TOWER.

The original tower of Kincade has disappeared so completely that there is uncertainty about its site.

The modern mansion was erected at three different times. The oldest portion, where the kitchen is, was built about 1690; the next oldest about 1750; and the modern large square portion, with its central staircase, its tower, and its four corner turrets, about 1812. The main idea of this new portion was taken from the Castle of Inveraray, which was destroyed by fire a few years ago. Kincaid was the first dwelling-house of any considerable pretentions which the late David Hamilton, architect, Glasgow, designed and carried forward. His later works were the Parish Church, in 1827, and Lennox Castle. From an examination of the foundation walls of the cellars under the south-west corner of the modern building Mr. Galloway formed the opinion that part of these must have been part of the old tower. The late J. L. Kincaid Lennox, however, always said that his father alleged that the site of the original tower was a few yards west from the range of the one-story building forming the stables, or about fifty yards west from the cellars.

John Kincaid, the Laird who died in 1835, was not the eldest son. Father and mother and brothers had been rather unthrifty, and John saw that it would be necessary to do something for himself, if he was to maintain the respectability of his family, so he took to farming and lime-burning at Auchinairn. He occupied the mansion-house there, and being of good family, respectable in personal conduct, and a good business man, he was made a Justice of the Peace in 1793. In course of time his elder brothers died, and he married Miss Cecilia Lennox of Woodhead, by whom he had a son, John Lennox Kincaid, who succeeded to the Woodhead estates on the death of his aunt. In his younger days he had often held the plough, and was a first-rate ploughman. He seemed to have been passionately fond of ploughing, and even when well up in years and Laird of Kincaid, he could never resist an opportunity of taking the plough for a few furrows, just to keep in his hand. This Laird always called a field to the west of the mansion-house, " The Law Park," as being where, in olden times, the barony courts were held.

In the historical MS. there is a charter by William Galbraith to Sir Patrick de Grahame, Knight, and his heirs, remitting to him 2¼ merks, payable annually from the lands of Kincade, and granting to him the Mill of Kincade. The charter is not dated, but was probably granted about 1285. The old Mill of Kyncade is, I presume, what is now termed French Mill. This name is said to have been given to it, either from its having been reconstructed by French Huguenots or from the millstones there used having been brought from France. The French burr stones have a close grit, adapted for grinding, and the best quality is got at Andernack on the Rhine and in Auvergne in France.

THE TOWER.

The Tower would appear to have been one of the oldest peels or castles in the parish, but there is now to be seen only remains of what were probably foundations of the outhouses. It has given its name to the Tower Burn, which since 1649 has formed the boundary between the parish and Baldernock, and the farm steading retains the name of Tower. The names of the burn and the steading alone remain to perpetuate the memory of the old mansion house of the proprietors of the Balegrochyr and Lethad or Lechade lands. The tower existed in all its glory before 1400, when the laird, having become embarrassed, took to borrowing. He gave his lands as security under a bond to the lady of Craigbernard. Little is known of this individual except that his name was Giles, son of Donald, and that he had been proprietor of the lands of Lethad and Balegrochyr. The Lethad lands probably comprised Back-o'-hill, Bargeny Hill, and the Tower. All of these were on one side of the Tower Burn, and the Balegrochyr lands were on the other. The name of Lethad seems to have become obsolete, as when Mr. Maitland, the present laird, was pointing out the site of the old tower to me in 1890, in reply to my enquiry, he mentioned that he had never heard the name, although his father was proprietor of the Tower. On 13th Feb., 1400, Giles resigned his patrimony to the bondholder, Alicia de Erth, lady of Craigbernard, who the same day granted a charter of the lands of Lethad and Balegrochyr to Sir William Graham, Lord of Kyncardine, who shortly afterwards acquired the castle of Mugdoch.

In 1458, Patrick Graham obtained from James II. a charter whereby the lands of Ballingrothane (Balegrochyr), Caristoune, Dougalstoune, Barloch, and various others, were erected into the barony of Mukok (Mugdoch). The old mansion house of Tower seems then to have gradually fallen into ruin. Not being inhabited, it would soon become a quarry for stones. Mugdoch Castle became the residence of the Earls of Montrose, and of the old tower not a stone remains above the ground. What remains were probably the foundations of outhouses forming a court in rear.

BALLYNCORRAUCH (BALCORRACH).

The charter in which Duncan Earl of Lennox granted these lands to his son Donald designates them as Ballyncorrauch. The name *Bal, ballyn,* implies a building then existing, but of what nature—whether this was one of the earl's minor castles or only a farm town—it is impossible now to determine. There is nothing which connects the old earls with this place; there are no charters extant which had been signed here, as they had been at the earl's residences at Strathblayn or Fyntre. The probabilities are that Donald would have to get a dwelling-house erected for himself. Such residences took then the form of castles or peels. Accommodation was required not only for the residence of the lord of the manor, but it had to be of sufficient strength and size to afford shelter and protection to his dependants in time of danger—whither his vassals and their followers (and perhaps their cattle) could resort in dire extremity. In a letter to Mr. William Brown, Mr. Galloway thus describes the site :—

"SITE OF BALCORRACH TOWER."

" A long straight line of stone dyke passes from the glen, a little north of the Bleachwork' buildings, eastwards, dividing the hill from the arable ground. In the first field, about half-way eastward, and near the dyke (opposite a lot of old thorn-trees growing in the hill ground), you will come on a plateau, upon which, I believe, the Tower stood. Near to the centre of it you will see a depression of the surface, curving down towards the site of the old church, which I think was the course of the access road. In front of the site there is still a sudden descent, where I fancy there had been a retaining wall which formed the face of a terrace plot and protection to the buildings. Other walls on the west and east sides and on the higher ground behind would enclose offices and garden. The position corresponds in a general way with the sites of all or nearly every one of the towers and castles within the Earldom at the beginning of the 15th century." The trees and terraces still to be seen on the hillside to the east of the Glen are all that remains now of Ballyncorrach Tower.

As 500 years ago every considerable barony had its meeting place, where the vassals assembled to have justice dispensed, we must look about us for the Law or Mute Hill. The Mute Hill, or Midge Knoll, would likely be the Court of the old Balcorrach barony. This mound has been spread to make arable ground, and is hardly distinguishable in time of growing corn crops, but its outlines are perfectly marked at other times, especially when the sun is low on the horizon and shines out brightly. The Law Mound was sometimes used as the hanging or gallows hill, and as we know that Highland reivers sometimes made a raid into the parish when engaged in cattle-lifting expeditions, we can easily conceive that where some of these depredators were caught, the owners of the cattle would be of opinion that hanging was the only cure, and their bodies might be left suspended from a gallows on the Mound here as a terror to evil-doers, the news of which would soon spread towards the head of Loch Lomond. There is, however, no record of a gallows hill at Balcorrach. The Midge Hole is a name which is full of perplexity to etymologists and archæologists. According to one version this is Image Hole, from a cross or image which stood on the roadside here in the old Roman Catholic times. Others laugh at this as very far-fetched, and say it is the Midge Hole; that there used to be a small pond for steeping lint, and it got the name owing to the swarms of midges which abounded here.

TOWER OF BENCLOICH.

Maldwin the Earl of Lennox granted by charter the lands of Glasskell, Monaebroch, with the patronage of the church of Monaebroch, to Malcolm, as detailed in page 174. The Kilsyth Livingstones were thus detached from the Livingstones of Callendar about 1450, and they held their Kilsyth lands for more than two centuries and a half. But they only gained a footing in Campsie shortly before 1660, when the proprietor of that time entered in possession of the lands of Bencloich, part of the lands of Easter and Wester Muckcroft, Tamfin, Carrower, Tambuy, which had all belonged to Lennox of Woodhead, having formed part of the family estate since 1421. Livingstone accompanied the Duke of Lennox on an embassy to France in 1601. He was knighted and made a Lord of Session, 1609, was sworn Privy Councillor and made Chancellor of Scotland in 1613. In this year 1613, through his influence at court, he obtained a charter from the King, which conferred on him the ecclesiastical patronage of the parish of Campsie. In 1621 he was made a Commissioner for the Plantation of Kirks. He died in 1627, and is supposed to have left behind him a considerable sum in hard cash. Son, grandson, and brother succeeded in turn to the estates. When his brother succeeded to the Kilsyth estates he was Sir James Livingstone Barncleugh, or Ballyncloich, or Bencloich. During the minority of his grandnephew, Sir James had carefully nursed the Kilsyth estate. This, with the savings of the Chancellor, he carefully used to advance his interests, lending money to Royalists to defray the expenses of the army under Montrose. When ruin overtook them after Philiphaugh he lent money to enable them to pay the fines levied on them. He took care to have ample security for his advances by wadset bonds over their estates. Under these bonds the lender had immediate possession as security. If at the end of twelve years the borrower had not repaid the money, the lender could then apply to the Court for declarator that the lands given in security had now become his. Sir James was grasping and ambitious, and he made the lending of his ready money on wadset bonds a means of rapidly extending his possessions, and obtaining a preponderating influence over the impoverished lairds who were now suffering severely for their loyalty and attachment to the Stuart or Royalist cause. The Earl of Montrose then of Mugdoch, Lennox of Woodhead, Stirling of Craigbarnet, Hamilton of Bardowie, and Napier of Culcreuch all suffered terribly at this time, and in their extremity they got into Sir James' hands. When Livingstone became proprietor of Bencloich, through Lennox's inability to pay the bond at the end of the twelve years, he proceeded forthwith to build for himself a tower on his newly-acquired possessions.

The Tower of Bencloich was erected on a site which had been well selected. The tower and offices occupied what was then a level platform of sufficient size to accommodate them all. There was a gorge on either side, formed by the Ferret or Glorat Burn. There appears also to have been a level field or lawn just below the house, while the gardens occupied the lower ground in front of this. There was an abundance of growing wood on the slope behind. There are trees still growing on the Ferret Brae, near the site of this tower, which at first sight may appear that these could not possibly have been planted in Livingstone's time. A close inspection will remove this impression, for it will be found that some of them may have been even older, for what are growing now have in some cases sprung from stocks of older trees and not from young transplants.

Bencloich Tower must have been a great eyesore to Glorat. Besides, a field belonging to Bencloich came far too near the doors and windows of Glorat to be agreeable to the inmates there. This field was afterwards excambed for a piece of Glorat ground near to Rowantreefauld. I am not aware of any representations of Bencloich being in existence. The style of the period in which it was erected was that of an ordinary square building about 35 by 25 by 30 high, with the pepper-box turrets projecting at corners. The ground floor was used for kitchen cooking and stores. The upper floor contained the family parlour, dining-room, and a small service room; the upper flat would be divided into apartments for sleeping, the access to these bed-rooms being by a screw stair. Small buildings adjoining would give the other needful accommodation. Debris from the lime workings about the end of last century and beginning of the present one covers over irregularly portions of the platform where the tower stood, especially at its sides and behind. These dirt hills, as they have been called, or mounds thrown up by mineral workings, have altered the surface so much as to make the place look utterly unsuited for the site of a tower. The tower would stand close to the old pit, which is situated a little to the west of the Ferret Burn, and which would be sunk after the tower had been swept away. The site is very near a small reservoir which was constructed by the Alum Company about 1856.

David Miller, or " Old Mains," as he was called, who died in Lennoxtown in April, 1851, has informed Mr. William Brown, my correspondent in Johnstone, that he had a distinct recollection of the tower and the gardens and pleasure-grounds by which it was surrounded. The tower continued pretty entire till about 1804. The late John Stewart, shoemaker, born in 1797—whom I remember as working with Mr James Glen—had no recollection whatever of ever having seen any tower, but he remembered the gardens very well. He had frequently pulled gooseberries and also plums from the bushes and trees growing therein. At a more recent date he remembers seeing an old plum tree growing in the precincts of an old lime kiln, in close proximity to what has now been ascertained to have been the site of the old tower.

The estate of Bencloich had been purchased in. 1783 by Sir Archibald Edmonstone, who had sold his estates in Ireland and had been created a baronet in 1774. The new proprietor found the small farmsteads and cottages on the estate almost in ruins. To save the expense and trouble of quarrying at the Ferrets and carting the stones to the new steadings and cottages, Mr. Alexander Mackenzie, contractor, received orders from the proprietor to tear down the tower. It was thus ruthlessly swept away, and the stones were used to build the farm steading of Mains, which is just a little to the west of it. The year 1805 is cut on the lintel of the south door at Mains. New steadings were erected between 1804 and 1812 at Drewmillan, Middle Muckcroft, West Muckcroft, and the Mill of Bencloich. George Brown entered on the occupancy of Mains Farm in 1821, and he had a distillery erected at the Mains about that time. Any stones then remaining about the site of the tower would be used up for this.

The tower was unoccupied after the forfeiture of Viscount Kilsyth's estates. The estates were sold, and were acquired by the York Buildings Company, who sadly neglected them. Old Mains had heard his father say that he had in severe snowstorms collected his sheep and put them into the kitchen of the old tower. This place was swarming with rats, which, however, did not prevent an old woman taking up her residence in it as a squatter. Strange to say, the rats, although very numerous, became very tame. The old woman learned to know them and actually gave them names. One in particular, which she called "Rumpy," would hasten to her whenever she called it, and for prompt obedience the rat was always rewarded with something to eat. People in the neighbouring farms did not care to pass near the old tower after nightfall. There were local traditions that the ghosts of the Livingstones, its former occupants, still haunted the scenes of their bacchanalian revelry.

The mineral workings, which have so completely effaced the old Bencloich Tower, were carried on at the end of last century. They were in the blue limestone seam, which there was about four feet thick. This lime was worked by a level, or mine, or ingoing e'e. After the portion of the outcrop was worked by open cast till the depth of the material above, called the tirring or baring, became so deep as to be expensive in removing, then another level had to be opened. The coal seam was from twelve to fifteen fathoms below the limestone. This had to be worked by pits, as coals were necessary to calcine the limestone, and the calcining kilns were between the tower and the limestone outcrop

ANTERMONY OR AUCHTERMONY.

The family of the Flemings of Biggar, Kirkintilloch, and Cumbernauld acquired the Antermony lands shortly after 1424. They then had built upon the site of the present mansion-house a small tower or substantial dwelling-house for the tacksman, who was usually a relative of the proprietor. The site then selected was about one hundred and seventy yards north of the public road, and this house in its various rebuildings and enlargements was henceforward the mansion-house of the estate. The Flemings became Earls of Wigton in 1606. They retained possession of their Antermony lands till soon after 1700, when they parted with them, and the Rev. Patrick Bell, minister of Port of Menteith, became the possessor. In all probability the Bells would take down the old house and re-erect a new house for themselves. The house then built by them forms the central portion of the present mansion, which has been very greatly enlarged by the present tenant, Mr Charles Macintosh King, and the house of the Bells is now flanked on both sides by extensive wings. The Rev. Patrick Bell married Annabel Stirling, daughter of John Stirling the ninth Laird of Craigbarnet, ar grand daughter of Sir Mungo Stirling of Glorat. Their son John Bell, born in 1691, became the celebrated traveller, and was one of the most distinguished of all the natives of Campsie. He adopted medicine as his profession, and having passed as a physician in 1713, he went to Russia in the following year, when only twenty-three years of age. His first appointment was that of physician to a Russian Embassy to Persia, where he was away for three years. He was then appointed to an embassy to China. What he saw and learned during his residence at the Court of China is perhaps the most valuable part of his book of travels, a book which when published made its readers acquainted with a country hitherto but imperfectly known. It was said of it that it was the one of the best and most interesting relations ever written by any traveller. Bell had abundant opportunities of acquiring information that was full of interest and information to his countrymen.

He accompanied Czar Peter the Great, his Empress, and a Russian army that went to the assistance of Persia, whose territory had been invaded by Afghans. He describes Circassia, and vividly pourtrayed the character of Czar Peter, whose habits and manner of life he had abundant opportunity of studying. When Russia and Turkey were at war in 1737 he went to Constantinople as a confidential agent of Russia on a secret mission. He returned to Russia the following year. He then lived in Constantinople as a merchant for several years. Being then 55 years of age, in 1746 he married Mary Peters—whose sister, Jane Vigors, Lady Hyndford, died at Craigbarnet while on a visit there, and is interred in the Clachan churchyard—and in the following year settled at Antermony, where his subsequent life was passed in ease and affluence. He is described as a warm-hearted, benevolent, sociable man, and he obtained from his friends and neighbours the appellation of Honest John Bell. It is a tradition in the district that he sometimes rode out attired in oriental costume. His memory is perpetuated by his book of travels, but his memorial in Campsie is the avenue of lime trees along the public road in front of Antermony and in the avenue to the mansion-house, the seeds of which he is said to have brought from abroad. In his travels abroad he had seen much distress from want of water, and finding the little hamlet of Aulton indifferently supplied with that necessary of life, he had a well built near the Waltry Burn to ensure a domestic supply to the cottagers in the summer droughts. A proposal, having for its object the restoration of this well by new cradling and cover, as a memorial of Bell, was not regarded favourably, the objection taken to it being that it might annoy the tenant of the farm by bringing idle people into his field. Having no issue, he sold Antermony to Captain John Lennox, reserving his own life-rent. This ran on till he was 89, and the captain seemed to think he was lingering on life's stage too long. Many of his most valuable effects were bequeathed to the Stirlings of Craigbarnet, where they are carefully treasured and highly prized. Annexed is an advertisement of 1827 :—

TO BE LET.

THE MANSION HOUSE OF ANTERMONY.—The house, which stands in a pleasant situation, amid fine old timber, consists of dining room, drawing room, five bedrooms, laundry, kitchen, &c., with good accommodation for servants and suitable offices, and there is a good garden with a fine south exposure.

Antermony is distant from Glasgow ten miles, two miles from the post town of Kirkintilloch, from which there is daily communication to Glasgow by coaches, and the great canal is within the same distance, where passage boats betwixt Edinburgh and Glasgow also pass within a mile of the house.

Woodhead House, 1st March, 1827.

Alton, Aulton, or Auldtown of Antermony exists now only as a farm steading, but down to the beginning of this century there was a little hamlet, which in the 17th century was even larger. It seems to have formed one of those village communities of small farmers, who for mutual protection and convenience had their dwellings and byres near each other. They would have their common barn and kiln, just as the Birdston feuars had. The conjecture of its etymology is that when the Flemings built their house at Antermony, the hamlet on the south side of the road would thenceforth take the name of the Auld town. It is so written in the titles when acquired by Captain Lennox. The houses of the hamlet were between Alton farmsteading westward and northwestward towards the road and Waltry burn. In old M'Kerroch's time, who was tenant of Alton before the Stevensons, a number of these old houses were pulled down and their stones used in helping to build the dyke along the south side of the road between Alton and the " castle." Other old cottages were pulled down about 1837-8 within the memory of men still living. Some of these had probably been built about 1773, and it was to give them a water supply Bell dug the well.

With a hamlet here from a very early period we are not surprised to find burying-places. The grant erecting the parish church, mentioned " the churches of Campsie and Altermurrin," and in another charter besides the parish church and " all adjacent chapels." It has been conjectured that at one time a chapel of some kind had existed probably in the vicinity of these burying-places. The late Mr. William Stevenson of Alton informed me that in his father's young days the old people then living about Auldton had seen people buried in two separate burying-places on Alton farm. The burying-place for the well-to-do people was a mound nearly opposite Antermony gate. There was another mound for the poor east from that about half way between Alton and Lochmill. The farmers before his grandfather's time did not plough over the mound opposite Antermony gate, and his grandfather always respected its sanctity. His father first threw it into the field and ploughed over it, and there is now no indication where it was. When it was first ploughed a number of human bones was disturbed. These Stevenson was alleged to have gathered together and burned. A report to this effect was current in 1836, but Stevenson did not wish the subject dwelt on. The term " castle " as applied to one cottage on the roadside near the bridge over Waltry Burn was used as a jibe when it was a-building, and had reference particularly to the high south wall. There is a King's Hill near Antermony Loch. This is an old local name and is given in the Ordnance Survey maps. I have never been able to ascertain how this name was bestowed in old times.

BALLANCLEROCH.

The earliest mention of Ballenacleroch is in a charter, given in extenso, No. 215, pages 411-3, of "The Lennox." The charter is by Sir William de Grahame to John Brisbane of a quarter of land in Campsy, called Ballenacleroch, 11th August, 1423. This is the year in which Sir William de Grahame parted with his lands of Ballegrochyr to Donald de Levenax of Ballecorrach. In the deed Donald was explicitly styled filius legitimus Duncani Comitis de Levenax. In the charter granting Ballenacleroch to John Brisbane the witnesses are—Hiis testibus nobili domino nostro et potenti, domino Duncano comite de Leuenax, Malcolmo Thoma et Donaldo filiis suis naturalibus, Johanne de Buchanne, &c.—Duncan, Earl of Lennox, Malcolm, Thomas, and Donald, his natural sons. The Brisbanes of Bishopton, who were owners of Balnaclerroch from 1423 to 1642, had obtained possession of their lands of Bishopton in 1332. They parted with this estate in 1671, and after passing through a number of hands, it is now the property of Lord Blantyre.

In 1481 we find a Thomas Brisbane infeft in the lands of Balnacleroch in virtue of a precept of sasine from William Lord Graham as superior. The next infeftment is in 1547, and is in favour of John Brisbane of Bishoptown, from William, Earl of Montrose; and so generation after generation of Brisbanes succeed as proprietors of the lands of Balnacleroch, with miln, miln lands, and pertinents. In 1639 John Brisbane, contemplating a sale, went to the Crown and obtained confirmation of his rights by royal charter. On 22nd October, 1642, John Brisbane of Bishopton seems to have considered himself now a Crown vassal, for of this date he sold the lands of Balnacleroch to Patrick M'Farlan of Keithton, to be holden of himself for 100 merks Scots for feu-duty; and on 27th August, 1652, Brisbane of Bishopton sold the superiority of said lands, and the 100 merks of feu-duty payable for them, to Sir Mungo Stirling of Glorat for no less a sum than £2500 Scots, a further proof of Brisbane now holding immediately from the Crown.

In 1652 Sir Mungo Stirling took out two charters, and in 25th November, 1653, he was infeft, so that he was Bishopton's immediate vassal ; but in 1656 the property of these lands came into the person of Isobel M'Farlan, daughter of Patrick M'Farlan, the original purchaser, and sister to James M'Farlan, to whom the fee was provided, and whose heir in general she was. In 1657, charter of resignation by Sir Mungo Stirling. In 1664, Isabel M'Farlan, with consent of her husband, Rev. Benjamin Burns, sold the lands to Mr. James M'Farlan of Kirkton or Keithtown. Sir George Stirling, in 1667, disposed of the superiority to James M'Farlan, who, having now acquired both the property and the superiority, instead of going to the Crown, applied to and obtained from the Marquis of Montrose, as superior, a charter, &c. 1703, a judicial sale brought about. Hugh M'Farlan, the son of the laird, became purchaser at the sale.

In the days of the Brisbanes there would be a mansion house or tower of some kind, and it has been said that the arch above the present kitchen court entrance was part of the refectory or kitchen of the older building, which some have fancied from the name, might have been a monastery. Local traditions linger about the Clachan to the effect that Ballancleroch, as the name was held to mean "town or building of the clergy," was church land, and that there resided in a sort of monastery here some of the clergymen connected with the church, or monks, and there is also a tradition of a subterranean passage between the house of Ballancleroch and the old church. I am bound to say that neither in the charters founding the church and endowing it, nor in the extant records of the diocese of Glasgow in pre-Reformation times have I seen anything to warrant such a conjecture. There are charters extant since 1423 in which this is never alluded to. There is no record of any monastery having existed here, and if the assumption is correct, that the arch is part of an older building, it must have been part of Brisbane's tower or peel.

The Patrick M'Farlan who purchased the lands in 1642 was a son of the M'Farlans of Arrochar. His grandfather had been knighted by James IV., and was also slain at Flodden. His father, George, went to Aberdeenshire and acquired some property there, but Patrick, wishing to be nearer his kindred, sold his Aberdeenshire lands and purchased Balnacleroch. He was succeeded in Balnacleroch by his daughter Isabel, who married the Rev. Benjamin Burns. Isobel, with the consent of her husband, sold the lands to her brother, James M'Farlan, who also acquired the rights of superiority. James married Mary Keith of Invermay, neice of the Earl Marischal of Scotland, and he built a new mansion-house, which now forms the northern wing of the present mansion and faces towards the glen. Above the entrance door may still be seen the armorial shield, party per pale, with the M'Farlan and Keith arms, and the initials underneath :—

· I. M.   M. K.

1665.

O

In connection with this Mary Keith there is in possession of the family a silver-mounted Malacca cane, with the inscription, "Innermay, 1709," which, nearly fifty years after her marriage, was presented to her by her family in the north. The M'Farlans were Whigs, the Keiths Tories, and the tradition is that when the cane was presented it was accompanied by the jocular remark that "The best use it could be applied to was to lay it across a Whig's back," looking laughingly towards her husband.

James and Mary had a son named William, who was assassinated just outside the door of Cadder Kirk,* but the circumstances under which this took place have now passed into oblivion. The importance of the family in the eyes of the Government of that day may be inferred from the fact that, on hearing of the sudden death of their son, King William III. wrote to the laird a letter of condolence and sympathy, in which he stated that the deceased had ever been a good friend of the king's, and that no efforts would be spared to bring the assassins who had perpetrated the outrage to justice. Unfortunately, what a few years ago was a historical fact, has now become mere tradition. In an old oaken cabinet in Ballancleroch were preserved many treasured family documents. Among these were this letter, signed William Rex. When the present laird was serving with his regiment in India, Ballancleroch was let furnished. One of the tenants,' neither valuing the old oak cabinet nor the family treasures which it contained, and evidently considering it old-fashioned for his refined tastes, had it removed from Ballancleroch and stowed away with other lumber in his Glasgow place of business, where it was unfortunately destroyed by fire when the Tradeston Flour Mills were burned down. The loss to the family was simply irreparable, and could not be replaced by silver or gold.

James M'Farlan and Mary Keith had another son, Hugh, who suddenly left home, and was heard of as serving as a subaltern officer under Marlborough. The reason of his flight was that, in a duel fought beside the old chesnut trees at Clashmore, he had unfortunately killed his opponent, a son of the Glorat baronet, and had also hastily buried him on the spot. A rusted rapier and a short dirk were found in Mr. John M'Farlan's time, near the spot where the encounter is believed to have taken place, and these were supposed to have belonged to young Stirling. As has been mentioned, the M'Farlans were Whigs while the Stirlings were Royalists. In the time of the Commonwealth the Cavaliers or Royalists had been in the cold shades of opposition ; but their turn came at the Restoration in 1660; and a few years afterwards King Charles II. had acknowledged the services of the Glorat family by conferring a baronetcy of Nova Scotia on the

---

* John Calhoune or Colquhoun, of Konmore, and James Wallace, younger of Possill, were the parties charged with having killed William M'Farlan, younger of Keithtown, in a most barbarous manner at Cadder. This was about 1687.

Laird. The turn of the Whigs came again at the Revolution in 1688. The politics of the M'Farlans were of service to their family on the occasion of this unfortunate duel. The slain man belonged to the side which had been dished by the advent of William of Orange; the slayer was of a good Whig family, whose influence was exerted on the side of the government; so the family were informed that no proceedings would be taken against the young fugitive. When the Clachan was a populous hamlet, and before its inhabitants were nearly "a' wede away," it was firmly believed there by the young and by the superstitious among the old, that young Stirling's ghost was to be seen wander-ing about Clashmore in the moonlight. In other parts of the parish there are stories of houses haunted by visitors from the unseen world, stories known in very limited circles. I refrain from giving any particulars of these, as it might be the means of putting certain families to inconvenience and perhaps be the cause of preventing young, timid, nervous female servants from taking situations. The age of superstition is not yet past. Hugh, who so suddenly became a fugitive, and in consequence a soldier, had an eye for the beautiful in nature. While with his regiment in the campaigns on the continent he must have admired the fine trees he would see. He brought home with him a number of young trees, which he had planted about the Ballancleroch grounds and in the approach to Campsie Glen. They were planted with care, and throve and grew till some of them became the finest and most beautiful of their kind in the west of Scotland. Very few in Campsie arc aware that those beautiful beeches that used to grow at the foot of the glen had been brought from the continent and planted there by a soldier laird of long ago, shortly after the Union of England and Scotland, completed under Queen Anne. Some have been recently cut down at the entrance to the Glen, and this clearance has entirely changed its aspect.*

The tombstone of Laird Hugh and his wife, Elizabeth Doig of Ballangrew, is still to be seen in the Clachan church-yard. It has the M'Farlan and Doig arms. The M'Farlan arms are— Ar. on a saltire wavy betw. four roses, gu. a crescent of the field. Crest—A naked man holding forth a sheaf of arrows ppr., a crown or., standing by it. Motto—"This I'll defend." The Doig arms are—Gu. a chev. ar. betw. two cinquefoils, erm. in chief and a sword paleways in base of the second. Two of the oldest stones of the M'Farlans were lifted to make room for

---

* It was one thing to throw open the Glen and make all visitors welcome, but surely the privilege is abused by the Railway Company bringing great crowds of excursionists and pouring them into the Glen and on to the hill sides without any acknowledgment to the proprietors, whose trees are frequently injured, and damage caused to fences and lands by the noisy crowds on Glasgow holidays. If the people of Campsie are to retain their privileges they should see to it lest inconsiderate excursionists endanger free access to the Glen.

interments of tenants on the estate, as I have been told by one who has actually seen fragments of these stones, commemorating the old lairds, lying near the west wall of the graveyard. The late Miss Catherine M'Farlan, as long as she lived, cared with affectionate solicitude for her father's monument. When I referred to this on page 68 as evidently well cared for, I was not then aware by whom it was kept in such beautiful order. Laird Hugh and Elizabeth Doig had a son, William, who married Hume Robertson, of Fermeside, but had no issue ; also a daughter, Anne, who married the Rev. John Warden, minister of the parish, but who afterwards was translated to the Canongate, in Edinburgh. When William was in possession of the estate, having no family of his own, he settled the estates of Ballancleroch and Dalgowrie by entail on the eldest son of his sister Anne, the Rev. John Warden M'Farlan, who succeeded in due course. He married Helen M'Dowall, and their son, John M'Farlan, advocate, Edinburgh, was laird from about 1785 till his death in 1846.

I find that I have made a mistake on page 173. It was not Colonel M'Farlan, the present laird, but his grandfather, Mr. John M'Farlan, advocate, who was sent for by Miss Elizabeth Margaret M'Farlan of Arrochar, the last of the race of the old M'Farlans, and the undoubted head of the clan. Some time before her death she had caused the message to be sent to him, and when he responded to the invitation and went to see her, she solemnly and with due formality handed over to him the cairngorm, the ring, and the seal of the chief, telling him that at her death he would inherit the headship of the Clan M'Farlan.

The house erected by James M'Farlan in 1665 had various modifications made on it from time to time, but was substantially the mansion-house till 1852. The late Miss Catherine M'Farlan, who only died in 1890, aged 83, recollected an older and smaller house that joined on to the older part of the present old house This was beginning to fall down, when her father, Mr. John M'Farlan, cleared it away entirely, and erected a plain square building across the large court, on the front of what would be the old peel in the times when the Brisbanes were the owners of the lands. There is still a very old ivy-covered arch at the entrance to the small court at the back door. This was taken out of the kitchen of the Brisbane house. The garden used to be on the north side of the house, on a slope down to the burn. It had grassy walks, and quaint cut yews and shrubs, and a sun dial stood on a pedestal. This was thrown into lawn about the beginning of the century, and the present walled garden nearer the glen was then formed.

Between Ballancleroch and the road to the Clachan there is a small field on the east side of the burn, which formerly belonged to the Lairds of Woodhead. This bit of ground is called " Croft-an-righ " the King's Field. Now, unless when James IV. visited Cragbernard in 1507, there is no record of any royal personage

having been within the boundaries of the parish to give the name
either here or to the little hillock at the west end of Antermony
Loch, which is called "The King's hill" in the Ordnance Survey
map. The field of "Croft-an-righ" was exchanged by excambion, the Laird of Ballancleroch giving a piece of land
beyond Haughhead for it, thus improving the amenity of Ballancleroch, and giving greater privacy to the grounds. In some
way this field has got associated with the letters INRI perhaps
from these letters having been used as phonetic abbreviation of
the an-righ.

John M'Farlan, advocate, died in 1846. He was succeeded by
his son John, a surgeon in Edinburgh. The Edinburgh doctor
looked forward to following the example of his father and retiring
to Ballancleroch to spend his latter days on his patrimonial
estate. In view of this he planned a reconstruction of the
mansion-house, the erection of a large addition, with Mary Keith's
house converted into a north wing. This was commenced in the
spring of 1852 and completed in the summer of 1853. The
extensive additions completely altered the aspect of the house and
left it as we see it now. The old entrance was closed and a new
avenue formed with gates and entrance lodge, at the west side of
the bridge over the glen burn. The Doctor's dreams were however never realised. He died on the 6th July, 1852, while the
building operations at Ballancleroch were in progress, and was
succeeded by his son, John Warden M'Farlan, the present laird,
who was born in 1824. The heir-presumptive to Ballancleroch
and to the chieftainship of the M'Farlans is Lieut.-General David
M'Farlan, C.B., who resides in London. He was in the Bengal
Artillery, and served through the Indian Mutiny. He was
engaged in the defence of Lucknow, and was twice wounded.
He also served in the operations on the North-West frontier of
India, and in the Afghan War under Sir Donald Stewart. His
services were such as to obtain for him three medals for these
campaigns and'the Companionship of the Bath. He commanded
a division of the Bengal army. Even when only a young subaltern, during the days of the Mutiny, he showed great courage
and presence of mind in some of the most stirring episodes with
the mutineers.

AUCHINREOCH.

The etymology, *achadh*, a field: *reigheachd*, level; or *ach-an-
reid-heachd*, "Field of the plain," indicates the level meadow land
in which this old house has been built. It stands with the outer
walls still intact, although the western gable is bulging out.
The roof of the front or newer portion has partially fallen in,
carrying away the dining-room ceiling, &c., and so has the roof
over the kitchen. There are no dates on any of the lintels, and
little information can be gleaned as to when it was first built.

One of the Buchanan lairds is credited with having enlarged it by building the front portion. It fell into a delapidated condition while the Laird Buchanan who died about 1823 was proprietor, and was abandoned by him when he had Woodburn built. The tenant of the Mains of Auchinreoch has occupied it sometime since, but it is now a ruin and deserted, and is popularly known as "The Haunted House." The situation is rather low perhaps, because only about 130 feet above the mean sea level, but it is beautiful in the extreme, the pasture is rich, the trees are fine, and the whole scenery suggests peaceful pastoral life. The lands at one time were owned by the Kincaids, and there is frequent reference to the lands and the proprietors in the ecclesiastical records, as, for example, the following :—

"Jul. 2, 1594.—The Presbiterie ordenis Johnne Kincaid of Auchinreoche, for byding fra his parroche kirk and fra the communione, remaining stubburne to the citationis and admonitionis of the kirk, and not presenting his barne to baptisme, to confess his offens the nixt Sondaye in his paroch kirk, standing in sum part of the kirk, as he salbe callit upone be his minister. And siclyk ordenis the said Johnne, under the pane of twentie lib money, to find souertie that he sall cum to his paroche kirk heireftir, salbe present at the communione, sall nocht byd admonitionis and citationis of the kirk, and sall present his barnis that God sall send to baptisme. Dec. 2.—The Presbytery ordains the minister of Campsie to baptize the laird of Kincaid's bairn next Sunday, on that condition that the laird presents it ; if not, he is neither to baptize it that or any other day."

THE PARISH VALUATION ROLL IN 1691.

In 1649 the parish of Campsie was considerbly reduced in area, probably at the instigation of Sir James Livingstone. A considerable portion was taken off its eastern part and added to Kilsyth, and a large slice was taken off its south-western part and added to Baldernock. After it had been thus docked of the Kilsyth and Baldernock portions, the total valuation in 1691 was £6437 2d., and the heritors and their estates were entered in the County Roll as under :—

1. Laird of Glorat for Glorat and Cragbernard,	...	£1336	15	2
2. Viscount Kilsyth, ..., ...	...	1173	14	6
8. Laird of Woodhead, ...	...	805	5	10
4. J. Macfarlane of Kirktoune, ...	...	586	17	4
5. Feuars of Mugdock (formerly Mar. of Montrose), 11 ploughs,		518	5	0
6. Auchinreoch,} Earl of Wigton's then under forfeiture,	...	402	13	0
7. Antermony, } Earl pleading to have them restored,	...	402	13	0
8. The Laird of Kincaid, ...	...	416	6	8
9. Balquharrage, (under bond, fell to W. Lindsay afterwards),		290	16	0
10. Birdston Feuars, ...	...	244	12	10
11. Laird of Keir for Hayston lands, ...	...	178	9	4
12. Birbeston, Woodhead, but under bond, ...	...	52	9	0
18. Cappieston, „ „	...	32	4	4
14. Balglass, Woodhead, then Cunningham's, recovered by marriage, ...	...	32	4	4
15. Ellishaugh, part of Birdston lands, ...	...	13	13	10

£6437 0 2

THE ELEVEN PLOUGHS OF BALGROCHAN.

THE ELEVEN PLOUGHS OF BALGROCHAN.

On the southern border, or "laigh side," of the parish, the noble family of the Grahames of Montrose have held lands since 1400, as has been stated at page 187. This is not the place to enter into great detail, but as the genealogies of the other old landed families have been mentioned I may briefly give that of the ducal house of Montrose.

The first Graham of whom there is authentic record was a Sir William, who was one of the witnesses to David the First's charter erecting Holyrood Abbey. The king gave this Anglo-Norman knight the lands of Abercorn and Dalkeith. A Sir David obtained the lands of Clifton and Cliftonhall, and from William the Lion the lands of Charlton, Barrowfield, and the lordship of Kinnaber, all in Forfarshire. In the reign of King Alexander II. another Sir David gave certain lands he had in Galloway in exchange for those of Dundaff in Strathcarron. There is still a ruined fortalice called Sir John de Græme's castle, about three and a half miles east of Fintry, associated with the Sir John the friend and supporter of Wallace, whose "right hand" he was called. His son, another Sir David, obtained from Malise, Earl of Strathearn, the lands of Kincardine, on the east border of the parish of Blackford. "Of Kincardine" now became one of the principle designations of the family, and the Castle of Kincardine was the principal dwelling-place, until it was demolished by the Earl of Argyll in 1645, when Mugdoch Castle became the principal seat of the family. Another Sir David had several grants from King Robert the Bruce, with whom he exchanged his property of Cardross for the lands of Old Montrose, in Maryton parish, Forfarshire. The titles of Earl, Marquis, and Duke of Montrose are taken from these lands of Old Montrose, in Maryton, and not from the town of Montrose, with which the estate had no connection whatever. This Sir David died in 1327. Patrick Grahame of Kincardine was made a Peer of Parliament in 1451, under the title of Baron Grahame. William the third Lord Grahame was created Earl of Montrose in 1504. He fell at Flodden in 1513. It was while this William, the first earl, was living at Mugdoch that the incident occurred which I mentioned in my lecture of 1886, and which I now repeat.

One day, in ascending the hill from Torrance, past Barraston Farm, the late Mr. George Miller of Acre Valley pointed out to me, cut in the lintel of the door, initials and a date, thus:—

A. H.   1609.   A. B.

As we went leisurely up the hill, I learned the story of these initials. It is this. Once upon a time, or, to be more precise, in the year 1508, an Englishman arrived at the close of the house of Mugdoch. He had a great opinion of his own prowess, and was in quest of adventures. The Earl of Montrose was residing at Mugdoch, and having enquired what was the object of the Englishman's visit, he expressed a wish to have some one to fight with, on whom he could show his powers. The Earl was in the humour to gratify him, and he mentioned that he had a shepherd on the hill whom he thought would be quite willing to accommodate him if he wanted "fechtin'." The shepherd was sent for, and in due time appeared, but when the Englishman surveyed him, it occurred to him, rather suddenly, that he was out of condition, that travelling had put him out of his usual form, but a few days' rest would soon restore him. This seemed quite reasonable, and a week's delay was arranged, the Englishman, in the meantime, to be provided with lodgings and plenty of meat and drink. At length the day came when the parties were to engage. The combat began, when the Englishman was not only thrashed, but killed outright by the shepherd. The Earl was highly gratified that his champion had come off victor, and in token of his gratification asked the shepherd what he could give him to show his appreciation of his pluck. The shepherd was quite prepared, and rather took the Earl aback by saying that he would like a charter of the Barraston land at George Maclom's back-door. The Earl granted the request, made a gift of the lands, which extend to 110 acres, the *reddendo* of the lands in the charter being a white rose, *si petitur tantum* (if asked), the superior to personally have this, he riding out of the place of Mugdoch on a white horse, with a cocked hat on, and clad in gilt spurs. The holding is, therefore, really a blench one, the rose having never been asked for. This is the story of Abraham Hannay and Ann Blyth, his wife, whose descendents still possess the land acquired in so strange a manner by their resolute and courageous ancestor.

The barony of Mugdoch marches with the baronies of Woodhead, Bardowie, Livingstone's old barony of Campsie, and others. There is an extant agreement, of date 1587, between the then "Erle of Montrose and John Lennox of Woodheid," settling the boundaries of their respectivs estates, which they had defined by the erection of an earthen ridge. This archaic march "dyke" may still be seen stretching across the Clochoore Moor, sometimes in a straight line, sometimes in a crooked one. In one place there is a rectangular diversion, intended to exclude what had apparently been a hut. This ridge is about four feet wide by two feet high, and in it there is inserted at intervals large stones. It can be seen best between Newlands or Cock-ma-lane farm and Mount Hooly, immediately overlooking Clochore. Its existence is almost unknown in Campsie, but its existence and history is known in the Torrance district, where all the antiquities of the laigh side of the Parish were well known to the eleven plough lairds, especially to the late Mr. James Maitland of Balgrochan, the late Mr. James Ferrie, and the late Mr. George Miller. Mr. John Buckie now remains the chief depository of local traditions.

On the 10th November, 1587, there was an agreement between the Earl and Laird of Woodhead setting the marches of the lands of Lethad, which the Earl's ancestor had obtained from Alicia, Lady of Cragbernard, in 1400. The career of James Graham, Earl and first Marquis can only be referred to briefly. Born in 1612, he succeeded to the title and estates in 1626, and three years afterwards, when only 17 years, he married a daughter of Lord Carnegie of Kinnaird. He first joined the Covenanters, then deserted them and became a supporter of the Royalist cause. After a short but brilliant campaign his army was defeated at Philiphaugh, and he left Scotland a fugitive in disguise. Some of the Campsie lairds actively supported the Royalist side. The son of the laird of Woodheid was serving under Montrose, and died shortly after the battle of Auldearn, probably from wounds or injuries received there. Being in urgent need of money, the Earl, as early as 1630, sought to raise funds by feuing off the Balgrochan and Balmore lands to those who were willing to give a grassum on condition of small feu-duty. There is some doggerel on this subject, which the late laird Maitland quoted one evening in my presence. I asked him to try and recollect it, but his memory failed him. All I could get was—

Twa centuries syne the Marquis o' Grahame
Gaed oot tae the wars at the heid o' his men ;
His income was sma', tho' h'ed titles enew,
And great part o' his lan' he had then to feu.

. . . .

The eleven ploughs o' Bo'grochan were acquired at that time
By eleven sturdy carles, as they ca'ed them lang syne.

. . . .

For the chiefs o' the borders at that time did keep
As mony blue bonnets as noo they keep sheep ;
An' Marquis o' Grahame, Montrose, and Dundaff
Had naething before him but feu the lan' aff.

The term plough, ploughgate, or ploughland requires a word of explanation. From a charter by William the Lion we gather that a ploughgate or carucate of land in Scotland contained 104 acres.* An oxgate contained 13 acres. A merkland was about one-third of a ploughgate. Converted into money value a 40s. land of old extent was in some parts of Scotland 104 acres. Cosmo Innes expressly limits this to Merse and Lothian. In this district a ploughgate is a 6s. 8d. land of old extent, and varies from 60 to 110 acres, according to the situation and the

*Notes—Lindores Abbey, p. 77

barrenness or fertility of the soil. It is one thing on Clochcore moor and another in the richer lands near the Kelvin.

The eleven ploughs contain the lands of Easter and Wester Balgrochan and Carlston, and extend from the march across Clochcore Moor to the river Kelvin, the southern boundary of the parish. The lands are differently valued, regard being evidently had to situation and fertility. Wester Balgrochan is assessed at £48 Scots per plough, Easter Balgrochan at £44 10s. Scots, and Carlston at £39 Scots. The original feuars holding of the Earl of Montrose were as under:—

No.	Amount of land.	Original Feuar.	Date of Feu.	Present Proprietors.
		LANDS OF CARLSTON (3 Ploughs)—		
1	6/8	William Reid, ...	1630	Thomas Reid.
2	6/8	Thomas Gray, ...	,,	Hon. Mrs. Lennox.
3	6/8	William Angus,...	,,	William Simpson.
		EASTER BALGROCHAN (4 Ploughs)—		
4	6/8	Mungo Stirling, ...	1630-1	G. Miller Trs., Hon. Mrs. Lennox, M'Nicol's Heirs, and R. Watson.
5	6/8	Richard Turner,...	,,	J. Buckie and Hon. Mrs. Lennox.
6	6/8	William M'Ildowie,	,,	J. Buckie, J. Ferrie's Trs., and Hon. Mrs. Lennox.
7	6/8	John Charity, ...	1631	J. Ferrie's Trs. and M'Farlan's Trs.
		WESTER BALGROCHAN (4 Ploughs)—		
*8	6/8	John Blair, merchant, burgess in Edinburgh. His wife in liferent and son George in fee,...	1643	Hon. Mrs. Lennox. Reprs. of late Jas. Maitland and J. Ferrie's Trs. (a pendicle).
9	6/8	John Marshall, ...	1632	Hon. Mrs. Lennox, J. Maitland's Repr., Trs. of H. and C. Alum Co., Trs. of J. Morrison, Trs. of J. Buchanan, J. Howie, Mrs. Baird or Morton.
10	3/4 3/4	Robert Wilson, ... W. Buie or Bowie,	,, ,,	Ferrie's Trs. and M'Farlan's Trustees.
11	3/4 3/4	Allan Marshall, ... William Blair, ...	1631 1643	J. Maitland's Reprs. Hon. Mrs. Lennox, Maitland's Reprs., H. and C. Alum Co.'s Trs., Agnes Peat, John Robertson Stevenson.

* In the titles of No. 8 6/8, called "Collier's Acre," from George Blair by George Maiklam (Maitland), in Barraston, in 1671, the original feuars, in 1643, are mentioned as Allan Blair and George Maiklam in Barraston. The probability is that John Blair was a creditor of theirs.

The foregoing are the eleven plough lands proper, but along with them there is also:—

Balgrochan miln, miln lands, and multures, feued in 1631 by Robert Farie miller, and Janet Brash, his spouse, in liferent. Now held by Ferrie's Trustees.

Poffle of Wester Balgrochan, called Sandyhole. Robert Imbrie (1630). Now held by Ferrie's Trustees.

Poffle of Wester Balgrochan, called Guildie Acre. Marista Marshall (1630), relict of John Angus at Cadder Bridge, in liferent, their daughter in fee. Now held by Ferrie's Trustees.

The Temple of Balgrochan. Richard Turner and Janet Provan, his wife in liferent, and W. Turner, son in fee (1632). Trustees of late G. Miller.

The eleven plough lairds of Balgrochan pay a somewhat archaic *reddendo* for their lands, each 6/8 land of old extent being a ploughgate, paying sundry sums for ferme meal, multer meal and bier, lyme craig, and coal, sheep, poultry, coals, &c., the whole amounting in money to £69 6s. 8d. Scots for each ploughgate or 6/8 land of old extent. Besides these payments they were bound to render certain services, such as a certain number of creels of peats from Craigallion Moss to the outer close of the place of Mugdoch. In cais of failzie, to pay 8s. Scots for ilk creel leiding yrof. They were bound to help to carry the "Erle's" furniture from Dundaff or Glasgow to Mugdoch. Ilk ane of the feuars was taken bound to cart coals from his place to Mugdoch. This used to be regularly performed. Although only entitled to cart to Mugdoch they went cheerfully to Buchanan. The procession of carts, with coals, &c., to Buchanan House was a red letter day for the plough lairds. Their procession was headed by a piper, and the refreshments given were so heartily partaken of that they had a wonderfully elevating effect on the lairds or their deputies. The Balgrochan eleven lairds' coals were not of good quality, and the supply was discontinued on this account. Collectively, they were likewise bound to supply one carriage horse to take Montrose from Mugdoch to Edinburgh. The feuars were bound to have their corn ground at the "Erle's" mill, and to wait twenty days for water if that was scarce. After the twenty days they could take their corn to any mill they pleased, they paying the knaveship for sae muckle as they can transfer. This knaveship is a sequel of thirlage, and is the "niefou'" given to the mill servant by whom the work is performed. By a feu charter of part of the Balgrochan lands, dated in 1631, the vassal in that part (Mr. James Maitland claimed this) was accorded the privilege and liberty of "hostelries and brewing, and making of banquets and bridals, but any wraith or stolen goods found upon his land" were to belong to the superior, the Earl of Montrose.

A family named Winning were the proprietors of the Tower farm at one time, but they sold it and emigrated to America about 1820. They had acquired the Tower lands from the

Montrose family, and all that they had to pay for them under their *reddendo* was a pound of black pepper, which was only to be given to Montrose himself, if he came to the farm riding on a white horse, and made the demand. The Winnings used to pride themselves on this, claiming that they, owing to services rendered in past times, probably in the wars under the Marquis, were the only lairds among the eleven ploughs who were really free lairds, as the pound of black pepper had never been asked for.

The result of the campaign in favour of King Charles II. by the Marquis of Montrose is well known. His army was surprised and completely routed at Philiphaugh in 1645, and he himself was executed at Edinburgh in 1650. His estates were forfeited. The Committee of Estates granted a Commission on 18th Apr., 1644, to George Buchanan, younger of that Ilk, to repair to the house and fortalice of Mugdoch, break open doors, break down the iron gates, and intromit with the cannon, powder, ball, matches, and other warlike furniture therein, for the use of the public.—*The Lennox.* vol i., p. 164.

The Committee of Estates granted a disposition, dated 17th Aug., 1647, to Archibald Marquis of Argyll and to his heirs of the lands and barony of Mugdoch, and ordained a charter of said lands be passed under the Great Seal in favour of the Marquis of Argyll. This was done, and he was infeft in November, 1647. The Marquis disponed the barony of Mugdoch to his second son, Lord Neil Campbell, who was duly infefted in them. The Barony was now called Neil's-town.

The castle of Mugdoch, with the lands of the barony, were restored to the Marquis of Montrose in 1656. The Marquis of Argyll was executed at Edinburgh 17th May, 1661.

It is well known that King Robert the Bruce granted a charter of the lands and barony of Lenzie, which comprehended Kirkintilloch and Cumbernauld, separating these lands from the shire of Stirling and annexing them to the county of Dumbarton. It is not so well known that, in 1388, King Robert granted to Sir Patrick Graham a warrant separating various lands belonging to him from the shire of Dumbarton and annexing them to that of Stirling. These lands were the carucate of Kilminevane and the lands of Clockbar, Dougalstoun, Barloch, Hayston, and the two Tavnachis, with the pertinents. The charter authorised the Sheriff of Stirling to compel, should it be necessary, the said Patrick and his heirs and possessors of the same lands to render the service due to the king for the said lands, and to receive these things, as was wont to be done within the shire of Dumbarton.

In 1839 the Duke of Montrose proposed to convert the services exacted by the original charters into an annual money payment, but the feuars did not then look on the Duke's proposal favourably. As far as I can learn an arrangement has since been carried out whereby all these services have been commuted for a sum of about 2s. per acre on the more valuable ground. The feuars of the eleven ploughs originally held their lands in run-rigs, which ran down in long strips from the march near Mount Hooly to the Kelvin; but on 27th May, 1735, it was divided up, under the act of 1695, amongst the various proprietors, by consent of the superior. In the original deeds the superior had given liberty to work the coal and lime in common, throughout the whole eleven ploughs, and this common right was not divided in 1735, nor has it been since. As there was no reservation of the iron-stone in the lands, it appears that each proprietor of the surface is entitled to the possession of the ironstone underlying that surface, but *quoad* the coal and lime they still remain *pro rata* as common property among the vassals *inter se*. On the south brae of Balgrochan, below the Clochcore ridge, the coal and lime crop out in horizontal strata, and for many years previous to, and even in the present century, each individual plough laird worked such lime and coal as he could then lay his hands on, for his own individual use and profit; but afterwards better times came, and a peaceable arrangement was made, whereby one man under a pecuniary consideration worked for all, the proceeds being divided *pro rata.* The late Mr. James Maitland became the tenant of the minerals in the first instance. Afterwards, at a meeting of the plough lairds. he asked their permission, as he put it, to take in a partner, and this having been agreed to, he sublet to the Hurlet and Campsie Alum Company for 15 years. On the expiry of this the Alum Company leased the minerals direct, the lordship on the coal and lime being divided among the proprietors in proportion to their interests in the lands.

The sums derived from the lordships varied considerably under the lease to the Alum Company. I have obtained a copy of the statement for the year 1877, which I give as showing the proportions of the various proprietors. In that year a sum of £155 9s. 5½d. fell to be divided, being the monies obtained from the Alum Company under their then current lease of the minerals. This was divided as under. Their lease expired in 1881, and has not been renewed by them. The minerals are not worked at present, which must be matter of regret to the " lairds."

CARLSTON (3 ploughs)—
Hon. Mrs. Lennox, W. Reid, and W. Simpson, each £14 2s. 1d , £42   6   3
EAST BALGROCHAN (4 ploughs)—

	Value.			Rent.		
Mrs. Hanbury Lennox, ...	£55	15	0	£17	13	4
John Buckie, ...	45	10	0	14	8	5
A. Clark, Meadowbank (now Macfarlane's Trustees),... ...	25	1	0	7	18	7¾
J. Ferrie (now Ferrie's Trustees),	19	7	0	6	2	6¼
Trs. of Hurlet and Campsie Alum Co.,	18	17	0	5	19	4½
G. Miller, ...	8	10	0	2	13	10
Nicol's Heirs, ...	3	0	0	0	19	0
D. Watson,...	2	0	0	0	12	8
				56	7	9¼

Carry Forward, ...   £98 14   0¾

Brought forward,	...	...	...	...	...			... £98	14	0¾

WEST BALGROCHAN (4 ploughs)—

J. Maitland,	...	...	...	£88	0	0	£25	17	1¾
Mrs. Hanbury Lennox,	...	...	55	0	0	16	14	9¼
J. Ferrie,	...	...	...	16	0	0	4	15	8
Buchanan, Leitchbank,	...	...	12	10	0	3	13	2
A. Clark,	...	...	...	8	0	0	2	6	10
Alum Company,	...	...	5	15	0	1	13	7¾
Howie,	...	...	...	3	10	0	1	0	5¾
J. R. Stevenson,	...	...	0	10	0	0	2	11
Downie's Heirs,	...	...	0	10	0	0	2	11
Peat's Heirs,	...	...	0	5	0	0	1	5¼
Balance,	...	...	...			0	6	4¾

56 15 4¾

£155 9 5½

In the earlier days of the working of these minerals the difficulty of getting rid of the water which collected in the workings was an almost insuperable difficulty. The Rev. Mr. Lapslie in his Statistical Account says their manner of working was to advance their ingoing e'e mine or day level as far as they could and then put down an air shaft. They mined across to the rise from their e'e, proceeding on the stoop and room system, the "rooms" averaged about seven feet square, and the "stoops" about the same. Generally they did not manage to get further than the first air shaft, as they then preferred to shift to a new entry from the surface where they could find water level.

The well-known Mr. Charles Macintosh, at one time partner with Charles Tennant of St. Rollox, and of the Alum Co., in his young days went to France, where he acquired a knowledge of the French process of tanning leather. He started works for tanning, according to this French process, near Barrastone, above Torrance. He also leased the ironstone there and after commencing to work the minerals, discovered the alum schist. There was not, however, as much water as he required, and so he followed the alum to the northern slope of the hill. Mr. Macintosh had become a partner in 1797 of a firm who started a work at Hurlet, for the manufacture of alum. When he had discovered the schist to be abundant in Campsie, an alum work was started there in 1805, by the same firm who were established at Hurlet. The style of the Hurlet firm was Macintosh, Knox, & Co., and the partners were Mr. Macintosh, Major Finlay, R.E. (a brother of Kirkman Finlay of Toward Castle), Mr. John Wilson of Hurlet, and Mr. James Knox. Mr. Charles Stirling (brother of the Laird of Keir) afterwards became a partner, and remained in both firms till 1829. Mr. Macintosh bought the lands in 1835 on which the Alum Works had been erected. This had formed part of Viscount Kilsyth's forfeited estate.

BURSTON, BURDSTON, NOW BIRDSTON.

BURSTON, BURDSTON, NOW BIRDSTON.

This little hamlet is not without an interest of its own in parish history. It has no great claim to antiquity, for the lands were only feued off between 1653 and 1658, the feuars forming themselves into a little community, after a fashion very uncommon nowadays. The families of the little hamlet had many vicissitudes, and an unusual number among them lost their lives by sudden and violent deaths, such as murder, suicides, drowning, and by other accidents. The families of the original feuars have now nearly all ceased to have any connection with the lands, with the exception of Mrs Forrest, *nee* Mary Muir. She alone remains of the old stock in the old home. One cannot help being struck with one thing that is continually recurring again and again, namely, the failure of heirs male in the succession, as exemplified in the Galbraiths, Donaldsons, Grahams, Grays, Samsons, Laings, &c. The names of old proprietors, and also of some of the feuars, have in this way become changed.

The lands of Burston were included in the Kincaid lands, which have been already referred to on page 183. The Kincaids of that ilk possessed the Kincaid lands in their entirety from 1280 till 1350, when " that fourth part of Kyncade which lies near the Kelvin in the County of Lennox " was carried away as her portion by a female Kincaid, who was married to a Galbraith of Craigmaddie Castle. Reference has been made already on page 183 to the once powerful family of Galbraith and the extensive estates owned by them. But of the marriage of 1350 there was no male issue, and, as already mentioned, the three daughters, co-heiresses, had the lands portioned among them.

A younger member of the Hamiltons of Cadzow was fortunate in wooing and winning Janet Keith Galbraith, one of these heiresses, and by his marriage with her he became laird of a third of the fine estate of the Galbraiths and also of the fourth part of Kincaid, which had been rent off in 1350. Their residence was Craigmaddie Castle, and this remained their dwelling-place till 1531, when the eighth Hamilton laird abandoned the old residence of the Galbraiths and his own Hamilton predecessors, and had then rebuilt for his own residence the old fort of Bardowie. The building of the new mansion-house seems to have run the Laird of Bardowie short of cash, for in 1534 he sold part of Ballindrocht, the lands of Hayston, Balquharrage, and others to John Stirling of Keir; but his son, the ninth Laird Hamilton, re-acquired them from Sir James Stirling of Keir. John Hamilton, the eleventh laird of Bardowie and Birdston, succeeded in minority to a fine unencumbered estate. In 1616, when very young, he married Mary Douglas of Mains, and by charter, dated 22nd May, 1616, with consent of his curators, he granted to his wife in life-rent the lands of Birdston and Bankier. John, the eleventh laird, heartily espoused the cause of Charles. He sadly embarrassed his estate by raising money to pay the troops serving under Montrose and fines levied on the defeated leaders by those who had triumphed in the civil strife.

Financial embarrassments, resulting from the political misfortunes connected with the losing cause he had espoused, placed both the Laird of Bardowie and also his eldest son, who had been out serving in person under Montrose in the Civil War, at the mercy of Sir James Livingstone, who constituted himself chief creditor, and also assumed the superiority in ward. In this capacity he endorsed the charters granted by John Hamilton to his Birdston feuars. It was probably well for the laird that he was related to Livingstone, as this may have saved him from losing his lands altogether. Sir James, however, took advantage of the position he held to advance his own interests, here as elsewhere, with the other estates on which he had made money advances. It has been alleged that he compelled the eldest son of the Laird to marry his sister, Anne Livingstone, under what he called "virtue of power of avail." At the same time, he is said to have made the wife of the then laird accept an annuity over Fluchart, an already overburdened part of the property, and renounce her life-rent interest in Birdston and Bankier, in order that it might be feued off and that he might get the grassums. This was the expedient resorted to by the Earl of Montrose with his Balgrochan lands, as has been mentioned on page 205. Hamilton of Bardowie decided to feu off that fourth part of the Kincaid lands that had been detached from that estate since 1350. Accordingly, he had them divided into eight lots, and parted with them to five feuars, between 1653 and 1658.

For information regarding these Birdston feuars I am greatly indebted to Dr. D. P. Stewart, Kirkintilloch, who was at one time an ardent archæologist, and is still a member of the Glasgow Archæological Society. While he was making enquiries into local history he obtained a memorandum from the late Mr Alexander Galloway, entitled, "Notes for Dr Stewart as to the lands of Birdston, and the families of the Muirs, portioners thereof. 4th December, 1860." The Doctor was aware that I was hunting up information about Campsie, and finding Mr. Galloway's memorandum one day among his papers, when looking for something else, he, with kind consideration, sent it on to me, and I have been greatly indebted to it for many of the details which have been embodied in the following paper. The names of the feuars and the dates of the feu-charters are :—1. William Muir, then in Bogquharrage, charter dated 21st October, 1653. Finding a small bit of haugh intervening between Hamilton's Birdston land and the Kelvin, this William, in the same year, acquired from James Fleming the lands of Ellishaugh, which in 1649 were bounded on the north by Mr Hamilton of Bardowie's lands of Redheuche ; on the east by the lands of Goyle, hence the name of the bridge over the Kelvin, Goyle bridge, and Adamsheugh or heuche, belonging to Lord Fleming; on the west by lands of Fleming of Waddilee and by Hayston lands; and on the south the Kelvin would be the boundary. William Muir aforesaid and his son Robert, 1658. 2. John Muir in Burston, charter dated 1656. 3. James Donaldson, charters dated 1656 and 1657. Donaldson also acquired the Wetshod poffle, charter dated 1657. 4. James Muir, 1658. 5. David Calder, 1658. Of these lands, James Donaldson held one half and the remaining half was held in the proportions of one-eighth by each of the three brothers Muir, and one-eighth by David Calder. The brothers Muir were said to have come from the neighbourhood of Rowallan Castle, between Kilmarnock and Stewarton, in Ayrshire, and were connected by lineal descent from the Mures, Barons of Rowallan. A member of this family, Elizabeth Mure, was first wife of King Robert II.

Donaldson, Calder, and the three brothers Muir had feued off the lands between 1653 and 1658. Each of them had small portions called crofts, or infield lands, as individual proprietors, and the outfield, or pasturage lands, were at first held in common. Instead of erecting their farm-steadings in the isolated fashion almost universally prevailing, they formed themselves into a little village community, in the old manner of this and other countries. They built their dwelling-houses in a cluster, for their mutual convenience and protection. They used a common barn, kiln, and stackyard. For domestic water supply they had the Easter and Wester Wells, which still remain, and a bit of bleaching-green around each of them. On the wester green may be seen still the large stone on which they beetled their lint.

In 1731, when the proprietors were Marion Donaldson, spouse of Archibald Graham ; James Calder, and the three Muirs, they, being all the partners, divided and disponed to one another the town and lands of Birdston, according to their interest and for their mutual convenience. Again, in 1773, the division of the common lands was agreed on and carried out, all the proprietors for the time being agreeing to this.

The great drawback to all these lands, then and now, was the frequent flooding by the Glazert and Kelvin overflowing their banks. To remedy this the courses of the rivers have been straightened and embankments formed to prevent the crops or cattle being swept away. During the years of his tenancy— 1810-1820—Mr Fergus, who was then tenant of Ellishaugh, had the embankment constructed which still surrounds it.

The anxiety with which the floods in autumn were regarded is evidenced in Muir's poem—

KELVIN, KEEP LOW.

(An invocation to that river, written during a heavy fall of rain, 13th August, 1809.)

Thy banks crowned with plenty the valleys adorn,
Thro' which thou oft leisurely strays,
Thy margin is fringed with fields of rich corn,
The husbandman's happiest bays.
Then think what a pity a prospect so fine,
That heaven hath thought fit to bestow,
Should fall to the ground by a mischief of thine—
Then Kelvin, I pray thee, keep low.

How oft have I seen thee in years that are past
The sickle in harvest deceive,
And all the fond hopes of the husbandman blast,
And drown them in thy muddy wave.
Repenting thy crimes, as true penitents should,
To-day be thou placid and slow;
For ruin attends thee when swelled to a flood—
Then Kelvin, I pray thee, keep low.

At present the peasant in peril beholds
His all uninsured in the field,
His cattle at home, and his flocks in the folds,
Expecting what autumn will yield;
Disappoint not their wishes, inundate them not
(If Providence orders it so),
The wealth of the peasant is painfully got—
Then Kelvin, I pray thee, keep low.

Owing to the drainage which exists everywhere in the valleys of the Glazert and Kelvin, the waters now rise very much more quickly than formerly, but they fall also much sooner than they used to do. The deepening of the River Clyde has had an influence in lessening the duration of the flooding of the Birdston, Hayston, and Balmore haughs. Two hundred years ago Birdston haughs were impassable in winter, but about fifty-five years ago the late Mr. J. L. Kincaid Lennox had a thorough system of drainage effected by deep ditches led into the Kelvin. This greatly improved the lands for cropping, but they still continued liable to flooding. When the Roman officers selected the line for the Antonine wall they would appear to have decided to make as much as possible of the streams on the northern front of the wall —the Kelvin, Bonny, and Carron. These streams and the haughs through which they flowed were utilised as an outer or first line of defence. Mr. Galloway hazarded a conjecture that by an embankment extending from below the Kirkintilloch fort across the haugh towards Hayston the Romans raised the level of the Kelvin and Glazert nineteen feet above their present levels. This would practically throw the haughs under water, the higher points would appear as islands, and the names of the farms to the eastward bear names which, according to their etymology, corroborate this theory. The names are Inchbelly, Innis-bal, the building or farm on the island; Inchterf, the bull island; Inchbreak, Inchwood, Netherinch. If such an embankment ever existed, all traces of it have long ago disappeared.

Without giving the details that might be expected in a process of writs, the history of the connection of the families of the five feuars of Birdston may be briefly narrated.

1. William Muir, Ellishaugh, 21st October, 1653. Birdston, ⅛th part. Crooked ridge poffle by said William Muir and his son Robert. In 1752, by contract of excambion, John Muir, then owner, and Malcolm Brown, Kirkintilloch, some small portions of land are interchanged for mutual convenience, probably in consequence of a change in the bed of the Kelvin. The lands of Wester Aulton were acquired by one of these Muirs. Another of the Muirs went to Glasgow, from whom sprang the famous Thomas Muir of Huntershill. Part of these lands was sold in 1825 to Robert Ferrie, after whose death this portion was bought by James Laing, flesher in Glasgow. Other portions were sold in 1815 by James Muir to John Morrison of Craigend, who again sold them, in 1834, to the Laird of Kincaid.

2. John Muir (feuar of 1656). In 1819, his descendant, William Muir, sold 10½ acres to Miss Lennox of Woodhead and John Kincaid. In 1837, 18 acres, called Bogsandy and Skimmerhill, were sold to R. Ferrie, who, in 1846, sold about 14 acres to Mr J. L. K. Lennox, and 4 acres to Mr James Laing. The remainder, after these sales, has now passed to the heirs of David Smith, Calfmuir.

4. James Muir (1658). Held by descendants till 1826, when trustees sold 5¼ acres to J. L. Kincaid, and, in 1828, remainder to Robert Ferrie, who had married a Margaret Muir. In same year Mr Ferrie sold 9½ acres to Mr Kincaid. The remainder was acquired by Mr Laing, after Mr. Ferrie's death. John Muir was born in 1720, the same year as Prince Charlie. In 1746 he went over to Kirkintilloch, where he saw the Highlanders, with Prince Charlie at their head, on the march from Glasgow to Falkirk. This John Muir was vested as heir of his father in 1794. He died in 1808. His eldest son John, the elder brother of the poet, had a sequestered corner consecrated as burial-place for his family in 1805, when he buried his wife. The poet wrote lines on the consecration of his burial-place, which are given on page 223 of his poems. A wall was subsequently built to enclose this tomb. There are four people buried here, viz., John Muir, the laird; Robina Baillie, his wife; Mrs Baillie, his wife's mother; and Mary Muir, his daughter, who died unmarried. William Muir the poet was the second son of John Muir, who died 21st October, 1808. The poet was born in 1766, and died in 1817. David Muir, a younger brother of the poet, married a Jeanie Gray, who, with her brother, was brought from America to live with her uncle, Mr John Gray. With her portion

David built a cottage, on which Mr Laing afterwards put a storey, and which is now known as Birdston Bank. His daughter Mary, Mrs Forrest, is the only one of the old stock of the Muirs now resident at Birdston.

In the early part of the century there were living here a number of families who were all descended from the original feuars. The name of Muir was so common that nicknames had to be had recourse to to identify the various individuals. A stranger asking for John Muir would be asked whether it was Farmer John or Printer John he wanted, and so one William was Nat'ral Willie, another William was the Poet, while a Muir who had gone through the curriculum at Glasgow College to qualify for the ministry, but who had lacked perseverance and become a stickit minister, was known as the Divine. It was not a little awkward for the young female Muirs, where Mary and Jeanie were the favourite names. There is an authentic story of a young love-lorn swain coming to see the Mary Muir by whose charms he had been smitten. Unaware of the number of Marys when directed to where Mary Muir lived, he asked, when the door was opened by the father, "Does Mary Muir live here?" "Yes, but which Mary are ye wanting?" He didn't know. What was she like? He could only describe her as pretty. "There's nae pretty Mary here." There were three Marys and three Jeanies. The Marys were named after the fathers and the Jeanies after the mothers where the names were different. There were Farmer John's Mary (who died unmarried, and was buried in the tomb already referred to), Printer John's Mary (Mrs Cunningham), and Dauvid's Mary (Mrs Forrest). Farmer John's Jean, or wee Jean, became the wife of Bailie Wallace, coalmaster. The others were Kate's Jean and Bell's Jean (Mrs David Smith). Farmer John's Mary had a sad disappointment, and died of a broken heart. She was getting ready to be married to the Rev. William Craig, a Relief minister in Dalkeith, but circumstances emerged which showed he had been a general lover and a very gay Lothario. The marriage was broken off; Mary fell into a decline; and Craig himself went down to a premature grave.

5. James Calder's one-eighth was possessed by his descendants till 1836, when David Calder, sometime weaver in Kirkintilloch, thereafter farmer at Inchbelly, Bridge-End, and then farmer at Millersneuk, sold them to R. Ferrie. Mr James Laing acquired them in 1846, after Mr Ferrie's death.

3. James Donaldson, the original feuar, per charter of 1657, does not seem to have lived long at Birdston, as in 1669 the owner is called Robert Donaldson. He was murdered one evening at his own road-end by a man whom he had met at an inn in Edinburgh, with whom, on being overtaken by him, he had travelled to his own dwelling. He is reported to have invited him to stay over-night in his house, but this was declined, and he was saying, "We part here, as I see my ain lum reeking," when the

stranger suddenly stabbed him with his rapier. He fell off his horse, which the stranger seized ; then taking Donaldson's pocket-book and a cape he had been wearing, he rode off. Tradition has it that his dog, then inside the farmhouse, was greatly excited while this tragedy was being enacted, and his wife asked the servant to let it out. Shortly afterwards Donaldson was found lying dead on the road. There is conflict of testimony as to where Donaldson was killed. The bulk of the evidence points to it having taken place quite near his own house. but Mrs Forrest tells me her father David Muir always told them that it was on the Inchbelly Road just where it crosses the Woodburn. The Rev. Mr Anderson took for his second wife a Jean Muir of Birdston, and Mrs Forrest and her sister were often at the Relief Manse of Kilsyth. When returning home, if in the gloaming, the girls always ran past the brig where they had been told Donaldson had been murdered.

The story is told by Law in his Memorials as follows :—

" November, 1669.—In this month did one Thomas Scott, ane English borderer, murder Robert Donaldson, of Birdston in Campsie, by cutting of his throat with his rapier, and then thrusting him off the horse, fell upon him and cutt it through and through with his knife, the man not being able to defend himself, though a strong man of body, his cloke being at that time so far buttoned down and hevie with the great rains he had received in his journey. This villan and incarnate devill did pretend great friendship to him in Edinburgh, and perceiving he had received money, pretended an errand to Glasgow, to whom the said Robert was very courteous, finding him a stranger and in the equipage of a gentleman, prooffered him lodging at his own house, having before dyned with him at Falkirk, and in the very rod that led into his house he surprizes him with this stroke, and murders him, carrying away his horse and money. Who afterwards was marvellously discovered in the search of Robert's servants after him, by his hood, which they knew that he had taken, which he had given to a carrier, and the day being rainy the carrier put on the hood, which the servants when they saw it quarrells it, and the carrier told it was such a man's ryding before (that was near to Haddington), whom they instantly surprise and apprehend, and he being struck with a terrible fear and horror confessed the fact, is hanged at Edinburgh, and his carcase hung up between Edinburgh and Leith. This Robert Donaldson was a good man and courteous to all."

I applied to a legal friend in Edinburgh to see if he could verify the alleged facts. He wrote in reply—" I find the case in the Justiciary Clerk's Office amongst the criminal records. The facts you give are mainly correct. Donaldson had come to Edinburgh to get money due to him, and he put up at the ' Salutation.' Scott also came there, from England, and heard what Donaldson's business in Edinburgh was. On 4th November

1669, Donaldson started for home, with £50 in his pocket. Scott overtook him on the road, both being on horseback, and they rode together to near Donaldson's house, when between 6 and 7 p.m. Scott killed Donaldson and took his money and his horse, and immediately rode back to Edinburgh; but he was pursued and apprehended. On 5th November, 1669, Scott was taken before the Lord Justice-Clerk, when he made a declaration before him, admitting his crime, and giving all particulars of it. He was forthwith placed before a jury, his declaration was read, and the evidence of Donaldson's nephew given, to the effect that he had seen his uncle's dead body. Scott was at once found guilty, and sentenced to be hung on the 12th November current, at the usual place in High Street, Edinburgh, his body to be afterwards hung in chains at Gallowlee, between Edinburgh and Leith. The record does not say whether the sentence was carried out, but there can be no doubt that it was."

This case is referred to as unique in our criminal annals, where a man was hanged on his own confession, with no legal evidence being adduced in proof of his guilt. The old road at this time followed the line of the trees going down towards the Muir tomb. The turnpike was made straight here afterwards. The next event in Donaldson's records is Wet Shod conveyed to James Marshall and Marion Donaldson, his spouse, in 1698. In 1747, Marion Donaldson, wife of Archibald Graham, in Birdston, is vested in these lands, as nearest lawful heir of her deceased brother, James Donaldson. In 1768, William Graham, grandson of Marion Donaldson, is vested as heir of the toun and lands of Birdston. In 1775, Marion Graham, wife of John Orr of Barrowfield; Christian Graham, and Helen Graham, wife of Thos. Buchanan, succeed their brother, and in 1776 sell to Thomas Buchanan. In 1782 Thomas Buchanan sells to John Gray, late of New York.

The lands now passed away from the descendants of the original feuar. Mr Gray, the new proprietor, had been in America and made money there, with which he now purchased Donaldson's half of Birdston. Mr Gray had only a daughter, Jeanie, who married a son of Bailie Morrison, Glasgow, who was also proprietor of the small estate of Craigend, in the east of Glasgow, near Shettleston. When his daughter got married Mr Gray built a cottage for himself immediately behind the farm. Into Birdston Cottage he retired, leaving the farm to be managed by his son-in-law, who lived in the farm-house. Morrison, who now farmed it, latterly became addicted to drink, and in a fit of jealousy committed suicide by taking laudanum. His widow then married a Dr Paterson, a medical practitioner in Kirkintilloch, and shortly afterwards they went to live at Dunoon, where the Doctor built one of the early houses. At the time of the first cholera Mrs Paterson was going to Glasgow, and went on board the steamer at Dunoon, in her usual health. She was attacked by apoplexy during the passage, and either died on board or immediately on being carried ashore at Glasgow. Morrison's son, Andrew, committed suicide at Birdston, and a married daughter, who lived at Lamlash, contracted smallpox, when returning in a steamer from Rothesay, where she had been visiting her husband's friends. The seats in the steamer were all taken up, and she sat down on a box, unaware that it concealed a coffin containing the remains of a person who had died of smallpox, and, as a result, she sickened and died in a day or two. On Mr. Gray's death his property was vested in trustees, who, in 1827-8, sold it to Mr. J. L. Kincaid, younger of Kincaid.

It is amusing for us of the present day to see the importance attached eighty years ago to proximity to the Forth and Clyde Canal as a means of access to Glasgow. The following advertisement appeared on 19th July, 1827 :—

LANDS IN CAMPSIE FOR SALE.

THE Lands of Birdston, which belonged to the deceased John Gray, consisting of about 120 acres. . . . The situation of these lands is otherwise extremely convenient, from ready access to Glasgow by stage coaches and the canal passage boats, and they are distant only about half a mile from Kirkintilloch.

Birdston Cottage, which Mr. Gray had built, was afterwards fitted up by Mr. Galloway for his residence when he came to Birdston. Early in the fifties, the late Mr. Robert Cowan, merchant, Glasgow, who was tenant of old Ballancleroch House for some years, took this cottage on a long cheap lease, and greatly enlarged it, at his own expense, as a residence for himself. Mr. Cowan was an elder in Campsie Church, where he sat in the front of the gallery. I can recall the pew, with Mrs. Cowan and her two sisters in it. At that time an old Mr. Campbell resided at Viewfield. Mr. and Mrs. Campbell and Mrs. Campbell's brother lived at Kincaid; the Middletons, who went to Kinfauns Castle, near Perth, were in Antermony, where they were succeeded by Monteiths, M·Farlanes, Readmans, &c., all of whom sat on the minister's left hand in the front of the gallery in Campsie Church. I can easily bring before my mind's eye the occupants of these pews from 1855 to 1864.

It is rather singular to notice that of that fourth part of the Kincaid lands that was parted with in 1350, by far the greater portion of it was regained by purchase, after having been out of the family for nearly 500 years.

One of the Calders, then tenant of Inchbreck Farm, when riding home by the Falls of Inchbelly Road, took the near road by Inchbreak and the Glazert Ford, opposite Birdston. The Glazert was in high flood, and the horse, having crossed the stream, slipped on the further bank, and both horse and rider fell back into the water, and were carried away, Calder being drowned before he could extricate himself.

On 31st December, 1846, Mr James Stevenson, then tenant of Birdston farm, was accidentally killed in a sandpit quite near his house. He had gone into the pit to look at some work, when, owing to frost, a sudden fall of sand took place, and he was in this way accidentally killed. After her husband's death, Mrs. Stevenson went to reside at Gateside with her family. Her son, Mr. William Stevenson, writer in Glasgow, was well known and highly respected in Campsie and Kilsyth. Birdston farm was then taken by a namesake, but no relative, Mark Stevenson, of the Boghead family, whose son, Mr. Robert Stevenson, has lately left the farm and gone abroad to the Pacific slopes with his family. A local newspaper intimates that recently 121 ploughs turned out to give a love darg to the incoming tenant, Mr. Prentice.

In the lecture on the Clachan and district (page 88) I referred to the many families of tenant farmers in the western portion of the parish who have gone from the district without leaving any descendants now connected with it. The departure of the Stevensons from Birdston brings prominently before me that this applies equally to this district. There have been Stevensons farmers in Birdston as long as I can recollect, now they have left like the Stevensons of Alton, Lyons of Balquharrage, Andersons of Inchbreak, and Marshalls of Bridgend. I wonder if in many parishes there has been such a complete change of tenant farmers as there has been in Campsie within the last generation.

Some Roman urns have been exhumed in the vicinity of Birdston, and a number of coins of the time of Elizabeth, James I. of England, and Charles I. were dug up one day by Farmer John when he was casting peats. They were contained in a copper dish, which is likely still at Birdston in Mrs. Forrest's attic, but the coins have all been scattered. The conjecture is that these had been concealed by some inhabitant, fleeing from the troops of Montrose, at the time of the battle of Kilsyth, in 1645, a few years before the lands were feued off as described.

WILLIAM MUIR. THE BIRDSTON POET.

How many in Campsie have read or even seen the poems on various subjects by the late William Muir, Campsie, published in 1818? The answer must be, very few indeed. Born at Birdston, 1766, he died on 21st October, 1817. Muir first tried a haberdasher's shop, but disliking the confinement and being too shy in manner, he served an apprenticeship to saddlery, going up to London and working there to perfect himself in his trade. Returning, he commenced business in Falkirk, but did not succeed, and was content afterwards to work journeyman. On Kirkintilloch Fair-day he went there and in the evening was calling upon a friend, who happened not to be in. On turning to come down the stair, it is supposed he had missed a step, as he fell to the bottom and was killed on the spot. He was interred in the family burying-place in Clachan church-yard, where a number of his admirers have erected a monument to keep his name from being forgotten, as mentioned on page 72. The death of his father in 1808 broke up the old home, as his brothers were all married. He seemed to feel leaving the old home acutely, and this often appears in his poems. He was often restless and depressed by an enervating melancholy. He was never married, and his biographers say that it does not appear from his papers that he ever felt the power of "that most felicitous or most calamitous of all passions, love." This must have been a loss of the most prolific source of poetic afflatus, which often not only stirs the emotional nature but also awakens and quickens the intellect. There is, therefore, an absence of passion in all his writings, and as his muse, unlike that of Burns and other Scottish bards, did not run into songs giving expression to the hopes and fears and joys and sorrows which were the common experiences of all, his fame is local, and his poems have failed to attain the immortality predicted by an admirer in a few lines that have been adopted as the motto of the book—

> " The pleasing sweets and charms of poesy
> That grace the flowing numbers of thy pen
> Shall gain for thee, thro' Albion's farthest ken
> A name through ages that shall never die. "

MR. ALEXANDER GALLOWAY.

In connection with Birdston some reference is due to the late Alexander Galloway, who resided there from 1836 till 1844, in the cottage which Mr. Gray had originally erected for himself. Mr. Galloway was born in 1802, of a Lanarkshire family, who trace their ancestry back over four centuries. His father was bred a civil engineer, but turned farmer. He gained a practical acquaintance with agriculture in his own home. After receiving a good education he became clerk to the factor on the Coltness estate. From 1826 to 1831 he was assistant to Lord Belhaven's factor, where he mastered the principles of levelling and land surveying. From this situation he passed to the office of Messrs. Dundas & Wilson, W.S., Edinburgh, the law agents of the Lennox family. Here his duties led him to study the charters on various West Country estates, and this gave him quite exceptional facilities for obtaining a great deal of interesting information regarding families and lands which was quite inaccessible to the general historical student. From among immense masses of details he gleaned much that possessed a general or local value, and this he turned to excellent account, contributing out of the fullness of his knowledge many papers to the Glasgow Archæological Society, of which he was one of the founders, and at the time of his death the acting foreign secretary, and some of these papers have been published in the Transactions of the Society. He also delivered two lectures on local history in 1863 and 1864 in Lennoxtown, under the auspices of the Campsie Mechanics' Institution. He spoke on Campsie antiquities when presiding at the reunion in Glasgow of the natives of Campsie and their friends. He prepared a memorandum on matters of parochial interest for Mr. Robert Blair, session-clerk, Clachan, for Dr. Stewart, Kirkintilloch, and I believe also for others. But I have been mostly indebted to his correspondence with Mr. William Brown, formerly of Westerton, now of Johnstone. This extended from 1868 till 1883. It contains many facts which could only have been learned by one having access to the charter chests. I have gleaned much in these letters—sometimes a casual remark, a date, the name of an individual or of a book giving a clue—and I have pleasure in acknowledging this indebtedness to Mr. Galloway's letters and my obligations to Mr. William Brown, who has permitted me opportunity of leisurely perusal.

From the office of Messrs. Dundas & Wilson, Edinburgh, he was appointed resident factor to Mr. J. L. K. Lennox of Woodhead, and he also subsequently had charge of the Craigend estate until the death of the late Sir Andrew Buchanan. He was factor for the Auchineden, Duntocher, and Bencloich estates for many years. He was in his 35th year when he came to Birdston as the resident factor on the Woodhead estate. Possessing great mental activity, he was an ardent student of history and archæology, of lands and the history and genealogies of their owners. Circumstances now directed his mental energies into tracing the family history of the Lennoxes of Woodhead, which required the laborious perusal of old charters, titles, and writs. He had thus unusual facilities for becoming acquainted with the details of local history and the traditions that had been handed down in families long connected with the parish. It was his good fortune to become acquainted with all classes, and to hear these speak of old times, old customs, and events of great parochial interest; but while hearing these, he omitted to make notes of them at the time, which he afterwards greatly regretted. He confessed he did not then appreciate them enough, but preferred plodding wearisomely among old parchments and other records of the past. Indeed, he says again in one of his letters to Mr. William Brown, that he generally gave a small portion of each day to what might be called "fancy" reading and writing, which was almost his only relaxation. He indulged in hardly any amusements, avoided all kinds of games, sight-seeing of ordinary kinds, or political meetings. One of his greatest and most enjoyed recreations was travelling abroad. He visited most of the countries of Europe, including France, Switzerland, Holland, Belgium, Austria, Germany, Italy, Denmark, Sweden, and Norway. He also travelled a great deal in Scotland, England, and Ireland. In this way he spent his annual summer holiday, and continued these excursions till within a very few years of his death. He had studied the language, literature, history, and people of many countries; he had an excellent knowledge of painting and music, and paid many visits to the best picture galleries in Europe, as well as to the best collections of antiquities and other objects of artistic or scientific interest. He read much in science, especially chemistry and geology. His relaxations, foreign travels, good music, and historical study were taken, to some extent, from a sense of duty, as being, in his opinion, needful for keeping up his strength and relish for the daily routine of his regular work.

He resigned the situation of factor on the Woodhead estate in 1844 to commence business as land-agent, accountant, and property valuator in Glasgow. In the following year the railway mania gave abundant employment to certain professions. He was in great repute as a landlord's valuator, and was constantly retained in disputes about the value of land required for railway purposes. Mr. Galloway left Birdston in 1844, not intending to return to the parish, but he was induced to resume his former charge of the estate in 1845. Stipulating that he should be free to reside in Glasgow, he fitted up Baldow farm steading as a dwelling-house, with a business office, and kept a housekeeper and a clerk there. Afterwards he advised Mr. Lennox to get a resident factor, and to employ him as a consulting land agent, an arrangement which continued till the death of Mr. Lennox.

He gave much study and research to philology and etymology of place names, bringing much knowledge and great patience to these subjects; he had a *penchant* in favour of Teutonic origins, and was fond of deriving from Danish or Norse roots, which sometimes led him to rather far-fetched conjectures. But apart from his Teutonic leanings, his distrust of monkish legends, and strong political and ecclesiastical antipathy to the Covenanters, he had accumulated, from his general reading, an immense mass of materials into which he strove to breathe a life that made their concentrated essence of great interest and full of information. He possessed great exactness in his writings and work, united with untiring industry and inflexible honesty, and his papers and notes were classified and arranged in perfect order, archæological papers, &c., apart from his business papers. It will be a great loss to Campsie if his notes are not left in such a state of preparedness that they can be given to the public. His own letters tell the story of his literary schemes.

In a letter to Mr. W. Brown, his correspondent at Johnstone, of date 11th December, 1868, he says—" I have squandered many precious hours, days, weeks, months, in searching for such food and handing it to others who liked to have it without any trouble in seeking for it in the same way. Few months pass without demands upon me from various quarters for details about families, landed property, &c." He took the keenest interest in his investigations at Ballagan, drew elaborate plans, and intended publishing his discoveries, but from want of leisure was unable to accomplish this. Writing to Mr. Brown under date 31st July, 1883, less than a month before his death, he says—" Several literary projects have come under consideration as a means of filling up time profitably or otherwise. Most probably I shall not live long enough to mature any of them, yet I may be able to arrange thousands of memoranda I have written and put aside during the last half century that may be considered by others as worth printing. If I cannot carry any of these the length of the press, possibly someone into whose hands they have fallen may make use of a portion of them in that line. One of the series of collections relates to the Campsie district, and may be more easily framed up than some of the others. If I am enabled to prepare it for the public I believe no one will feel more interest in it than yourself." In a letter, dated 3rd June, 1879, addressed to Mr. William Houston, he wrote—" My residence place during the last thirty years has been in big Glasgow, and in Campsie it was hardly ten years, yet Campsie is still vastly dearer to me than any other part of the world, notwithstanding that I am not known to five per cent. of its population, and cannot expect that after a few years, more or less, I shall be known or remembered by any of them. Meantime, having pleasure in every contribution to true history, especially of Campsie, I again thank you for your letter."

Mr. Galloway died 14th August, 1883, and was buried at Lennoxtown. A handsome tombstone has been erected by his daughter, the design of it being that of an old cross in Cirencester, which was found among his papers. The plans from this drawing were prepared by Mr. John Honeyman, architect, and the stone was put up by Mr. J. Mossman. It bears this inscription :—" In memory of Alexander Galloway, factor for many years on Woodhead, Craigend, and other estates, Born near Symington, 13th June, 1802; died in Glasgow, 14th August, 1883. And of his children, William, born 11th July, 1840, died 24th July, 1840; Alexander William, born 28th February, 1845, died 8th March, 1845 : Eliza Margaret, born 10th October, 1846, died 18th February, 1855."

THE REV. JOHN GOVANE

AND

"SESSIONAL AFFAIRES."

Q

THE REV. JOHN GOVANE

AND

SESSIONAL AFFAIRS.

THE ecclesiastical records of the parish, from its formation up to his time, were carried off or destroyed by the Rev. George Milne, when he was expelled in 1688. Milne was a zealous Episcopalian, and the people would not tolerate him after the Presbyterian party had got the upper hand at the Revolution of 1688. But from a collection of Diocesan records and muniments connected with the see of Glasgow, which had been removed for safety to France at the Reformation, stored partly at the Scots' College and partly in the Chartreuse of Paris and, as far as they had not perished, restored to this country in 1798, by the patriotic exertions of Abbé Macpherson, and published under the editorship of Joseph Bain, F.S.A. Scot., and the Rev. Charles Rogers, LL.D., we obtain many incidental references to Campsie.

The records of the Glasgow Presbytery contain notices of Campsie, over which the Presbytery exercised the spiritual oversight which formerly belonged to the office of the bishop, and directed the minister, or dealt themselves with grave cases of discipline, and insisted on the minister getting his rights with dilatory heritors, giving their counsel when asked by minister or session. Extracts from the Registers of the Presbytery of Glasgow, 1592 to 1601 and 1603 to 1626, have been published by the Maitland Club. The original records were nearly destroyed and have been much injured by fire. I have been privileged to obtain from Sir Michael Connal, on loan, his MS. copy of notes of the Presbytery minutes, taken by the Rev. Dr. Porteous, Glasgow, before they were injured, a volume which will be of great service should I ever deal with the Church history of the parish as a whole, by re-writing and extending my lecture of 1886 on that subject.

The ecclesiastical history of the parish is full of interest. From the Reformation in 1560 to the Revolution in 1688 Roman Catholicism, Prelacy, and Presbyterianism contended with varying fortunes for ascendency. The parishioners took sides keenly in the great conflict, and the depositions, imprisonment, banishment, and expulsion of the clergymen who were acting as parsons or ministers attest the earnestness of the parties and the fluctuating success that attended the course of the prolonged struggle.

In 1688 Presbyterianism obtained a complete supremacy, and became the established religion of the country, and since that time the story of the succession of ministers, while lacking much of the excitement of the former period, attains interest from the personalities of the various ministers, their different methods of work, and their gifts as preachers, the causes and results of dissent in the parish. From 1661, when, rather than conform to Prelacy, many ministers were ejected from their livings by the then dominant Episcopal party (Mr. Law, the minister of Campsie, being among those deposed), up till 1688, a period of twenty-one years, there had really been two clergymen ministering in the parish, one (Mr. Milne) in the church, who also occupied the manse, and the other (Mr. Law), who, notwithstanding his ministrations were proscribed, his attached people erected for him, near the Burn House, a dwelling-house and little meeting-place. The existence of these was brought before the notice of the Duke of Lauderdale, and on 26th March, 1678, the Council " expect that they will cause demolish the meeting-house in that shire erected for Mr. Law, as they did for those in the shire of Ayr." Notwithstanding, he continued to meet with his own hearers, preaching to them in conventicles, in the glens, on hillsides, or by night in the friendly shelter of some barn or farm outhouse. Meeting under circumstances such as these both preacher and hearers were in earnest, and the people were edified, and their numbers were not only not diminished but actually were multiplied.

The Revolution of 1688 gave the parish peace, and when Milne had been got rid of the people called Law, who, however, was then engaged, as one of the leaders of the Church, in attending to the interests of the Church and of the Scottish people in the settlement then being made by William and Mary, and he could not come. He was afterwards called to Edinburgh, accepted the call, and became one of the leading ministers in Edinburgh.

The Rev. John Govane was next thought of. He had only been licensed in June, 1688, and was ordained minister of Campsie in December of same year. Govane came from a true blue Covenanting stock. It was said of him that he was present at Bothwell Brig. He had suffered imprisonment in the Bass Rock for attending field meetings and conventicles. He had actually been seen speaking to his own brother-in-law the Rev. F. Forrester, who was, however, then a proscribed preacher For no other offence than merely speaking to his brother-in-law (according to Wodrow) he was incarcerated for two years in the prison of Stirling. He was therefore a man of strong convictions and had the courage of his opinions. In regard to scholarship he had been an earnest student and had gained a bursary at Glasgow College, which was held by him for three years. He took his degree in 1676, and was Preceptor of Hutchesons' Hospital in

1679. He was strongly attached to Presbyterianism. What was unusual in those days, he had studied medicine, perhaps having intended at first to become a medical man, and had changed his mind during his curriculum, and had finally chosen the ministry. In Campsie he threw himself heartily into his work, he was an excellent preacher, and Wodrow refers to him in his Church history as "the present worthy and useful minister of Campsie." He was also a popular pastor, and, what soon made his visits more appreciated, he was always ready to impart the benefits of his knowledge of medicine. In time, no matter what was the nature of the trouble or the social condition of the patient, all classes eagerly availed themselves of his medical skill, which was ever freely at the call of rich and poor alike. To the latter this was indeed a great boon, as when he prescribed for his people he never charged any fees for his visits, but gave his advice always and sometimes even the medicine gratis. He made his people welcome to his medical and surgical knowledge, and rejoiced at being able to relieve their physical ills as well as minister salvation to their souls. In his personal habits of life he was most abstemious. He is said to have lived at his own home like a hermit, and must have been in practice a vegetarian, as " he lived narrowly, and except at the Sacrament flesh was not in his house throughout the year." No wonder, says Wodrow, that he left £6000 sterling. He was ordained in 1688, and he died 17th Sept., 1729, aged 71, after having been minister of the parish for a period of 41 years. It seems to be assumed that the sum of money left at his death had not been acquired by inheritance, but was the accumulated savings of his lifetime. Now, while I admit there would be many in the parish who would take his services without any recognition, yet, on the other hand, there would be sufficient independence and gratitude among his parishioners, the heritors, farmers, cottars, &c., as to make them readily send him presents of farm produce, peats, cloth, &c., in return for his medical services. These presents, extending over a period of forty years, would help to account for the large sum he had amassed, and which he left at his death.

A careful perusal of the records of the kirk-session will impress on the reader that Mr. Govane was a man of God, of sincere piety, devout, and with a strong sense of duty. As Moderator he was calm, impartial, clear headed, and of strong common sense, always averse to precipitate action, always ready to put a fair or charitable construction on questionable conduct. As long as he was Moderator rich and poor were dealt with alike—there was not one law or practice for the big landed proprietor and another for his ploughman or dairymaid. The Laird of Dumbiedykes need not have asked him " wad siller do naething? " if that meant passing the session without the usual routine.

The ecclesiastical records of the times after the Reformation disclose many singular memorials, cases of discipline which appear very strange in the present day, and much that, if not useful or instructive, is at least curious and amusing. One thing is quite clear, there was no regular civil administration of justice or steady universal enforcement of the criminal laws. Murders, riots, and feuds were common, and even those who had committed murder were left unpunished if they were not dealt with by the Church courts. It thus came about that the Presbyteries took upon themselves the administration of both civil and criminal law. They prosecuted murderers and all kinds of criminals, and took cognisance of brawling in families and breaches of the peace. In every church the kirk-session exercised peculiar jurisdiction as well as dealing with breaches of the moral law. Delinquents had to appear at the pillar of repentance in the church or at the church door, sometimes bareheaded, barefooted, and barelegged, or clothed in sackcloth or the penitential white linen sheet. The church was not only a house of prayer, it was a place of preaching the gospel and of explaining to the people the principles at issue in the civil and ecclesiastical questions occupying the public mind. But it was far more. Within the walls, Sabbath after Sabbath, delinquents performed penance, and were rebuked and admonished before the congregation. The work of the "serker" or searcher, in the first minute of the kirk-session under Mr. Govane's moderatorship (page 233) points to duties almost equivalent to those of a Roman Inquisitor, while many of the cases dealt with by the session would now be brought before a police or sheriff court. Culprits had to appear for three several Sabbaths, and on the third occasion absolution was formally pronounced. Very frequently the devout-minded would be grieved and the frivolous entertained by such appearances.

In Mr. Govane's time the session were most assiduous in the discharge of their duties. The cases dealt with are given sometimes in great detail, but the whole tone of meetings is most creditable to the members of the session. A perusal of their records conveys the idea of men solemnly sitting as a judicial court, seeking to elicit truth and administer justice, and dealing with erring ones falling under the discipline of the church with an earnest desire that it should lead to confession, sincere penitence and repentance, and re-admission to church privileges, from which they had been temporarily debarred. When anyone was brought before Mr. Govane's session, charged with some transgression, the "Moderator entreated him to speak the truth, and not add sin to sin by covering it; that he would consider he had to do with a heart-searching God, who would soon or syne discover the hidden things of dishonesty; to be ingenuous in his confession of guilty, and to give glory to God." Witnesses when called were also warned. The formula in the minute bears— "Called and compeared (so-and-so), and being purged of malice, partiall counsell, or good deed done or promised to be done, deponed," &c. Cases there were where the woman charged refused

to attend when cited, or when appearing refused to answer the
questions addressed to her or to disclose the paternity, as, for
instance, in August, 1690, one on being expostulated with about
her disobedience in former citations, declared it was not her fault,
for she was most willing but durst not, being severely threatened
by the man who had got her into this condition, which was confirmed by the elder of the quarter. Gentle remonstrances were used
in the first instance, if these did not suffice pressure was brought
to bear. Where the woman persisted in concealing the name of
her partner in guilt through fear or from other causes, recourse
was sometimes had to measures for wringing a confession which
is calculated to shock public opinion nowadays. A surgeon
giving evidence before the session, who, being in professional
attendance in a case of child-birth, and his patient being in his
judgment *in periculo mortis*, stated that "before I would deliver
her, in the most solemn manner called upon her to declare who
was father of the child." In another case a midwife in attendance had made a similar appeal, and she likewise testified before
the same court.

The *Book of the Sessional Affaires* commences with the
first meeting at which the kirk-session met formally under Mr.
Govane's moderatorship. The sederunt of 24th June, 1689, consisted of the Moderator, Mr. John Govean, John Buchanan, William
Tournor, and D. Young, Elders. The first minute begins thus :—
"After prayer, it was thought fit to chuse John Young, in
Muckcroft, clerk, and accordingly he was called for and unanimously chosen, and the said John Buchanan, being the serker at
the tyme, is appointed to continue, the rest being of great age and
likewise at a great distance, till more elders be obtained." In
regard to the Moderator's unacquaintance with the place it was
recommended by the Moderator to the said elders that they have
serious thoughts about some to be added to the eldership, and
give in the report with all expedition. Then followed the arrears
of cases of discipline that had accumulated during the vacancy.
Also the said day Janet Cleg was dilated as guilty of fornication,
&c. ; also Agnes Murray was delated the same day to be guilty
of the like ; also Christian Crom is delated as guilty of fornication.
After conferring on the subject the elders agreed that Malcolm
Brown, in Lennox Miln (then a meal mill), and John Shearer, in
Capieston, were suitable parties for the office. The importance
they attached to this may be inferred from their resolution that,
in connection with the ordination of elders, 15th October, 1689,
it was ordered that upon Thursday ensuing a "considerable tyme
be set apart for prayer for ye Lord's countenance, direction, and
assistance in that important affaire." In a few years the matter
came up again, as will be seen from the following minute:—9th
September, 1701.—The said day, in regard to the paucity of the
number of the elders and the inability of some of them to attend
the session, and upon the account that they had no deacons,

enjoyned the Elders to make enquiry in their respective districts and quarters, anent those persons that they think most fit and qualified, both in regard to their knowledge and Christian lives and conversation, to undertake such offices, viz., of an elder and deacon, and to give a list thereof against next session.

In due course the elders reported on the most suitable individuals in their respective districts, and at a subsequent meeting it is reported of those designed to be ordained elders and deacons that their names were read from the pulpit, and nothing to this day objected. It is therefore thought fit that Sabbath next they be ordained, and, as previous and preparatory thereto, that upon Thursday ensuing a considerable time be set apart for prayer, for the Lord's countenance, directions, and assistance in that important and weighty affair.

On next Sabbath, 5th January, 1702, John Brown, William Miller, Alexander Miller, John Calder, John Blair, James Brown, and Robert Morrison were ordained elders, and John Young, Thomas Patrick, and David Robison were ordained deacons. It was arranged that the deacons should attend the meetings of the session, but only take part in the business that pertained to their office, and not vote in session business.

At the meeting of elders and deacons, after the ordination, the sederunt was as follows:—On 5th January, 1702, Mr. John Govane, modr.

Elders.	Elders.	Elders.
John Muir.	Robert Reid.	Andrew Fergus.
John Bennie.	John Brisbane.	Patrick Macklom.
Malcolm Brown.	James Lennox.	James Booll.
William Muir.	William Reid.	William Muir.
John Brown.	John Blair.	James Brown.
William Miller.	Alexander Miller.	Robert Morison.
John Calder.		

David Robison, *Deacon.*
John Young, *Deacon.*
Thomas Patrick, *Deacon.*

Lybel.—7th June, 1702.—The said day James Lennox, elder, gave in a lybel against Janet Brown, for her scandalizing him and his family publicly, before many witnesses, saying that he was a covetous wretch, and that he had one face to God and another to the Devil, and that he was not worthy to be an elder, and that they that made him an elder might have made him a cowherd. Five witnesses were adduced to prove the charge. Called on to plead, Janet could not deny them altogether, but refused the greater part. She objected to some of the witnesses, and in reply to the Moderator challenged proof—"Let them prove it; it would never be proved." Fresh witnesses were cited, further depositions taken, and the case is fully detailed. Libel found proven.

Alehouses.—April 15, 1690.—Also ye said day the elders are appointed to go through the alehouses in the Clachan and places adjacent, by turns, immediately after the ringing of the last bell (Sabbath afternoon), to see if any be found there drinking, or unnecessarily absent from ordinances during the summer time.

This injunction is repeated again and again, and is carried out by the elders, as we find—Reported by the elders who went through the alehouses and places adjacent that they found James ———— at home. Questioned him how it came he did not attend ordinances. Replied his cloathes were so ill he thought shame to come into the church, but he said he came ordinarily to the back window and heard. James and a number of others who were found not attending ordinances were duly cited to attend the next meeting of session, when they were dealt with. At that time and long afterwards ale was the universal beverage in Scotland. It was displaced by taxes imposed on malt in the end of last century, which were very unpopular at the time, witness—

> We'll mak' our maut, we'll brew our drink,
> We'll laugh, sing, and rejoice man.

To obviate the increased cost of malt the ale was made weaker and less exhilarating, and was gradually superseded by the use of whisky.

Testimonials.—On 4th June, 1690, public intimation was made to heads of families that no new servants be received into their houses from other congregations without testimonials. Elders to take notice of any such in their bounds. This is again repeated on the 17th May, 1691, with the addition, "as they will be answerable," addressed to the heads of families. 31 May, 1716.—Intimation from the pulpit that such as get servants from other congregations take care that they bring testimonials along with them. When a domestic servant was leaving the parish she applied to the minister or elder for her testimonial. The case was taken up at the session.

25th July, 1691.—Janet Provan appeared and required a testimonial. She being found free of scandal to our knowledge it was recommended to the clerk to give. Also a testimonial is appoynted to be given to Janet Gardner, in New Milne, being free of public scandal.

Compeared Margaret Forsyth, Robert Provan's wife, demanding a testimonial to go to Ireland. The session taking into consideration that there was a surmise of their being guilty before marriage thought it fitt particularly to enquire yr anent. The sd Margaret being called in and interrogat she denied yt there was any such thing. Ye clark is appoynted to give you a testimoniall, mentioning yr marriage day.

20th May, 1696.—It is recommended to the elders in yr several districts to make strict enqurie anent strangers come to the parish at the term, and require testimonialls.

1st February, 1697.—The same day called and compeared James Brown, and being enquired how he came to keep Joan M'Gregor, qo had no testimoniall, notwithstanding of public intimation from the pulpit yt no servants yt, are strangers be admitted without testimonialls, and yt the elders had required it once and again. He was appoynted to promise a testimoniall, and deliver it to ye elder of the quarter.

William Fergus for keeping Margaret Knight lykways Margaret M·Farlan, and William Bryston for keeping on Mary Gordon without a testimonial. This had been done although the elders had once and again been at them requiring testimonials. Fergus and Bryston cited to appear and be dealt with.

7th June, 1702.—Janet Somervell is sharply rebuked for her forgot testimonial. She was ordered to remove out of the parish and told that public intimation would be made from the pulpit of her carriage, that none might receive her, under pain of being proceeded with before the session.

The ordinary mode of citation was by the beadle. In cases of persistent contumacy the elder waited on the employer and requested his influence to get a servant to obey the summons to attend the session. If this failed, the accused was summoned by name by the minister from the pulpit, in the face of the congregation. If this failed, recourse was had to the civil magistrate, which was always effectual. The censures of the Church in Mr. Govane's days were not an empty form that could be disregarded with impunity.

1697.—William Lapslie was called before the Session in the usual manner by citation by the beadle, but disregarded his three warnings by that official. He was then summoned by name by the minister, in the face of the congregation, but remained persistently contumacious. The deposition of witnesses from the session of St. Ninian's were publicly read before the congregation, and Lapslie was summoned to appear before the Presbytery of Glasgow. This citation he also disregarded. Reported to Sheriff at Stirling, who sent an order to imprison him until he found bond and caution to be obedient to the session's demands, whereupon Lapslie got alarmed and caved in, and gave the required satisfaction to the session. In 1698, the year following, in a case that the Session had issued a citation, Janet Graham, the accused, was contumacious and ignored the Session. The case was taken before the Justices of the Peace, at Stirling, whereupon Janet came to the Moderator and entreated him that the session would free her at Stirling and she would give all obedience.

Attendance at Church and Sabbath Desecration.—In 1697 great activity is shown by the session in taking up the cases of those who had been irregular in their attendance at church. They were called upon by the elders and remonstrated with, and if they failed to amend were then cited before the session. The visits of the elders had apparently not met with much success in some quarters, for, having heard their reports, the session appointed two elders to go to those residing at Balgrochan and other two to Baldow and expostulate with them ; to hold forth their sin and danger in slighting and contemning ordinances, withal certifying if they continue to absent themselves they will be called before the session. This formal call resulted in all of the defaulters promising better attendance in future. Some of the absentees gave as their excuse for non-attendance that they required to stay at home and attend to their cattle. This was stated at the meeting, where it is minuted :—Reported that some stay from ordinances feeding their horses and kynd on the Sabbath day, during the time of sermon. Elders to take notice of such and rebuke them ; and this failing, they were to be proceeded against in a public way.

1700.—Reported yt Joan Matthed, servitrix to Alexander Miller, did always stay at home from ordinances on the Lord's Day, bearing companie to one William Livingstone, she is to be cited, and acknowledged yt she had been a considerable tyme absent from ordinances ; but yt it was not her dislyke of ordinances obliged her to stay at home, only she had been sicklie, and as for her frequenting the companie of William Livingstone she denies it.

The foregoing refer merely to non-attendance, but breach of the Sabbath, by performing acts lawful on other days but not on the Sabbath day, was held as profaning the day by . . "unnecessary . . works about our worldly employments."

Nov. 19, 1691.—The same day reported that Thomas Bennie and Marion Brown are guilted of breach of Sabbath in coming to David Young's house, in Baldorran, upon a Sabbath night, seeking cloves and clevers to guide their lint. They are appoynted to be cited to the next session. These two appeared and confessed their fault, and promised to have regard to the Lord's Day, and they appearing penitent were passed with a sessional rebuke, " Certifying them, if found guiltie of the lyk that they should not so easilie pass."

On 3rd Sept., 1696.—Called but not compeared James Kincaid and his servants, whereupon they are cited a second time to the next session. 10th Oct.—Called but not compeared James Kincaid, and his servants, wherefore, &c. 18th Nov.—Called and compeared James Kincaid and acknowledged that he had caused carry in and thrash some bear for straw to his horse that day. He is appointed to appear before the Congregation next Sabbath and receive a public rebuke. This was the Laird of Kincaid, and his servants having neglected to provide straw for his horses he seems to have sent them out either to the field or to the stackyard for a few sheaves of bear, which he caused them to thrash on the Sabbath day. His punishment was standing on the stool of repentance, and receiving a solemn rebuke in public, because, according to one version, on his arriving home on

Sunday morning from a journey, and finding no food for his wearied horse, he sent the groom out to the next field, to cut and bring in some, which, by his master's orders, the groom thrashed on the spot, as it was entirely owing to his own negligence.

23rd May, 1708.—James Book delated to be guilty of the breach of the Sabbath by taking a cow to the bill.

22nd August, 1708.—Called and compeared John Buchanan. Being interrogated if it was true that he speaned his lambs on a Sabbath night, he said it was true, but he was obliged to do it, for he had no where to put them. It being the first fault, and promising not to do the like for the future passed with a sessional rebuke.

Not only was the due observance of the Sabbath rigorously enforced, but the Fast-days had also to be kept almost as strictly. At the meeting of session 14th June, 1691, it was recommended to the respective elders to enquire how the last Fast was observed. On 28th June, 1691, it was reported by the elders that they heard nothing anent the breach of the Fast, but it had been observed.

Matters evidently were not quite so satisfactory a few years after, as the following extracts show:—April, 1702.—Reported that John Scot in Balgrochan should have caston peitts the Fast-day before the communion, wherefore he is to be cited to the next Session. The maid servant was called to prove the charge. Being interrogated, said it was too true, and that it was against her will, for John Scot compelled her, which Scot admitted. He had to appear before the congregation, while the maid got off with a sessional rebuke.

November 22nd, '92·—The same day Robert Dunwiddie delated as being drunk in Kirkintilloch upon a Saturday night and coming home in the Sabbath morning, wherefor he is appointed to be cited, &c.

8th May, 1697.—The sd day William Fergus in Royt Fair is delated as guilty of drunkenness in Kirkintilloch on ane Saturday night.

24th May, 1697.—Fergus compeared and confessed his drunkenness, and professed sorrow for it, and promised he should never be found in the lyke, wherefore the session thought fitt to pass him with a sessional rebuke, it being the first tyme, certifying if he should be found in the lyke for the future he should not get so easilie past.

October 28, 1697.—The same day William Angus is delated for being drunk and swearing in Kirkintilloch; William King is delated for drunkenness in Kirkintilloch on Saturday and coming home on the Sabbath morning with two horse and bringing meal in a sack; William Bolloch, at same session, as to being drunk in Kirkintilloch upon Saturday and coming home on Sabbath morning with his meall.

August, 1700.—Delated William Fergus for drinking to excess

in Kirkintilloch after two o'clock on the Sunday morning
and wandering through the street wanting the bonnet, and
vomiting.

19th August—It was reported that James and John Ronald
and Francis Calder should have been guilty of horrid swearing
and cursing as they were going to Drumond with lyme. Cited,
and passed with a sharp sessional rebuke.

Another case is recorded wherein the parishioner is charged
with fighting with his brother and being drunk in Kirkintilloch
and with calling names. In some of the cases, when the language
used is specified, it is evident that for coarseness and offensiveness
it could hardly be surpassed at the present day.

Not only were the parishioners strictly looked after, but when
visitors from the neighbouring parishes of Kilsyth and Kirkintilloch got too convivial when seeing their friends, the same was
duly reported to their respective kirk sessions in order that they
might be dealt with.

1701.—Report was sent to the minister of Kilsyth anent Andrew
Livingstone, James Gray, and John Buchanan, giving account of
their being too late on a Saturday night about the Roit Fair and
their being overtaken with drink.

A charge is made against a female servant of the Lady Bal-
qurage. Cited and before the session she pleads guilty, the other
party being a Kirkintilloch man. " And ye clerk was enjoyned
to signifye it to the session of the Lenzie."

Enforcing attendance at church, and the production of " testimonials " by all incomers ; seeing to it that not only Sabbath
day but also Fast-days were rigidly observed ; that none tarried
in the alehouses while they should have been at afternoon church ;
and the general cognisance of petty misdemeanours, drunkenness,
and defamation of character—all of these put together did not en-
gross the attention of the session to the same extent as the constantly recurring breaches of the seventh commandment by all
classes in the parish. The Campsie kirk session did all in their
power to raise the moral tone of the community, with only partial
success. Two cases might be cited to illustrate the method of
procedure.

20th November, 1702.—Isabel B., delated to be with child,
wherefore she is to be cited to next session.

13th December.—Being interrogated if she was with child,
answered affirmatively ; being further enquired to whom, replyed,
Malcolm Wilson in Killwonant. She is cited *apud acta*, and the
said Malcolm is cited to next session.

3rd January, 1703.—M. W. appears and denies guilt. Intreated
by the Moderator to confess and give glory to God by a free and
ingenuous confession, and not to add sin to sin by a denial, he
answered he was never guilty with that woman at no time nor in
no place. Isobel is now called in and informed that Malcolm
denied guilt with her. She says in his face he was guilty, and

that his conscience could tell him so much. As Malcolm still denied, the Moderator desired her to condescend, in order to fixing guilt on him, on time and place and other circumstances as far as she could. She then appealed to his conscience if he were not guilty on three several occasions which she minutely specifies— day, date, and circumstances—but he still denies. After deliberation the elders of the district are appointed to discourse with Malcolm to see if they can bring him to confess if guilty, and they were then both called in and cited to attend next session.

31st January, 1703.—Reported that the elders appointed to confer with Malcolm Wilson discoursed him, but could gain no ground upon him in order to confession, and with all that he alledged that if the matter were thoroughly searched into others might be found guilty with her, upon which he was called in and questioned thereanent, answered she was intimate with George M'Farlan and John Ben, and that they had, as she said herself, given her gloves, or at least one of them, &c. The Moderator said, "Can you make these things good? Ye would consider that ye are speaking before a Judicatory, and therefore would take heed that you say nothing save what you can make appear." So he replied it was reported him for a truth, and he names certain individuals whom he refers to as witnesses. Isobel is called in, denies the countercharges, and asserts she bought the gloves referred to. After giving details as to time and circumstances, Malcolm again denies having had any dealings with her. He would declare this upon oath, though he were going to eternity the next moment. He and she are cited *apud acta*, and their respective witnesses are to be cited to the next session.

21st February, 1703.—Witnesses examined. Malcom is told that his witnesses have not made good what he asserted. He could not help it, tho' belike it could not be proved, yet it was well known she was a light woman. The Moderator said he should be careful and take heed not to affirm anything to the prejudice of any person's good name but what he could make good, and that was not the way to clear himself by aspersing others, and therefore entreated him to be free and ingenuous in his confession if he was guilty. He replied he was ready to declare upon oath he never had carnal dealings with her. Isobel called and informed he still denied, said she could say no more, but God and his own conscience knew it was truth. The session, after deliberation, thought fit to give him the forme of an oath in formidable terms, seeing he professed himself willing to give his oath and referred it to the Moderator to draw up one against next session, and withal that the Presbyterie should be acquainted with it before it was taken. Malcom was cited to the next meeting.

1703.—At next meeting Malcom called. Intreated by the Moderator to be free and ingenuous and not add sin to sin by an obstinate denial of the truth. Answered that though he were to die in a hour he could say no more than he had said, that he was never guilty. The Moderator then caused the Clerk to read this form of oath (the Presbytery allowing the same)—"I, Malcom Wilson, does swear, by the great and eternal God, that I am not guilty of the sin of fornication with Isobel Boyl, and if I be, let me never find mercy, but be damned eternally, let me never thrive in this world, but some visible judgment be seen upon me." Enquired if he was ready to take that oath, he said he was just now if we pleased. The Moderator told him it was to be done in a more public way, and that he seemed too precipitate in offering, yet they would allow him time to consider, and referred it to his serious consideration for a fortnight, and cited him to attend next session.

10th April.—Malcolm appears but declines to take the oath. Said he was advised and now determined otherwise, because such who in like case had given their oaths, tho' never so innocent, were by the most part reputed guilty and so their credit for ever broke. But if she would give her oath that she never had carnal dealings with any other than him, he would take with the child, and do all duty as if it were his own, and so would keep his credit. The Moderator told him it would be accounted odd and strange if he were innocent to leave it to her declaration, especially as he had asserted once and again she was of bad fame, but he adhered and referred it to her oath. She is cited to next meeting.

30th April.—Compeared Isobel, and being told the state of matters, expressed her willingness to purge herself by oath. The session delay till the Presbytery may be consulted.

23rd May.—Presbytery judge it a matter for the oath to be taken before the congregation. Both cited to next session.

7th June.—Malcom refuses. Refers it to her. If she will swear him guilty he will give his bond that he will satisfie the church and do all duty to her and the child. Isobel is willing— cautioned—the form of oath is read over to her and she is to consider it till next session.

27th June, 1703.—Is willing to do it not only before the congregation but all the world. Is appointed to appear before the congregation on Sabbath first and give her oath of purgation.

25th July.—Reported that she appeared before congregation. Oath was read over, and she answered the questions affirmatively. Has other eight days to consider oath.

14th August.—Reported appeared. Moderator till that day eight days to consider and lay seriously to heart that oath.

8th Sept.—Appeared and gave her oath. The minister told the people they might now judge charitably of her. Appointed to appear before the congregation Sabbath first to be rebuked. Malcolm is cited to next session.

27th Sept.—Isobel appeared and got her first rebuke. She is to confer with James Lennox and Robert Marshall, two of the elders, who are to report to next session.

17th Oct.—Elders reported her sensible of her sin, and she being present and professing sorrow for her sin is appointed to appear before the congregation Sabbath first to be rebuked and absolved. This case was taken up on 20th Nov., 1702, and only concluded 17th Oct., 1703, having occupied the anxious consideration of the kirk session for eleven months and a half. It illustrates the great patience and also the determination of the kirk session.

23rd July, 1704.—Janet Paul delated as guilty of fornication, wherefore she is to be cited. 13th August.—Confessed was with child to one of the heritors, who is cited for 8th September. He compeared and confessed. Appointed to appear before the congregation Sabbath cum eight days, to be rebuked. It was not uncommon to deny stoutly charges which were afterwards confessed. "She thought shame" was the extenuation put forward.

October, 1704.—The Laird appeared before the congregation and was rebuked for the first tyme. At interview with elders professing his grief for his sin he was appointed to appear before the congregation Sabbath cum eight days to be rebuked for the second tyme and absolved. Reported appeared, 19th November, 1704.

A great variety of miscellaneous business comes up from time to time, from which I quote a few typical cases.

March 13, 1690.—The session, taking to their consideration that some had been proclaimed in order to marriage for the first and second tyme and no more, and nt. all that Justices of Peace being wanting in the parish, the penalties could not be obtained from those who were guilty of fornication before marriage, appointed that henceforward the parties to be proclaimed give in two dollars for consignation, and that cation be no more admitted.

26th July, 1691.—The session, considering the mortcloath is old and torn, yt their is a necessitie to diminish the pryce, did appoynt yt henceforward ten shillings Scots be exacted for each time of its going out.

12th August, 1691.—Such difficulty in obtaining the money for the mortcloath. Appoynted henceforward should not be given out but upon ye receipt of readie money for it.

1st March, 1699.—Cristan M'Lay is delated for using of charms, particularlie directing one Girzell Maiklom to get Sabbath meall to end or mend a child. She was cited, and being enquired anent her using charms, particularlie directing to seek Sabbath day's meall, she denyed yt she bade Girzell Maiklom seek it, only she told her yt she had heard of such a thing yt had done good. The Moderator told her the evil of using of charms or advysing any to use ym. And so she was past, she promising never to be found the lyke again.

25th September, 1707. — Alexander Galbraith compeared desyring baptism to his child. The session, considering his irregular marriage in being married with a curat, appointed him to appear before the congregation Sabbath first to be rebuked for the same, in order to his getting the benefit of baptism to his child. Alexander duly appeared and was rebuked according to church order for his being irregularly married by a curat without proclamation.

14th September, 1788.—J. Carr. Irregular marriage with a woman named Clachars, in Kirkintilloch, who owned same. Was rebuked before Kirkintilloch session, and on that account only paid the kirk dues of this parish. Same meeting another couple summoned and appeared for an irregular marriage. Were sessionally rebuked, but on account of their poverty and on the promise of good behaviour in the future only ordered to pay the kirk dues, which they accordingly did.

29th June, 1800.—Two women, as they were both desirous to leave the parish as soon as possible, the session allowed them to appear before the congregation and be rebuked twice in one day. The session, however, do not intend that this shall pass into a precedent.

December 11, 1807.—C—— S——, daughter of a farmer, owned her irregular marriage with a labourer in Glasgow, producing at the same time a certificate showing that they had been married by a Justice of the Peace, and stating that as she had returned to her father's house, with an intention not to cohabit any longer with him, and he was prohibited from coming into her presence, she would consider it a particular favour if Mr. Lapslie and the session would take the fine and accept of her acknowledgment, instead of requiring her husband and herself to appear together before them. Agreed to, from motives of delicacy, to authorise Moderator to receive her acknowledgment.

26th August, 1800.—A couple appear and acknowledge an irregular marriage. Having owned one another as man and wife, and having paid a fine of seventy shillings, they were passed.

1795.—John Lapslie, tenant of Inchterf, having left a legacy to the parish, which the former kirk-session had retained, the new kirk-session take steps to recover this, and the old session, now of the Relief Church, was found liable, and the treasurer had to refund the money.

£55 of Lapslie legacy in Thistle Bank; two years' interest at four per cent., £4 8s. Pious books bought with this, namely, two dozen Confession of Faith and 2 and 7-12 Testaments, which exactly exhausted it.

1797.—Abram Angus, feuar, Balgrochan, called on David Gemmell, schoolmaster and session clerk, and asked for a sight of the register of baptisms. Was shown the same, in which he discovered the name of his son William, who, by his age, was liable to be balloted for under the Militia Act. He insisted on the Registrar altering the date or expunging his son's name, but this being refused, Angus forcibly seized the record and tore therefrom the leaf in which his son's and other names were recorded, which leaf he carried off and destroyed. The matter was reported to the Crown agent, who ordered a precognition. John Lennox of Antermony and John Stirling of Craigbarnet granted warrant, but the matter was settled extrajudicially by Angus offering to pay twenty-one pounds sterling as a fine.

1809.—John Lennox of Woodhead, in celebration and permanent commemoration of this joyful and auspicious day, in which our gracious and beloved sovereign, King George III., enters on the 50th year of his reign, makes a donation of fifty guineas to be added to the poor's fund of the parish. Reported that the capital of the poor's fund of Campsie now amounts by this generous donation to £775 6s. 3d.

1813.—On 28th November, Miss Lennox gave a donation of £117 10s. to the poor's fund, thus making up a capital sum of £300 to the fund from this family.

1826.—Total stagnation of trade and manufactures and want of work for operative classes. Dr. Macleod, in the session, called attention to a numerous and distressed portion of the people, who, from the infirmities of age or bodily disease, are unable to avail themselves of the relief tendered; especially of a numerous class of poor lonely females, many of whom are advanced in life, and whose ordinary means of industry, arising from pirn and bobbin winding, and also from muslin sewing, are entirely destroyed.

NOTES AND CORRECTIONS.

Page 3. *Armorial Bearings on Lapslie's Tombstone.*—After his marriage Mr. Lapslie had so strong a desire to be able to subscribe *Armigero* that he obtained armorial bearings, which are registered thus :—" Lapslie.—Rev. James Lapslie, Campsie, Co. Stirling, 1797. Or, an eagle displ. gu. beaked and membered sa. surmounted by a fesse engr. az. charged with a bezant betw. two buckles of the field. *Crest*—a passion cross gu. *Motto*—Corona mea Christus."
Rev. James Lapslie.—The late James Glen, shoemaker, Lennoxtown, was a good scholar and a beautiful writer, and acted as amanuensis to the Rev. James Lapslie for a long time, whose hand shook so much he was unable to write. His signature before his death was almost illegible. Mr. William Brown has informed me that James Glen had stated to him that Lapslie had written out a history of the parish going back 900 years, and all that he had written had been destroyed by some pranks of his wild sons.

Page 11. *Rats.*—Mr. Lapslie used occasionally to hold meetings at Milton. On these occasions Forrest, the miller, had as many dead rats collected as he could obtain, and had them distributed where Lapslie was to hold his meeting.

Page 44. *Dr. Macleod of St. Columba's.*—I learn on good authority that a memorial volume of Dr. Macleod's life and remains is almost ready for the press. It will be printed for private circulation only.

Page 59. *The Clachan.*—Since the lecture on "The Clachan and District" was printed, through Mr. James Millar I have heard of a Mrs. M'Ewan, who has resided in the same house in Glasgow for nearly fifty-two years. Her father, who was named Barr, left Darnley to become foreman with Mr. M'Kinlay at Glenmill bleachwork, where he had a free house and coal. Mary Barr (Mrs. M'Ewan) had been first a "tearer" at Lennoxmill, but she was afterwards employed at Glenmill. Her mother was a highland woman from Islay, and Dr. Macleod was therefore very friendly with the family, who lived in the house subsequently acquired by Sandy Norris, quite close to the manse. Mary romped with the manse children, and says she has many a time carried Geordie and Donald on her back. Norman was then too big for that sort of thing. She speaks familiarly of " the boys with their bits o' kilts and bare legs, braw laddies. Donald was a real nice, wee, fat laddie." When the old church was dismantled she lifted a bit of wood one day, which she had made into a little box. It is in constant household use and was shown to me. Mrs M'Ewan is very intelligent, and has a splendid memory. She is full of anecdotes of " Auld Kirkton," from whom she received a bible before he went to Rome on one occasion. On his return he made particular enquiry as to the use she had made of it. The bible is still carefully treasured. She was a great favourite with the Muirs in the inn, and was frequently requisitioned as an assistant. She remembers the arrival of the first omnibus that had been seen in the Clachan, and has seen as many as sixteen carriages standing at the inn, all out filled with people making holiday. Some of the visitors brought their own provisions, and the ladies of the party laid their table-cloth and picnicked in the glen, having tea only in the inn. But the greater part wanted dinner also. When the joints in the larder were unequal to the demands and no butcher meat could be got— on a Sunday, for instance—the Clachan poultry were killed, girls were set to pull the feathers, to pull and shell peas, &c. Being a bright, intelligent girl, she was often sent for to act as a guide to parties visiting the glen. Her instructions were—" You'll show these people the glen. Let them see 'The Ladies' Linn,' 'The Spout o' Craiglee,' 'The Lover's Loup,' 'The Bed o' Wild Leeks,' 'Jacob's Ladder,' and 'The Covenanters' Cave.' " I asked what story she told of "The Lover's Loup." Mrs. Muir's version was that two sweethearts were sitting at the turn in the road looking down the glen; they had some difference, and the man threw himself over the steep descent. I replied the version I had heard as a boy was that the lover had been at the turn of the road, and that he had seen his sweetheart down below at the water side walking with a rival, and that he had, under these circumstances, taken the wild leap towards the pair at the bottom. The bed of "wild leeks" is a mass of garlic, the white flowers of which look beautiful, but let the admiring beholder beware of touching the flowers, which leave a strong and disagreeable odour on the hands. "The Covenanters' Cave" is more popularly known as "The Big Linn." The water falls over a projecting ledge, and one can pass under this projecting rock from one side to the other. This used to be a favourite bathing place, and diving under the fall added additional zest. Mrs. M'Ewan recollects the Resurrectionist times well. One morning, as her brother was going to his work at Glenmill, he saw Rabbie Reid's body sticking half out of its grave in the kirk-yard. A tall farmer had recently died, whose body was wanted, and the body-lifters had mistaken the grave, and whenever they had ascertained this they left the body half drawn out. The cause of the sudden cessation of operations in the case of Rabbie Reid's corpse was believed to be the knowledge of the fact that he had died of a contagious disease, and the Resurrectionists were afraid of touching the body, which they had lifted in mistake. Their operations were neither seen nor disturbed by any watch, if such had been set that evening. On another occasion, coming home along the Howe Loan, she heard on a frosty night a most unusual rumbling, crunkling sound. There was motion, but no sound of wheels. To avoid meeting those causing the noise, whom she considered to be Resurrectionists who had been lifting a body in the Clachan, she first thought of hiding in M'Farlan the carrier's hay rick, but bethought herself they might want hay, and what if they discovered her hiding there? So she turned and posted herself below the Haughhead bridge, near the entrance to Ballancleroch, where she fancied she was sure of avoiding them wherever they turned. "And what do ye think cam' o'er the brig and splashed at ma very feet—me a bit lassie, cowering there in terror—what do ye think now?" the recollection stirring her whole emotional nature. I professed to be unable to conjecture. "Weel, just the barrel o' ma ain father's sow. They had poisoned the sow, and had rolled the barrel along to the bridge and thrown it over, and me hiding there!" She ran through the Kirkton policies and got home, where she fainted. She had many stories about the kirk-yard. One of a farmer's wife, who had been driven almost to distraction by the stories about body-lifting. Her husband had been recently buried, and the thought that his grave might possibly be desecrated had caused such distress and nervous excitement that nothing short of actually opening the grave would satisfy her. One day Donald Blair and his assistants opened the grave in her presence. When they came to the coffin and struck it the sound indicated that the coffin was full. "Take off the lid." This was done, and the body was declared to be there quite undisturbed. Nothing would satisfy her short of the evidence of her own senses, and she did not wish the coffin raised to the surface. A ladder was procured by which, with the assistance of the bystanders, she was enabled to descend into the grave, satisfy herself that the grave had been undisturbed, and actually identify the remains as those of her husband, besides whose remains she wished her own to lie. The mental distress and nervous excitement were at an end, and she went up with her mind at rest.

A Mysterious Murder.—Mrs. M'Ewan and her mother were one evening walking in the Ha' End. when they both heard faint cries of murder! murder! proceeding from up the Ward Brae or the glen. They were both frightened, and Mary caught her mother's arm and supported her till they got into their own cottage. She then raised an alarm in the clachan. A number of men got lanterns, and they went up the glen to the turn of the Craw Road, but heard or saw nothing. A dog belonging to Ferguson the shepherd, who resided at Allanhead, one day uncovered some human remains —the hair and teeth of a young woman. It then transpired that a strange. fair-haired young woman had been seen leaving the Clachan in the company of " Scuffy " Brown the evening that the cries of murder had been heard, and the suspicion of some foul play having occurred took possession of the Clachan. Search was afterwards renewed and in a soft bit of marshy ground a box was discovered with the body of a young woman crushed into it. No legal proceedings were taken beyond some enquiries, but the Clachan folks had no doubt in their minds, and this deepened their aversion to Scuffy, who was regarded as the murderer. The young woman had been enquiring the way across to Fintry, and had incautiously mentioned that she was taking home her half-year's fee, which she had secreted in the " tourie " on her crown. Scuffy, it was considered, having overheard about the fee had volunteered to shew her the way till she got on to the Craw Road. No further tidings were heard of her till the dog discovered the spot where the body was lying concealed. The young woman had left her trunk at Bulloch's shop, Lennoxtown, where it lay long unclaimed. Mrs. M'Ewan's husband was a mason from Crieff, who came to the building of Lennox Castle, where he was employed for some years. The masons at the castle were paid 24s. per week, while in Glasgow the summer wages were only 18s. per week ; in winter less, with broken time when weather was unfavourable. Mary was married in 1837, and has lived in Glasgow, since about 1839.

Page 68. *Mr. John M'Farlan's Inscription.*—This inscription was written by Lord Jeffrey and his own son David, the father of Lieut.-General David M'Farlan, and not by Lord Brougham or Lord Cockburn.

Page 78. *Clachan Characters.*—I have omitted Bettach Scott and Wee Black Meg, who lived with her. Mrs. M'Ewan says Bettach had a free house and other than visible means of support. Meg's father had been brought from India by Captain Lennox, as his servant, and then became the black footman at Woodhead. He was always called Lennox. Meg was therefore a Eurasian, her dark hair and dusky skin indicating Hindoo paternity.

Page 81. *Spots of White Paint symbolical of Tears.*—The late Miss Catherine M'Farlan recollected the Auchinreoch pew in the Clachan Church being painted black after the laird's death, and white spots of paint dotted all over it, to symbolise tears.

Page 83. *The Craw Road.*—The new Craw Road was formed towards the end of last century mainly through the exertions of Mr. Dunmore of Ballindalloch and Mr. Peter Spiers of Culcreuch, &c. The gradients were made so that wheel traffic could go over it. The old road, with its steep gradients, was made at a time when nearly all traffic across Campsie Muir was carried on horseback. The term a "load of meal," meaning thereby two bolls, is not yet obsolete, as in these old times two bolls were the load for a horse. Coals formerly were carried on horseback in sacks, and a load of coals was 3 cwts.

Page 87. *David Wilkie.*—The Rev. Norman Macleod knew Wilkie, and it has been said that he was the prototype of "Jock Hall," in his story of *The Starling.*

Page 97. *Parish Mills.*—The dwellers in the barony were not only compelled to have all their grain ground at the barony mill, but the vassals were held bound under their charters to assist in bringing home the mill stones, in upholding the mill, and repairing the mill dam and inlaid, or mill lade.

Page 101. *James M'Gilchrist in Portugal.*—Mr. James M'Gilchrist has informed me that the incident did not happen to him. Though I am mistaken in the individual addressed the incident is a true one.

Page 104. *Jamie Foyer and the 42nd.*—The Campsie militia contingent were drafted into the Perth militia, and in the year 1811 six hundred men volunteered from the Perthshire militia into the 42nd—

From the Perthshire Militia to serve in the line,
The brave forty-second we sailed for to join.

Mr David Russell, of 175 Slatefield Street, Glasgow, an old sergeant of the 42nd, wrote in 1888 an interesting series of sketches in the *Kirkintilloch Herald*, and compiled a most interesting chronological summary of the Regimental history for the *Glasgow Evening Times* on the eve of the unveiling, at Aberfeldy, by Lord Bredalbane, in 1888, of the monument to the Black Watch, with the object of interesting the present residents of Campsie and Kirkintilloch in the natives of these parishes who so gallantly served their country in the Highland regiments, particularly the 42nd and 71st. The Robert Perry in whose arms young Foyer breathed his last was said to have been a Campsie man. Mr Russell hoped thereby to have some suitable memorial erected to their memory. Up till the present time his good intentions have been without result.

Pages 132-134. *List of Ministers.*—The list of ministers given does not profess to be complete. I have been reminded that Mr. Alexander Mackenzie, lime-work contractor, Lennoxtown, referred to on page 190. had a son, the Rev. James R. Mackenzie, who was minister of the Scottish Episcopal Church, Helensburgh, 1835-44. He died in the latter year, and was buried at Lennoxtown. The name of James Allan, who was a minister in New South Wales, has been added at foot of page 156.

Page 169. *Coal and Lime Workings in the Parish.*—Both coal and limestone were worked on each side of the Glazert, near New Mill Farm steading eastward, a century ago, on the estates of Glorat and Kincaid. The workings were resumed on the Glorat side, east of New Mill, about 1860, but were soon given up. The site of these lime kilns is now covered by the house and grounds of Fingarry. Campsie limestone has always had a good name. It is said that it was used in the erection of Glasgow Cathedral. At present sampled fairly and analysed carefully for trade purposes, it gives—

Lime, - - - - - - -	91·45
Lime carbonate, - - - - -	3·45
Oxide of iron and alumina, - - -	4·10
Insoluble matter, - - - -	1
	100

Page 179. *James Stirling out in the '45*—"Burry" was in personal attendance on the Prince when he was in Edinburgh. In the Memoirs of the Jacobites of 1715 and 1745, by Mrs. Thomson, vol. iii., it is stated that when Prince Charlie rode through St. Anne's yard into Holyrood House, "he was joined upon his entering the Abbey by the Earl of Kelly, Lord Balmerino, Mr. Hepburn of Keith, Mr. Lockhart, yr. of Carnwath, Mr. Graham, yr. of Airth, Mr. Rollo, yr. of Powhouse, Mr. Stirling of Craigbarnet, and several other gentlemen of distinction."

Page 183. *Glorat.*—The heir apparent to Glorat is Sir Charles Stirling's son, George Stirling, born 4th September, 1869, who was educated at Eton College and Sandhurst Royal Military College. He was gazetted a second lieutenant in the (56) Essex Regiment, November, 1889, which regiment he joined at Cyprus in January, 1890, and where he is now (May, 1892) serving. The portion of Glorat built in 1879 is named the Ladies' Tower.

Page 193. *Burying Places.*—There is a tradition of interments having at one time been made in the Sterriqua Farm, on Kincaid Moor, and of some slight skirmish having taken place there when Cromwell's troops were quartered in Glasgow. The Kincaid Moor was taken in about the beginning of the present century, and divided between the farms of French Mill, Sterriqua, and Temple.

Page 209. *Rights of Pasture on Common Lands.*—Many of the lands at Torrance had rights of pasturing so many cows, or of pasturing and grazing cows and a horse, or a mare with a foal, on certain specified common moors.

CALICO PRINTING IN CAMPSIE.

Bntoch's

CALICO PRINTING

IN CAMPSIE:

BEING

SKETCHES OF ITS RISE AND PROGRESS IN THE PARISH,

WITH

JOTTINGS AND REMINISCENCES CONCERNING
EMPLOYERS AND EMPLOYED, TRADES,
STRIKES, FRIENDLY SOCIETIES, &c.

BY

JOHN CAMERON, J.P.,
KIRKINTILLOCH.

KIRKINTILLOCH:
D. MACLEOD, *HERALD* OFFICE, COWGATE STREET.
1891.

PREFACE.

A PORTION of the following pages was read as the opening lecture of this winter's course of the Campsie Young Men's Association. At the request of the editor of the *Kirkintilloch Herald* the MS. was placed at his disposal. The copious notes published in that newspaper from week to week have awakened an unexpected amount of local interest, and have been the means of placing additional information within my reach.

I have incorporated in the lecture some of the newly-acquired facts and anecdotes. I have also included extracts from some of the letters I have received. At the suggestion of a number of old Campsonians, who are no longer connected with the parish, but who still take the deepest interest in its concerns, I have been induced to publish it in a more compact form than the columns of a weekly paper.

I am collecting information concerning the parish, and will be glad to receive notes on any matters affecting Campsie. I take this opportunity of cordially thanking all who have assisted me with materials for the present paper.

SOUTH BANK HOUSE,
KIRKINTILLOCH, *January,* 1891.

CALICO PRINTING IN CAMPSIE.

INTRODUCTORY.

CALICO PRINTING has been practised from time immemorial in India. In that country, it is alleged, manufacturing processes have undergone little change for nearly three thousand years, and not only was the art of using mordants well known, but also that of resist pastes, in order to preserve the cloth from the action of the dye-bath.

Pliny, the Roman author, who lost his life at the age of 56, owing to the eruption of Mount Vesuvius, in August, 79 A.D., describes in his "Natural History" the processes that prevailed in his time in Egypt. In Book xxxv. chap. ii. he says : " Robes and white veils are painted in Egypt in a wonderful way : being first imbued, not with dyes but with dye-absorbing drugs, by which they appear to be unaltered, but when plunged for a little in a cauldron of boiling dye-stuff, they are found to be painted. Since there is only one colour in the cauldron, it is marvellous to see many colours imparted to the robe, in consequence of the modifying agency of the excipient drug. Thus . . . the cauldron is made to impart several dyes from a single one, painting while it boils."

About the middle of the Seventeenth Century commercial enterprise made the nations of the West acquainted with the brilliant colours of the Orient, and attempts were soon made in Europe to imitate them. France lost much and this country gained immensely by the Revocation of the Edict of Nantes, in 1685, by which the French Protestants were obliged to flee to this and other countries for shelter. To their adopted countries they carried their intelligence and skill, introducing arts and manufactures hitherto unknown amongst ourselves. The merit of originating calico printing in England belongs to a Frenchman, who commenced it in a small work on the banks of the Thames at Richmond, in 1696. Afterwards a large establishment was started at Bromley Hall in Essex. It was only in 1768 that it was introduced into Lancashire, where it has since developed to such a wonderful extent.

When the chintzes of Malabar were first imported by the East India Company, the silk weavers of Spitalfields, roused by the fear that their craft was in danger, assailed in a riotous manner the East India House. In deference to the clamour for protection for the native industries, Government imposed heavy duties on the importation of Indian calicoes, and in 1700 went further and prohibited their importation altogether. But calico print-works were now erected, and their productions were finding their way to the home markets, to the dismay and alarm of those interested in the silk and woollen industries. These trades succeeded in persuading Parliament to pass a law in their interests, and in 1720 the wear of all calicoes, foreign or British, was prohibited. This was going too far, so in 1730 a new enactment was made on the subject, whereby British calicoes, only made of cotton weft and *linen* warp, were permitted to be printed and worn, subject to an excise tax of 6d for every square yard of calico printed, stained, painted, or dyed. This tax was afterwards reduced to 3½d per yard, and subsequently repealed. It was not until 1774 that cloth made entirely of cotton was allowed to be printed, although it was known to be better adapted for taking in the colours equally than mixed webs of cotton and linen. Oppressive fiscal laws and stupid restrictions hampered this great industry till 1831, when they were repealed. Its development has proceeded by leaps and bounds ever since.

CALICO PRINTING IN SCOTLAND.

Calico printing was not introduced into Scotland until 1738. The Cart, the Clyde, the Leven, and the Glazert, and in later times the Blane, were seized on as affording the necessary water supply. The discoveries of James Watt and the steam engine gave other motive power than the fall of water, but a plentiful supply of pure water was indispensably necessary for the processes then in vogue, more particularly for bleaching, &c. These processes were extremely tedious. The cloth was spread on the grass, and exposed to the air, light, and moisture. Weeks and even months were at first occupied in the various processes of bleaching. These consisted of steeping in alkaline lyes, which was called bucking, washing clean, then steeping in buttermilk. Afterwards it was discovered that by substituting water acidulated with sulphuric acid for the sour milk, a great saving of time was effected, so the sulphuric acid superseded the milk. Spreading it on the grass and watering it, and leaving it exposed to the atmosphere was called crofting. All this was changed mainly by the skill of two men—Charles Tennant, then a bleacher at Darnley, near Glasgow, and Charles Mackintosh, one of the founders of the Alum Company, and for some years a resident in Antermony House. They discovered that a weak solution of chloride of lime effected as much in a few hours as had, up to that time, required as many weeks or even months. The idea of saturating slaked lime with chlorine was suggested by

Mr Mackintosh, then at Crossbasket. Tennant took out a patent in 1798 for a liquid compound of chlorine and lime, but this patent was set aside by a combination formed of almost all the bleachers in Lancashire. The case was tried before Lord Ellenborough and a jury. The verdict of the jury and the decision of the judge was given on the ground that bucking with quick-lime and water was not a new invention, or, in other words, that because one part of the process was not new the whole patent should be set aside, a decision contrary both to law and equity. The following year Mr Tennant obtained another patent for impregnating dry hydrate of lime with chlorine gas. This invention was not contested; so the manufacture of solid chloride of lime, generally known as bleaching powder, was commenced at St. Rollox, Glasgow. It was found that this process combined economy, celerity, and safety; and its use became universal.

The cotton trade was the result of the inventions of Hargreaves, Arkwright, Crompton, Carpenter, and others; improved and perfected by other mechanicians. The use of cotton, for the production of tissues, was very limited before the time of Arkwright, whose first patent was only taken out in 1769. But from the discoveries in making cloth from cotton have grown up " the largest manufacture, the largest trade, some of the largest cities, the largest revenue, and the largest national prosperity in the world." They certainly have given rise to calico printing. These combined have created an enormous demand for cotton. When the Campsie Works were being erected in 1785-86, the total imports of cotton into this country was less than twenty million lbs., no part of which was furnished by America. The price of cotton yarn, 100 hanks to the lb., was 38s per lb. When Dalglish, Falconer, & Co., restarted Lennoxmill, in 1805, the price of this cotton yarn had fallen to 7s. 10d. per lb.

ITS BENEFITS TO CAMPSIE.

Since the introduction of Calico printing into Scotland the whole practice has been changed again and again, in the methods of printing, bleaching, dyeing, and finishing, and also in the materials of the colours and dyestuffs. Yet in all these changes very little inconvenience has been caused to those employed. The parish of Campsie owed much to its printfields, and landowners, farmers, merchants, and the working classes have all shared in the prosperity they have brought. Their introduction, progress, and success must possess interest to all natives of the parish; and in Lennoxtown, in an association the great majority of whom are interested directly or indirectly with Lennoxmill, it seemed an appropriate subject for my lecture on the occasion of the opening of your winter course. After this lengthy introduction, I shall take up the three Fields, in the chronological order of their commencing. But I shall linger longest on Lennoxmill, and give full scope to my own personal reminiscences or gleanings, gathered from many sources and from many old personal friends, who have kindly assisted me. The collecting of the details has been a labour of love and a source of pleasure, and I take this opportunity of thanking all who have so readily helped me.

KINCAID, OR EASTER FIELD.

A firm of Glasgow merchants, who carried on business under the style of Henderson, Semple, & Co., were the first to introduce calico printing to the parish, in the year 1785. It would appear that they commenced operations at first in a very small way at Cannerton, and hence the name of the Cannerton Field was at first applied to Kincaid Printfield, where they proceeded to erect works on a larger scale. They feued the land required for their purposes from Mr. Kincaid of that ilk, on a 99 years' tack, paying for it at the rate of £3 per acre. They dug a reservoir 120 yards long by 70 yards wide for maintaining a supply of water in summer, and also obtained a supply from the Glazert by a lade. Henderson, Semple, & Co., after carrying on business for a few years at Kincaid, gave it up, and the laird of Kincaid had the works, which they had erected on his land, thrown upon his hands.

PIONEERS IN REFORM.

It was while Henderson, Semple, & Co. were carrying on business in Kincaid that, after a meeting held at Milton, in November, 1792, at which Thomas Muir of Huntershill was the principal speaker, an association in favour of reform was formed, which was the first political organisation of the kind ever instituted in the parish. Its members were chiefly drawn from the workers in Kincaid and Lennoxmill printfields, to whom the honour of having been local pioneers in a great cause must be accorded. Their society was called the Friends of the People. When Thomas Muir was put on his trial for sedition, Rev. James Lapslie tendered himself as a witness for the prosecution, but among the witnesses for the defence I find the names of the following Kincaid people:—John Buchanan, foreman; Robert Hendrie, Patrick Horn, James M'Gibbon, printers; Smollett M'Lintock, John Edmund, block-cutters, &c.

DISCREET VALOUR.

There is a story told yet in Milton of a great Radical gathering that was held at the top of the Cannerton Brae. The speakers strongly denounced the Government of the day, and appealed to their hearers to be up and doing, and these sentiments were greatly applauded. The applause was interrupted by a sound as of horses trotting briskly through the Birdston Haughs. The suspicion that the authorities might have heard of the meeting, and were sending cavalry to take the ringleaders, seized the crowd. There was no longer doubt that it was the sound of horses' hoofs coming from Birdston. Might there not be a party in the Nappy Loan or between them and Milton? Acting on sudden impulse and panic, the crowd bolted through the fields, crossed the Glazert, and gained the Antermony Road by the "Castle," from which the approach of the troopers could be safely watched. Imagine their disgust when they saw the cause of their sudden flight, all unconscious of the commotion he had caused, riding on a bare-backed cart horse, leading other two horses, one on either side of him. This was Hetherington, the carter, who had been over at Kirkintilloch having the horses shod—horses well known to them all, being regularly employed carting coals from the pits at the "Derries" to the Wester Field, as Lennoxmill was then commonly called. The brave words followed by such a display was long a good joke at the expense of the extreme reformers.

THE INGLIS FIRM.

Henderson, Semple, & Co., had in their employment as clerk a young man named David Inglis, a native of Glasgow, who had been in his youth a clerk in a Glasgow warehouse, and had at one time occupied the same lodgings and slept in the same bed with Michael Rowand, afterwards the well known banker in Glasgow. Mr. Inglis' late employers had acquired the land and had then erected the works themselves, but he now obtained a lease of the works as they then stood from Mr Kincaid. Mr Inglis started under the great disadvantage of insufficient capital to carry on his work. He struggled on manfully, however, but with very indifferent success, as he was obliged to compound three times with his creditors, on the last occasion paying a dividend of 2/6 per £, which obtained for him the nickname of "Half-crown Davie." In course of time Mr Inglis assumed his son Henry as a partner, changing the style of the firm to D. & H. Inglis. Henry did not remain long in the business, dying when comparatively a young man. After his death Mr Inglis obtained the assistance of his son David, who had gone out to Spain, where he was engaged in the wine trade. When carrying on business with his son David he had the good fortune to have a large legacy left him by a medical friend in Edinburgh. This, according to popular report, amounted to a sum of forty thousand pounds. In the midst of his embarrassments he was wont to say he had been born with a silver spoon in his mouth. When the good time came at last he retired from business, and built a villa at Ardrossan, where he died a few years afterwards.

Mr Inglis belonged to the old school, now happily almost extinct, who interlarded conversation with habitual swearing.

He was a vigilant critic of the doings of his work-people. One very decent man, very tall and very thin, married a bonnie little woman, who was comely in face, but very stout. This pair Mr Inglis characterised as " the kirn and the kirn staff." He had to let a worker, Rigg, but popularly called Raggs, know his opinion when at the Chartist Sunday meeting. Bob Wingate, a layman, had christened Riggs' child, " John Frost Raggs." Mr. Inglis declared it was a bad mixture, " Frost " and " Raggs."

Mr. Inglis kept a good table, dined at four o'clock, drank his pint of port every day, and when he came down to the work at five o'clock used stronger language and was more exacting and difficult to please than in the forenoon. At his dinner parties he seems to have insisted on each of his guests finishing his bottle of old port. When Dr. Finlayson was one of the party this was a terrible ordeal for the doctor, who was a very temperate man, and he could not stow away a whole bottle with impunity. The circumstance was the occasion of a good deal of chaffing among the circle who met round the dining table at Kincaid. Indeed, in this connection a wonderful change has taken place in social customs. In the first quarter of this century the doctors in the district were rather convival and too fond of whisky toddy. A shrewd local observer has said that the women in the parish were mostly to blame for this : their mistaken kindness fairly demoralising them, for they insisted on administering a dram at every professional call. They never grudged the whisky. but some of them looked rather blank when the doctor reminded them that his professional account was still unpaid, having probably been overlooked.

After his father's retiral Mr. David Inglis, jun., obtained the services of Mr. Alexander Duncan, then of Ruthvenfield, near Perth, as managing partner. On Mr. Inglis's death, Mr. Duncan's father and brother Archibald, and brother-in-law Pender, gave up their work at Ruthvenfield, and they all joined in carrying on Kincaid. I remember the brothers Duncan well, as they occupied the Kincaid pew in the Parish Church. They were tall handsome men, with wavy raven locks, high foreheads, and gentle, refined manners. Hamlet's description could be applied to them both, particularly to the elder, Alexander :—

> See, what a grace was seated on his brow :
> Hyperion's curls ; the front of Jove himself ;
> An eye like Mars, to threaten and command.
>
> *　　*　　*　　*　　*　　*
>
> A combination and a form indeed,
> Where every god did seem to set his seal
> To give the world assurance of a man.

The two brothers had married two sisters. The ladies were very handsome; indeed, the two couples reminded me of the "fair women and brave men " of the poet. A number of their work people came with them from Ruthvenfield. While they took the greatest interest in all their workers, they regarded these with special interest, and this kindly feeling was cordially reciprocated. A female teacher was employed by the firm to hold a school in the Red Row for girls and little children. Mr. A. Duncan and Mr. Pender took great interest in the Sabbath school, in which they had classes. The Messrs. Duncan did business largely with Messrs. John Monteith & Co., of Glasgow. Some of my present audience will remember Mr. Monteith residing first in Antermony House and afterwards in Ballancleroch. Mr. Monteith's connection with the Western Bank of Scotland is well known. The large unsecured advances to his firm was one of the causes of its stoppage. When the bank closed its doors in November, 1857, Mr. Monteith's firm at once suspended payments, and this ruined the Messrs. Duncan, and caused the stoppage of their works. The Messrs. Duncan removed to England, and Kincaid was unoccupied for two years.

During the block-printers' strike, in 1834, which I refer to at length under Lennoxmill, where the Enniskilling Dragoons were quartered, a detachment of twenty men from the 82nd Regiment was protecting Kincaid; and a similar number of the 68th Regiment had Lillyburn under their care. These soldiers were billeted in Milton, and were on duty there for about six months. They were relieved weekly, the reliefs marching to and from Glasgow on certain days, and always at the same hours. Of course the boys of those days soon learned this, and were waiting to see the " sodgers." At this time also, officers from the Criminal Investigation Department, Edinburgh, were posted at Milton, during all the time the military were occupying the village. They were to act only in the event of disturbances taking place, or any breach of the law.

CALDWELL & RITCHIE.

In 1860 Messrs. Caldwell & Ritchie transferred their works from Kelvinhaugh Field, Glasgow. The partners, who now became tenants of Kincaid, were Finlay Caldwell and William Ritchie. Previous to 1852 they had been engaged with Messrs. Neil & Co., calico printers, Pollokshaws, Mr. Caldwell in charge of the block printers and Mr. Ritchie as colour maker. In 1852 they resolved to commence business on their own account, encouraged thereto by the good times and the very remunerative prices then prevailing. They accordingly started in Kelvinhaugh. Prosperity attended the new " Field," their business increased beyond the accommodation which Kelvinhaugh afforded, hence they transferred to Campsie in 1860, when they took a nineteen years' lease of Kincaid Field. On its completion in 1879, as both partners had only sons in the business, the original partners retired that year in favour of their sons, who continued under the same style.

In the autumn of 1884 an extensive fire consumed the warehouse and entire finishing department, and threw some hundreds
of workers out of employment for a few months. The Field was,
however, speedily rebuilt and remodelled, the utensils and machinery that had been destroyed being replaced by others of the
latest and most improved kinds. Mr. James Caldwell retired from
the firm in 1888, when he ceased to reside in the parish. Mr.
William Ritchie, jun., is now the sole partner. He has built for
himself a beautiful house on the Waltry burn, which he has
named Waltry. Mr. Ritchie, sen., has been spared to enjoy a
well-earned leisure, and to see the continued prosperity of the firm.

LENNOXMILL.

In 1786, the year after Kincaid had been started by Henderson,
Semple, & Co., another Glasgow firm, who traded under the style
of Lindsay, Smith, & Co., took a lease of 30 acres of land for a
period of 99 years, at a rental of £3 per acre. On this land they
forthwith proceeded to erect a printfield. The site of the new
work was adjacent to a mill called Lennoxmill. It was at first
called the Westerfield, to distinguish it from Kincaid or the East-
erfield, but in course of time it came to take its distinguishing
name from the old meal mill. The Rev. James Lapslie, in his
account of the parish, mentions that it was considered to be well
planned and laid out, and for that day " uncommonly commodious."
There was no village of Lennoxtown then, and the starting of
a public work gave a great impetus to the building trades to provide accommodation for the workmen. Lindsay, Smith, & Co.
had the terrace at Whitefield erected. Demand was soon followed
by supply, and the Newtown of Campsie, as distinguished from
the Clachan, or old town, rapidly sprang up and developed into a
thriving village, as the houses were occupied as soon as they were
finished. Shops followed, to supply the necessaries of life. The
two " Fields " caused a great demand for labour, and this abundant employment for young as well as older workers attracted
families from other districts less favourably situated in this respect.
A spirit of activity and progress became general and characterised ·
the people of the district in all their dealings.
The transformation effected in two or three years was something astonishing and at first acted like an irritant on Mr. Lapslie, the minister of the parish. The quiet secluded valley, with
its lairds, farmers, and graziers, its millers, weavers, and cottars,
was suddenly filled with the stir and energy of an industrial centre.
The total population of the parish in 1789 was only 1627. In
1793 it had risen to 2517, mainly owing to the abundant employment to be obtained in the printfields having attracted families to
the parish. According to the *Statistical Account* the two Fields
employed the same number of " hands." In each work there

were 37 block printers, 37 tearers (all boys), 22 copperplate printers and assistants, 160 pencillers, 16 cutters and engravers, 2 millwrights, 8 labourers, 8 furnace men, and 2 excise officers. In 1793 the wages paid to the various classes of workers were as follows, per week :—Block printers, 18/ to 21/ ; copperplate printers, 17/ to 20/ ; engravers and cutters, 18/ to 21/ ; labourers 7/ ; pencillers (women), 5/ to 6/ ; masons, 11/ ; millwrights, 10/.

In the *Statistical Account,* Mr. Lapslie laments what he calls the sudden transition from strict to loose manners by those attracted by the employment to be had in the " Fields," who, he adds, were not attentive to regularity of conduct. But, he admits, this soon improved ; the worst gradually left and the more sober and industrious remained ; so that by 1793 things had greatly improved, morals having become more regular than they had been when the works were commenced.

I have been unable to glean any information regarding the individuals who composed the firms who introduced calico printing at Kincaid and Lennoxmill. Lindsay, Smith, & Co. is a name few in Lennoxtown have ever heard of, yet they were the pioneers of an industry which called Lennoxtown into existence, which has ever since been mainly dependent on Lennoxmill for its prosperity. Owing to commercial embarrassments, Lindsay, Smith, & Co. stopped their works about the beginning of the present century, when their connection as individuals with the parish would appear to have ceased entirely. The workers betook themselves elsewhere in search of employment ; the houses recently erected and hitherto fully occupied were left tenantless, and soon fell into disrepair, the broken windows and empty houses giving the village a most forlorn and deserted appearance, which happily it has never since presented. Lennoxmill was unoccupied for some years, notwithstanding its abundant water supply and the existence of dwelling-houses for the workers, which offered great inducements to those in the calico printing trade, or who contemplated starting public works requiring water and house accommodation.

THE DALGLISHES.

The stress of circumstances, which caused the stoppage of Lindsay, Smith, & Co. was also operating at Balfron, where, about the same time, Mr Dunmore and his partners, after carrying on business as calico printers at Endrick Field, closed their works and dissolved the partnership. As Endrick Field, through the Dalglishes and J. Dennistoun, has an interest for Campsonians, I may here trace the source of the connection. A firm styled Dalglish & Hutcheson, had a printfield on the Clyde at Fleshers' Haugh, Glasgow Green, which they occupied for some years previous to 1790, In *Old Glasgow and its Environs,* Senex refers to it, and I mentioned that it was probably to that Field that the late Mr Dalglish referred, when, at a public meeting in Calton, during his first canvass of the city, he mentioned he had a family connection with the East-end, and consequently some claim on the East-enders as originally one of themselves.

A correspondent, on seeing a report of the lecture which appeared in a local newspaper, thinks I am mistaken in thinking the Dalglishes had anything to do with a printfield in the Fleshers' Haugh. He says :—

"I have always understood that Mr. Dalglish was at one time a weaver in the Calton, and when business prospered with him he married a Miss Jane Clyde. It was in honour of this lady that Clyde Street, Calton, Glasgow, received its name. A Campsie woman, Jane Clyde Russell, whom I knew in Glasgow, informed me she was named after Mrs. Dalglish, and assured me that it was quite true that Clyde Street, Calton, had got its name after her."

But to return to Endrickbank. In 1790 Charles Park of Parkhill let to Robert Dunmore of Ballindalloch in tack for 999 years the lands of Duniechip, as well as the portion cut off the estate by the new road to Glasgow. In 1792 Charles Park fues to Robert Dunmore the above lands, the feu-duty being £14 8s 9d and duplication. Robert Dunmore, the same year, fened them to a company consisting of John Monteith, Gilbert Hamilton, James Dennistoun (who was born at Newmill of Glorat, in 1752), Robert Scott Moncrieff, William Scott Moncrieff, William Dalglish (elder brother of the Robert Dalglish who was senior partner at Lennoxmill), James Buchanan, and Robert Dunmore, all merchants in Glasgow. This co-partnery carried on business as John Monteith & Co. The feu-duty was £61 3s 6d, and duplication. In 1802, John Monteith & Co. purchased from the trustees on the sequestrated estate of Robert Dunmore the lands of Endrick Field. After an occupancy of about ten years, Endrick Field was closed and the partnership dissolved. James Dennistoun, one of the partners, was a Campsie man, and it is not unlikely that it was owing to him that the attention of the brother of his partner, William Dalglish, was first called to the suitability of Lennoxmill, then standing vacant. William Dalglish retired from the printing at the dissolution of the Endrick Field firm, but his younger brother, Robert, along with Mr Patrick Falconer, and a younger brother, Alexander Dalglish, determined to enter the trade. They commenced business under the style of R. Dalglish, Falconer, & Co. They leased the works formerly occupied by Lindsay, Smith, & Co., and land to the extent of 33 acres. They acquired the plant of John Monteith & Co. at Endrick Field, which they had conveyed to Lennoxmill. They had the steam boilers transferred with other plant, but these could not pass on the highway owing to the branches on the large oak tree of Blairquhosh, which had therefore to be cut off to allow the passage.

Great changes have taken place in connection with the firms carrying on calico printing since the beginning of the century, but since 1805 the style of the company occupying Lennoxmill has remained the same. Three generations of Robert Dalglishes have followed each other in the partnership. The two older generations always manifested the keenest interest in the welfare of the village of Lennoxtown, and they did much to promote its best interests. A little detail concerning the founders of the firm will be interesting to all the natives of the parish, especially to those who may have been connected personally or through relatives with Lennoxmill.

Robert Dalglish, the principal founder, was born in 1770. He was trained to business in the warehouse of Mr. Andrew Stevenson, muslin manufacturer, Bell Street, Glasgow. He had the reputation of being a shrewd, cautious, sensible man, who was looked up to and esteemed by all who knew him. He resided at first in Glasgow, his department being the commercial one, but he was even then a frequent visitor at the Field. He took great interest in his work people and also in the education of their children. In some cases he would personally examine the boys in order to test and judge of their proficiency. Where they were found to be very deficient he had them frequently sent to school at his own expense : this, too, in working hours.

While living in Glasgow he seems to have come under the influence of Dr. Chalmers, then of the Tron Parish, by whose fervid preaching he was much impressed. He remained on intimate terms with him afterwards, when he was residing at Lennoxmill Cottage. In Chalmers' *Memoirs* we find in his diary, under date 1820, Tuesday, 11th July—"Mr. Robert Dalglish's chaise came to take us out to Campsie; after tea walked to Campsie Glen. Wednesday—Went to Muckle Bin. I had nearly laired among the soft moss of the hill, and in the struggle the horse fell on its side. Previously, in throwing back its head, it struck my face, and set my nose bleeding. After dinner, express from Kilsyth, intimation of Dr. Rennie's death. I took a warm bath in the evening in one of the immense circular vats of the manufactory. It was fortunate it was not a dyework, or else I might have come out a bottle-green colour."

Mr. R. Dalglish was Dean of Guild in Glasgow in 1825-6. As Preceptor of Hutchesons' Hospital he laid the foundation stone of a Glasgow Bridge on 18th August, 1829. Mr. Dalglish entered the Glasgow Town Council, and was Lord Provost of that city, in 1832, when the Reform Bill passed. In a book published a few years ago, giving the portraits and biographical sketches of one hundred prominent men in Glasgow and the West of Scotland, the writer of Mr. Dalglish's life remarks that he was far from being a reformer, yet that he, in order to keep control over the exciting movements which preceded the passing of the Reform Bill of 1832, put himself at the head of the reforming movement, presiding at the meetings at which the reformers agitated in its favour. He even headed one of the greatest processions, where the people made a great popular demonstration ; towns, parishes, societies, craftsmen, with 500 flags and 200 bands of music ; the numbers, including spectators, were reckoned at from 80,000 to 100,000.

. Peter Mackenzie, in his reminiscences, tells of Provost Dalglish receiving, in his blandest manner, at his new, elegant, self-contained house on the south side of St. Vincent Place, a deputation who wished to have the city bells rung and an illumination in the evening when, in March 1831, the Reform Bill had passed its second reading by a majority of one. Old Peter likewise describes the Provost's illumination : 3,000 jettees in front of his house, with " Let Glasgow Flourish " sparkling out in the centre, &c. ; surmounting this were figures of Trade, Commerce, and Manufactures hailing Reform. In every view, for effective display, Provost Dalglish's house bore away the palm.

Mr. Alexander Dalglish had charge at Lennoxmill. He resided directly opposite the Field gate, the lower flat of the same house being occupied by Mr. Wylie. By his first marriage Mr. A. Dalglish had a son who was popularly known as " Dandy James," who took his place as one of the managers for a few years after his father's death, but he left Campsie, it was understood, to go to England. He returned and married a niece of Mungo Park, the celebrated traveller.

Mr. Alexander married as his second wife Mrs. Buchanan, a widowed sister of Mungo Park, a tall, handsome lady, who is still remembered by many. After her husband's death Mrs. Dalglish resided in Glorat, from 1840 till 1847, when she died. Alexander Dalglish belonged to the old school. He was commonly called " Saunders," and fancied he required a short rest at " twal hours," when he regularly adjourned to take his " meridian." He liked companionship at this important function, so he was generally accompanied by Mr. Wylie or one of the foremen. After a slight refreshment, duty was resumed in the Field. By and by his nephew, Mr. Robert, came to take a greater charge of the management, which passed to Mr. Gardner, who succeeded Saunders when the latter became unable to undertake all the duties.

Two of the original partners of Endrick Field, on the dissolution of that concern, recommenced business, viz., John Monteith and Robert Scott Moncrieff, the firm being that of John Monteith & Co., the founders of the great manufacturing business at Blantyre. The old firm of John Monteith & Co. consisted at one time of these two. Monteith was energetic and pushing, his partner timid and nervous, so Moncrieff was paid out and Mr. Patrick Falconer assumed in his place, and the firm became Monteith & Falconer. Falconer had a knowledge of French and a smattering of German, so Monteith proposed that he should attend the great fairs in Germany, which would afford a favourable opportunity of disposing of their goods in the Continental markets. In *Popular Traditions of Glasgow*, p. 156, Mr. Andrew Wallace tells a story how Mr. Falconer, when on a business mission to Germany, was arrested on landing in Holland, then occupied by the French. He was suspected of being a spy, and was carried before the French general. He was surprised at the Frenchman's minute enquiries concerning Glasgow, who at last, having requested to be left alone with the stranger, dropped French and spoke out in guid braid Scotch—"But, ma freen, do ye ken auld James Monteith of Anderston." "Ou aye, general, I ken him brawly, for he's my ain partner's faither." The general was Mortier, who had been educated in Glasgow University. His father and Mr. Monteith had considerable dealings, and, bringing his son on a visit, left him for three years to pursue his education. After a long talk about Glasgow bodies, Falconer was allowed to pass on his way through the French lines unmolested.

Quitting his partnership with Monteith, Falconer now joined Robert Dalglish and his brother in the new enterprise at Lennoxmill. Mr. Patrick Falconer was an elder in Dr. Chalmers' church. He is said to have been a singularly godly man. He was author of a book entitled, *Intellectual Difficulties of Christianity*. He rarely visited Lennoxmill, and was therefore little known in Campsie. In Dr. Chalmers' *Memoirs* there is an allusion to him in his diary under date 1818—"Went out to Mr. Falconer's country place, where I dined and staid all the evening. Mr F. is among the most eminently spiritually-minded men I ever met."

In *Glasgow and its Clubs* Dr. Strang relates the following incident:—"It is told of a well-known calico printer in this city, when the presence of excisemen was required at the works to stamp goods with His Majesty's seal, that he was in the habit of inviting these functionaries to breakfast, and of course, as he was a religious man, to family worship. Both the temporals and the spirituals were at that time most unusually prolonged, and the officers having forgotten to take their stamp along with them, a very profitable use was made of it during their absence." I have already mentioned the fact of Provost Dalglish having been an intimate friend of Dr. Chalmers, as well as a member of his church, and that Mr. Patrick Falconer was one of his elders. I was formerly under the impression that Dr. Strang's story had a reference to one of the Lennoxmill partners, but I am assured that this was not so. In justice to Lennoxmill we must clear it of this impeachment.

Provost Dalglish had two sons, on whom devolved in course of time the management of the business. Andrew Stevenson Dalglish was born in 1793, and died in 1858. Robert was born in 1808 and died 20th June, 1880. Little was known at Lennoxmill about the elder brother, but his personality was felt during the great strike which took place in 1834. The energy with

B

which he threw himself into the struggle, and the ability and ingenuity he displayed in obtaining workers, in protecting them, and making the most of some very unpromising material, made him the object of fear and dislike to the strikers and their sympathisers. When by his firmness and determination he had at last gained the victory he became temporarily unpopular, and the ill-feeling found vent in the doggrel of local rhymers, which has now sunk into oblivion.

Mr Stevenson Dalglish after this became prominent as a citizen of Glasgow, and ceased to be associated with Lennoxmill. He was a great admirer of the Duke of Wellington, and took an active part in getting up the statue to him, by Marochetti, which stands in front of the Glasgow Royal Exchange. Partly in recognition of his exertions in this matter, and partly as a mark of esteem, he was entertained by his fellow-citizens at a public dinner in the Trades' Hall, in Oct., 1844. His portrait is on one of the *bas reliefs* on the Queen's statue in St. George's Square. For this honour he was indebted to the grateful memory of Baron Marochetti, the artist of this statue and also of the Iron Duke's. Stevenson Dalglish was one of the most active sergeants of the Glasgow troop of yeomanry, and according to Peter Mackenzie rode one of the most spanking grey horses ever seen in Glasgow, for which he was frequently offered 300 guineas or more.

In the *Stray Leaves* of Alexander Rodger we find allusion to Campsie matters. There is one song especially, entitled, " Come, fye, let us a' to the guzzle," where both Provost Dalglish and his son are referred to. Sandy Rodger used to come out to Torrance about the year 1820, where, I am informed, he taught a singing class.

> And there will be jolly John Geordie,
>   The king o' the calico nobs ;
> Wi' Robin,* the proud cotton lordie,
>   Sae fond o' nice pickings and jobs.
> And tere will be Norman M'Tartan,
>   Wha in her nainsell be a host,
> Wi' face red and round as a partan,
>   To greet us wi' some yeuky toast.
> And there will be braid-backit Steenie,†
>   Whase bouk made the Glazert recede,
> Ae nicht, when pursuing some queenie,
>   He plumpit in, heels over heid.
> The holms and the haughs were o'erflooded,
>   The hay ricks were carried awa,
> The beasts to the hills quickly scudded,
>   Or else they'd been droon'd ane an' a'.

Another of Rodger's songs hits at a popular minister of Campsie:—

> And there will be bare-legged gillies
>   Frae Morven, frae Mull, and Tiree ;

---

* R. Dalglish, late Provost.
† S——n D——sh, Esq., a very portly gentleman, who once fell into the Glazert and caused it to overflow its banks.

As rampant and rough as young fillies ;
Shust come ta great wonder to see.

Robert, the younger son—Mr Robert, as he was called—learned
the business practically in the " Field," where he seems to have
been well liked. When cholera broke out in Campsie in 1833 he
was very active in taking both precautionary and remedial
measures. Along with James Kincaid, for many years the
beadle in the U.P. Church, he went through the village of
Lennoxtown, and personally attended to the fumigation, disinfec-
tion, and ventilation of houses where the disease had been. At
the time of the strike, he remonstrated with the workers and gave
them warning in a friendly spirit, that the effect would be the
erection of machinery to do the work hitherto performed by them.
This they treated with incredulity, believing such a result to be
quite impossible. In his endeavours to effect a peaceful termina-
tion to the dispute he even took a number of the leaders into the
" Store " and treated them.

There is one anecdote illustrating Mr. Robert's kindness of
heart which I had from the recipient himself, who spoke with a
warm feeling of gratitude to his old employer and benefactor. A
little boy, aged seven and a-half years, the son of a widow, was
sent to work as a " tearer." In the course of time the boy wanted
to learn the trade of block-cutting, but this could not be accomplished until he had paid the entry money of £7 7s. to the trade
union. He could obtain no assistance from his mother or from
relatives, yet, he resolutely set himself to what seemed at first a
hopeless task. After pondering one plan after another, as a last
resource he resolved to try and borrow the money from his
employers. So he went to the counting-house in Lennoxmill and
addressed the request to Mr. Robert, that he should advance
the money necessary to obtain his apprenticeship at the trade
he had selected. Pleased with the boy's appearance, impressed
with his transparent honesty of purpose and his sturdy independence and self-reliance, he laughingly turned to the clerk and
said—" M'Intyre, let him have the money, but take care that he
pays his instalments regularly." Before, however, it was half
paid back the balance was voluntarily cancelled. The boy learned
the block-cutting by-and-bye. Owing to the strike he left
Campsie and found his way to Glasgow, where, by his business
abilities and sterling character, he long held a leading position in
the calico printing trade in the East-End. When he retired from
the active duties of his calling it was not to enjoy ease, but to
give his best services to promote works of philanthropy and education as a member of the Glasgow School Board, of which he is
still a member. He retains his keen interest in Campsie
undiminished.

Mr. Robert Dalglish, after living for some time in Lennoxmill
Cottage, purchased Kilmardinny in 1853, and thenceforth made
that his home till about 1878, when he returned to live at the

Cottage once more, on his taking into his own hands the active duties of management of the "Field." In 1857 he came forward as a candidate for the representation of the city of Glasgow in Parliament. He stood as an independent Radical. Buchanan and Dalglish were returned, Hastie, who had been one of the sitting members, losing his seat. The poll was, Buchanan, 7069; Dalglish, 6764; Hastie, 5044. Mr Dalglish was returned in 1859, 1865, 1868, and retired in 1874. His portrait was given in *Vanity Fair* in 1873, when he was termed the most popular man in the House of Commons. He bestowed great attention on all Glasgow concerns, and his hospitality to the members of deputations and others from Glasgow who had occasion to go to Westminster on municipal or other public business of the city was princely.

Mr. Dalglish is held to have committed an error of judgment in coming back to Lennoxmill and undertaking its management; especially in parting with all the old foremen and employees who had grown grey in the service of his firm. His personal management was not generally considered a success. Indeed, this could hardly have been expected. While he was away in London at his Parliamentary duties the business entirely changed. The years of splendid prosperity that preceded the American civil war, when Lennoxmill was in the very fore-front of the trade—when it had almost a monopoly of some of the most lucrative work—were followed by years of keen competition, when other houses came forward and wrested much of their trade from Lennoxmill. A process of reconstruction of the works was commenced then, having its object to lessen labour and cheapen production. This has now been completed under the present skilful and energetic manager, Mr. Oliphant Brown, who had the good fortune to be assistant manager to Mr. John Cowan in Lancashire.

After Mr. Dalglish's death the works were taken over by a limited liability company, who now carry on the business as R. Dalglish, Falconer, & Co., Limited.

In noticing the personal history of the partners I have anticipated events, and now revert to them in chronological order.

MR. BARCLAY.

The Messrs. Dalglish brought from Balfron two of their principal employees, and put them over Lennoxmill as managers. One of these was Mr. Wylie, who had charge of the printers, and whom I recollect well; an old man, going regularly down in the forenoon, wearing a shepherd's tartan plaid, evidently impressed with the belief that things would not get on unless he went down to keep everything right. The other, Mr. Robert Barclay, was colour-maker and dyer. Mr. Barclay must have been an intelligent, energetic, deeply religious man. He threw himself with great heartiness into every good work that had for its object the religious and social improvement of the villagers. He himself initiated many of the schemes, and organised public meetings to promote them. Among those mainly founded by him were a Bible and Missionary Society, Mutual Improvement and Friendly Societies. He, along with Mr. Alex. Fraser (eldest son of the worthy teacher), John Shand, and others, originated the Y. M. Association, which has had a most useful history. After he left this Association was given up, but it was resuscitated a few years after by a few earnest young men in Lennoxmill. The chief moving spirits were John M'Vicar, machine printer; John Cowan, colour-maker; and John M'Luckie, then a pattern drawer. These three hunted up the old minutes of the association, and took the preliminary steps to have it resuscitated. In this they were completely successful. Among the earliest names enrolled were Rowland Hill Eadie, John Service, and other well-known names.

THE FIELD KIRK.

But, reverting to Mr. Barclay, his earnest personality first attracted, then influenced, and deeply impressed several younger men, who became his fellow-workers, and who carried on his good works after he left the locality. Mr. Barclay was an elder of the Relief Church. This church originated in an unpopular presentee being placed as minister of the parish. Its membership, as long as Mr. Lapslie lived, embraced many heritors and the principal farmers in the parish; but the greater number of these, on the advent of the Rev. Norman Macleod, in 1825, returned to the "Auld Kirk" in the Clachan. But long before this exodus took place, probably mainly owing to the moral and personal influence of Mr. Barclay, a much closer connection was formed with Lennoxmill. During the long period in which Mr. Gordon Wilson managed the works, with rare ability, and sagacity, and conspicuous success, the Relief and the Field were getting more closely identified. I have no intention of saying a single word in disparagement of the pastor or people of the Relief congregation, whose religious profession was adorned by consistent lives and active Christian work, but it cannot be denied that to those unconnected with the Relief the intimate connection with Lennoxmill came to be attributed to the fact that Mr. Gordon Wilson was one of its members, and wielded, probably quite unconsciously, a preponderating influence. His position in Lennoxmill made him the most influential man in the church. His subordinates there naturally attached great weight to his opinions and sought to give effect to his wishes. This fact exercised considerable influence, according to popular opinion, in determining new-comers, who had obtained situations in Lennoxmill, to join the Relief. To such an extent did this obtain, that in popular parlance, the two churches were the Hill Kirk and the Field Kirk. Where there was ecclesiastical rivalry, accompanied by unfriendly feeling, the Field Kirk became Wilson, Kay, & Co., which I have often heard it called. It certainly was amusing that people from other parts of the country, on getting employment in Lennoxmill, went almost as a matter of course to this Kirk. English and Irish Episcopalians from Lancashire, Established Churchmen from the Western Islands, who had never heard of the Relief body till they came to Campsie, at once joined its membership, apparently as a matter of course. Besides the manager nearly all the heads of departments were connected with it. One outspoken foreman boldly avowed that he went to the Relief for the sake of his work, to the Hill Kirk to see and be seen, and to the Roman Catholic Chapel for the sake of his soul. It was at one time considered to be for their interests in the Field to attend the Relief Kirk, and take all their provisions, &c., at the Store.

Mr. Barclay left Lennoxmill owing to some expression of opinion by one of his employers that he occupied himself too much with outside work, and that it would be better if he concentrated his energies on his duties at Lennoxmill. After this he removed to Glasgow, where he was manager for many years in Dalmarnock Print Work. His removal was a great loss to Lennoxtown, not only to the Field but also to the parish, where he was highly respected. He continued throughout his long life actively to promote the good of his fellow-citizens.

BLEACHING.

When Lennoxmill was re-started in 1805 the cotton pieces were bleached by exposure in the fields around, which became literally whitefields. In these fields were placed sentry boxes for the shelter and protection of the excisemen appointed to watch that the duty of sixpence per yard was duly paid. The grass-bleach was the work of natural agencies—rain, dew, and sun ; aided by copious sprinkling of water in dry weather, and turning occasionally on the grass. The process was tedious, but the durability of the cloth bore favourable comparison with that subjected to the speedy processes of modern chemistry. The fields in which the cloth was bleached were protected by beautiful beech hedges, which ran in lines east and west, indeed they were called "The Lines," the remains of which are still visible between Whitefield and the "Grey Stane." One who has wrought there informs me these "Lines" were swarming with birds' nests, and that it was delightful to be employed out there in the summer time.

A PREMIUM ON SOAP.

Not only was printed cloth then taxed, but certain materials used in the various processes had excise duties levied. On soap, for instance, from 1782 till 1816 the duty was—Hard soap, 2¼d ;

soft soap, 1¾d per lb. In 1816 the duty was raised from 2¼d to 3d per lb on the hard soap. But a rebate to manufacturers came to be allowed. Mr Gordon Wilson has told me that he has gone to the Supervisor's office in Kirkintilloch and been repaid at one time the sum of £1300, as drawback for one year on soap alone that had been used in the Field.

COLOUR PRINTING.

The first work attempted by Dalglish, Falconer, & Co. at Lennoxmill was, I have been informed, handkerchiefs, indigo blue with a white spot. When fairly into working order, in those early days, the turnout of finished goods was limited as compared with present times. Then one man and a boy could only print, in one colour, six pieces of 25 yards each per day. If there had been eight colours in the pattern, then eight men and eight boys would have been required to print the six pieces, making 150 yards in all. Improvements came to be effected gradually in the various processes. A great step was made in advance when colours for dyeing were printed by cylinders first, and after the cloth had been dyed, other colours necessary to complete the design were afterwards put in by block printing. Imperfections in the printing were filled in by pencillers. What a contrast that presents to what can now be done in any of our parish print-fields with one cylinder machine. With coal tar colours, including alizarine, all the different colours can now be printed by the machine at one run, and as many as 700 pieces of cloth have been run through the printing machine in a single day. In connection with this point I have received the following letter from a practical man :—

"You would be safer, before practical people, to say from 200 to 300 pieces of 30 yards each. Probably your informer was thinking of once on a time, when a great effort was made to see how many pieces could be done in one day at Lennoxmill, by a two-colour printing machine, not an eight-colour one."

A CRISIS IN "THE VALE."

We now pass on to the era of the Reform Bill in 1832. At that time there were two of the leading printing firms situated in the Vale of Leven. These were the Stirlings of Cordale, and the Messrs. Kibble of Dalmonach. The Stirlings printed "furnitures," bed curtains, drapery in large patterns, and were turkey red dyers also. Messrs. James and John Kibble did fine muslins and cambrics in fast colours. When undoubtedly one of the leading firms in the country, and to outward appearance prosperous, they unexpectedly suspended payment, about 1835. The works were accordingly closed, and, after a time, sold.

LENNOXMILL PUT ON ITS METTLE.

This event became an important epoch to Campsie, for the Lennoxmill firm seized the opportunity, acquired the copper rollers, blocks, plant, and patterns of the Dalmonach firm. Having secured these, they also succeeded in getting the great firm of Graham, Alexander & Co., of London, to transfer to them the trade which they had sent to Dalmonach. But after a fair trial. of Lennoxmill workmanship, their new customers expressed dissatisfaction with its style and finish, which they alleged compared unfavourably with that formerly produced by Kibble at Dalmonach. Dalglish, Falconer & Co., thus put on their mettle, determined to remove all cause of complaint, and made great exertions to improve their workmanship in the Field. To secure this they went in quest of the most skilled workmen who could be obtained. This task was rendered comparatively easy, owing to the number of highly-experienced men who had been thrown out of work at Dalmonach. The Messrs. Dalglish now offered inducements to those considered most suitable, which caused them to enter their employment at Lennoxmill, many obtaining posts as foremen, or higher wages. It was at this time that Mr. Kay, foreman engraver, and Mr. Cooke, foreman printer, came to the Field. This soon effected improvements, but Graham, Alexander & Co. were still complaining that the colouring was deficient and not up to that of the old Dalmonach firm. The obvious cure for this was to obtain if possible the same skill that had given such satisfactory results at Dalmonach.

Messrs. Dalglish learned that a clever young colour-maker was still retained, engaged in winding up matters for the Messrs. Kibble at their works. Messrs. Dalglish applied to this young man, and in order to induce him to come to Lennoxmill made him a very tempting offer. This was accepted, and on the 26th October, 1836, the young man, Mr. Gordon Wilson by name, came to Lennoxtown to enter on his new duties.

THE DISCONSOLATE EXILES OF THE LEVEN.

After their removal to Lennoxtown some of the natives of the Vale of Leven did not take kindly to their new surroundings. Like the exiled Jews in Babylon, they longed for their own "Vale." Like the Jews they relieved their home-sick pinings by pensive wanderings by the Glazert banks. One of their number gave vent to his feelings in a poetic effusion, the first four lines of which, being a parody on a well-known psalm, caught the public ear, and lingered long in the memories of a generation who have now, with very few exceptions, all passed away. These lines were:

> By Glazert's streams we sat and wept,
>   When Leven we thought on ;
> In midst thereof we dashed our heads
>   The big grey stanes upon.

Shortly after the events narrated, Messrs. James Black & Co. acquired Dalmonach, and the re-opening of that work gave an opportunity for some of the home-sick ones to return. The greater number, however, remained at Lennoxmill, which accounts for a warm feeling of regard still entertained for the Vale of Leven and its natives. The Vale of Leven men must have given great satisfaction, for the firm went there afterwards for Mr. John Barr, now of Lennox Cottage, who was brought from Leven in 1845 to take charge of the pattern room, issuing orders for printing, seeing these executed; with charge also of the printing machines. When loss of sight caused Mr. Barr to retire, he was much missed, and it was found very difficult to replace him.

In 1835 there were only 6 or 7 machines and about 200 tables in Lennoxmill, on which the work was done by hand by block printers. The patterns were cut in relief on the blocks, or various strips of flattened copper wire were inserted edgewise, and then filed and polished into a horizontal plane. These blocks were worked by hand, and block printing was then one of the leading skilled handicrafts in connection with the calico printing industry. There was excellent remuneration at piece-work rates for such skilled labour. By working steadily the block-printers could easily make what was then considered a very high wage, but in their own interests they formed a trade union, and agreed among themselves to a self-denying ordinance, whereby they restricted their earnings to seven pounds per month, and latterly to only six pounds per month. The wages, I am informed, averaged about 35/ per week, off which the "tearer" had to be paid about 2/6 per week. The pay was made up monthly to a regular date. The printers were paid for all work passed previous to, and including, the Tuesday preceding the pay Saturday. The work performed during the pay week, but after the Tuesday, was technically called a "dead horse," and formed the nucleus, or nest egg, of the following month's pay.

TRADE ENTRY MONEY, SHOP FINES, AND PAY-OFFS.

The trades' unions of the present day are great friendly societies, making provision for want of employment, for disablement by sickness or accident, or in case of death. Some unions seek to enhance the value of their members' labour by restricting their day's work, or by combination to influence the rate of wages. The block-printers confined their attention exclusively to the latter, and to regulating the terms of admission to their trade and the amounts to be paid at entry. If £10 were paid down, the persons paying that were free from all subsequent payments to their trades' union. But if they only paid the minimum sum of £7 7s, they had to "pay off" whenever they were liable. Not only block-printers but block-cutters and engravers had to pay such entry money. In some cases half-entry of £3 10s. was exacted before a member was allowed to commence work in a new shop, if he had left his former printfield of his own accord. If the work was closed, or employment could not be had, the half-entry was not exigible. Almost every conceivable circumstance was made the occasion of a trade or shop fine or pay-off. The signs of an incipient beard in the apprentice were carefully watched, and when it was at length pronounced to be " the genuine article," the oldest apprentice tendered his services as barber, the victim was seized, seated, daubed over his face and scraped, and then had to pay out the usual half-crown for the first shave. When a man got a new suit of clothes, when he left off day's wages and was put on piece-work, when his work was changed, when his apprenticeship was out, when he got married, when his wife had a baby, a bottle of whisky had to be procured to stand treat to his shopmates, and men and women all partook, sometimes to excess, even within the gates in working hours.

These shop fines were exacted in Lennoxmill, Kincaid, and Lillyburn. Mr. John Brown, who formerly resided at Burnhouse, but who is now living at Whitefield, has told me the following, illustrating the rigour with which they were enforced, he himself having been one of the victims in the case in point. John Bauchope, block-printer, residing at Craighead, Milton, was employed at Kincaid. His child died, and he was off work for two or three days till after the funeral. When he went back his shopmates would not allow him to resume work until he had paid for a bottle of whisky, as a fine for having had a death in the house— Bauchope, or Bauk, as he was called, point-blank refused to pay, declaring that there might be some excuse for exacting a pay-off in the event of a birth, but for a death, it was cruel, it was inhuman. Afraid that they might be done out of their treat, and thinking that even if they succeeded, one bottle was rather · too little, some of the printers resorted to an expedient to entrap John Brown, then serving his apprenticeship as a block-printer. With a plausible excuse that the goods were wanted at once it was proposed to Brown to finish Bauchope's "piece,"—willing to oblige and unsuspicious of any trick, he proceeded to do so. Whenever he commenced he was saluted, " Hallo! my man! what business has an apprentice to work in a journeyman's place, and at a journeyman's job too? a fine! a fine!" Bauchope had meantime gone to the manager, Mr Heys, and indignantly protested that cannibals would have shown more humanity; this was not the conduct of men but of devils. Mr Heys, however, recommended him to pay for his bottle, to say no more about it, but quietly resume work; accordingly, he came back and gave in—both Brown and he had to pay their fines.

The sums thus levied at entry, half-entry, and in pay-offs were not paid into sick aliment or death and funeral expenses, but were entirely expended on eating and drinking. Seven apprentices have been known to begin their servitude at one time, and seven guineas had to be paid by each before they were allowed to begin their apprenticeship, and forty-nine guineas were in hands at one time to be swilled and guzzled. Such occasions presented great temptations to all in the trade. A very few refrained altogether—many enjoyed themselves in moderation, but others, it is to be feared a majority, went to excess. The late Rev. Dr. Edwards has informed me that before he left Lennoxtown he has seen men lying about at Bulloch's corner drinking whisky out of milk boynes. The bouts continued as long as the money lasted. The effect was most demoralising to all concerned, and the families of the revellers were the greatest sufferers, in the long run.

THE STRIKE, 1834.

We now come to the period of the great strike, an event fraught with disaster to those who, with little consideration or counting of the cost, so rashly decided to proceed with it. We have already referred to the Block-printers' Trade Union. From a monthly levy of 1s. 6d. per man and 9d. per apprentice a large annual income had gradually accumulated, until a sum of about £6000 or £7000 was at the credit of their funds. This was considered a very large amount, and gave the printers the idea that with it to fall back upon they could at any time bring their employers to their terms. Block-printers were paid so much the "over," that was the number of times the block had to be repeated across the "piece." It was generally four or five overs; this at 2d. per over was 8d. or 10d. on a piece of cloth 24 yards long. Narrower pieces of only 3 overs but 28 yards long had recently been introduced, and they had been paid at the same rate per piece and per "over" as those only 24 yards. The printers considered this a grievance, and claimed $\frac{1}{2}$d. per piece for the extra 4 yards. As new styles came out differing from the old ones for which the over prices had been settled, the employers complained that the printers were fractious and exaggerated the differences in style and length of pieces, and they resisted the claims for extras on the innovations, and refused to pay them. I have been assured by one of themselves, the late Mr. John M'Nee, Eastside, Kirkintilloch, that the workers in Kincaid, where he was then employed, would not have been effected to the extent of 2/6 in twelve months by the matters which were then in dispute, and which led to the strike. He was one who was deputed to wait on Mr. Inglis on behalf of the men. "What do you think about it yourself now, John?" "Oh! I am quite satisfied, but I am but one." Heat and temper got into the discussions. Strong speeches were made on behalf of the men, and the flourishing state of the funds was dwelt on. The more cautious and prudent workmen, who knew the miseries which a strike involved on their families, even when it was successful, and if it lasted only a few weeks, advised patience, and were opposed to the strike. But they were threatened, and found it prudent to leave the district for a time.

Without realising the magnitude of the struggle they were entering on, a strike was decided on, and the block-printers came out at Lennoxmill, Kincaid, and Lillyburn, with the sympathies and best wishes of the majority of their fellow-workmen. The engravers were neutral, a course which led to important results after it was all over. The employers were determined not to yield, and entered keenly into the struggle. This became protracted, and the strikers gradually scattered over the country in search of whatever employment could be got. New print-works were started about this period at Paisley, Barrhead, and Kilmarnock, where some found employment; many, however, forsook their old trade and never returned to Campsie. The places vacated by the strikers were gradually filled up, weavers from Kirkintilloch, Camlachie, Millguy, or Milngavie as it is now termed, furnishing a large quota of the new hands, or "nobs," as the strikers called them.

Amongst the "nobs" who came to Kincaid was Mr. James Martin, in these latter days a member of the Glasgow School Board and the Glasgow Town Council—now Bailie James Martin of Gallowgate Street. A Campsie man still living has seen "Jeems" marching in the counter-demonstrations, when the "nobs" showed themselves in the village streets. When the employers' recruiting parties had obtained workers willing to accept their terms, the new hands had to be marched to Lennoxmill under protection.

On one occasion the scouts of the strikers reported the advance of the "nobs," who were being brought over the south hill to the Field. The strikers and their sympathisers immediately mustered on the north bank of the Glazert in great numbers, opposite the stepping-stones, which were a little to the westward of the present bridge, in hopes that they would in this way intimidate them from their purpose of taking employment in the Field, and, if they persisted, many urged violent measures and were prepared to oppose them by force. However, the "nobs" were got into the Field in safety, thanks to the good generalship of Mr. Stevenson Dalglish, and lodgings were provided for them there. They were, however, greatly annoyed and harassed inside the gates by fellow-workmen, who sympathised with those "out." They were hooted, jostled, and intimidated if they ventured outside, either singly or in small parties. This prevailed to such an extent that "the powers that be" had to be called in to preserve the public peace, and protect the new workers from persecution. Hostile collisions occurred between opposing parties, which resulted in legal proceedings, convictions, and imprisonments, which only further embittered the excited feelings.

Demonstrations were made by sympathisers from Milngavie and neighbouring towns and villages, who marched in procession through Lennoxtown and encouraged the strikers to persevere. So high did the excitement reach that it was said it had been threatened to set fire to the works at Lennoxmill. This threat brought matters to a crisis, and an application was now made to the civil authorities for a military force capable of protecting both the Field and those employed in it. A detachment of the Enniskilling dragoons was at once despatched, and was quartered inside the Field, in what became subsequently known as "The Barracks" in Lennoxmill. Kincaid and Lillyburn were also placed under military protection. Meanwhile Mr Stevenson Dalglish was exerting himself to the utmost to get the vacant places filled up. Where men could not be obtained, he assigned work to women which hitherto had always been considered men's work.

Every expedient was devised to save labour. It is an old proverb that necessity is the mother of invention. Machinery was devised and introduced to supersede manual labour. One of the expedients tried for the first time was Coubrough's Printing Machine, the inventor claiming in its favour that it could print 300 or 400 pieces per day. While all this was going on, the firm straining every nerve to get work carried on as usual, the strikers making demonstrations to baffle them, a rather ludicrous incident happened in front of the Field gate. The village being apparently perfectly quiet, the dragoons had ridden out to exercise their horses, and had gone up the Craw Road, leaving a solitary horseman on duty in the Field. A crowd suddenly gathered in front of the gate, determined apparently on effecting an entrance by forcing or carrying the gate by assault. But the garrison was equal to the occasion. Signalling to the gatekeeper to open the locked gate, he put his horse to the gallop, and charged out into the crowd, brandishing his sword and striking out freely with the flat of his blade. The crowd gave way, completely cowed, and before the other troopers returned, had gradually dispersed. Mr. William Craig of Balglass had witnessed the whole incident, the sudden tumult and the hasty dispersion, and on his jeeringly taunting one of the ringleaders for running away in such a cowardly fashion from one man, the strike leader's reply was " Faith, man, it was time to rin awa', when the cauld steel was at your wame." After this, although the strike dragged on for weeks, the spirits of the strikers gradually sank, as they began to realise they had the worst of the struggle.

AMATEUR THEATRICALS.

There has always been a number of admirers of the drama in Lennoxmill. Before 1830 a goodly number of young men employed in the Field used to go to Glasgow after work hours to attend the theatre. They walked there and back, and resumed work next morning at 6 o'clock. There was an amateur performance of Allan Ramsay's " Gentle Shepherd," in Robertson's Hall, about 1830. "Rob Roy" was performed in the Lennox Arms' Hall in 1831. James Biggar was the "Dougal Cratur," John Lindsay was the Bailie, and with Wattie Paterson, D. Crawford, Malcolm Kincaid, and others, made up a very respectable company. Indeed, Biggar as Dougal and Lindsay as the Bailie were said to be exceptionally good. Mr. James Millar, of Glasgow, was asked to be Helen M'Gregor, but his mother would not allow him. When the strike took place a number of these amateur actors formed a company to "star" the country districts, in order to raise funds in support of those who were out on strike. They went to Fintry, Killearn, Balfron, Callander, and Doune, in all of which places they had a friendly reception, good houses, and liberal responses to their appeals on behalf of the families of the strikers. Their success was owing to a combination of talents in the company. Biggar was an excellent bugle player, and was full of fun. Wattie Paterson played the trombone. He also walked up and down the outside, with a long whip in his hand, shouting, "Walk in, ladies and gentlemen." Others played various musical instruments with considerable skill. Malcolm Kincaid was quite an expert juggler, and clever at all kinds of sleight-of-hand tricks.

In later times I remember Robert M'Gilchrist and James Brodie going frequently to Glasgow after working hours to hear famous actors in parts which they were studying, with a view to reproducing the plays at home. Their services and those of the other members of later companies of amateurs, and the great financial success of their performances in clearing off the debt on the Town Hall, and for other public objects, are well known and too recent to require notice here.

MOSES M'LAY.

Before leaving the subject of the strike I must pay a passing tribute to one of the men who became prominent when the struggle had been entered on. This was Moses M'Lay, block-printer, Crosshill. When Dalglish, Falconer & Co. started, he came with them from Killearn. He had wrought previously at End-rick Field, walking to Balfron and home again every day. He was a man universally respected, and was appointed treasurer of the Strike Funds, as the printers declared they could "lippen him wi' the bawbees." He never resumed work in Lennoxmill after the strike, but continued a life of Christian activity and great usefulness. He was known as a praying man, and was in request as a visitor of the sick, to whom he was unwearied in declaring the consolations of the gospel. Mr James Millar has told me this anecdote about him.

"When I was a child I had a sore illness, and was thought to be dying. A kind neighbour, old Grannie Gault, used to come and sit up all night to relieve my mother's watch and let her get some rest. One night, when it seemed that I was dying, Moses M'Lay was sent for, and came at once. He knelt down and engaged in prayer. Suddenly Grannie Gault ceased rocking the cradle; both my mother and she thinking that I was gone. She touched Moses, and said—'Oh, Moses, stop! he's deid.' All were gazing earnestly, hoping against hope, when I suddenly opened my eyes. My dear mother often told me the story, when I was grown up, and how Grannie said, when they were full of joy at the favourable 'turn' of the trouble— 'He's a braw broo'd loon; he'll gar some woman sigh and lay bye her supper.'"

Moses M'Lay died in 1837, aged 56, having caught typhus fever from an individual whom he had been called in to pray for. Although not then employed in Lennoxmill, Provost Dalglish wrote to express his high respect for his character and his regret that he was unable to attend the funeral. The late Rev. John Edwards, D.D., said of him he hardly ever knew any man for whom he had a higher respect. I find Mr. M'Lay's name enrolled on the list of Elders of the Relief Church, among other Campsie "Worthies," who did much in their day and generation to promote spiritual life in the parish.

COLLAPSE OF STRIKE.

On the collapse of the strike, when the men gave in the masters could not abandon those who had come to them in their hour of need. The nobs had to be retained, so there was no room for the old hands, many of whom had to leave the parish in search of work, while others found employment at other vocations. The block-printers brought irretrievable disaster on their trade, as employers had stimulated the minds of mechanicians to devise new methods of executing the work. This gave wonderful impetus to machine cylinder printing, so that in about twenty years after the strike, block printing was entirely discontinued in Lennoxmill, and the allied trades of block cutters, &c., were all cast adrift. It was in 1856 that block printing was entirely given up in Lennoxmill. At the period of the strike Mr. Archd. Duncan was an apprentice engraver. He was working late one evening, when he was warned to be prepared to co-operate in protecting the work in the event of an attack, which it was feared was likely to be made upon it. That same evening the dragoons arrived. Of course their appearance made a sensation, and was an incident not likely to be forgotten by any one who saw it—or saw the commotion it caused in Lennoxtown. Messrs. Dalglish felt grateful to the engravers for their benevolent neutrality. The same entry-money was exigible from the apprentice engravers as from the block-printers. The engravers themselves first reduced their entry by one half. Latterly the entry money was abolished in all the trades in the Field.

TURKEY RED. THE MACBEANS, FATHER AND SON.

Up till the stoppage of Messrs. Kibble & Co. in Dalmonach, turkey-red dyeing had been carried on in Lennoxmill, but at that time the future of turkey-red dyeing did not appear very bright, so, with the accession of orders from Graham, Alexander, & Co., the firm decided to discontinue it. The turkey-red dyeing was under the sole charge of a Highlander, Mr. M'Bean, who came from near Inverness. Mr. M'Bean brought from the north a little colony of strongly-built young men, of whom I only remember Hugh M'Donald, once an engraver, now a herbalist in Glasgow. Mr. M'Bean's son entered the Glasgow warehouse of the firm, where he showed great business aptitude and was highly appreciated. Other firms also came to see his worth, and he passed into the service of Messrs. James Black & Co., where he rapidly came to the front. Happily married and in the enjoyment of domestic felicity, with bright prospects for the future before him, his health failed, and he died young. After his death his young widow, with her little daughter, returned to her own people in Inverness, where I had the pleasure, a few years ago, of partaking of her hospitality.

I have received the following interesting reminiscences from an old Field man, now occupying a distinguished position. Rightly to understand this we must recollect that the Factory Act, regulating the employment of women and children, was only passed in 1833. It was amended and regulated in 1844. The Ten Hours Act was passed in 1847, and the Children's Labour Act in 1853. Also, that calico intended for printing had to be " singed " to clear it of fibrous down. It was passed quickly over cast iron at a red heat. Another process was passing it over hot drying rollers. After the cloth had been printed it required to be dyed. This was done in three operations—1, dunging; 2, maddering; 3, clearing. I remember when the Fintry carts used to came to Lennoxmill full of cow dung, then in great request. All pieces madder dyed were passed through the dung vats, then washed, then streamed in the lade to get rid of the dung; bran, soap, and other ingredients being used to clear the whites after the dyeing. These explanations are necessary for those unacquainted with the processes in Lennoxmill to follow the details described in the following communication :—

MR. JOHN YOUNG'S REMINISCENCES.

" I went to the Field in the year 1833, as message boy in the printers warehouse. This was the year before the Printers' Strike and the year that the " Big Lum " was built Elie Cooper, an Englishman, was head foreman over the printers and old Andrew White under foreman. I was in the employment of the firm for 26 years, until I came here in 1859. I have a clear remembrance of many of the events of the first cholera. Mr Dalglish, senr., was then Lord Provost of Glasgow. I remember that he brought out to the works a lot of plaster cloth and camphor. The plaster cloth was cut to a shape to fit the breast and belly, the camphor was worn in a small woollen bag, to prevent infection. My father, Thomas Young, made wooden moulds for cutting the plasters, so as to fit various sizes of people.

" Saunders Dalglish I remember well, from the time I was 6 or 7 years of age. He was a kind old man, who used to walk back and forward on fine summer evenings, between the Field Road and the Pond. If any boys were at play he would offer them pennies to have races on foot, or running their hoops, or for playing ball. He died before the strike took place.

"Robert Barclay I also knew well. When I was 10 years of age I had the misfortune to be thrown from a horse one winter's night, whilst Archie Miller and I were getting a ride from my uncle's house at Torrance. Both of us were thrown. I had the larger bone of my right leg broken, under the knee, and had to lie on my back for six weeks at one stretch. This was during the period of the strike.

"During my three months' confinement Robert Barclay kept me supplied with as many story books from the Sabbath School Library as I could manage to read. I used to work with Mr. John Wylie, then colour-maker, as assistant boy, while he was making experiments on different shades of colour, and I liked this very much, as we were in a room all by ourselves.

"I had several jobs in the works before I commenced my apprenticeship of seven years to print-cutting. One of these jobs was working in the "warm end" of the blotching-house; there we had to stand over nearly red-hot plates, and keep stretching out the cloth as it kept passing over the drying rollers.

"Another boy and I took it by turns, 15 minutes at a time. I have seen when I came out to cool that I could hardly touch the metal buttons on my clothes, they were so hot. This was then done only with a certain class of goods and I don't think is ever done now.

"Another job I had, gave me an opposite experience. It was working at the Lade, streaming cloth in the water. This was pleasant in the summer months, but not in the winter. All the same, we had often to stand over the boards and the cold water from 6 a.m till 12 p.m. on many occasions.

"I will ever remember one very cold night, when the thermometer fell nearly to zero, that my comrades and I were all frozen to the boards, cloth and all. Our leggings were covered with ice, and fingers benumbed with cold. My comrades and I latterly were crying, and had to be lifted from the boards to which they were frozen. When I reached home about 2 o'clock in the morning, my mother rose, and when she saw the frozen condition I was in, she commenced crying too, with sorrow. She said she would never let me go back to that job again although the family should starve. This was the year Lennox Castle was building, and we had six weeks of frost without any thaw. This exposure to cold I've had to endure for 16 hours on a stretch, for the magnificent pay of 6d per day and 1d per hour for overtime. Strong, full-grown, healthy women at similar work had then only 10d per day, and 1½d per hour for overtime. The works at that time were allowed to work night and day when busy. Even the youngest workers were compelled to work two or three nights per week. That was the time the firm was making money, getting good prices in the market, and paying a third less for labour than what was then given in other printfields near Glasgow. . . . I was sorry to learn from various sources that, years after I had left, trade had begun to decline, and that Lennoxmill, for the first time in my remembrance, was obliged to go on short time. . . . On the whole—with very few exceptions indeed—I can testify that Mr Dalglish was well and faithfully served by all his employees, foremen, and managers. While their industry built up his fortune, it can never be said it was afterwards lost through any fault of theirs."

When Mr. Dalglish was away in London he seemed to lose touch with the advancing spirit of the age. He let many of his best workmen drift away to other districts, where they received better remuneration; and, besides, many of his best salesmen in Glasgow and Manchester were allowed to leave and enter the warehouses of rival houses, who paid higher salaries.

C

THE KING'S BIRTHDAY.

I am not aware whether the employees in Lennoxmill now show their loyalty by observing the Queen's birthday, but when George the Third was king it was the correct thing for all good citizens to observe it as a holiday, and in this way testify their loyalty. There was a treat in the evening to all Lennoxmill workers, and the firm presented all the apprentices and boys with a sum of twopence, to be expended by them at pleasure. This was spent on fire-works if loyal, or on good things if selfish, and they were treated also at the expense of the firm to a glass of toddy, if they cared to have it. Very few in those days refused either the twopence or the glass of toddy.

TEMPERANCE MOVEMENT.

Public rejoicing and social festivity were inseparably associated with drinking customs. Scenes of excess, as I have already mentioned, frequently accompanied the payment of entries by new apprentices, and other occasions, such as half-entry and pay-offs. These evils were fostered by the system of paying the wages in public-houses. These practices connected with pay-offs, &c., had long grieved the hearts of such men as Robert Barclay and his coadjutors, who were intent on effecting social and moral reforms. Hitherto they had felt themselves powerless. They hailed the arrival of the pioneers of a new movement to promote temperance. In the year 1829 there was convened a public meeting in the Relief Church, to explain the objects and advocate the claims of temperance. This meeting was called to hear addresses by Mr. William Collins, the father of the well-known Sir William Collins, who was accompanied by a Mr Cruickshanks, known as the converted Dundee Carter, and whose personal appeals were very effective in gaining adherents. The results of this meeting were far reaching. Two men became zealous converts to the new cause, and threw themselves heart and soul into the work of spreading its principles and advocating their adoption. These were Mr Alexander Fraser, the eldest son of Mr Fraser, teacher, and Mr James M'Pherson, shoemaker. Mr Fraser had served his apprenticeship as an engraver in Lennoxmill. He then went to a printwork in France, but after two or three years returned to Campsie as foreman engraver, studied for the ministry, and was ordained in connection with the Congregational Church, first in England, then in Ewing Chapel, Waterloo St., Glasgow. Failing health caused him to remove to a more genial climate. Mr Fraser's co-worker, Mr James M'Pherson, left afterwards for Glasgow, and then became employed in home mission work by the widow of the famous Lord Byron. His daughter is the well-known Miss M'Pherson, the story of whose life and philanthropic work in taking destitute boys and girls to

Canada is well known in all the churches. It is briefly detailed in the *Sunday at Home* for September, 1882. With such apostolic fervour did these two men devote themselves to this work while in Campsie that they purchased a pony and gig to take them to the neighbouring villages after their day's work was over. As a result of their arduous labours a great change for the better was soon visible. This was greatly assisted by the system of entries being discontinued, and by the adoption of payment of wages in Lennoxmill in working hours. It is a pleasure to have this opportunity of doing an act of justice to these two noble men, by recalling their self-denying exertions to a generation in Lennoxmill, to whom their names are already almost unknown.

Since the "Notes" of the lecture was published in the local newspaper I have received the following letter :—

"HOME OF INDUSTRY,
"29 BETHNAL GREEN ROAD, LONDON E.
"DEAR SIR,
"A newspaper with your lecture to the Campsie Y.M.C.A. has been forwarded to me. Accept my thanks for the honourable mention and kindly reference to my beloved father's memory. I have had such a full life since his departure to glory in '51· His last words were, "Jesus, Jesus," breathed into my ear as his dying arms were around my neck. He was a genius and a devoted Christian of great reality. His life work I have by God's grace sought to carry on, for the best welfare of the young, and it has been a right royal life. My sisters, Mrs Merry and Mrs Birt of Liverpool, have co-operated with me. Together, we have aided 8,200 destitute to a land where they are now in comfort and plenty. It is the Lord who has taken up weaklings, "poor yet making others rich." Life seems so real around me in this dying mass, 200,000 in this parish, that to look forward to our coming Lord, hastening His return by winning souls, rather than by going back on these old times, helps one to endure. We as a band endeavour to influence some 10,000 to 12,000 weekly in direct gospel work. Thanking you again, believe me, yours sincerely,   "ANNIE MACPHERSON."

PAYMENT OF WAGES.

Up till about 1832 a system prevailed in Lennoxmill of giving to the foreman in each department the money required to pay the wages of those in the department under his charge. This was on a Saturday afternoon, and all went to public-houses in the village, where it was divided, and the workers paid. Of course it was necessary to obtain change, so this and the use of a room was afforded in return for their patronage. It was expected that every one using the room would spend something for the good of the house, or contribute a small sum as payment. Under such a system it was quite possible for a clever but unprincipled foreman to cheat both his employers and his employees. Such a system of payment of wages encouraged drinking to excess, as many workmen spent too much of their hardly earned wages before they left; the carousal kept them at home on the Sabbaths, and it was often continued well into the following week. Realising the evils attendant on this system of pays, Mr. R. Dalglish had matters put on a more satisfactory basis. He arranged that every man, woman, and child separately, should be paid by a clerk during working hours, a practice strictly followed out afterwards. A decided improvement at once resulted. The pay was made on Thursday up to the Saturday preceding. The workers were more regular and punctual at work on the Friday mornings than they used to be on the Mondays or even the Tuesdays, and the pay on Thursday has continued to be the custom ever since.

FRIENDLY SOCIETIES.

Friendly societies were introduced and mainly promoted by Messrs. Robert Barclay, Alex. Fraser, James M'Pherson, Robert Morrison (block-printer), John Glen (engraver), John Wylie, Matthew M'Culloch, Adam M'Luckie, and others. The constitution of the society that was the first formed was, I understand, drawn up by Messrs. Barclay and M'Pherson. In the event of any member becoming ill and unable to work, the society became bound to pay 20/ per week, as long as the member was unable to work. There was the fatal mistake, in neither introducing a limit to the liability of the members, nor specifying a period after which the sick allowance would decrease, and in due course terminate altogether. The success of this society led to the formation of another one, on a smaller scale. The weekly payment was smaller, only 1d per week, and so in proportion was the sick benefit, which was 7/ per week. In this penny society there was unlimited liability of members for the allowance to sick, and there was no stated period at which this should terminate. Mr. William Eadie, foreman mason, long acted as secretary.

Alexander Farquhar, a labourer in Lennoxmill, became a member of both societies. He became unwell, alleged he was unfit to work, and he then became entitled to 20/ a week from the one society, and 7/ per week from the other. His wages in Lennoxmill would be about 12/ to 14/ per week, so that his sick allowance was fully double his ordinary weekly wages. He never resumed work, but became a permanent burden on both societies, and outlived nearly all the original members. As the membership decreased the calls on those remaining became heavier, till these amounted to from 3/ to 4/ per week. The matter was tested in court, but the members failed to get rid of their liability. Such a constant drain on their funds prevented the accession of new members, and for a time brought all Friendly societies into local disrepute. Such incidents led to the existing societies being placed on sure foundations, and none of these now in favour, such as Foresters, Shepherds, Free Gardeners, &c., entail such liabilities. The Penny Society by a final effort collected about £60, for which amount Farquhar compromised his claim. Before his death the original society was reduced to about four members, who made up his weekly aliment among them.

The Rev. John Gillon, Roman Catholic clergyman, now took up the idea and instituted a society among his own people, the St. Patrick's Society. He took an active interest in this and personally superintended its operations for many years. It was not confined to his own flock, and many Protestants joined it, as it was kept in a flourishing condition. In recognition of his exertions in connection with this matter, and also his devotion in visiting during the third cholera epidemic, the inhabitants of Campsie (and I am assured chiefly the Protestants) presented him with an eight-day clock in a mahogany case, on the door of which a suitable inscription was engraved on a silver plate. After this, so generally was he esteemed by all classes, Mr. Gillon was often called the Protestant Priest. Shortly after this he was transferred to Dundee. His successor would have gladly acquired the clock, but Mr. Gillon prized it too highly to part with it in his lifetime.

A secession from the St. Patrick's Society afterwards took place, headed by John Kinloch, a Field man, and John Morrison, shoemaker, Rowantreefauld. It was they who then originated the Campsie Yearly Friendly Society, which still exists in a prosperous condition. This society, I understand, breaks up at the close of every year and is then reconstituted.

There was another society which, after a prosperous course for a few years, suddenly went down, owing to want of concord among its membership. Mr. John Walker, for many years in charge of the white warehouse, and latterly of the finishing of the cambrics, was identified closely with this one—the Oddfellows Friendly Society—and he took a very active part in its management. With a large membership and a flourishing condition, a proposal was made to raise the weekly contribution one penny per week. This met with strong opposition, and, in consequence of the diversity of opinion, a disruption took place. Both parties laid claim to the regalia, or wished it divided between them, and the meeting closed with a "scene." It was the intention of both parties to reconstitute the society on a new basis, but as time passed, their good resolutions cooled down, and these schemes led to no practical result.

Another movement, which had for its objects the cultivation of habits of thrift and forethought, was that of the Penny Savings Bank. Mr. John Gardiner long took a deep interest in its success. Mr. Gardiner had charge of the finished warehouse and of the despatch of orders.

FIELD MEN WHO HAVE GOT ON.

The ups and downs in the lives of the workers in Lennoxmill contain much that is romantic, and a modern novelist might find among them materials amusing and instructive. A few instances only can I mention here. One young man, who wrought as a block-printer for a short time in Lennoxmill, left, to return about

25 years later as a partner in the oldest parish printfield, and his son is now one of the M.P.s for Glasgow. A block-printer named Simpson was employed in the Field. In order to avoid marrying a girl who had loved " not wisely but too well," he suddenly resolved to leave Lennoxmill, and go south to England. He was then so hard up that he had to borrow a pair of shoes. In the south he got his chance, and in time became sole proprietor of Foxell Bank Printworks, Lancashire, then one of the leading works in England. Many years afterwards he re-visited Campsie, full of old memories, with a heart warming to old associates. He called on all his old cronies whom he found alive and invited them to a splendid supper, where he hospitably entertained them. It was found that the average age of these Campsie callants was over 74 years. Amongst their number were old Johnnie Leckie, grocer, and old John Glen, engraver, then very aged men, but hale and hearty in spite of their years. So many have gone from Lennoxmill to the printfields in Lancashire that a social gathering of the natives of Campsie and their friends can be held in Manchester.

JOHN YOUNG, F.G.S., HUNTERIAN MUSEUM, GLASGOW UNIVERSITY.

John Young served his apprenticeship to print-cutting, and worked as a journeyman at this trade till the firm gave up block-printing. He then passed to the wright shop. In 1855 the meeting of the British Association for the Promotion of Science was held in Glasgow, over which the Duke of Argyle presided. Mineral and geological collections were formed in Glasgow for this meeting of the Association, and a man skilled in the rocks and fossils of this district was required to superintend, classify, and generally take charge of the valuable collection. By request, Mr. John Young was allowed to go to Glasgow to undertake this duty, which was performed to the great satisfaction of the *savants*. At the expiry of five months, he resumed his old duties in Lennox-mill. Becoming interested in geological science, he had early commenced to study the geology of the Campsie district, and form a collection of its various rocks and fossils. Little did he think that these pursuits of his leisure hours should afterwards lead him away from his native home to a new and active sphere of life. This it has done, but it has not made him forget his early days in Lennoxmill. While he was arranging the collection referred to the authorities in Glasgow University discovered his worth, and whenever the opportunity occurred they offered him the charge of the Hunterian Museum, a most congenial occupation. Mr. Young has become the life and soul of the Glasgow Geological Society. He gave a lecture to that society in 1858, entitled, "On the Geology of the Campsie District," and, the same winter, he re-delivered it in the Mechanics' Institute, Campsie. At the request of the Glasgow society, this lecture has been extended and printed, and now forms Part I., Vol. I., of the society's Transactions. He gives a full sketch of the physical features of the Campsie district, along with lists of the various fossils found in the strata, and descriptions of the rocks and minerals. When he left for Glasgow, Sandy Cowan, who was also a print-cutter, and also a student of geology, returned to Lennoxmill to fill the vacancy. Poor fellow, he accidentally cut his leg with a chisel a few weeks afterwards, and died from the effects of inflammation of the wound.

MR. JOHN COWAN.

When I was a scholar in Mr. James Gray's Sabbath school, I was a short time in Mr. Young's class. From that I passed to the class of Mr. John Cowan, from which I was taken and made a teacher. Mr. Cowan had been one of the three who resuscitated the Y.M.A. The essays, discussions, and intellectual life awakened there made the want of a public library and reading-room to be greatly felt. So the Mechanics' Institute was evolved, as a consequence of the operations of the Y.M.A. In the establishing and early management of the Institution Mr. Cowan took an active interest. He was also an ardent temperance reformer. Mr. Cowan went to England to push his way upwards. His great skill and administrative ability soon asserted themselves. He was placed over large print-works in Lancashire and Derbyshire. His high character, incorruptible integrity, and pawky Scotch humour revealed to those coming in contact with him one of the best types of a Scotchman, and what is better, a Christian gentleman. He has now retired from business. I had occasion to be in Hull recently. Learning that I was coming, he had a kind invitation awaiting me at the hotel, asking me to dine and stay over night with him at Wycliffe House, Anlaby Road, where he is residing now, with one of his married daughters. He sends by me a very kind message to the younger generation, who are now members of the C.Y.M.A., and also to some of his former friends in Campsie.

MR. WILLIAM GARDNER.

One who was a class-mate with me, Mr. William Gardner, died in his early manhood. He had already attained the position of manager to the Messrs. Heys at Barrhead. Speaking to Mr. Gordon Wilson about Mr. Gardner, shortly after his death, Mr. Heys declared he had never had a better manager in his work.

A son of Mr John Barr, so well known in Lennoxtown, is at present manager of Mr. Potter's Printworks, at Dinting, near Glossop, which are the largest in the world.

MESSRS. JAMES AND ALEXANDER YOUNG.

In Rumney's Printworks, at Stubbins, near Ramsbottom, James and Alexander Young are employed, the latter as managing partner. I am informed that the ingenuity of the brothers Young has devised various new methods of printing, the most recent being one by which exquisitively fine patterns can be printed on glass, wood, iron and other hard smooth substances that can be used in the internal decoration of houses, steamships, &c. I have myself seen beautiful specimens of their workmanship on both glass and wood. A crate of glass, containing 30 sheets, 36×48, can be printed in a quarter of an hour. It would rather surprise some of our local calico printers to see a sheet of glass, as large as a dining-room table, printed from copper rollers before you could say "Jack Robinson." The brothers, James and Alexander Young, are living in the Rossendale Valley, where they are keen supporters of Lord Hartington. In compliment to the district and constituency, they have named their invention the "Rossendale." I see this noticed briefly, under the head of "New Appliances and Improvements," in the *Plumber and Decorator and Journal of Gas and Sanitary Engineering* for 1st September, 1890. Referring to the productions of the Rossendale Glass and Wood Decorating Co.; office, 53 Portland St., Manchester, the article says :—

"Decorated glass, turned out in first-class style and permanent to boot, can now be placed on the market at an astonishing low price. The scope of the invention renders it possible to produce perfect coloured decorations for windows, which, in effect and permanence, are on a par with ordinary enamelled glass, and ranging up to, in artistic colouring and effect, the most elaborate leaded or stained and painted glass windows. On plain ground sheet glass or plate glass it is the easiest thing in the world for the patentees' machinery to turn out *ad lib.* glass decoration with the quality of permanence. Another development is the printing on wood of venetian blinds," &c.

There has been a great demand for this new class of "prints" from our colonies, from China, Japan, &c. I understand the process has been patented, and I trust the Messrs. Young will reap the reward of their ingenuity as inventors.

The Lennoxmill young men have come well to the front in other branches and professions, but I cannot enter into detail now. I can only mention one case, that of the late John Service, D.D., Glasgow. I remember when he was in Lennoxmill, employed as a clerk in the Counting-House, and I became a member of the Y.M.A. shortly before he left to attend the University.

A great many former Campsonians are to be found in connection with the printworks around Manchester, they being employed, either as skilled workmen, or as foremen in the various branches, or as the managers of the works. Many of them cherish the old Campsie associations.

I have an old cutting from the *Lennox Herald* of a gathering which took place a few years ago in Manchester, and which I may now quote :—

"On Saturday night a number of Campsonians, with other Scotch friends, residents in Manchester and district, held an inaugural festival in the Merchants' Hotel, Oldham Street. Covers were laid for eighty. Mr. John Cowan presided and gave the sentiment of the evening, 'Campsie.' Mr James Smellie gave 'Scotland, our Native Land.' Songs were sung by Mr. Robert Dalglish, engraver (one specially composed for the occasion), and Thomas Mackay; and recitations by Josiah Kay and William Kay. Among others present, the names of James Cowan, H. M'Innes, Hamilton Humphreys, Brodie, M'Adam, Paton, M'Kinley, Robertson, and M'Kean will be well remembered in Lennoxtown."

At this meeting Mr. Thomas M'Kay sang a "Field" song, written by William Smith, a genial native of Campsie, who was in his youth a handloom weaver, but for many years an employee in Lennoxmill. The song is, I believe, well known.

"We seldom meet oor frien's to greet,
    And troubles they are mair than twa;
Oor chequered life's replete wi' strife,
    And will be on this earthly ba'.

Chorus—We're a' met and happy set,
    Nor frae oor hames so long awa';
And since we a' sae weel agree,
    Oh, wha can think to gang awa'?" &c.

There used to be an annual re-union in Glasgow of the "natives of Campsie and their friends." Why they are now given up I do not know. Some of the meetings have been very enjoyable.

MR. JAMES MILLAR'S SPEECH AT CAMPSIE RE-UNION OF 1872.

Of the "natives" of Campsie whom the committee asked to preside at the re-union in Glasgow, the very first they delighted to honour was Mr. James Millar, Monteith Row, Glasgow, who served his apprenticeship as a block-cutter. I have already referred to the manner in which he raised the £7 7/ of entry money. He left the Field about the time of the strike. In the course of a most interesting address as chairman, about 1872, I think, Mr. Millar said—

"This is the sixth Re-union of the Natives of Campsie which I have attended in Glasgow. The first was held in the Wheat Sheaf Inn, Adelphi Street, in the year 1835. The second was held in the following year, 1836, in the Black Bull Hall, at the foot of Virginia Street. Both of these meetings were in the form of a supper and ball, and with many of the guests, I remember, inspiring bold "John Barleycorn" made the fun grow fast and furious. After an interval of thirty years we met in this hall three years ago. Our present Re-union is the fourth meeting in this hall of Campsonians and their friends, and your present Chairman is the only native of Campsie, who has hitherto been called on to preside at these social gatherings."

Mr. Millar, after giving a historical sketch of the parish, referred to the print-works, and spoke as follows:—

" There is more skilled labour required in a print-work than in any other kind of manufacture I know of. There is to begin with, the designer, who designs the pattern; the engraver, who cuts this on steel and copper; or the block-cutter, who indents it in copper, or brings it out in relief on wood. Then the chemist and colour-maker, who prepare colours in endless variety of shades; the printer, who applies them to the cloth; then bleachers, dyers, finishers, mechanics, blacksmiths, joiners, tinsmiths, plumbers, masons, and a great variety of unskilled labour, men, women, boys, and girls, to say nothing of clerks, salesmen, &c. All these may be seen any day in a print-work, forming a busy hive of human industry, the products of whose labour go to every quarter of the world, and decorate the persons of women of every clime and colour."

COAL SUPPLY.

Coals used to be supplied to Lennoxmill from Scull100ngour, from the pits at the Derries, near Baldorran, Milton, and the Alum Coy.'s mines. About sixty years ago Mr. William M'Farlane, of Muckcroft, leased the coal and lime in Newlands, Clochcorr, Balglass, and South Birbiston, working them from an " ingaun e'e " in the Culloch Slap mine, near the rifle targets. Mr. Matthew H. Muirhead, Kirkintilloch, is the present lessee. Mr. M'Farlane obtained the contract for the supply of Lennoxmill, and at once proceeded to throw a wooden bridge over the Glazert, to accommodate his traffic. This was the bridge that continued to span the water until the railway was extended to the Blane Valley, when Mr. M'Farlane's bridge was replaced by a new one, at a level to suit the railway passing beneath it. The supply of coals was continued till the Campsie branch was opened, when a wider area of selection was opened up. I remember Mr. M'Farlane, whose conversational hobby was the Church, ministers, and their sermons. In Mr. Wm. Partington's interesting communication, apropos of Mr. M'Farlane, he says :—

" You mention William M'Farlane of Muckcroft; he was a relative of my wife's father, and a very good, Christian gentleman. I will give you two anecdotes about him. He had a pet gander at Muckcroft, which often accompanied him to his office at the coal mine. Arriving there, he would say to it, ' Awa' hame, ye scoundrel,' and away it would fly off back to the Muckcroft. Some time before Mr. M'Farlane's death, an evil-disposed person cut the gander's head off, threw it into his lobby, greatly to the worthy man's distress. At the mine he had a byng of coal lying, and a number of poor people used to go up and help themselves to the coals. This got so prevalent that complaints were made to the police to have it put a stop to. The police accordingly caught a number gathering coals, and reported the matter for Mr. M'Farlane's instructions. He, however, rather sympathised with the delinquents, told the policemen. ' They were just some o' my ain men's folks,' and added, ' Gie awa', ye beadle bodies, I dinna like ye.' "

FIRES.

One of the largest fires that ever occurred in Lennoxmill was, I understand, when the Turkey-red stove was burned. As that occurred before 1834 very few remember it now. I myself vividly remember one night when, about ten o'clock, the Field bell rang. There was at first a startled look—"What can that mean?" then a cry of "Fire! the Field's on fire!" In about five minutes the whole village had turned out, and from the corner of the Field Road to the scene of the fire, there was a solid mass of human beings. This fire originated in some sparks reaching the beams of cloth in the grey loft at the top of the new machine shop. It was beside the big beam engine, and near Willie M'Callum's boilers; but, although a big blaze, there was not very much damage done.

The next big fire was the ageing-room, which communicated by a gangway with the large wooden house built over the pond, and called "the ark." This was a large fire; the glare attracted people from a wide area around. The damage was covered by insurance. This would be about 1857 or 1858.

Willie Gray's muslin-room, or "back style," was also a big fire. The Field fire brigade did splendid service on this occasion. In particular, honourable mention should be made of Robert Walker, foreman mechanic, David M'Donald, John Mulholland, William Smith, and, indeed, every man not only in the fire brigade but in the Field, nobly did his duty. Often at great personal risk they exerted themselves to the utmost, and succeeded in preventing the fire from spreading to where it would have consumed the work.

I have had a photograph of this fire posted to me from Lennoxtown. There is a printed narrative on the back of the photo:—

"BURNING OF WAREHOUSE No. 65—12th December, 1871.—Fire broke out a little after seven o'clock p.m. Steam was immediately kept rushing through the dye-house roof. . . . The steam pipes were broken and a strong head of steam kept on. These means, perseveringly persisted in, speedily had the desired effect. All danger to surrounding buildings was removed by ten o'clock.

"Some remarkable instances of hardihood were displayed. One man kept his post, though seemingly enveloped in the flames and hot steam, steadily playing on an iron door of communication. Another went under the burning building and smashed the main steam pipe with a fore-hammer; indeed, all exerted themselves to the utmost.

"Lennoxtown, 20th December, 1871."

On making enquiry who was referred to as having kept his dangerous post at the door, I was informed, "Davoc M'Donald looked after his post like a hero."

Some time after this, part of the old machine shop was destroyed by fire. Fears were entertained that it might spread to the white warehouse and finishing departments, but it was fortunately checked before this could occur.

There was another large fire after the concern had been made a limited company. The finished warehouse, full of goods ready for despatch to London, was consumed. The money loss in this case was much greater than in the other fires. Here, again, the members of the fire brigade displayed great courage, and shewed efficient organisation and discipline.

VOLUNTEER MOVEMENT.

It is impossible in connection with Lennoxmill, and the public spirit at all times shown therein, to omit to notice the volunteer movement. When the movement had been fairly launched in the country, Mr. Dalglish called a meeting in the works, and offered to clothe and equip a company of 80, with a band of 20. The only stipulation Mr. Dalglish made was that all the members must be employed in Lennoxmill. This offer was at once acceded to. A company of 80 men was enrolled, Mr. Gordon Wilson, the manager, being captain. Drill was commenced forthwith, and entered into with such spirit, that the Lennoxmill corps could hold their own, both at drill and shooting, with any existing in the county. Indeed, in discipline, martial bearing, and physique, the Lennoxmill Company might have been taken as belonging to a "regiment of the line." They had one great advantage in having the Lennoxmill Brass Band—numbering 20 performers—in connection with their corps. This band was then in a high state of efficiency, under Mr. Edward Conner, an employee at the works, an excellent musician, and capital conductor. This band was of great service in public functions. For instance, when the Hon. Mr. Hanbury Lennox arrived with Mrs. Lennox after their wedding, both companies of volunteers formed a guard of honour, and, headed by the band, escorted them to the castle.

PLEASING TRAITS OF CHARACTER.

One pleasing trait of the workers in Lennoxmill was their sturdy independence and intense dislike to parochial relief. There was an *esprit de corps* in the work and a feeling of brotherhood, so that when accident, protracted disease, or family distress rendered the bread-winner incapable of work, a hearty response was made. When it was a case for taking through a subscription sheet, £10, £15, or £20 would be quickly collected, a sum which generally sufficed to tide over the particular emergency. An outsider like myself rarely heard of these, but I can recollect having heard that during the Crimean War all the workers gave a day's pay on behalf of the wives and children of the soldiers who had fallen in battle or perished by disease. On this occasion the sum of £70 was collected, and Mr. Gordon Wilson had the pleasure of transmitting this handsome sum to the treasurers of the fund.

A HORSE STORY.

Previous to 1849 the whole traffic from and to Glasgow was carted. Mr. William M'Gilchrist, the Field carter, had a beautiful grey horse, and when passing his house in the Field Road his wife used always to speak kindly to the horse and often gave it a piece of oat-cake, of which it was fond. One day, as the horse was passing, Mrs. M'Gilchrist was stooping over a boyne at the door steps, and did not notice the horse. "Badger," unaccustomed to such coldness, seized Mrs. M'Gilchrist by the dress, lifted her up, and gave her a shake, then set her down. When she had recovered from her astonishment she hastened into the house, brought out a whole "farl," and presenting this, with kind speech and gentle patting, soon soothed "Badger's" ruffled feelings, and he never tried such a prank again.

GAMES AND MATCHES ON SATURDAY AFTERNOONS.

Before I close, I advert to the games and amusements of my boyish days, which are now entirely changed. "Smugglers," "rounders," and shinty were popular games long ago. I can recollect once at a New-Year time a team going from the Field to play a shinty match with the Vale of Leven. They went away in high spirits, sanguine of success, but returned crest-fallen, badly beaten. I can only recollect two of the players in this match, Hugh Kane and David Armstrong (baker). I remember when quoits was a favourite game. When I was a boy there were two brothers, named M'Crone, blacksmiths in the Field, whom I recollect being the local crack players. "Bullets" was another favourite game. There were matches on the Saturday afternoons, sometimes between individuals or between different "shops" in the Field, or frequently with players from Kirkintilloch. I was present as a boy at a great match on the Cumbernauld road, when three players aside represented Campsie and Kirkintilloch respectively. Thomas Meikle and John and Malcolm Brown were, I think, the Field champions. For Kirkintilloch—W. Graham (the "Kornel"), Stewart, and Miller. Kirkintilloch won the match and the stakes of three or five guineas by two hails to one.

MR. WILLIAM PARTINGTON'S REMINISCENSES.

I have received a long letter from Mr. William Partington, from which I make the following extracts :—

"FOREST WORKS, BULWELL, Dec , 1890.

"In the published 'notes' of your lecture I have not observed any reference to the

"CAMPSIE MECHANICS' INSTITUTION,

which owed its birth and management almost exclusively to those who were employed in Lennoxmill. This was instituted in 1848, and was one of the best things that Campsie has ever experienced for the improvement of its rising young men. The institution was well managed by a number of excellent, intelligent, working men, such as John Cowan, George Somerville, Thomas Wilson, W. Shiel, James M'Crie, Jamieson Provan, &c., &c., not forgetting your humble servant. There was a meeting in the Field park to consider the question of a

TOWN HALL.

Some proposed we should beg as much money as would build it. I proposed we should raise the money by subscription and in 10s. shares. This plan was adopted, and the hall was built, and opened by the Hon. Mr. Hanbury Lennox. Mr. R. Dalglish, M.P., was also very liberal in helping us to build the hall. The total cost was £1340. We were £600 in debt when the hall was finished, but we got up concerts, private theatricals, &c., &c., and we wiped off the debt, and the Hall Co are now able to pay a dividend. There is another useful thing of which I have seen no notice taken, the Field Park, used as a public recreation ground.

FIELD PARK.

" I was the means of getting this park for the workers in Lennoxmill. I went to Mr. Gordon Wilson and offered him £10 for the use of it, when I did not know how or where I should ever raise the money. I represented to Mr. Wilson what a great benefit it would be. He received me very favourably, and suggested that I should embody all I had said to him in a letter addressed to Mr. R. Dalglish, and if Mr. D. consulted him he would not throw any difficulties in the way. In reply, Mr. Dalglish acceded to my request, and gave a free grant of the Field Park, not only to the workers in Lennoxmill, but for the benefit of the inhabitants of Campsie.

" Should you ever at any time be anywhere near Nottingham, be sure to come to Bulwell and call at Forest Works, and you will get a hearty welcome. And now I must close. With kind regards,

" Yours sincerely,
" WILLIAM PARTINGTON."

I have enjoyed the use of the Field Park in my younger days, but I never knew to whom the public of Campsie were indebted for procuring this from Mr. Dalglish.

All old Campsonians will be pleased to see from the foregoing letter that Mr. Partington is as bright and cheery as ever, and that he has not forgotten the parish or the local institutions in which he took such a deep interest while residing in Lennoxtown.

MR. GORDON WILSON.

I have already referred to the circumstances under which Mr. Gordon Wilson left Dalmonach and in 1836 entered on his lengthened period of service at Lennoxmill. As colour-maker, manager, and partner, he remained there till March, 1877, and during this long period the firm enjoyed great prosperity, not a little of which was due to his good management and the able manner in which he was supported by Mr John Barr, another Vale of Leven man, and the foremen of the various departments. I remember hearing Mr Dalglish say, when he was addressing a meeting in the Field Park, that in the event of Glasgow electing him a Member of Parliament, he could go away to London and leave Lennoxmill in the full charge of Mr. Wilson, in whom he reposed the utmost confidence. I have often had occasion to refer to Mr. Gordon Wilson in the course of this paper. I cannot refrain from noticing two recognitions of his public services, that

were accorded to him on the occasion of his retiring from Lennoxmill and leaving Lennoxtown to take up his abode in Kirkintilloch.
One from gentlemen unconnected with the work, and the other
from the workers in Lennoxmill. The first of these was a public
dinner. A very representative committee, consisting of Mr. Ritchie
of View Park, Mr. James Ross, Baldow, and the Rev. William
Wood, made all the arrangements, and to suit general convenience
of friends coming long distances to attend, it was held in a Glasgow hotel. Mr. Alexander Macnab of Lillyburn presided. Mr.
James Wright of Myrtle Bank, Kirkintilloch, was croupier. Fifty
gentlemen assembled to do honour to the guest of the evening.
The other was in the Town Hall, Lennoxtown, when a large and
enthusiastic gathering of the workers in Lennoxmill was held.
Here a beautiful illuminated address was presented, also a massive
silver tea tray with suitable inscription, and a brooch and earrings
for Mrs Wilson. Mr. Archibald Duncan presided, and made the
presentation. The clergy were present in the persons of Dr.
Munro, Rev. W. Wood, and the Rev. J. H. Magini, I shall allow
the address to speak for the donors :—

"We, the workers in Lennoxmill Print Works, avail ourselves of the
opportunity this meeting affords to present an Address to you, expressing,
though imperfectly, the feelings on the occasion of your separation from us
as our Manager.

"That arduous and honourable position you occupied for the long period
of fully forty years.

"You came among us a very young man, and though there are few left
now who were workers then, we have sufficient to testify that from first to
last your character and disposition have been always the same.

"We found you, Sir, ever anxious to encourage any good movement
among us; ever ready to assist and encourage us in times of trouble or
difficulty, and ever jealous of our reputation.

"Regretting, as we now do, your separation from amongst us, it still
affords us satisfaction to know that your feelings incline you to remain in
our neighbourhood, and we feel assured that the happiness and prosperity
of Campsie will always interest you.

"In now, Sir, saying Farewell, we earnestly desire for yourself and your
Family, happiness and prosperity. May you be long spared together, and
as years roll on, and separations necessarily take place, may that good
Providence which has sustained and supported you hitherto, be your Guide
and Counsellor to the end.

"In connection with this Address, our Chairman will present you with
a token of our remembrance which will remain with your Family when you
are gone, and testify to your children that your honourable and consistent
walk in life was highly appreciated by that people among whom you spent
so many of the best of your days.

"Signed, in name of the workers,

"ARCHIBALD DUNCAN, Chairman of Committee.

"Lennoxtown, 6th April, 1877."

ALLOCH PRINTFIELD.

There existed at one time a printfield at the Alloch Dam,
which is situated between Glorat Mansion House and Glorat Mill.

The work was situated between the dam and the row of beech trees. John and George Brown, now living at Whitefield, remember the block-printing building. They remember that the doors had holes in which the finger was inserted and the catch lifted and the door thus opened. Operations must have been conducted on a very small scale, and in a very primitive fashion. The calico printer who then carried on the business was, as far as I can gather, a Mr. Monteith. Accompanied by his wife, he went to Glasgow with the finished goods, which were conveyed in a barrow. The barrow returned laden with raw materials, and when this was filled to its utmost capacity, the calico printer's helpmeet, besides her own " parcels," carried out the finer dyestuffs on her back as she walked home from Glasgow. Although the water supply was abundant there were disadvantages in the situation, and after a few years the work was discontinued.

HAUGHHEAD PRINTFIELD.

There was a printwork erected at Haughhead, on the Fin Glen burn, opposite Kilwinnet Farm. The members of the co-partnery who started this Field were William Hart, Duncan Ferguson, William Archibald, and James Donaldson. The time selected for commencing—shortly after the block-printers' strike—does not seem to have been favourable. After continuing for three or four years, operations were discontinued. In later years the old print-field was twice occupied as a power-loom factory. It did not continue long enough to make much mark on the parish history.

LILLYBURN PRINT-WORKS.

This work has had a more varied and eventful career, especially in its earlier history, than either Kincaid or Lennoxmill, the other and older printworks of the parish.

About sixty years ago it was carried on as a print-work by Mr. Bankier, who left it to go to Glasgow to engage in business as a calenderer. In this he seems to have succeeded. He found his way into the Town Council, became one of the City Magistrates, and was widely known as Bailie Bankier.

When Bankier left Lillyburn, Sir Samuel Stirling of Glorat, his brother, Captain Stirling, and Mr. John Gray of Oxgang, entered into partnership, and commenced business as distillers, converting the print-works into a distillery. This did not prove a successful speculation, and was discontinued in 1828. Stories are still current as to the abundance of whisky in Milton and Mount of Glorat in those days, and how easily it could be got from the distillery, from which it was almost openly carried off in pails and watering cans. When this firm ceased to carry on business,

Lillyburn was taken by the Messrs. Dawson, then and still of Linlithgow, who continued it for a few years as a distillery, and then abandoned it. It is not a little remarkable to note the complete disappearance of the distilleries which formerly existed in this district. In Kirkintilloch there were several, and there were others in Campsie besides Lillyburn.

George Brown, farmer, had a distillery at the mains of Bencloich. John Forrest was both miller and distiller, at French Mill; some of the buildings connected with it may still be seen adjoining Milton Station. In Kirkintilloch there was Freeland's "Old" Distillery; one at Habbie's Howe, opposite the old foundry; Finlay's one at the Holm; one at the Loch; one at Duntiblae, on the Waterside Mill lade; besides two breweries, Jaffray's and that of Mr. James Wood. These distilleries explain the great number of tombs in the Old Aisle erected to the memory of Englishmen. who were here as officers of excise.

The reason of the total disappearance seems to be that small works, however prudently and economically carried on, are unable to compete in production, as regards cost, with large works, where a profit of 1d or 2d per gallon on a turn-out of millions of gallons, puts out of the market the productions of works only producing thousands, and where there is an on-cost of perhaps 9d or 1s per gallon, as against greatly reduced costs in the large distilleries.

The next tenants of Lillyburn were Messrs. George M'Farlane & Co., who re-converted the distillery into a printwork, as it had been originally. Mr. M'Farlane had made a fortune as a calico printer near Hurlet, and now put his sons into Lillyburn. They were not acquainted with the practical work, and did not give its management any close supervision. They seem to have been imposed upon in many ways, if the stories still current in Milton are to be credited. The inevitable result of want of knowledge, of supervision, and of ordinary prudence soon followed, and they discontinued business, after having, according to popular report, lost a very large sum during the twelve years the works had been carried on by them.

Lillyburn works were now exposed for sale, and in 1843 were bought at a public sale by Mr. Alexander Macnab, the head of the firm who now carry on business there.

Mr. Macnab's father, the late Mr. James Macnab, began life as manager to his uncle, Mr. D. Ferguson, at Milncroft, near Glasgow. In a few years he was asked to take the management of larger works at Strathblane, belonging to Messrs. Sharp & Buchanan. After a few years, he joined his brother John, the late Mr. Thomas Boyd, along with a Mr. Smellie, and they commenced business as calico printers at Bellfield, Kirkintilloch, under the style of Boyd, Smellie, & Macnabs. The firm took a lease of the works for nineteen years from the late Mr. Thomson. Mr. Boyd and the Messrs. Macnab soon found reason to complain of their partner Mr. Smellie. Calico printing was quite uncongenial to his tastes and his sporting proclivities. At every public ball, at every wedding to which he could obtain an invitation, at dances of all kinds he was sure to be present. He was also musical, and an excellent player on the violin, and was in consequence in great request at social and festive gatherings. He was a fine looking man, and when attired in the full dress of the period, with white hat and top boots, he was a " dandy " of the first water.

He had a passion for dogs, having sometimes as many as forty in his possession at one time. Three of these dogs, of the famous Kirkintilloch " Blue Pauls," were matchless fighters, and were never beaten. These were "Courage," "Crib," and '· Tiftae." The story of the "Blue Pauls," descended through the male line from a Campsie dog, may be told here, although unconnected with calico-printing at Lillyburn. A regiment changing quarters marched through Kirkintilloch shortly after 1820, when there was left behind, strayed, a fine bitch, believed to be the property of one of the officers. This dog was of a very peculiar kind, which beat all the fanciers to determine the breed. The most plausible conjecture was that it was a cross between an English bull and some other terrier, probably Bedlington. It was large in size, and a more game animal never walked. It would face anything. It became the property of what would be called now a syndicate of the "Fancy," of which a man named Shaw, who kept the Beehive Tavern in Townhead, was a leading man. Dr. Robertson of Campsie had a famous white bull dog, " a beauty," and said to be perfect in all the points. From a cross between this Campsie dog and the strayed regimental waif sprang the race that for a few years were famous as the Kirkintilloch Blue Pauls.

There used in these days to be great dog fights at Bishopbriggs for large sums of money, sometimes even for £40 or £50 a side. This breed was never beat, and so famous did it become that orders came from every part of the country, even from abroad, to procure dogs of this strain, for which large sums were offered. The strain was soon spoiled by chance indiscriminate crossing, and the qualities that had made the parents valuable were lost in their " messan " descendants. How could Mr. Smellie be expected to plod at Bellfield when excited with the chances of " Courage " or " Crib " ? After the copartnery had existed for two years, he retired from the Bellfield firm.

During the currency of their nineteen year's lease, great success attended Boyd & Macnabs, and according to popular report a great amount of money was made by the Bellfield firm. Their manufactures were fortunate in obtaining a favourable name; "Bellfield prints" being not only well known in Scotland but also in Manchester and London. When Lillyburn came into the market the lease of Bellfield had not expired, and the firm were not at liberty to leave until it had run out. Mr. Alexander Macnab therefore secured it in the meantime, and as soon as they were at liberty to do so, the Messrs. Macnab transferred their business from Bellfield to Lillyburn. Mr. Boyd went to Barrhead, whither a number of the Kirkintilloch employees followed him.

Before the advent of Messrs. James and John Macnab, nothing had succeeded at Lillyburn. Since that time, however, the reputation which the firm had gradually and surely built up at Bellfield has been maintained and increased. The business not only continues to flourish, but actually at the present time the works have been largely extended, new machines fitted up, and the very best appliances and latest improvements adopted. The present style of the firm is Alexander Macnab & Co., and the partners are understood to be Mr. Macnab, his two sons, and Mr. John Hunt.

Mr. Macnab is the first gentleman in the parish who has adopted the use of electricity for lighting purposes, and not for lighting only, as it is used in the drawing-room of Lillyburn to play the piano! *Apropos* of electric lighting I have been informed that Mr. Alexander Macnab nearly fifty years ago gave the first public display of the then newly discovered light in Kirkintilloch. He took his apparatus up to the Town Steeple, and from the sounding boards above the clock dials exhibited a light that was seen for miles around.

At a time when lectures were fewer, and on that account perhaps more highly appreciated, Mr. Macnab gave about 30 lectures on chemistry, electricity, and magnetism, and was always ready when requested to deliver a lecture or a speech when any good object was to be promoted. As a Justice of the Peace, member of School Board, and now as County Councillor, Mr. Macnab still continues to take an active interest in public affairs. He is a great traveller. Egypt, Ireland, Italy, France, and Germany have been visited by him, and on his return he generally gives the result of his observations in a popular lecture, when there is the additional attraction of photographs of the scenes described, illustrated by a powerful magic lantern. On these occasions a rare treat is enjoyed by those privileged to hear about and see representations of the scenes described.

While these sheets are passing through the press, I am reminded that when the late Mr. R. Dalglish left "The Cottage" he went to live at Dumbreck House, Paisley Road, and thence to Kilmardinny. A few days ago I met a well-known townsman of Kirkintilloch, who has told me that he was engaged herding in Campsie when Waterloo was fought. I took the opportunity of asking him if he remembered the meeting at Cannerton in 1820. "Fine, man; I mind it, we ca'd it Knocky Buckle Brae. I canna keep frae

laughin' yet, as I min' o' "Printer John," as he was ca'd, he was
among the first to tak' to his heels; but he halted, turned round,
and shouted "Stan' firm, lads, stan' firm." Having given this
excellent advice to others, he disregarded it in his own case, and
ran away as fast as his legs would carry him. "Printer John"
belonged to a once well-known family in Birdston, and was so
called to distinguish him from "Farmer John."

COTTAGE HOSPITALITY.

When Mr. Dalglish resided at "The Cottage" he cultivated
friendly relations with his foremen in the Field. He had them
frequently at his hospitable table—and there are many queer
stories concerning these convivial evenings. Once, after a night
of it, the guests had great difficulty in finding the gate. One of
them wandered off the road and came to a tree. Mistaking this
for the wall outside the gate. he bethought him that he should
keep touch of the wall along the "Doddle Raw," which would
lead him very nearly home. He commenced his journey, steadily
tramping, always keeping his hand on the tree. He must have
walked a long time round and round the tree; but at last more
light and increasing sobriety enabled him to take his bearings
afresh, and find his way to the road. It was discovered next
morning that there was a beaten path round the tree. The weary
traveller had unusually large feet, and he was afterwards frequently reminded how admirably they were adapted for road-
making purposes.

My paper on "The Rev. James Lapslie and his Times," read at
the opening of the Y.M.A. course last winter, was the means of my
obtaining many new facts and anecdotes concerning him. It has
been the same with "Calico Printing"; and in drawing these long
rambling, discursive jottings to a close, I have to express my gratification at the reception given to the "Notes." Since they
appeared, much additional information has accumulated, and this
pamphlet has attained its present proportions. If time and space
had permitted, many other details could have been noted, and
other interesting topics touched upon.

manu...
"Bellfiel...
also in Man
market the le...
not at liberty
Macnab there

Lightning Source UK Ltd.
Milton Keynes UK
UKOW06f2320220817
307732UK00011B/720/P